THE CAMBRIDGE COMPANION TO

Feminism has dramatically influenced the way literary texts are read, taught, and evaluated. Feminist literary theory has deliberately transgressed traditional boundaries between literature, philosophy, and the social sciences in order to understand how gender has been constructed and represented through language. This lively and thought-provoking Companion presents a range of approaches to the field. Some of the essays demonstrate feminist critical principles at work in analyzing texts, while others take a step back to trace the development of a particular feminist literary method. The essays draw on a range of primary material from the medieval period to postmodernism and from several countries, disciplines, and genres. Each essay suggests further reading to explore this vital field. This is the most accessible guide available both for students of literature new to this developing discipline and for students of gender studies and readers interested in the interactions of feminism, literary criticism, and literature.

ELLEN ROONEY is Professor of English and Gender Studies at Brown University, Rhode Island.

THE CAMBRIDGE
COMPANION TO

FEMINIST
LITERARY THEORY

EDITED BY
ELLEN ROONEY

CAMBRIDGE
UNIVERSITY PRESS

CAMBRIDGE UNIVERSITY PRESS
Cambridge, New York, Melbourne, Madrid, Cape Town, Singapore, São Paulo

Cambridge University Press
The Edinburgh Building, Cambridge CB2 2RU, UK
Published in the United States of America by Cambridge University Press, New York

www.cambridge.org
Information on this title: www.cambridge.org/9780521001687

© Cambridge University Press 2006

First published 2006

Printed in the United Kingdom at the University Press, Cambridge

A catalogue record for this book is available from the British Library

ISBN-13 978-0-521-80706-7 hardback
ISBN-10 0-521-80706-9 hardback
ISBN-13 978-0-521-00168-7 paperback
ISBN-10 0-521-00168-4 paperback

CONTENTS

NOTES ON CONTRIBUTORS

LINDA ANDERSON is Professor of Modern English and American Literature at the University of Newcastle upon Tyne. She is the author of *Women and Autobiography in the Twentieth Century* (1997) and *Autobiography* (2001), and has co-edited (with Trev Broughton) *Women's Lives/Women's Times* (1997) and (with David Alderson) *Territories of Desire in Queer Culture* (2000).

NANCY ARMSTRONG is Nancy Duke Lewis Professor of English, Comparative Literature, Modern Culture and Media, and Gender Studies at Brown University. She is the author of *Desire and Domestic Fiction: A Political History of the Novel* (1987), (with Leonard Tennenhouse) *The Imaginary Puritan: Literature, Intellectual Labor, and the History of Personal Life* (1992), *Fiction in the Age of Photography: The Legacy of British Realism* (2000), and *How Novels Think: The Limits of British Individualism from 1719 to 1900* (2005).

REY CHOW is Andrew W. Mellon Professor of the Humanities at Brown University. The author of numerous publications on literature, film, theory, and the study of modern China, Chow has written regularly on women's and gender issues as they pertain to cross-cultural and cross-ethnic representations in journals and edited collections, and her work has been widely anthologized and translated into major Asian and European languages. Her new book, *The Age of the World Target: Self-Referentiality in War, Theory, and Comparative Work*, is forthcoming in 2006.

ANN DUCILLE is Professor of English and African American Studies at Wesleyan University. She is the author of *The Coupling Convention: Sex, Text, and Tradition in Black Women's Fiction* (1993) and *Skin Trade* (1996), as well as numerous essays on race, feminism, and popular culture.

ROSEMARY MARANGOLY GEORGE is Associate Professor in the Department of Literature at the University of California, San Diego. She is the author of *The Politics of Home: Postcolonial Relocations and Twentieth-Century Fiction* (Cambridge University Press, 1996) and editor of *Burning Down the House:*

Recycling Domesticity (1998). Her scholarship on postcolonial feminist and other issues has been published in *Diaspora*, *differences*, *Cultural Critique*, and *Feminist Studies*. She is currently working on a book project entitled *Troubling the National: Readings in Indian Literature*.

GERALDINE HENG is Director of Medieval Studies and Associate Professor of English at the University of Texas at Austin. She is the author of *Empire of Magic: Medieval Romance and the Politics of Cultural Fantasy* (2003). Her medieval-feminist publications include "Feminine Knots and the Other Sir Gawain and the Green Knight" (*PMLA*, 1991) and "A Woman Wants: The Lady, Gawain, and the Forms of Seduction" (*Yale Journal of Criticism*, 1992). She has also written "'A Great Way to Fly': Women, Nationalism, and the Varieties of Feminism in Southeast Asia" and (with Janadas Devan) "State Fatherhood: The Politics of Nationalism, Sexuality, and Race in Singapore." Her current book project is "The Invention of Race in the European Middle Ages."

NICKIANNE MOODY is Principal Lecturer in Media and Cultural Studies at Liverpool John Moores University. Her research interests are primarily in cultural history and popular culture, and she is convenor of the Association for Research in Popular Fictions. Her publications include work on library history, young adult fiction, electronic media, and the representation of disability.

KATHERINE MULLIN is Lecturer in Twentieth-Century Literature at the University of Leeds. She is the author of *James Joyce, Sexuality and Social Purity* (Cambridge University Press, 2003) and has published articles on Joyce and sexuality in *Modernism/Modernity* and *Textual Practice*.

ELLEN ROONEY is Chair of the Department of Modern Culture and Media, and Professor of English and Gender Studies at Brown University. The author of *Seductive Reasoning: Pluralism as the Problematic of Contemporary Literary Theory* (1989), she is currently co-editor of *differences: a journal of feminist cultural studies* and associate editor of *Novel: A Forum on Fiction*. She has written on feminist theory, the Victorian novel, and cultural studies and is completing a new book, *A Semiprivate Room*.

BERTHOLD SCHOENE is Professor of English and Director of the English Research Institute at Manchester Metropolitan University. He has published on questions of postcoloniality, contemporary Scottish literature, gender theory, and literary representations of masculinity. His books include *Writing Men: Literary Masculinities from Frankenstein to the New Man* (2000) and *Posting the Male: Masculinities in Post-War Contemporary British Writing* (2003). He is currently completing *Plural Identities in Contemporary British Fiction and Film* (forthcoming in 2006). He is also the editor of *The Edinburgh Companion to Contemporary Scottish Literature*, which will be published in 2007.

RASHMI VARMA teaches postcolonial studies and feminist theory at the University of Warwick. She is the author of *Unhomely Women: The Postcolonial City and its Subjects* (forthcoming in 2006) and co-editor (with Robyn Warhol et al.) of *The McGraw Hill Anthology of Women Writing Globally in English*. Her recent publications include "Provincializing the Global City: from Bombay to Mumbai" in *Social Text* (2004) and "Untimely Letters: Edward Said and the Politics of the Present" in *Culture and Politics* (2004). She is a member of the London-based group Women Against Fundamentalism.

ELIZABETH WEED is Director of the Pembroke Center for Teaching and Research on Women at Brown University. She is founding co-editor of *differences: a journal of feminist cultural studies* and editor of several books on feminist theory. She is currently working on a project entitled "Reading for Consolation: Poststructuralist Theory and the Waning of Critique."

KARI WEIL is Associate Professor of Humanities at the California College of the Arts. She is the author of *Androgyny and the Denial of Difference* (1992) and numerous articles on nineteenth-century French literature and culture. She is currently working on a book on the horse in nineteenth-century France.

ELLEN ROONEY

Introduction

Feminist literary theory resists generalization. Perhaps because feminism has been such a prolific intellectual current and also because feminist critics have produced work of such extraordinary diversity, a remarkable range of scholars have tried to abstract the essential elements of feminist literary theory over the past two decades and more. Some of these scholars have worked in the mode of the collection or anthology, others by attempting their own synoptic analyses; at least one published a collection studying already existing critical anthologies.[1] Virtually all such efforts have been subject to strenuous critique and symptomatic reading, but they have simultaneously made important, even profound, interventions in the academic field of feminist criticism and beyond. Indeed, it may well be a rule of intellectual life that those books that are at some point most energetically critiqued, or even condemned, are precisely those whose very powerful impact must be, at whatever cost, undone, displaced, disavowed, in order to enable new work to find its point of departure.

Nevertheless, a glance over the history of efforts by feminist literary theorists to summarize their collective project reveals a marked and growing concern over the very possibility of such a synoptic view, a concern mirrored in the questions readers raise about the terms of inclusion and exclusion that govern any attempt to define the borders of feminism. The effort to propose a definition, genealogy or history of feminist literary theory, whether for the sake of pedagogy, political clarity or even to establish an intellectual rationale for the field as a whole, threatens to simplify what is, in a stubborn, perhaps ineradicable way, complex. In the proposal of a general account of feminist literary theory's proper form there is something that feminist theorists themselves do not relish.[2]

This may be in part because formulating useful generalizations about theoretical problematics so rarely seems to feature the kind of attention to textual detail or "literariness" that literary critics (including of course feminists) usually prefer as their intellectual practice. Barbara Johnson acknowledges this longing for literariness – and connects it to the question of difference – in the preface to *The Critical Difference*:

> Difference is, of course, at work within the very discourse of theory itself. Indeed, it is precisely contemporary theory that has made us so aware of this. Theoretical pronouncements therefore do not stand here as instruments to be used in mastering literary structures. On the contrary, it is through contact with literature that theoretical tools are useful precisely to the extent that they thereby change and dissolve in the hands of the user. Theory here is often the straight man whose precarious rectitude and hidden risibility, passion and pathos are precisely what literature has already somehow already foreseen.[3]

Johnson warns her readers away from the expectation (or fear) that she will permit theoretical paradigms to pass themselves off as master texts, dominating literature and dictating in a mechanical, uninterrogated way the practice of reading. In the theoretical *tour de force* of readings that make up her book, Johnson scrupulously attends to the power of literature to read theory, to elude in some essentially unpredictable way even the most subtle theoretical problematic, and thus to contribute to a retheorizing, a reinscription with a difference, of theory's established points of departure. This difference that literature or "textuality" discloses within theory is bound up, she notes, with traces of affect: with pathos and passion, with a less-than-stable uprightness and with something laughable, as well. The literariness within theory does not conform to a strictly logical order.

Textuality, broadly defined in this way, is what makes not just literary but cultural studies generally, including feminist cultural studies, something other than sociology or ethnography. This is not merely an aesthetic distinction or a matter of taking pleasure in the text (otherwise known as "loving literature"). We lose the *evidence* of textuality when we read past or around its effects, when we "read without seeing," as Derrida puts it in his (perhaps) feminist book, *Spurs*.[4] Feminist literary scholars seek in everything they read the textual details that an empirical or sociological approach privileging a kind of "information retrieval" finds merely disruptive;[5] as a result, they may be particularly resistant to seduction by masterful abstractions of feminist theory's particularities. The exclusions that reductive generalizations can never entirely avoid disturb them.

Johnson's view is by now familiar to students of literature. That literariness inhabits theory; that theory is, in fact, a genre of literature and not a pure metalanguage; that reading transacts an exchange between theoretical texts and literary works, rather than simply applying theory to an abject text the better to illustrate theory's profundity: these propositions are widely acknowledged, if not always consistently put into practice. Feminist literary theory belongs in a fundamental way to literary studies and thus participates in its disciplinary debates. (This is not simply a matter of being confined by disciplinarity; disciplines are knowledge-producing forms, with their own capacities for renewal and transformation.) But this emphasis on the way in which literature inhabits theory has a particular relevance to contemporary feminist literary theory insofar as it also inhabits feminist theory in general and participates in the interdisciplinary projects of women's studies and gender studies. On the one hand, literature and literariness, rhetoric and reading, are inescapable terms for feminist literary theory, especially in its academic avatars, which is the primary form in which it will be considered in this volume; Johnson encourages us to keep feminist theorizing attuned to the ongoing challenges of the literary. On the other hand, feminism has had an important and in many ways painful historical relation with the processes of abstraction and generalization that are most often (though too reductively) identified with theory as such, a history that is also the history of feminist literary studies.

The connections between difference and textuality – and the threat represented by their loss – have a particular resonance for feminist theory (in the academy and beyond). To take the United States as an example, the habitual definition or abstraction of "woman" by dominant white and middle-class feminist theorists in terms that excluded women of color, women of the working classes, and women living outside the metropolitan centers has marked feminist theorizing in virtually all its forms. This theoretical exclusion has by now been "interrupted" (to use Gayatri Spivak's term) by many critiques, emanating from figures ranging from Barbara Smith, Elizabeth Spellman, bell hooks, and Spivak, to Cherríe Moraga, Trinh Minh-Ha, Hortense Spillers, and Chandra Mohanty, to name only a handful. The racism and class bias, heterosexism and neocolonial privilege that underwrote these exclusions have been carefully disclosed and mapped; feminist theories that have eschewed similar exclusions and abstractions have been elaborated.

This critical work, however, has also engendered the insight that systemic exclusions are not easily repaired by a simple additive approach, by the "inclusion" of once marginalized women and communities in a renovated theoretical totalization. Indeed, the logic by which an essentially white feminism stands at the origins of feminist theory, renewing and reforming itself in response to the critiques of somehow belated women who introduce *their* differences into the established discussion, has radical shortcomings. These include (1) its distortion of the original work of feminists of color and postcolonial feminists for whom the fusion of questions of gender and questions of race or empire was not an afterthought (a topic Ann duCille analyzes in her essay in this volume); (2) its erasure of the racial, national, sexual, and class inscriptions of white, middle-class, heterosexual feminists, who thus appear to have an unmediated and logically as well as politically prior claim to feminism as such – they are consequently confirmed as the unacknowledged norm;[6] and (3) its implicit underwriting of the additive approach (add race, add class, add religion, add "and so on") that sustains efforts to define women as such. As Sabina Sawhney remarks, the steady addition of "another item to the list of all 'others' – all finally to be incorporated into some version of a global McSisterhood" – cannot be any feminism's program.[7] If even well-intentioned gestures of inclusion leave undisturbed the assumptions that produced exclusions in the first place, how is feminist theorizing to proceed? What shall it take for its object?

Reading Johnson's remarks in the light of feminism's history of theory opens the question of how the problems of generalization and difference are bound up with the problems of textuality and rhetoric. How does feminist literary theory respond to the claim that the very definition of theory is subject to something other than a "straight" reading, that theory might be queered? What does the resistance to generalizing and abstracting mean for feminist literary theory? Is the persistent difficulty of presenting an overview of the field a symptom in its own right, a warning about the state of feminist theory today? Is there something "literary" about this difficulty? And what is feminist literary theory? I will tackle the last question first, since any conceivable answer requires us to enter the precincts of generalization.

Feminist literary theories

Women read. They write, too, of course: literature and criticism and theory (plays, newspaper columns, manifestos, annual reports). But it can be argued that feminist literary studies depends upon the premise that women read and on the conclusion that their reading *makes* a difference. (We will return to the importance of making.)[8] Feminist literary theory maintains that women's reading is of consequence, intellectually, politically, poetically; women's readings signify. This feminist insistence on the interpretative consequences of women's reading is quite different from the conclusions drawn by earlier commentators who also noticed women reading. For example, the rise of the English novel, in the eighteenth century, was accompanied by a stream of diatribes opposed to women's reading: on the social hazards of allowing women to read; on the importance of monitoring and censoring women's reading; on the threat that women's pleasure in reading represented to female virtue and domestic order. Similar attacks on women's literacy are of course still commonplace in many places around the globe; not all women read. Jane Austen mocks these polemics on women's reading when she represents Mr. Collins's horror as the Bennet daughters hand him a novel to be read aloud after tea; to humor their guest, the family agree instead to a selection from *Fordyce's Sermons*. Such censorious concerns were aroused by fears of the impact that novels might have on their female readers: on their chastity, their docility, their submission to (often patriarchal) authority. By contrast, the woman reader as feminist is drawn to the promise that women reading will have an impact on texts.

Women read. Might we find in this remarkably simple slogan a rubric for the shared paradigm of feminist literary theories? Or do these two deceptively simple words also require to be read? Perhaps, as Hazel Carby observes about the project of black feminist criticism, this appealing slogan must be "regarded critically as a problem, not a solution, as a sign that should be interrogated, a locus of contradictions."[9] Indeed, as she advances her interrogation of the forces shaping academic black feminist theory, Carby stresses that the meanings we can attach to the flat observation that black women read are not obvious or unified: "Black feminist criticism has too frequently been reduced to an experiential relationship that exists between black women as critics and black women as writers who represent black women's reality. Theoretically this reliance on a common, or shared, experience is essentialist and ahistorical" (p. 16). Carby's observations are exemplary of the feminist theorist's opening up of the "experience" of the woman reader. No sooner has the point been made that women read and that their reading introduces a difference into literary history and criticism, than the meanings of both women and reading are put into question. Women readers have not always made the difference that feminist criticism looks for.

What does the feminist critic mean when she says "women"? Biologically female persons? Individuals who have been socialized as "feminine"? Does that socialization vary when we understand women as always already raced, classed, and sexualized, and by *contradictory* processes, which introduce differences within every construct of identity, so that there is no singular woman reader, or singular white woman reader, or singular black woman reader, or singular lesbian reader?[10] Does the invocation of "women" announce simply that the category of gender is at work, conceptualized in an "intersectional" model that focuses on the interlocking (not parallel) constructions of race, gender, class, and sexuality, in an encounter in which each term is determined and determining?[11] Or perhaps "women" signifies sexual difference as it is figured by psychoanalysis or the critique of phallocentrism, which aligns femininity with the divided subject and invokes it to herald the ruin of any concept of identity or identity-based reading.[12] This last option stresses the differences *within* femininity and masculinity, differences that phallocentrism masks in order to leave us with the illusion of a firm opposition between men and women and the fantasy of a feminine essence, of Woman as a unitary subject. Peggy Kamuf elaborates the literary-critical consequences of this deconstruction of the binary masculine/feminine in her essay "Writing Like a Woman." Kamuf challenges the "tautology," popular with many feminist critics, that "women's writing is writing signed by women,"[13] and she argues that this logic presumes that the literary text has "a father," that is, a legitimate parent who "represents ... a clear intentionality, realized or given expression in the written work and recovered through the work of interpretation" (p. 297). In Kamuf's analysis the presupposition that identity and intentionality rule meaning is a specifically patriarchal myth that masks the instability and fluidity of all identity, including the identity of the woman reader. This last possibility raises the question of whether the practice of a "feminine" reading that abandons the myths of identity can be restricted to readers who are gendered as women in their social roles. Is the woman reader a critical hypothesis that is available to any and every reader, including men?

The phrase "any reader" is for its part no more transparent than the term women. As the impossibility of assigning a singular or proper identity to the "women" who read looms larger, another question arises: what does it mean to read? Does reading decipher textual codes firmly in place in a text that reflects its author's intentions? If so, is the reader's task to articulate those intentions as fully as possible? Or can the author's consciousness, her actual experience and deliberate ends, be bracketed, provided that we attend to historical contexts and ideological problematics? Without insisting that the text's meanings are contained by its author's explicit intentions, we might still preserve the fundamental objectivity of reading by placing texts firmly in historical contexts, in cultural fields or among socio-political forces that provide a horizon for interpretation. This kind of historicist model is powerful in literary studies at the present moment, and it has always been a rich source of interpretative insight for feminist readers. But is this process itself too indebted to the sociological reductions of the literary that we questioned above? Is there danger in the tendency to shrink textual effects to the already known, to what Ann duCille has called "the discursively familiar, . . . faithful representations of lived experiences in the social real"?[14] Formulated as ideology critique, such an approach can have a powerful, demystifying impact. But it may also threaten its textual examples with irrelevance: if ideological ruses are always already understood in advance, if ideology stands, as theory aspires to, in a position of mastery over the text, reading itself is redundant, another tautological reiteration of what our theory of ideology has already rendered obvious and familiar.

Another possibility is the one held out by Johnson's jokes at theory's expense and made explicit in her *The Feminist Difference*:

> literature is important for feminism because literature can best be understood as the place where impasses can be kept open for examination, where questions can be guarded and not forced into a premature validation of the available paradigms. Literature, that is, is not to be understood as a predetermined set of works but as a mode of cultural work, the work of giving-to-read those impossible contradictions that cannot yet be spoken. (p. 13)

This reader has an active relation to the text, one that attends closely to the play of its signfiers, its contradictory movements, its capacity to surprise. Reading in this perspective is transitive: reading a text changes it. If women readers "make" a difference, it is because they read to undo previous phallic paradigms of interpretative mastery and to disclose as yet unimagined textual possibilities, possibilities that invalidate our "available paradigms" and leave ambivalence, conflict, and contradiction in place for us to explore. Literature as that which "figures the impossible" (Spivak, *Critique*, p. 112) is not literature that is apolitical or quietistic, for conflict and contradiction inhere in feminist politics; but it is a scene in which the already known can no longer be taken for granted.

In this last formulation, reading as a mode of work, as attention to the impasse, to the figuration of the impossible, threatens the transparency of categories like the (lesbian) woman or (black) women or even gender (in postcoloniality). Insofar as such categories imagine identity as rooted in an experience beyond representation, a unified experience given by some unmediated practice and not both formed and undone by language, literature is the site of their deconstruction as well as their renewal. Feminist reading here begins to complicate and unravel the very premises that first enabled it to get a purchase on textuality. Self-questioning and an unwillingness to settle in a single location are characteristic of feminist literary theories. They have not found skepticism to be paralyzing, for it is not only the identity of the woman reading that has been rethought. When feminist readers begin to argue that the women's readings matter to the meanings of literary texts, they are willy-nilly caught up in an argument about the manner in which men read (in the present and the past tense). Indeed, the feminist readers expose, by the difference of their interpretations, the *masculinism* of prior readings and readers. These prior readings had presented themselves not as the products of men accustomed to masculine privilege (so accustomed that their privileges appeared to them simply as nature), but as reading itself, objective, humanistic reading, where men (or certain men, to be more precise) were presumed to represent the human. Mary Ellman's *Thinking About Women* cannily called this pseudo-objective reading "phallic criticism." Masculinity itself *as a gender* (rather than in the form of the generically human) is made visible in her critical rereading. Can we argue, then, that when a masculinist reading is exposed as such, we may presume that the agent of that exposure is a feminist critic? This, whether she is a woman or a man? And does this mean that the slogan "women read" should be rewritten as the slighty less elegant "feminists read"?[15]

It is clear by now that we can position "feminist reading" as the essence of feminist literary theories' program only in a very particular sense. While the feminist is always someone committed to the exposure of the masculinist (whether in the works of men or women), both of these terms – feminist and masculinist – are contested, as is the practice of reading, as I have been arguing. Feminist literary theories, then, are the theories of feminists struggling against masculinism and among themselves over the meanings of literature, reading, and feminism. While it is not possible to define the essence of feminist literary theory, there are a range of (competing yet characteristic) practices that emerge in the course of these struggles. By their presence in this contestatory field, one can recognize the feminist literary theorists.

Let us consider just two of the forms that this struggle may take: the interrogation of tradition and the revaluation of the aesthetic. The feminist interrogation of tradition and literary canons has taken multiple forms, and it will come as no surprise that the strategies feminist theorists have adopted are not entirely compatible with each other. Some critics have approached the problem by nominating marginalized or entirely forgotten women writers for a place within the standard canon, arguing that the excluded writers meet its traditional criteria. Others have proposed counter-canons of radically distinct traditions, seeking to dismiss once-revered figures from the syllabus. These approaches are corrective, righting the wrongs of exclusion and misreading, and they are obviously connected to feminism's "gynocritical" (Showalter) interest in women writers. On the other hand, some feminist theorists have mounted a sharp critique of the very notion of the tradition; they neither seek to place women in hegemonic canons nor to build counter-canons, arguing that any narrative of tradition (or traditions) will inevitably reinscribe ahistorical and essentialist assumptions about women's experiences.[16] This sharp dissent from the momentum of canon building frees reading from the teleologies of tradition and from the entrenched stereotypes of canonicity.

A second topos that appears in the wake of feminist reading – as a direct result of feminist reflection on the question "what is it to read"? – is the critique of hegemonic aesthetic assumptions. Some feminist theorists propose rivals to the terms of hegemonic masculinist aesthetics, for example, championing sentimentality in the face of modernist distaste and condescension, or defending the marriage plot and a narrative preoccupation with subjectivity against a patriarchal nationalism's preferences for protest literature. Alternatively, a critique of the aesthetic may involve turning toward once-belittled forms, such as autobiography, slave narrative, diaries and *testimonios* (genres to which women in certain periods and places have had significant access), in order to disclose their substantial but overlooked aesthetic value. Or feminist literary theory may champion an avant-garde, as in the case of what French feminist Hélène Cixous calls *écriture féminine*, which she finds brilliantly embodied in the works of Jean Genet and James Joyce. All of these approaches intervene to redefine aesthetic value. But certain feminist critics have dismissed proposals to renovate the aesthetic, relegating aesthetic judgment to the history of taste. From this perspective, aesthetic values are inevitably compromised by ideology. Literary studies should report the facts of literary history understood as the evolution of imaginative discourses over time, just as history proper attends to social discourses. Historians do not dismiss objects of study on the grounds of aesthetic judgments, and the forms of feminist literary theory that emerge from this perspective would follow their lead, taking the form of cultural history.

Even this brief overview confirms that the perspective of the feminist reader has not tamed the heterogeneity of feminist literary theories. We can acknowledge the irreducible conflict in the field with the familiar gesture of pluralization: replacing the potentially monolithic concept of feminist literary theory with the multiplicity of feminist literary theories allows us to renounce any effort to totalize them or misrepresent them in a singular form. This is not a trivial gesture; the sheer wealth of material engendered by feminist literary studies across fields and national traditions, especially in a globalizing moment when "transnational literacy" (Spivak) is an urgent project, presents an empirical challenge that simply cannot be overcome. No approach can summarize this protean body of work or claim to represent it in its totality, and to signal this partiality in the form of the plural is useful. But, as even these two brief examples suggest, the difficulty of defining feminist literary theory is not, in the end, a matter of sheer quantity. The internal conflicts and varied, indeed, *contradictory* approaches (renovate the aesthetic/eradicate the aesthetic; reform or counter the canon/abandon the fiction of the canonical) that mark feminist literary theories are more daunting to the project of generalization than the sheer number of workers in the field.

Just as feminisms themselves are the work of widely divergent groups of women (and men), including women who oppose one another politically, work in different national traditions and transnational interstices, and face divergent social and political challenges, so feminist literary theories arise in multiple, contradictory, and even *opposing* contexts. The most sincere and well-meaning effort to represent feminism's heterogeneity by means of inclusive lists and expanded examples can only defer the inevitable moment of risking generalizations and testing their effects. Whenever we propose any definition, when we undertake to impose a name, to institute any identity or concept whatsoever, we must articulate some form of exclusion; identity, even in its most mobile and flexible forms, emerges from difference. And so we return to the problem of generalization with which we began. But now we are in a position to examine two radically opposed generalizations about the discursive field of feminist literary studies – and to consider their possible articulation.

To begin in the most abstract and what seems to be the least conceptually controversial register: while feminist literary theories represent remarkably wide-ranging, diverse, and contradictory projects, they are also increasingly pervasive and potent. Their impact on both the academic study of literature and the public discourse on letters and culture over the past nearly forty years has been deep and thoroughgoing and genuinely global in scope. Even a passing acquaintance with academic literary studies, course syllabi, degree programs, literary journals, and scholarly presses in a range of countries makes it clear that there is virtually no field of literary history, no national tradition, no subfield or genre that has been left entirely untouched by the discourse of academic feminist literary studies; outside the academy, as well, the impact of feminist thinking about literature is undeniable. What is more, the work of feminist critics in literature has influenced scholarship in a wide range of related fields, from history and anthropology to cinema studies and sociology, even as adjacent fields have influenced and critiqued feminist critics. Feminist literary theories have contributed both to the reorganization of the traditional study of national literatures and to the work of transnational cultural studies and theory.

Indeed, the visible impact of feminist criticism's intellectual-political-institutional projects has been so remarkable that it has made some of its own proponents curiously nervous. The assumptions, questions and intellectual programs put into motion by feminist literary theory are so entrenched in some contexts (in the US academy, for example) that more than one feminist has been moved to wonder if such institutional success, especially within university settings that early feminist scholars had hoped to challenge and even reorder, may represent a kind of historic defeat. Have feminist energies been coopted on the very site where once a revolution in the production of knowledge had been planned?[17]

This line of questioning is not new. In 1987 Lillian Robinson wrote a crisp and unsentimental essay entitled "Feminist Criticism: How Do We Know When We've Won?"[18] Faced with so many and such varied projects inspired by feminist insights, yet often pursued by critics with no explicit commitment to feminism in a directly political sense and no apparent experience of the women's movement outside the university, Robinson felt it not at all premature to ask: "is there a place for research . . . on women's literature, that, while not being explicitly feminist, nonetheless is not explicitly anti-feminist either?" ("Feminist Criticism," p. 141). She concluded that "any work that places the study of women writers at the center has an objectively feminist effect. Extending the canon . . . has a feminist effect almost regardless of the nature of the arguments and connections that are made or ignored about the work itself" (p. 142). The strong form of Robinson's diagnosis goes further, to claim that "the intellectual challenge posed by . . . women's studies . . . is so potent, even where unacknowledged, that at the present time it creates the historical context in which all discourse on women occurs" (p. 144) within literary studies. This conundrum of a powerful if sometimes unacknowledged influence is obviously not felt with equal force in every institutional location; still, the principle may interest feminist scholars working to transform even radically different contexts. But we need not evoke feminists critics at work in less congenial sites than Robinson's to raise doubts about her observation. Indeed, even as feminism's influence grows, a radically different evaluation of feminist literary studies has emerged, a bleaker, not to say, grim diagnosis of its health.[19]

The violence of the letter

"What must be done at the place of the speaking subject, in light of all 'I' know now, and what is its *name*?"
–Hortense Spillers, *Black, White and In Color* (2003)[20]

As this introduction has stressed, it is utterly commonplace to observe that feminist literary theories are protean, heterogeneous, conflictual; one theorist wonders if there is "a *necessary* ambivalence within feminism today" (Johnson, *Feminist*, p. 2)? But I think it fair to say that some of the recent commentary on conflict in feminist literary studies has become alarmist. To cite one prominent example of this genre of lament, consider the American feminist theorist Susan Gubar's "What Ails Feminist Criticism?" A brutal paraphrase of Gubar's argument would go as follows: feminist literary studies, in its Anglophone formation, is in a dire state, suffering from "a bad case of critical anorexia."[21] This terrible situation is the result of "rhetorics of dissension" (p. 901), and the feminist authors of these rhetorics are, on the one hand, postcolonialists, African Americanists and other proponents of critical race theory, and, on the other, poststructuralists.[22] These writers, according to Gubar, have produced "diatribes" and "disparaged" (p. 886) the work of other feminist critics; their scholarship has been "framed in such a way as to divide feminists, casting suspicion upon a common undertaking" (p. 880).

Critical anorexia is allegedly a direct result of the way in which "racialized identity politics made the word *women* slim down to stand only for a very particularized kind of woman, whereas poststructuralists obliged the term to disappear altogether" (p. 901). But Gubar's dour diagnosis concludes with a puzzling remark: "How paradoxical that during the time of feminist criticism's successful institutionalization in many academic fields it seems to be suffering from a sickness that can end in suicide" (p. 901). This acknowledgment of "success" echoes references scattered across her essay that praise the very scholars Gubar otherwise denounces, celebrating their innovative work, their "remarkable discernment" and all they have taught us about writers and paradigms once missing from feminist canons (pp. 880, 900, 883). "Ambivalence" is too mild a word for the conflict these diverging remarks embody: flush with unprecedented success, "we" (and of course, everything is at stake in that feminist "we") yet tremble on the verge of self-immolation.

The flaws in these arguments have been systematically addressed by others. Robyn Wiegman's trenchant response, "What Ails Feminist Criticism? A Second Opinion," challenges Gubar's account on all fronts. Wiegman points out that Gubar's nostalgic narrative of feminist criticism's Edenic past "sacrifices the complexities and discontinuities of feminism's institutional history for a plot formula that denigrates academic feminism's internal conflict while simultaneously refusing to cast its dynamically mobile and historically transforming intellectual and political formation in positive terms;"[23] Wiegman argues that Gubar's resistance to an intersectional analysis, one that pursues an "ongoing and always present critique of feminism's universalization of white women as woman" (p. 369), causes her to "misdescribe" the archive she indicts and to mistake intellectual and political substance for a matter of "rhetorical good manners" (p. 368). Reluctantly (and here reluctance may be the better part of wisdom), Wiegman also touches on what she calls the essay's "emotional" level, describing the way in which Gubar "crafts whiteness as an injured identity" and thus reads the critical intervention of black feminist theorists like Hazel Carby in the question of racial domination as an "accusation."

Wiegman's critique is largely persuasive. I would like to press it into service to return to the problem of "generalization" in feminist theory, by reconnecting this notion of "accusation" to the work of rhetoric in the light of a general claim Wiegman places in a footnote. She argues there that contemporary feminism's mode of critique "is fundamentally a homosocial circuit in which *feminism* signifies from the conflicted terrain of relations among women" (p. 363). This is another answer to the question "what is feminist theory?" But how are rhetoric and accusation articulated on this conflicted terrain?

Before going any further down the path that these questions suggest, I should stress that I cannot fathom the recent alarm about the state of feminist criticism. The criticisms Gubar and others level against certain theorists collapse in the face of the sheer pervasiveness and energy of feminist analysis in literary studies, due in part to the interventions of these same theorists. Critical anorexia is nowhere evident. The very opposite condition pertains. Feminist criticism and theory are omnipresent; familiarity with their arguments is presumed in myriad fields and genres of academic literary study in the United States and the United Kingdom and in many other sites. Of course, we might conclude that this institutionalization is in fact a sign that, whatever remains of "feminism" in feminist literary theories, it is no longer a threat to business as usual in a society that has yet to grant women equality. Gubar is not alone in deploring feminism's "depoliticization," although the theorists she indicts are urgently concerned with politics. If feminist literary theories are no longer "insurgent," are they in some sense no longer feminist? Can a feminist criticism that holds a *dominant* place in the university be a feminist criticism? Has feminist literary studies *generally* and long since become merely another approach to academic research? Is it now simply work that, for the purposes of reading, takes up at least one of a loosely related string of concepts, including "gender," "sexual difference," "sexuality," "masculinities" and "femininities," and, of course, "women" and "men," but without any feminist *political* content per se? Is a creeping political neutrality the fount of the bleak assessments of feminism's literary projects?

Gubar's polemic is actually on behalf of generalization. She is disturbed by any work that "divides" feminists, actively resisting the intuition that this division was always already in place, but also curiously unmoved by the notion that feminist literary studies is perhaps only possible in a precisely polemical sense, not in terms of what is agreed upon and shared, but in terms of what is battled over, even fiercely and angrily battled over. If feminist literary theories are the theories of feminists struggling against masculinism and among themselves over the meanings of literature, reading, and feminism, as I have suggested, the conflicts Gubar recounts are signs of vigor. Her own text offers considerable evidence suggesting that such battles do not simply set people in opposition; struggles involve people in one another's claims, arguments connect. But Gubar reads past these connections insofar as they disable generalization. She condemns scholarship that "cast[s] suspicion on our common undertaking" for the same reason, this time mistaking the durable history of this doubt, "our" longstanding lack of commonality; but also, most importantly, she forgets that dissension and the fragmentation it sows amount to a dissemination of feminisms, the diaspora of feminist discourses in a myriad of sites and problematics. When feminism divides, it multiplies; yet, despite her catalogue of the multiplicity of feminist arguments, Gubar fantasizes that they shrink the field, even starve it.

Her intervention is not, perhaps, primarily a matter of emotional injury, but more of the order of a political and intellectual misreading, a miscalculation overdetermined by her longing for generalization. (Perhaps generalization appears to Gubar as the necessary ground for political activity and thus as a cure for depoliticization?) The absence of a common project is not read recursively as the presence of a series of overlapping projects, never adequate to one another, and, even, in some cases, opposed, yet *all* of them *feminist*. This is peculiar, to be sure, given that generalization appears so prominently in many texts as contemporary feminist literary theory's greatest fear, representing, as it does, one of its greatest missteps, its most intellectually and politically costly misrepresentation. Hence the particular resistance to even its own efforts to generalize or abstract its forms. Feminists have learned to suspect and to worry about generalization because some of feminism's most harmful theoretical and political errors have had to do with overgeneralizations and overreaching abstraction, distorted histories and misbegotten theories universalizing woman, and indeed, with every feminism's potential attraction to the universal. But their resistance has also to do with the recognition that any project of inclusion organized around the figure of woman is doomed always to overlook some specificity, some genre of femininity, of "being woman." Generalization cannot be banished, as my own analysis certainly reveals; but feminist literary theorists' response to generalization will always be a rereading on behalf of difference.

Robinson knew this very well; she anticipated with pleasure the unraveling and reweaving of a certain feminism's generalizations. She wrote

> women differ from one another . . . every generalization about women's writing that was derived from surveying only relatively privileged white writers is called into question by looking at writers who are not middle class and white. It may be that some of these generalizations will hold. My

> suspicion is, however, that most do not. This is even more likely when, say, black women's literature is assimilated into a general American canon that was hitherto predominantly white and male. The addition not only enriches the canon, it changes our sense of what the canon is and what it is about.
>
> (Robinson, "Feminist Criticism," p. 146)

This sentence is distinguishable from many in Gubar's essay because of the confident "our" in the phrase "changes our sense of what the canon is." This is *not* an artifact of Robinson's earlier historical moment, but due rather to her comfort with the notion that opposed positions in literary theory will both claim feminism. Feminist theories continue to engender such oppositions. While certain feminists persist in writing about "women," however qualified their referent, others insist that this practice is itself the essence of patriarchal thinking, and still others propose "women's studies as a force that could revolutionize the very structures of knowledge," in part by "pos[ing] the question of what a feminist practice of study might be, beyond the recognizable themes: women and sexual difference."[24] This level of heterogeneity obviously strains any simple coherence that the *name* feminism might claim, and there are many, many such examples. Indeed, it sometimes appears that none of the quarrels of feminist literary theory has ever been resolved; the field is at this point so large, so diverse, and so entrenched that it simply expands to accommodate each new debate, allowing almost every possible view to occupy some critical space, somewhere. Does this amount to an admission that feminist literary studies is only a matter of tattered family resemblances, growing ever frailer, with no proper object?

Accusation and rhetoric are the terms to which I would like to return to answer this question. I invoked the textuality of theory at the outset of this discussion in order to embrace rhetorical analysis as an antidote to overgeneralization. Feminist literary theories, exposed in their "precarious rectitude," "passion and pathos," will continue to develop and dissolve under the pressure of our literary readings. But attention to the rhetoric of feminist theories themselves has another effect. It enables us to read "accusation" as a mode of address.

The rhetoric of recrimination that demoralizes Gubar emerges in a rather different light in this reading. Indeed, I would propose that we read feminist literary theories across the board in terms of the modes of "feminist address" – or the failures thereof. By feminist address, I do not mean the invocation of an empirical audience, already assembled and merely waiting to recognize itself in a representation held up to it as a mirror; feminist address is not a matter of mere inclusion or of identity politics. Rather, attention to the workings of address permits us to investigate feminist constructions of audience, of interpretative communities and subjects, of dialogue and dissension, beyond identity politics. In the place of a focus on the identity of the feminist speaking subject, we can attend to the idioms in which this feminist subject addresses her audience(s).[25] Reading forms of address is not the same as policing a discourse for inclusion because the emphasis is on how rhetorics of address create constituencies, that is, form feminist subjects, rather than simply accommodate them. Thus we should recognize feminist address in its performative sense, as an apostrophe to the reader that is constructive, *that brings into being a feminist position by means of a reading*. This of course makes it an address that cannot be guaranteed in advance. And it may even begin in accusation.

Gubar cites Carby as one of the theorists "impelled to disparage any feminist theory founded on equality" (p. 889). Wiegman attributes Gubar's tone deafness here to wounded racial identity, and her diagnosis may be correct. But if we look to the text of Carby's uncompromising critique of white feminist scholarship, we find that it is framed by two remarkable *addresses*. The first is its title: "White Woman Listen!"[26] The second is its final sentence: "of white feminists we must ask, what exactly do you mean when you say 'WE'?" Gubar overlooks the fact that she has been asked a question. The elaboration of an answer is an infinite task, but I will say unequivocally that this exclamation and this question represent anything but disparagement. On the contrary, they constitute an invitation, a direct feminist address that rests on no unearned generalization of woman and offers no guarantee of a "common undertaking." Feminist address can never do more than propose a position and await its reading. Such readings will not permit us to master conflict; generalization will remain a difficult if necessary passage. It would be sentimental to suggest that the fact that we continue to speak to one another at all is in itself an emblem of reconciliation or resolution. But the figure of address is essential to feminist theories because feminist theorists are constantly proposing new locations for feminist subjects, a new "we." These subjects are always in motion, and address is a powerful means for announcing and renouncing them.

In the scene of address, the speaking subject is both the locus of power and dependent upon her addressee, her audience, the "you" to whom she speaks and who says "you" to her. Many theorists have commented on the instability of these intricate structures and argued that part of their fragility stems from "the relation between direct address and the desire for the *other's* voice."[27] This desire is neither innocent nor purely friendly; power is at work here, along with rhetorical play and dangerous ambivalence. An unstable address threatens to produce confusion between the speaker and the addressee, between the putative subject and her apparent object, an "object" she nevertheless hopes to animate, to make speak. This confusion or impasse is an invitation to reading. If "one of the goals of what we so ambiguously call 'women's studies' [is] to call into question the oppressive effects of an epistemology based on the principle of a clear and nonambiguous distinction of subject and object of knowledge" (Gallop, *Lacan*, p. 15), we should attend closely to the rhetorics of feminist address. When feminists read the figures of women reading, they disrupt the distinction between the subject and the object of knowledge. You will recall that when Johnson sought to celebrate the ambiguous place of literature within theory, she punned on theory's rectitude, on theory as the "straight" man to literature's comic, a queer player. The "straight" is not in any simple sense the opposite of the gay or the lesbian in this scene, for what unsettles the straight man is the work of a difference situated within theory, itself now a rather queer subject. The feminist subjects that literature and literary theory propose for the future are also without essential features; they are potential subjects we must inscribe in our own texts and discover in our interlocutors' polemics. These figures cannot be read straight, and so feminist literary theories remain signs to be interrogated, which is another mode of address. The names of the feminist subjects who will reply cannot be known in advance.

Feminist theory without guarantees

"And then there is using everything."
– Gertrude Stein, "Composition as Explanation" (1926)

Feminist literary theories are the collective conversations – often contradictory, sometimes heated – of feminist readers concerning the meaning and practice of reading, the intersections of subject formations such as race, class, sexuality, and gender, and the work of literature. Feminist literary theory has successfully intervened in literary studies as a whole, recasting once commonsensical understandings of genres, the canon, and the aesthetic; in this respect, it is no longer radical because it has transformed its field. But a disciplinary focus can provide only a partial insight into the current state of feminist literary study. The common ground between feminist literary theory and contemporary theoretical problematics such as postcolonial theory, poststructuralism, and queer theory is also critical; in fact, this intersection is central to feminist theory's interdisciplinary reach.

No survey of this field can be exhaustive, but a companion to the study of feminist literary theory must capture both the disciplinary and the extra disciplinary features of its practices. The range and inventiveness of these practices is readily discerned in the subject matter and approaches of the essays collected here. They provide an opening onto important debates within the discipline of feminist criticism, even as they investigate its interactions with powerful theories that originate elsewhere. The academic contexts for the production of these essays are European and North American universities, but their content and form are not circumscribed by these geographical coordinates, and the critical and political perspectives brought to bear by their authors are as heterogeneous and politically diverse as the meanings of reading.

As feminist theory emerged in literary studies, it interrogated the most basic concepts of the field, including the notion of the canon, the definition of the aesthetic and of the reader, and the meaning of "theory" itself. Ann duCille's essay, "On canons: anxious history and the rise of black feminist literary studies," introduces the question of tradition by turning it back on the field of black feminist literary studies and the traditions it claims. Beginning in the eighteenth century and tracing the struggles and the writings of African American women into the present, duCille argues that the emerging black feminist critics of the 1970s, along with white feminist critics, failed fully to acknowledge a "lengthy history of black feminist agitation and writing," a tradition of foremothers who have still not been properly embraced. She argues that these early writer-activists conceptualized race and gender together, understanding "the political empowerment of the Negro race" as a "*feminist* as well as an antiracist imperative," and she demonstrates that feminism still contends with the "notion of separable gender and racial identities," a concept that reinscribes the white woman as a norm and forces black feminist literary theory into reactive postures that distract it from its own urgent work.

Geraldine Heng's "Pleasure, resistance, and a feminist aesthetics of reading" addresses tradition from the perspective of the feminist-medievalist *as reader*. Heng argues that the historically remote materials of medieval literature draw the feminist critic into an intricate dance in which political critique, pleasure, and a historical conception of the text produce a unique aesthetic that combines "acquiesence" and "resistance." She traces the trajectory of feminist approaches, from resisting readings and symptomatic analyses that disclose the unspoken assumptions of canonical works to the counter-canons of medieval women's writings. Marking the impact of queer feminist readings and "postcolonial" formulations of race, nation, and empire in the medieval period, Heng argues that "feminist theorizations of difference, subject-formation, and a historicized politics of location offer strategies by which *an entire culture in transition* might be grasped."

My own essay, "The literary politics of feminist theory," seeks to represent the varied political stakes at work across the field of feminist literary theory. Feminism in all its academic idioms returns repeatedly to the question of politics, to the possibility that feminist criticism is neutralized or compromised by its increasingly comfortable position in the university, by its hesitancy to engage in a properly materialist analysis of the real conditions of women's lives, or simply by its intellectual "mainstreaming" as a new common sense (Robinson, Wiegman, Messer-Davidow). This essay reflects on the terms in which feminist theorists have debated both the meaning of literary theory *as* practice and the responsibility of the critic; it argues that certain feminist quarrels about the politics of theories have their roots in the radically different assumptions that feminist literary theorists bring to the problem of representation. Who does feminist theory represent? How are its powers of representation figured, and how does feminist theory calculate the weight of its own intervention? Such a calculation is the burden of every critical position, whatever the content of its claims, but it is particularly urgent in the case of feminist literary scholars, for whom the consequences of our work in the world "outside" the university has always been at issue.

Part II of the Companion turns its attention to the impact of feminist literary theory on the fundamental elements of literary studies, matters of genre, periodization, and form. Nancy Armstrong addresses the novel, perhaps the genre whose understanding has been most radically reconfigured by feminist questions. Armstrong's essay directly addresses this striking transformation; "What feminism did to novel studies" recounts feminism's emergence as a force that reoriented "novelistic" reading, shifting critical attention from the "lack" in the male protagonist to the question of "what female protagonists lacked." Armstrong examines the difference that this shift made – and failed to make – in terms of what might count as lack. She argues that feminist literary theory "has transformed not only the field of novel studies, but our notion of what it means to have access to political power as well."

Linda Anderson's "Autobiography and the feminist subject" looks at a genre strongly related to the novel, yet implicated in a unique way in feminist practice beyond the bounds of the strictly literary. She traces the "almost symbiotic" relationship between feminism and autobiography, pointing to the crucial role that autobiographical writing played in feminism's development as a "privileged space for women to discover new forms of subjectivity." Anderson traces the complex trajectory of feminist theorizations of this autobiographical space, from a field of feminine difference (traced in the "relationality" that seems to be so marked in women's autobiography) to Carolyn Steedman's conception of autobiographical memories as "'interpretive devices,' ways of interrogating the 'truth' of theory," rather than as personal confessions. Anderson demonstrates the powerful impact of feminist literary theory on critical thinking about auto-biography; she also discloses the ways in which autobiography interrogated feminism and became "the site for major theoretical debates about the subject" as questions of identity, difference, and the role of the reader of autobiography became increasingly complex.

Katherine Mullin's "Modernisms and feminisms" unpacks the "tangled and often contradictory relationship between two notoriously complex ideological forms." Mullin uncompromisingly traces the explicit masculin-ism of many of the leading figures of literary modernism, even as she notes the "historical coincidence" of the emergence of feminist agitation and women's increasing presence in the public sphere between 1890 and 1930. Although the polemical male modernists often described their project in antifeminist terms, Mullin notes that while modernism was forging an aesthetic radicalism that in some respects responded to feminism's political radicalism, women writers were finding a place within the new literary movement. She argues forcefully that feminist literary theorists have revised our traditional conceptions of modernism as a period dominated by Joyce, T. S. Eliot and Ezra Pound, disclosing the women writers, from Virginia Woolf and H. D. to Gertrude Stein and Nella Larsen, who invented a modernism of their own. These writers consciously attended to realms of female experience that male modernists openly disdained and deliberately carried out their own radical experiments in form.

Kari Weil's essay, "French feminism's *écriture feminine*," takes the ques-tion of linguistic form and the political intervention that can be made by literature to be of central concern. Weil draws us firmly into the field of textuality as it has been conceptualized in poststructuralist theory. She argues that after the advent of French feminism, the focus of feminist literary criticism shifted from "the status of women as producers of litera-ture [and] the representation of women's experience in literature [to] the production of the 'feminine' in literature." This sea change involved a new attention to the body, pleasure, and difference, including, of course, sexual difference, now understood as a textual effect. Weil traces the prehistory of this new concept of representation, setting the theorists and writers dubbed "French feminists" in the United States within a French national context that is home to many other feminisms and to various poststructuralisms. She then discusses the work of four major figures, carefully teasing out the arguments and rhetorics with which they approach questions of subjectivity, essentialism, women's language, and desire. She sees in their experimental poetics and radical theorizing a feminist "provocation [that] has immense political and aesthetic possibilities that are still untapped today."

Nickianne Moody's "Feminism and popular culture" takes up another provocative field of aesthetic and political possibility: feminist theory's relationship with popular culture studies, which have developed alongside feminist literary studies, sometimes in intimate cooperation, sometimes in productive conflict. Moody is frank about the way in which some feminist observers have condemned popular culture, reducing its influence to a kind of propaganda against women's rights and interests. Her essay carefully traces the intricate readings that feminist scholars of popular culture have provided to debunk this alternately dismissive and alarmist view and to clarify the ways in which women (and men) *use* popular culture. To be sure, she emphasizes that popular texts – films, music, magazines, television, romance fiction – can be the occasion for subjection to stereotypes and oppressive norms; but she also demonstrates the myriad ways in which critical readings can emerge. She powerfully demonstrates the degree to which feminist literary studies has learned to appreciate the "popular" traditions of women's writing and the work of ideology in "high" culture, even as she discloses the "polysemic, porous" quality of popular culture, a textual heterogeneity that both guarantees its "popular" appeal to a wide audience and offers an opening to the critical reader.

The final section of the Companion turns to the intersections and articulations between feminist literary theories and other major theoretical problematics in cultural studies. Feminist theory has engaged, critiqued and, learned from theoretical work in other disciplines and subfields, even as it has helped to develop and elaborate those fields, introducing them to concepts of gender, representation, and textuality. Rey Chow's "Poststructuralism: theory as critical self-consciousness" shifts our attention from literary genres and the problem of tradition to the question of feminist theory's "contentious" relationship with poststructuralism. Chow reads that relation through the problem of the subject, a topic that feminist literary theory returns to repeatedly, whether in the form of the "deconstruction" of woman or the status of the "personal criticism" or the genres of autobiography and memoir. Chow sees in the work inaugurated by Derrida an "effort to radicalize (the meaning of) meaning as conventionally derived from various stable forms of *identities*, including the text, history, and thought, as well as the subject itself." Querying the bracketing of referentiality that is part and parcel of this radicalization, she asks: "what are the wider political implications of such intense acts of *self-referentiality?*" and finds in the poststructuralist work of Michel Foucault an alternative challenge to reference, one that is less vulnerable to a solipsistic textualism, but permits critical self-consciousness to address itself to representation and to the production of knowledge itself.

In "Feminists theorize colonial/postcolonial," Rosemary Marangoly George argues that postcolonial feminist theory works, on the one hand, to interrupt the discourses of postcolonial theory and liberal Western feminism and, on the other, to guard against the theorizing of the "Third World Woman" as a monolithic, singular figure. Focused on the structures of colonial relations of power and insistently "bringing the world" into the arena of Western scholarship, these crucial interruptions fund a range of literary and theoretical projects: the expansion of a canon both masculinist and Western in its biases and blind to "what cannot be represented in elite texts"; the theorization of the contradictory place of the female subject in colonialism and in decolonization; the "persistent embedding of gendered difference in a larger understanding of race, nationality, class, and caste." George reads a sequence of essays by the theorist Gayatri Spivak as signposts marking the trajectory of postcolonial feminist literary studies, which she finds turning with increasing interest to the questions of diaspora and transnationalism, even as it reflects soberly on location and on its own "relation and proximity to power."

Rashmi Varma's essay, "On common ground?: feminist theory and critical race theory," traces the rise of "feminist critical race studies" through a fifty-year history of interchanges, critiques, and negotiations concerning the theorization of race and gender. Drawing upon a vast range of scholarly work in critical legal studies, black feminist literary theory and history, critical multiculturalism, Chicana theory and literature, black British feminism, and globalization and citizenship studies, among others, Varma outlines the commitment of feminist critical race studies to "analyzing the ground of representation, especially as it pertains to how we read literary and cultural texts and their discourses on race and gender." Feminist literary theory contributes to this rethinking of representation in various ways. For example, the "reconstruction of black women's intellectual and literary traditions by writers and literary critics" such as Alice Walker, Barbara Christian, and Hazel Carby, central to articulations of black feminist theory, has contributed a powerful strand to feminist critical race studies' historical understanding.

At the same time, frameworks from literary analysis – for example, the concept of narrative – have enabled scholars to reinterpret textual power; critical race theory, for example, draws on narrative theory to expose the way in which the law inscribes notions of racial power as legitimate. Critical race theory has also complicated and revised earlier feminist theorists' conceptualizations of subjectivity: Varma argues that "one of the most salient contributions of the struggle to forge a 'women of color movement' in the United States was the understanding that feminist theory could not presume a priori the subjects of feminism." In the present historical moment, marked by a "reconsolidation of national borders and identities along racial and cultural lines" and the forces of economic globalization, Varma argues that it is crucial to think of identity as a powerful textual effect, socially constructed, but potent: "The task of a feminist critical race studies is precisely to help us to *read* the weave of race and gender in society."

Elizabeth Weed's and Berthold Schoene's essays mine very different archives and outline diverging, if not in some respects opposing, views of the large and unwieldy topic of sexuality, which remains critical to so much feminist thought. Weed's essay, "Feminist psychoanalytic literary criticism," focuses on the uses of psychoanalysis for a diverse group of critics. She argues that "all the players – feminism, psychoanalysis, reading, literature" – in the field have complex histories and uneven relations with each other. Teasing out these relations, Weed notes the shared engagement with the problem of meaning; the predominance of the concept of sexual difference; the shifting of advantage, such that, for a time, psychoanalysis reigns over literature, citing it for the sake of its "example," whereas, at another moment, psychoanalysis appears as text, resembling literature itself more than a theory of literariness. Weed discloses the many varieties of feminist psychoanalytic thought, ranging from the Lacanian to object relations to the more recent turn toward the problems of racism and racialization, and proposes that psychoanalysis as the possibility of rereading remains an "incitement" to feminist critics.

Berthold Schoene's "Queer politics, queer theory and the future of 'identity': spiralling out of culture" takes a very different point of departure – Michel Foucault's *History of Sexuality* – and a very different approach, tracing the consequences of Foucault's argument that sexuality is a discourse, a complex of incitements and disciplines intimately bound up with power, "a vast complexity of . . . power which for the most part [is] entirely beyond our control." Schoene proceeds to delineate the development of the queer movement and the dispersion of queer theories. "Intent on disrupting anything too smoothly commonsensical or straightforward," Schoene writes, in a marked echo of Weed's essay, "'queer' stands for recalcitrance and strategic fractiousness." He examines the possibilities and the hesitancies that mark "a politics of radical anti-identity" and the theorizations of figures from Michael Warner and Eve Sedgwick to Calvin Thomas and Judith Butler. Rather than focus on queer theory's innovations within literary criticism, Schoene discloses the way in which literary and feminist theorists have shaped the emergence of the elusively and allusively queer subject.

NOTES

1. A brief, unrepresentative sampling of such work over the past twenty years might include: Elaine Showalter, ed., *The New Feminist Criticism* (New York: Pantheon Books, 1985); Cheryl Wall, ed., *Changing Our Own Words: Essays on Criticism, Theory and Writing by Black Women* (New Brunswick: Rutgers, 1989); and Sally Munt, ed., *New Lesbian Criticism: Literary and Cultural Readings* (New York: Columbia University Press, 1992) as anthologists; Toril Moi, *Sexual/Textual Politics: Feminist Literary Theory* (London: Methuen, 1985), and Ruth Robbins, *Literary Feminisms* (New York: St. Martin's Press, 2000), as single authors providing introductions; and Jane Gallop's *Around 1981: Academic Feminist Literary Theory* (New York: Routledge, 1992), the study of feminist anthologizers. Gallop observes the odd temporality of feminist literary theory's "emergence" and notes the early (originary?) concern that it may be "impossible" to "theoretically 'account for' the entirety of feminist criticism in its breadth and diversity" (p. 23).
2. Theorists from many disciplines and traditions have asked "what counts as theory?" as Katie King argues in *Theory in Its Feminist Travels: Conversations in U. S. Women's Movements* (Bloomington: Indiana University Press, 1994), pp. 1–54. King asks: "what are the different investments in the multiple historical objects deployed/displayed under the sign of 'theory'" and "what generic or unmarked forms of 'theory' are challenged or altered by, or hide local or marked 'theory'" (p. 2)?
3. Barbara Johnson, *The Critical Difference: Essays in the Contemporary Rhetoric of Reading* (Baltimore: The Johns Hopkins University Press, 1980, pp. xi–xii.
4. Jacques Derrida, *Spurs: Nietzsche's Styles*. trans. Barbara Harlow (Chicago: University of Chicago Press, 1979), p. 85. Derrida makes this point while chastising Heidegger for misreading Nietzsche, specifically, for ignoring the "idea's becoming female" (p. 85).
5. See Elaine Marks, "Feminisms Wake," *Boundary* 2 12:2 (1984), pp. 99–110; Rey Chow, "The Politics and Pedagogy of Asian Literatures in American Universities," *differences* 2:3 (1990), pp. 29–51; and Gayatri Spivak, *A Critique of Postcolonial Reason* (Cambridge, MA: Harvard University Press, 1999). Spivak points out that the "information-retrieval approach to 'Third World' (the term is increasingly, and insultingly, 'emergent') literature . . . often employs a deliberately 'non-theoretical' methodology with self-conscious rectitude" (p. 114).
6. In "Feminist Politics: What's Home Got to Do with It?," in Teresa de Lauretis, ed., *Feminist Studies/Critical Studies* (Bloomington: Indiana University Press, 1986), Biddy Martin and Chandra Mohanty object to the way in which "critiques of what is increasingly identified as "white" or "Western" feminism unwittingly leave the terms of West/East, white/nonwhite polarities intact . . . the reproduction of such polarities only serves to concede 'feminism' to the 'West' all over again" (p. 193).
7. Sabina Sawhney, "Authenticity is such a Drag!," in Diane Elam and Robyn Wiegman, eds., *Feminism Beside Itself* (New York: Routledge, 1995), p. 205.
8. See Elizabeth A. Flynn and Patrocinio P. Schweickart, eds., *Gender and Reading: Essays on Readers, Texts, and Contexts* (Baltimore: The Johns Hopkins University Press, 1986); and Judith Fetterly, *The Resisting Reader: A Feminist*

Approach to American Fiction (Bloomington: Indiana University Press, 1978). Schweickart firmly emphasizes "feminist *criticism* – that is, *readings*" (p. 38), arguing that "feminist critics need to question their allegiance to text- and author-centered paradigms of criticism" (p. 39).

9. Hazel Carby, *Reconstructing Womanhood: The Emergence of the Afro-American Woman Novelist* (New York: Oxford University Press, 1987), p. 15.

10. For a glimpse of the difficulty of "speaking 'as a'" lesbian without invoking "media-induced images of what a lesbian is" or one's "own idealizations of what a lesbian *should* be," see Barbara Johnson, "Lesbian Spectacles: Reading *Sula, Passing, Thelma and Louise* and *The Accused*," in Johnson, *The Feminist Difference: Literature, Psychoanalysis, Race, and Gender* (Cambridge, MA, and London: Harvard University Press, 1998), p. 157–64.

11. See the legal scholar Kimberlè Crenshaw's formulation in "Demarginalizing the Intersection of Race and Sex: A Black Feminist Critique of Antidiscrimination Doctrine, Feminist Theory and Antiracist Politics," *The University of Chicago Legal Forum* (1989), pp. 139–67; and Valerie Smith's literary theorization, *Not Just Race, Not Just Gender: Black Feminist Readings* (New York: Routledge, 1998).

12. See Jane Gallop, *The Daughter's Seduction: Feminism and Psychoanalysis* (Ithaca: Cornell University Press, 1982); Jaqueline Rose, *Sexuality in the Field of Vision* (London: Verso, 1986); and Elizabeth Abel, Barbara Christian, and Helene Moglen, eds., *Female Subjects in Black and White: Race, Psychoanalysis, Feminism* (Berkeley: University of California Press, 1997).

13. Peggy Kamuf, "Writing Like a Woman," in Sally McConnell-Ginet, Ruth Borker, and Nelly Furman, eds., *Women and Language in Literature and Society* (New York: Praeger, 1980), p. 286.

14. Ann duCille, *The Coupling Convention: Sex, Text, and Tradition in Black Women's Fiction* (Oxford: Oxford University Press, 1993), p. 9.

15. Denise Riley's *"Am I That Name?": Feminism and the Category of "Women" in History* (Minneapolis: University of Minnesota Press, 1988) is among the most lucid accounts of the formation and deconstruction of the category of women in feminism. My rewriting of the formula "women read" owes an obvious debt to Riley's revision of Sojourner Truth's question/claim, "Ain't I a Woman?"

16. See duCille, who states in *The Coupling Convention* that "*The Coupling Convention* is not an act of recovery or reconnaissance. It assumes no single tradition and, in fact, argues against the notion of *a* black tradition, *a* common black female experience, or *a* shared black women's language" (p. 9). Mary Eagleton turns the argument against the paradigm of great books: "To talk of the female tradition of writing can reinforce the canonical view which looks upon literary history as a continuum of significant names. Rather than disrupting the individualistic values by which the mainstream has been created, feminist critics may merely replace a male First Eleven with a female one: so you can study Aphra Behn instead of Dryden, Edith Wharton instead of Henry James, Dorothy Wordsworth instead of William." See Mary Eagleton, ed., *Feminist Literary Theory* (Oxford: Blackwell, 1996), p. 4.

17. See Ellen Messer-Davidow, *Disciplining Feminism* (Durham: Duke University Press, 2002); Silvestra Mariniello and Paul A. Bove, eds., *Gendered Agents: Women and Institutional Knowledge* (Durham: Duke University Press, 1998);

and Robyn Wiegman, ed., *Women's Studies on Its Own* (Durham: Duke University Press, 2002); the latter focuses on women's studies, but many of the essays touch upon questions of disciplinarity/interdisciplinarity in terms relevant to feminist literary studies, which, for all their differences, has close ties to women's studies.

18. Lillian Robinson, "Feminist Critism: How Do We Know When We've Won?," in Shari Benstock, ed., *Feminist Issues in Literary Scholarship* (Bloomington: Indiana University Press, 1987).

19. Linda Kauffman's introduction to her collection *Gender and Theory: Dialogues on Feminist Criticism* (Oxford and New York: Blackwell 1989) begins by citing comments by feminist theorists Carolyn Heilbrun, Sandra Gilbert, and Elaine Showalter. These major figures object to the way in which feminist criticism has been "scorned, ignored, fled from, or at best reluctantly embraced" (Heilbrun), to the fact that significant feminist transformations are buried by a "business as usual" attention to male theory (Gilbert), and to appropriations of feminist criticism by allegedly sympathetic men (Showalter), all cited in Kauffman, pp. 2–3. This suggests that there may be no moment in feminist literary theory's history *prior* to its fall into disrepair or disrespect.

20. Hortense Spillers, *Black, White and In Color: Essays on American Literature and Culture* (Chicago: University of Chicago Press, 2003), p. xvi.

21. Susan Gubar, "What Ails Feminist Criticism?," *Critical Inquiry* 24 (Summer 1998), p. 901. A revised version appears in Gubar, *Critical Condition: Feminism at the Turn of the Century* (New York: Columbia University Press, 2000).

22. This opposition itself does not hold up to any scrutiny: there are postcolonialist critics who are poststructuralists, there are poststructuralists who are African Americanists, and so forth; Gubar would likely agree with this point, but her reading of these two currents almost requires her not to make it. Critical race theorists who are also poststructuralists have little patience for essentialisms or identity politics, which does not prevent them from criticizing racism or unearned universalizations.

23. Robyn Wiegman, "What Ails Feminist Criticism? A Second Opinion," *Critical Inquiry* 25 (Winter 1999), p. 366.

24. Jane Gallop, *Reading Lacan* (Ithaca: Cornell University Press, 1985), p. 18.

25. See Judith Roof and Robyn Wiegman, eds., *Who Can Speak? Authority and Critical Identity* (Urbana: University of Illinois Press, 1995); and Ellen Rooney, "What's the Story? Feminist Theory, Narrative, Address," *differences* 8:1 (1996), pp. 1–30.

26. Gubar remarks on the title, but only to observe that it revises Richard Wright's *White Man, Listen!*.

27. Barbara Johnson, *A World of Difference* (Baltimore: The Johns Hopkins University Press, 1987), p. 185. See Emile Benveniste, *Problems in General Linguistics* (Coral Gables: University of Miami Press, 1971), on the "I" and the "you" in the "instance of discourse" (225); and Jonathan Culler, "Apostrophe," in *The Pursuit of Signs* (Ithaca, NY: Cornell University Press, 1982), pp. 135–54.

PART I

Problematics emerge

I

ANN DUCILLE

On canons: anxious history and the rise of black feminist literary studies

"Twice in the history of the United States the struggle for racial equality has been midwife to a feminist movement. In the abolition movement of the 1830s and 1840s, and again in the civil rights movement of the 1960s, women experiencing the contradictory expectations and stresses of changing roles began to move from individual discontents to social movement in their own behalf. Working for racial justice, they gained experience in organizing and in collective action, an ideology that described and condemned oppression analogous to their own, and a belief in human "rights" that could justify them in claiming equality for themselves."
– Sara Evans, *Personal Politics* (1980)

Black feminist literary studies, like black women themselves, has had a troubled relationship to the larger rubric "feminist." The trouble stems in part from the history of elitism and exclusion that attends the development of feminism as a social and intellectual movement in the United States and as a politics of reading in the academy. In the nineteenth century, decades before the term feminist came into popular usage, the mainstream woman's rights movement spoke and wrote of itself in the singular to reinforce a sense of sisterhood in female body, mind, and spirit. In actuality, however, the use of the singular woman reflected a shortsightedness that bordered on tunnel vision, a sense of self and sisterhood that was – well – selfish. The universal "woman" this early movement embraced was generally white, middle to upper class, and based in the eastern portions of the United States. It did not include the pioneer women pushing their way west or the native women displaced in the name of Manifest Destiny. Nor did it include poor white women or immigrant women from the working classes. And it most certainly did not include the female slaves whose inhuman condition was so inspirational for the white proto-feminists who saw in the captives' oppression a metaphor for their own domestic slavery.

That the plight of black slaves served the kind of instructive and inspirational functions for white women that Sara Evans describes in *Personal Politics* is, however, not the sole or even the primary paradox inherent in the abolitionist origins of mainstream, first-wave feminism in the United States.[1] Also ironic is the fact that black women, who were often relegated to the margins of the woman's movement, and at times completely excluded from it, arguably had a keener sense of gender, as well as racial, inequality; a more nuanced, sun-up-to-sun-down, fieldhand and household experience of the sexual division of labor; and a longer and more complex history of what could be called feminist activism. Our continuing failure fully to acknowledge this lengthy history of black feminist agitation and writing has real consequences for all of contemporary feminist thought and activism, and for mainstream feminist discourses, as well as for black feminist criticism and theory.

Coming as they did from matrilineal and patriarchal African societies where the sexes often maintained separate, though by no means equal, systems of power, property ownership, labor, and wage earning, black women did not have the same tradition of dependence on men or submission to male authority that white women had. What they had instead, in many instances, was a tradition of self-reliance, sisterhood, women's networks, and female entrepreneurship that was not completely eradicated by the conditions of slavery in the New World. Nor was the slave cabin a patriarchal realm in which husband ruled over wife and child as provider and protector. Women were the more likely heads of slave households, though this labor-intensive role was defined by responsibilities, not power.[2]

Like black slaves, white women in the United States in the nineteenth century, regardless of their social standing, did not enjoy the full rights and privileges of citizenship. This was particularly true of married women for whom holy wedlock represented a kind of "civil death" that denied them independent legal status and gave their husbands dominion over their lives, their labor, their property, and even the children born into their marriages. Given this lack of political entitlement, it is not surprising that white women were attracted to the cause of equal rights, but even as they appropriated slavery as a metaphor for their own oppression, the priorities of their campaign against male domination were fundamentally different from those of black women. Whereas white female activists were concerned with the right of married women to own property, for example, black women were concerned with the basic human right not to be literally owned as chattel. As white women lobbied to change divorce laws, black women lobbied to change the laws that prohibited slaves from marrying. While white women sought definition outside the roles of wife and mother, black women sought the freedom to live within traditional gender roles, to claim the luxury of loving their own men and mothering their own children: "to get to a place where you could love anything you chose," Toni Morrison wrote in *Beloved* (1987), "not to need permission for desire."[3]

The publicly articulated campaigns of black women to own their own bodies, their own labor, their own land, their own desire can be traced back at least to the eighteenth century, if we include such figures as the pioneering poet, orator, and former slave Lucy Terry Prince (*c.* 1724–1821). Best known for her one poem that has survived, "Bars Fight" (1746), an eyewitness account of an Indian raid in Deerfield, Massachusetts, Prince lived a long and remarkable life that included many public challenges to the prevailing patriarchal order. Her frontier home in Guilford, Vermont, is said to have been a center for civil rights and literary activity in the years following her marriage in 1756 to Bijah Prince, a much older freed black man of means who purchased her freedom. In 1785, at a time when white women generally did not speak at meetings and other public forums or openly challenge male authority, Prince successfully appealed to no less than the governor of Vermont and his council for help in ending the harassment of her family by John Noyes, a wealthy, influential neighbor who went on to become a state legislator.

What persuaded the governor and his lieutenant and councilors to side with a black woman over a powerful white statesman or even to hear the black woman's case? The former slave's lack of standing within the category "woman" (and certainly within what would later be designated the "Cult of True Womanhood") may have afforded Mrs. Prince access to the public sphere, including the right to speak for her husband, which most white women would not have been allowed to claim. It is also true that, although by no means egalitarian, the colonial frontier was in some ways less gender and racially stratified in the eighteenth century than more "civil society" would become in the nineteenth. Relaxed gender conventions and racial codes aside, Lucy Prince's legendary oratorical gifts no doubt helped her to win the day with the Governor's Council, but the case also may have turned on the particularly cunning representation that the petitioner made to His Excellency on behalf of her husband and children. Apparently, Mrs. Prince argued that unless the governor ordered the Guilford selectmen to protect her and her family from the further destruction of their property and disruption of their livelihood, the Princes would be unable to sustain themselves and would therefore become dependent on the charity of the town. In other words, Mrs. Prince may have prevailed, at least in part, by playing the welfare card, by appealing not to the state's fair mind but to its pocketbook.

Prince also has been widely credited with at least two other remarkable feats of feminist insurrection and public oratory: successfully arguing her own land dispute case before the US Supreme Court and addressing the Trustees of Williams College in an unsuccessful attempt to persuade them to admit her son regardless of his race. Legend even insists that when her suit against another white male neighbor, Colonel Eli Bronson, reached the Supreme Court, the presiding justice, Samuel Chase, praised Prince for delivering a better oral argument than he had heard from any Vermont lawyer. There are numerous secondary accounts of these last two exploits but little or no primary documentation to support them. Prince may have petitioned some august white male body in pursuit of higher education for one of her three sons, and she may have argued before some court – even a high court. It is unclear, however, that either audience was the Trustees of Williams College or the Justices of the US Supreme Court, as legend would have it. In fact, by the time Williams was incorporated as a college in 1893, Prince's oldest sons, Caesar and Festus, who are alternately cited as the subjects of her plea, would have been thirty-six and thirty, respectively. Even her youngest son Abijah, who is not named in any of the Prince stories, would have been twenty-four. One recent source suggests that the institution in question may have been the Williamstown Free School, which later became Williams College, and that the judicial body before which Prince appeared may have been the US Circuit Court over which Justice Samuel Chase presided during its May 1796 session in Bennington, Vermont.[4]

Lucy Terry Prince was a remarkable figure by any reckoning, but she was by no means as anomalous as the valorized historical record would suggest. Rather, she represents a determination and an independence of spirit that were not uncommon among black women, even slave and indentured women, long before either the woman's rights campaign of the 1830s and 1840s or the women's liberation movement of the 1960s and 1970s. Many of their names and deeds have been lost to recorded history, but countless black women devoted themselves to the causes of abolition, woman's rights, suffrage, and temperance in the fight for gender as well as racial equality.

Speaking to a mixed audience in Boston in September of 1832, Maria Stewart, a free black woman and a tireless advocate for equal rights, became the first American woman of any race to deliver a public address. Her subject on that occasion was the Colonization Movement, which proposed to send blacks back to Africa, but Stewart has also been identified as one of, if not the, first American-born women, again of any race, to lecture publicly on the subject of woman's rights.[5] Indeed, many of Stewart's essays and speeches are veritable feminist manifestos that draw on strong female biblical and historical figures in imploring women to recognize and realize their full social, intellectual, and political potential.

Not only did black women like Stewart voice their protests in public forums, they also wrote out their resistance in fiction as well as exposition. Their literary offerings focused on subjects such as female education; the oppression, habitual rape, and sexual exploitation of women; the proscribed sexual relations between the races; and even, in the case of Harriet Wilson's 1859 novel *Our Nig*, the taboo topic of interracial marriage between white women and black men. As its full title suggests, *Our Nig; or, Sketches from the Life of a Free Black, in a Two-Story House, North, Showing That Slavery's Shadows Fall Even There* also tackled the similarly taboo topic of northern racism.

Despite prohibitions against them, sexual relations and in some cases marriages between white women and black men were more common than civilized society was willing to acknowledge. As early as 1663, a Maryland statute forbidding such liaisons noted that "divers freeborn *English* women, forgetful of their free condition, and to the disgrace of our nation, do inter-marry with negro slaves."[6] Sexual relations between white men and non-white women appear in early American fiction to be sure. Harriet Wilson, however, was not only the first African American to publish a novel in the United States,[7] she was also the first American writer to base a novel on the subject of intermarriage between a black man and a white woman. But while it opens with the story of a white woman forced by poverty to accept the marital protection and financial support of an African man after her white lover abandoned her, *Our Nig* goes on to indict the pervasive master mentality that made even free-born black women articles of trade. Both employing and subverting the conventions of the "woman's novel," Wilson dares to tell the autobiographical tale of the white woman's thrown-away mulatta daughter and the abuse she suffers as an indentured servant, not Down South but Up North, and not at the hands of a southern planter but at those of a New England lady. As Henry Louis Gates, Jr. suggests in his introduction to the 1983 reprint of *Our Nig*, the theme of white racism in the North could not have been popular with white or black abolitionists and may account for the novel's disappearance for more than a hundred years.[8]

Like *Our Nig*, Harriet Jacobs's 1861 autobiographical narrative, *Incidents in the Life of a Slave Girl*, boldly indicts the value system, as well as the sexual preoccupations and predilections, of the civilized society that put white women on a pedestal and black women on the auction block. Using the pseudonym Linda Brent, Jacobs recounts her life story and "the wrongs inflicted by Slavery," including the seven years she spent hiding from her lascivious master in an attic that was little more than a crawl space. But like Harriet Wilson, Jacobs also addresses the extent to which the jealous mistress conspired to make the plantation household a perilous place for black women. Ultimately, however, as the black feminist scholar Frances Smith Foster has pointed out, although it, like other antislavery texts, confirms the prevalence of rape and concubinage, Jacobs's narrative of resistance and escape is "a story of a slave woman who refused to be victimized."[9]

When it was reclaimed and authenticated by Jean Fagan Yellin and reissued by Harvard University Press in the late 1980s, *Incidents* quickly became the most sacred black woman's text of the nineteenth century. As such, this single autobiography easily eclipsed the body of work produced by Frances Ellen Watkins Harper. One of the better-known, though much-maligned, names from the nineteenth century, Harper actively participated in the antislavery, equal rights, and temperance movements of the day. She left behind a written record that includes volumes of poetry, essays, and speeches, as well as four novels and what is believed to be the first short story by an African American, "The Two Offers," published in 1859, the same year as *Our Nig*. "The Two Offers" is particularly interesting for the way it juxtaposes the marriage relation and antislavery activism as options for women. A tale of two cousins, the "Two Offers" is a parable of sorts whose title refers both to the two marriage proposals that one cousin receives and the different offerings that the two women – one wife, the other activist – make to society.

Harper does not mince words in critiquing marriage as a potentially self-limiting institution for women. "Intense love is often akin to intense suffering," she writes, "and to trust the whole wealth of a woman's nature on the frail bark of human love may often be like trusting a cargo of gold and precious gems to a bark that has never battled with the storm or buffeted the wave."[10] One could argue that Harper's equal rights activism and her consistently subversive critique of both racial ideology and gender conventions anticipated by a hundred years the rise of a radical black feminism. Yet, something I will address later in this essay, Harper was more often read and rejected as a mimetic, sentimental moralist in the early days of black feminist literary studies, which has yet to claim her fully.

Like Harper, Mary Ann Shadd Cary was a major player in many of the political, social, and intellectual initiatives of her day: abolition, woman's rights, temperance, public education, the black emigration movement, and a woman-centered black nationalism. A journalist, activist, teacher, and reformer, she was the first African American woman to publish and edit a newspaper, the long-running Canada-based *Provincial Freeman*, and the second to become a lawyer. Although she is by no means a household name, even among feminist historians, Shadd Cary is a more accessible subject than most nineteenth-century African American women, according to her biographer Jane Rhodes, because, like Harper, her story has been preserved through her own writings. "As a journalist, lawyer, and activist [Shadd Cary] left behind a collection of writing that provides a window on her life, her political ideas, and the world around her," Rhodes explains in her 1998 biography. "Few nineteenth-century African American women produced a written record that has survived the passage of time. This lack of documentary sources has been a key obstacle in the writing of black women's history."[11]

Rhodes is right, of course: the historical record is thin. But it is also true that women's historiography and literary studies have not always been about the business of ferreting out and claiming African American women as pioneering exemplars of feminist art and activism. More often, such studies, including some of those by black feminist scholars and critics, assume that African American women in the nineteenth and early twentieth centuries were primarily concerned with "what they [saw] as their strongest oppression – racism."[12] Although carrying the burdens of both race and gender difference, these early writers and activists, in the words of one black feminist scholar, made a "clear and forced choice" to fight racism first and sexism later.[13] In her intercultural study of American women writing between 1890 and 1930, Elizabeth Ammons, a white feminist scholar, similarly insists that the paramount issue for black women was race. "While they suffered because they were women," she argues, "they suffered more and primarily because they were black: If one or the other of the two issues had to take priority, it had to be race."[14]

Frances Harper is often invoked to substantiate these claims about black women's priorities. Of the heated, at times vitriolic, debate over black manhood rights versus female suffrage following the Civil War, Harper reportedly remarked: "When it was a question of race, she let the lesser question go. But the white women all go for sex, letting race occupy a minor position . . . If the nation could handle only one question, she would not have the black women put a single straw in the way, if only the men of the race could obtain what they wanted."[15] In a close, contextualized reading, however, Harper's remarks are less a blanket advocacy of racial over gender politics than a commentary on the historical blindness and overt bigotry of white feminists whose vehement opposition to black men's gaining the right to vote before them was often cast in racist terms. Like many black women activists of her day, Harper realized that the abolition of slavery had little altered the social and economic conditions of the majority of black people. What she endorsed was the political empowerment of the Negro race, which for her and others like her was a *feminist* as well as an antiracist imperative.

Historically, only black women and other women of color have been called upon to sort their suffering and divide and prioritize their racial and gender identities, as if such a splitting of the self were possible. This notion of separable gender and racial identities has been a thorny issue in black feminist studies almost from the beginning. In 1988 Elizabeth

Spelman, a white feminist philosopher, lent her voice to the critique, identifying the assumption of a divisible self as one of the major problematics of mainstream feminism. "Western feminist theory," she wrote in *Inessential Woman: Problems of Exclusion in Feminist Thought*, "has implicitly demanded that Afro-American, Asian-American, or Latin American women separate their 'woman's voice' from their racial or ethnic voice without requiring white women to distinguish being a 'woman' from being white."[16] As I will argue in a moment, this "problematic" – that is, this divide-and-conquer way of thinking about race and gender – had serious consequences for the development of both black and white feminist studies in the 1970s and 1980s. However inadvertently, it treated abolition in the nineteenth century and black liberation in the twentieth as feminist issues only when advocated by white women.

Under slavery black women were bred like chattel to increase the master's labor force. Rape, concubinage, and forced impregnation were part of what made the peculiar institution thrive. Black men, women, and children were all victimized in the process, but women were exploited in gender-specific ways that took advantage of their female bodies and their childbearing, rearing, and wet-nursing capacities. Subjugated, then, in ways as particular to their gender as determined by their race, nineteenth-century black women writers, activists, and intellectuals were finely concerned with the rights, roles, and responsibilities of women, as well as with the emancipation and betterment of the race. For them, however, "woman" was necessarily a complex and inclusive category, as well as a double consciousness that cut across (rather than between) their racial and gender identities. For the more elite black female thinkers and writers and for the masses of uneducated, impoverished, enslaved black women they represented, the race question did not exist separate and distinct from the woman question and vice versa. Their commitment to uplifting the race was inextricably linked to a commitment to improving the social, cultural, moral, and material conditions of women.

The best-known, although by no means the earliest, example of this double-edged political consciousness is Sojourner Truth's impromptu address at the Akron Woman's Rights Convention in 1851. Unaccustomed to speaking at meetings, the white women present were effectively silenced by the fire and brimstone of the Methodist, Baptist, Episcopal, Presbyterian, and Universalist ministers who came to the convention to remind the equal rights agitators of man's superior intellect and woman's proper place in the home. In rising to rebut the ministers' claims, Sojourner Truth, who as an tinerant preacher and antislavery activist was no stranger to public speaking, drew on her own embodied experiences as a slave forced to plow the fields and bear the lash like a man, without any of the protections conventionally accorded the so-called weaker sex. Her words, mediated and some say mutilated through the recollection of Matilda Joslyn Gage, who presided over the meeting, read in part:

> Dat man ober dar say dat womin needs to be helped into carriages, and lifted ober ditches, and to hab de best place everywhar. Nobody eber helps me into carriages, or ober mud-puddles, or gibs me any best place! And ain't I a woman? Look at me! Look at my arms! I have ploughed, and planted, and gathered into barns, and no man could head me! And ain't I a woman? I could work as much and eat as much as a man – when I could get it – and bear de lash as welt! And ain't I a woman? I have borne thirteen chilern, and seen 'em mos all sold off to slavery, and when I cried out with my mother's grief, none but Jesus heard me! And ain't I a woman?[17]

Despite the civil rights origins of the movement, many of the conference participants did not welcome Truth's presence and did not want her to be allowed to speak, lest the cause of woman's rights be mixed up with the cause of "abolition and niggers." Nevertheless, Truth prevailed, and the speech she delivered that day, with its "Ain't I a woman?" refrain, went on to become a kind of feminist battle cry used to proclaim the power and entitlement of white women, rather than to explain the particular predicament of black women. As Phyllis Marynick Palmer pointed out in the early 1980s: "White feminists who may know almost nothing about black women's history are moved by Truth's famous query . . . They take her portrait of herself . . . as compelling proof of the falsity of the notion that women are frail, dependent, and parasitic. They do not, we may notice, use Sojourner Truth's battle cry to show that *black* women are not feeble."[18]

But of course, the point wasn't simply that black women were not feeble. However readily they later slipped from the lips of white women, Truth's words were actually a scathing indictment of the racist ideology that positioned black females outside the category of woman and human while at the same time exploiting their "femaleness." Her words also commented ironically, and pointedly, on the failed sisterhood that sought to silence her within and exclude her from the very movement that women like her inspired, enabled, and initiated. But Truth's words and the sentiment behind them were not hers alone. They were part of a shared discourse among black women who were or had been slaves and others who joined them in the suit for freedom and equality. In asking "Ain't I a woman?," Truth offered a more potent, embodied recasting of what was actually a popular abolitionist motto – "Am I not a Woman and a Sister?" – derived from antislavery emblems that date back to the late eighteenth century.

In her 1989 study of these emblems, *Women and Sisters: The Antislavery Feminists in American Culture*, Jean Fagan Yellin offers an insightful critique of the failed sisterhood between black and white women activists. She argues that by conflating the oppression of black and white women, nineteenth-century white feminists obscured the crucial material differences between the two groups. Black women, especially those who had been slaves, experienced no such confusion. "For them," Yellin writes, "the discourse of antislavery feminism became not liberating but confining when it colored the self-liberated Woman and Sister white and reassigned the role of the passive victim, which patriarchy traditionally had reserved for white women, to women who were black."[19] In other words, even as they attempted to assert their own subjectivity, white antislavery and woman's rights activists often reduced slave women to objects, emblems, and figures of speech. But black women remained determined to assert their own womanhood, their own identities, and their own humanity. On another occasion when her gender identity was questioned, Truth physically embodied her "Ain't I a woman?" response. When a member of the audience at an antislavery meeting in Indiana suggested that she was actually a man, she opened her blouse, exposed her sagging breasts, and invited the Doubting Thomas to nurse from the nipples that had suckled many white infants.

Black women like Sojourner Truth, Harriet Jacobs, and Harriet Wilson insisted upon telling their own stories. In so doing, they not only revised and expanded the concept of womanhood; they also took back the particularity of slavery, embodying with their own lived experience what white feminists had reduced to a metaphor.

＊ ＊ ＊

The story I have been telling would be merely old news, hardly worth rehearsing here, were it not for two factors. The first is the regularity with which this ancient history has repeated itself through successive waves of feminist discourse. The second is the extent to which this ancient and *anxious* history worked to define black feminist literary studies as a defensive, reactionary discourse, rather than as a visionary one in which African American women are the initiators of feminist activism, intervention, and aesthetics, rather than merely the inspiration for them.

Growing out of the civil rights and black liberation movements of the previous decades, the 1970s gave rise to a burgeoning body of black feminist writers and critics who became actively engaged in reclaiming lost, dismissed, and otherwise disparaged texts by African American women. This cultural reconnaissance mission was entirely in keeping with the revisionary agenda of mainstream US feminist criticism, which in its early years, according to Elaine Showalter, "concentrated on exposing the misogyny of literary practice: the stereotyped images of women in literature as angels or monsters, the literary abuse or 'textual harassment' of women in classic and popular fiction, and the exclusion of women from literary history."[20] But black feminist literary studies had other marching orders as well. It not only had to correct the omissions and distortions of male-dominated literary and critical traditions, it also had to contend with the myopia of white feminist scholars who, like their nineteenth-century precursors, took "woman" to mean "white woman" and, in Deborah McDowell's words, "proceeded blindly to exclude the work of Black women from literary anthologies and critical studies."[21] Much like their nineteenth-century ancestors, black women artists, activists, and intellectuals of the 1970s and early 1980s found themselves and their literature doubly disparaged. They were, on the one hand, marginalized within a male-centered African American literary tradition because of their allegedly "feminist" preoccupation with women's issues; and on the other hand, they were excluded from the developing mainstream feminist literary canon because of their assumed preoccupation with the politics of race.

Black women had begun entering the professoriate in small but unprecedented numbers in the late 1960s. The antidote to the out-of-print texts and the critical vacuums they encountered in attempting to teach African American women's literature was for them to produce their own art and criticism, along with recovering "lost" volumes by black female authors. It is worth noting, however, that the canon construction to which black feminist studies devoted itself in its infancy began less with reclaiming its past than with celebrating its present. That is to say, the earliest black female-centered anthologies and critical studies (the term "feminist" was rarely used initially) focus less on reclaiming the lost works of nineteenth-century foremothers than on showcasing the work of contemporary, living black women writers and on recasting recent historical periods like the Harlem Renaissance and the Black Arts Movement of the 1960s in women-centered terms.

In fiery 1960s rhetoric, the preface to the first of these anthologies, Toni Cade's *The Black Woman* (1970), announces a break with the past and with male cultural constructs. It also voices its impatience with and distrust of white feminism:

> We are involved in a struggle for liberation: liberation from the exploitive and dehumanizing system of racism, from the manipulative control of a corporate society; liberation from the constrictive norms of "mainstream" culture, from

the synthetic myths that encourage us to fashion ourselves rashly from without (reaction) rather than from within (creation). What characterizes the current movement of the 60's is a turning away from the larger society and a turning toward each other. Our art, protest, dialogue no longer spring from the impulse to entertain, or to indulge or enlighten the conscience of the enemy; white people, whiteness, or racism; men, maleness, or chauvinism: America or imperialism . . . depending on your viewpoint or your terror.[22]

A fiction writer herself, Toni Cade (later Toni Cade Bambara) gathered together poems, short stories, and essays by twenty-six contributors – not all of whom were professional writers – whose work seemed "best to reflect the preoccupations of the contemporary Black woman" in the United States: racism, sexism, education, gender relations (p. 11). In addition to Cade, the most recognizable literary names among the eclectic list of contributors are those of Nikki Giovanni, Audre Lorde, Alice Walker, and Shirley [Sherley Anne] Williams. Their work is presented without critique, but the preface and several of the essays articulate the politics, rather than the aesthetics, that govern the volume and the sense of alienation and exclusion that inspired it.

"For the most part, the work grew out of impatience," Cade declares. "It grew out of an impatience with the half-hearted go-along attempts of Black women caught up in the white women's liberation groups around the country . . . And out of an impatience with the fact that in the whole bibliography of feminist literature, literature immediately and directly relevant to us wouldn't fill a page" (pp. 10–11). Cade also wonders out loud – or, rather, in print – whether "the canon of literature fondly referred to as 'feminist literature' – Anaïs Nin, Simone de Beauvoir, Doris Lessing, Betty Friedan, etc." – holds much relevance for black women.

She was hardly alone in associating the term "feminist" with what was increasingly characterized as the white women's liberation movement, despite its origins in the civil rights and black power initiatives of the 1960s in which "black women struck the first blow for female equality."[23] Cade also had plenty of company in insisting that black women could not depend on "this new field of experts (white, female)" to represent their truths and experiences (p. 9). Rather, they had to look to themselves and to each other for definition, and they had to create their own vehicles for cultural and intellectual expression.

The Black Woman: An Anthology was envisioned as "a beginning." Numerous other anthologies and critical studies of black women's writing followed, including two important collections edited by the pioneering black feminist scholar Mary Helen Washington, *Black-Eyed Susans: Classic Stories by and about Black Women* (1975) and *Midnight Birds: Stories of*

Contemporary Black Women Writers (1980). At the same time, black women writers were furiously producing remarkable fiction. Toni Morrison and Alice Walker both published their first novels in 1970: *The Bluest Eye* and *The Third Life of Grange Copeland*, respectively. Morrison followed up her stunning debut with such master works as *Sula* in 1973, *Song of Solomon* in 1977, and *Tar Baby* in 1981. In 1973 Walker published an important collection of short stories, *In Love and Trouble*; her second novel, *Meridian*, appeared in 1976, followed by a second collection of short stories, *You Can't Keep a Good Woman Down*, in 1981, and her third novel, *The Color Purple*, in 1982. She also published three volumes of poetry during the decade and several influential essays – many of them in *Ms. Magazine* – including "In Search of Our Mothers' Gardens" (1974), which would become the title of her 1983 essay collection, and "In Search of Zora Neale Hurston" (1975), which recounts her pilgrimage to Fort Pierce, Florida, two years earlier to find and honor Hurston's unmarked grave.

As an editor at Random House in the 1970s, Toni Morrison fostered the careers of several young black women writers, including Gayl Jones, who published her first two novels, *Corregidora* and *Eva's Man*, in 1975 and 1976, and a collection of short stories, *White Rat*, in 1977. In addition to *The Black Woman* in 1970, Toni Cade Bambara published three other books during the decade – two collections of short stories, *Gorilla, My Love* (1972) and *The Sea Birds Are Still Alive* (1974), and a novel, *The Salt Eaters*, in (1980) – the last two also with Random House under Morrison's editorship.

Black women scholars such as Mary Helen Washington, Nellie McKay, Barbara Christian, Trudier Harris, Frances Smith Foster, Claudia Tate, Hortense Spillers, Mae Henderson, Cheryl Wall, Deborah McDowell, and bell hooks – many of them new assistant professors in colleges and universities that had never before had black women on their faculties – scrambled to keep pace with the creative contributions of their black female contemporaries. Beginning in 1979 with *Sturdy Black Bridges: Visions of Black Women in Literature*, edited by Roseanne P. Bell, Bettye J. Parker, and Beverly Guy-Sheftall, and Barbara Christian's literary history, *Black Women Novelists: The Development of a Tradition, 1892–1976* (1980), dozens of anthologies and critical studies swelled the shelves of libraries and bookstores.

Among the most influential of these texts was an interdisciplinary collection of essays provocatively titled *All the Women Are White, All the Blacks Are Men, But Some of Us Are Brave*, edited by Gloria T. Hull, Patricia Bell Scott, and Barbara Smith, which appeared in 1982. In keeping with its stated aim of defining and institutionalizing black women's studies as an academic discipline, the book includes bibliographical essays and course syllabi, along with sections on black feminism, racism, black women and the social sciences, and black women's literature. As the black feminist critic Hazel Carby later pointed out, the idea of black feminist studies as an independent field of inquiry was ambitious, if not dangerous, in the early 1980s, given the already marginal status of women's studies within the university. "On the periphery of the already marginalized" was a precarious position from which to assert the autonomy of black feminist studies, Carby argued. Moreover, as the editors themselves acknowledge, pioneering work on African American women had been undertaken by white scholars such as Yellin, who was a contributor to the anthology, as well as by black women scholars. Building on the cautionary undercurrents of Mary Frances Berry's foreword to the volume, Carby suggested that a more practical course for black feminist inquiry might be to join forces and resources with women's studies and African American Studies in interrogating gender and racial oppression.[24]

Today, more than twenty years after the publication of *But Some of Us Are Brave*, the extent to which women's studies and African American Studies have been transformed by black feminist inquiry remains unclear. Women's studies majors still complain that the literature and history of black and other women of color are ancillary rather than central to the field's core curriculum. African American studies – sometimes now called Africana Studies or African Diaspora Studies – is still divided by gender hierarchies and dubious battles of the sexes, though the public discussion of these rifts and faultlines is generally less heated than it was at various points in the 1980s. What is clear is that by the end of the decade, black women writers and black feminist critics and scholars had produced complementary bodies of work that had opened a new line of inquiry, if not an autonomous field, and shaken up, if not transformed, the study of gender and race in the academy.

In some ways, however, the furious intellectual labor necessitated by a history of exclusion and neglect made the new field of black feminist criticism a reactionary discourse as much at war with itself as with competing methodologies. That is to say, black feminist literary studies emerged on some level as a politics of reading without a particular politics, a discourse diverted from the essential task of defining its own interpretative strategies by the need to jockey for position within American, African American, and women's literary traditions. In fact, Toni Morrison charged in 1986 that "most criticism by blacks only respond[ed] to the impetus of the criticism we were all taught in college." She urged black scholars to go "into the work on its own terms" – that is, to avoid the critical fallacy of bypassing the book at hand for criticism that merely inserts the text "into an already established literary tradition."[25]

"Tradition. Now there's a word that nags the feminist critic," Mary Helen Washington declared a year later. For Washington, the devil of the term lay in the way it had been used to expunge black women from the historical record. "Why is the fugitive slave, the fiery orator, the political activist, the abolitionist always represented as a black *man*?" she asked. In her view, the answer resided in the fact that men held the power to write history and to define traditions.[26]

What would eventually come back to haunt black feminist critical studies, however, was its early insistence on claiming a single organic black women's literary tradition glued together by shared experience and common language. The idea of such a tradition received its first and most powerful articulation in Barbara Smith's pivotal essay, "Toward a Black Feminist Criticism," which originally appeared in the lesbian feminist literary magazine *Conditions: Two* in 1977. Writing from what she identified as a black lesbian feminist perspective, Smith argues for a critical practice that assumes the interrelatedness of racial and sexual ideology and the existence of an identifiable tradition of black women writers. What defines this tradition, in Smith's view, is the authors' common approaches to writing, their shared political, social, and economic experiences, and their use of specifically black female language. Along with calling attention to the heterosexism of black literary studies, Smith also argues that the black feminist critic should "think and write out of her own identity and not try to graft the ideas or methodology of white/male thought upon the precious materials of Black women's art."[27]

One of the most important – and ultimately most controversial – moves of Smith's essay is its suggestion that black feminist criticism should, by definition, read against the dominant heterosexist grain, allowing for, if not insisting on, alternative interpretations, most specifically the lesbian reading. She then proceeds to offer such a reading of *Sula*, which she argues works as a "lesbian novel" both because of the "passionate friendship" between the central female characters and because of Morrison's implicit critique of male-female relationships and the heterosexual institutions of marriage and the family. So saying, Smith seems to imply that any positive fictive portrayal of "women in pivotal relationships with each other" amounts to "innately lesbian literature," even if/when the characters are not actually "lovers" (p. 11). Although provocative and enabling, in the absence of a clear definition of either "feminist" or "lesbian," Smith's interpretative strategy seems to conflate the two; it also blurs the line between the text and its reading(s), between authorial intent and reader response. That is, in asserting that *Sula* works as a lesbian novel – that "consciously or not," Morrison poses "both lesbian and feminist questions" – instead of merely demonstrating how a lesbian reading works for *Sula*, Smith leaves the door open for the author to say that the critic is seeing something that is not there (p. 3).

As Cheryl Wall points out in the introduction to her 1989 anthology of essays, *Changing Our Own Words*, Smith's landmark explication of black feminist criticism gave name and shape to the perspective from which many black women artists and intellectuals were writing and thinking in the 1970s. Other black feminist critics – most notably McDowell and Carby[28] – would later point out and attempt to plug up some of the holes in the critical methodology Smith proposed. Carby, for example, was among those who identified the reliance on a shared identity and a common black female experience as an incestuous, self-limiting interpretative strategy. Black feminist criticism, she warns, "cannot afford to be essentialist and ahistorical, reducing the experiences of all black women to a common denominator" (pp. 9–10). In addition to the restrictions it places on the discourse itself, such a methodology too closely resembles the inherently exclusionary politics of experience that makes it possible for mainstream feminist criticism to ignore the different experiences of women of color.

But there was something else about the critical practice that began to call itself "feminist" in the 1970s. While it took back, blackened, and politicized the term, it did not historicize it by connecting it to the pioneering black feminists of the nineteenth century, with the possible exception of Sojourner Truth. Still in the revolutionary mode of the 1960s, black feminist literary studies shot from the hip-huggers in the beginning. When it did become anxious enough about its origins to go back in search of its mothers' gardens – to use Alice Walker's metaphor – it too often stopped at the front porch of Zora Neale Hurston, the self-proclaimed queen of the Harlem Renaissance, who had died in 1960 out of print and out of favor. Replicating the great author/great book model of mainstream canon construction, the new black feminist criticism resurrected Hurston as its literary foremother and her 1937 novel *Their Eyes Were Watching God* as its classic text in much the same way that white feminist criticism had reclaimed Kate Chopin and *The Awakening* and Charlotte Perkins Gilman and *The Yellow Wallpaper*. And like its white counterpart, it often reconstructed its picked-to-click precursor in a cultural and intellectual vacuum that treated her as if she gave birth to herself, Alice Walker, Toni Morrison, and the entire identifiable tradition of black women writers.

What was often lost or at least overshadowed in the translation was the work of Hurston's precursors and contemporaries such as Alice Dunbar-Nelson, Nella Larsen, Dorothy West, Marita Bonner, and Jessie Fauset, and of other black women writers whose settings are urban or whose characters are middle class. (There are striking similarities between Dunbar-Nelson's unpublished novella, "A Modern Undine," and Hurston's fourth novel, *Seraph on the Suwanee* [1948], suggesting an anxiety of influence that, to my knowledge, no one has yet explored.) Also largely missing in action in this emerging discourse in the early 1970s was the fiction of a number of nineteenth-century black women writers. There is considerable irony in this last elision in particular because these early writers had already fought some of the same battles over sexism and racism, over failed sisterhood and the double jeopardy of race and gender difference, and over the exclusionary practices of the black male and white female communities that should have been allies. Not only had their black feminist ancestors traversed similar ground, they had also come to similar conclusions about the need for self-expression, self-representation, and, in a manner of speaking, self-publication. And they, too, had undertaken their own efforts to combat stereotypical representations of black womanhood by publishing their own counter-narratives.

In particular, the 1890s (what Harper dubbed the "Woman's Era") was the site of furious literary activity on the part of African American women similar to the productivity of the 1970s, but, if anything, written against an even stiffer grain and published against even greater odds. In the 1970s and 1980s black women were a commodity on the cusp of becoming in vogue, though by no means in power, in the academy and the publishing industry. In the 1890s black women were not in favor with anyone anywhere, except perhaps within the separate women's clubs, political organizations, and educational networks they built to continue the fight for both racial and gender justice. Their crusades intensified and solidified at the turn of the century in the wake of the failures of Reconstruction, the rise of the Ku Klux Klan, the proliferation of lynch law and Jim Crow, and the increasingly patriarchal character of their own black communities.

Challenging the white male authority and racist characterizations of plantation tradition writers like Joel Chandler Harris and Thomas Nelson Page, Pauline Hopkins, writer, political activist, and literary editor of the *Colored American Magazine*, urged black women and men to use literature as an instrument of liberation. "*No one will do this for us,*" she wrote in the introduction to her first novel, *Contending Forces: A Romance Illustrative of Negro Life North and South* (1900); "*we must ourselves develop the men and women who will faithfully portray the inmost thoughts and feelings of the Negro with all the fire and romance which lie dormant in our history,* and, as yet unrecognized by writers of the Anglo-Saxon race."[29]

In attempting to help "raise the stigma of degradation" from the race, Hopkins's "little romance" tackles all the major political and social crises of the day: the systematic rape and sexual exploitation of black women, lynching and other mob violence, women's rights, job discrimination, and black disenfranchisement. Much the same is true for the fiction, prose, and poetry of Frances Harper, whose body of work consistently addresses the interplay of racial and sexual ideology. Published in 1892, the same year as Ida B. Wells's antilynching manifesto *Southern Horrors: Lynch Law and All Its Phases* and Anna Julia Cooper's feminist manifesto *A Voice from the South,* Harper's political novel *Iola Leroy; or, Shadows Uplifted* was long believed to be the first novel published by an African American woman. But even before it was dislodged from its premier position by the recovery of *Our Nig* and other earlier novels (Amelia Johnson's *Clarence and Corinne* [1890] and Emma Dunham Kelley's *Megda* [1891]), and eventually three other earlier novels by Harper herself, *Iola Leroy* garnered little cultural capital from the designation "first."[30]

There are, of course, exceptions to the tendency to ignore the black feminist past – the work of Frances Smith Foster, for one, and later Claudia Tate and Carby. More often, however, early black feminist criticism either ignores nineteenth-century writers like Harper and Hopkins or dismisses them for writing sentimental fiction in the Anglo-American mode – "courtesy book[s] intended for white reading and black instruction," Houston Baker calls them, even though the stated audience for many of these works is the black community.[31] Unlike Hurston's colorful prose (whose misogyny was overlooked or explained away), their fiction was condemned for not being authentically black or feminist enough, despite its consistently critical stance toward the heterosexual institutions of racism, rape, sexual blackmail, lynching, and, in some instances, marriage itself.

In 1988 the Schomburg Library, in conjunction with Oxford University Press, reissued dozens of previously lost and out-of-print texts by nineteenth-century African American women. Gates, the general editor of the collection, noted in his foreword that black women published more fiction between 1890 and 1910 than black men had published in the preceding half-century. He questioned why this "great achievement" had been ignored. "For reasons unclear to me even today," he wrote, "few of these marvelous renderings of the Afro-American woman's consciousness were reprinted in the late 1960s and early 1970s, when so many other texts of the Afro-American literary tradition were resurrected from the dark and silent graveyards of the out-of-print and were reissued in facsimile editions aimed at the hungry readership for canonical texts in the nascent field of black studies."[32]

Gates may not know why so few of these renderings were taken up in the late 1960s and early 1970s, but there are some obvious possible answers. It is not just that many of these texts were accessible only in rare book rooms, as Gates acknowledges. It is also – perhaps even more so – that these books were known only through their *mis*readings and through the bad rap that the "women's fiction" of the period had received historically, mostly at the hands of male critics – white and black. But an even fuller answer to Gates's conundrum may lie in that nagging word "tradition." None of this nineteenth-century fiction easily fits within the 1970s model of an identifiable black feminist literary tradition, a tradition that, by definition, privileges the "authentic" voices and experiences of black women of the rural South such as Hurston's heroine Janie Crawford in *Their Eyes Were Watching God*. Articulating the sentiments of many black feminist critics, Sherley Anne Williams invokes this privilege in her preface to the 1978 reprint of *Their Eyes*, where she describes her discovery of the novel in graduate school as a close textual encounter that made her Hurston's for life. "In the speech of her characters I heard my own country voice and saw in the heroine something of my own country self. And this last was most wonderful because it was most rare."[33]

Self-expression as a cultural imperative is one thing, but however wonderful, however rare, self-recognition as a critical prescription is inherently limiting and exclusionary. Written in an intellectual rather than a vernacular tradition – in the master's tongue rather than the folk's – nineteenth-century narratives contain neither the specifically black female language nor the valorized black female activities that Barbara Smith identified as emblems of authentic black womanhood. In other words, within the 1970s black feminist dream of a common language, this early writing was judged grammatically incorrect, out of step with the established tempo of the literary tradition. Ironically, however, this canon construction of the close encounter kind also excluded some of the work by the very same writer it had claimed as its founding mother, Zora Neale Hurston. While Hurston's second novel, *Their Eyes Were Watching God*, was heralded as the quintessential black feminist text, her fourth novel, *Seraph on the Suwanee*, was panned along with nineteenth-century narratives like *Iola Leroy* and *Contending Forces* because of its move away from folklore and its focus on white characters instead of black.[34] Inexplicably, by the logic of 1970s and 1980s canon construction, Hurston was a card-carrying black feminist writer when she published *Their Eyes* in 1937 but not when she published *Seraph* in 1948.

With the wisdom of hindsight, it is easy to look back three decades and wonder how black feminist literary studies managed to trip over its own roots in the process of becoming – how a discourse that evolved, at least in part, in response to tunnel vision and exclusion managed to become prescriptive and exclusionary itself. But that may be the very nature of becoming, of making something new, particularly in a highly politicized moment when black women's art stood for so much more than its own sake. Reflecting on her own pace-setting critical manifesto of 1977, Barbara Smith has said recently that her perspective was influenced by "the bold new ideas of 1970s lesbian feminism" ("Toward a Black Feminist Criticism," 3).

At the dawn of not only a new century but also a new millennium, black feminist criticism is in need of bold new ideas like those that called it into being thirty years ago. The discourse has weathered many storms: protracted debates about who may do it (black women, white women, black men), accusations of racial heresy from the brotherhood (feminism = antimanism), a resistance to the rise of theory in the academy (what Barbara Christian called the race for theory[35]), and charges that its "racialized identity politics" and unrelenting critiques of white universalism hindered dialogue, divided white women from black, and derailed the common feminist enterprise.[36]

But if black feminist criticism has weathered these and other storms, it may also at this moment be beached on the grounds of its own unresolved questions and contradictions. Third-wave black feminism, a young colleague of mine insists, is more organic than its predecessors. It is much less reactionary, far less anxious about the rejection and exclusion of brother and sister traditions. It looks to itself for definition with all the bright sparkling confidence of youth and is largely unconcerned about foremothers, precursors, and pioneers of the past. This introspective self-assurance is a good thing, perhaps even a coming of age, of sorts, of a discourse that now has the luxury of generations. As they say, however, those who ignore the past are destined to reinvent the wheel. And many of us who have weathered storms ourselves are wondering just what is new in twenty-first-century black feminist literary studies.

Further reading

Elizabeth Abel, Barbara Christian, and Helene Moglen, eds., *Female Subjects in Black and White: Race, Psychoanalysis, Feminism* (Berkeley: University of California Press, 1997).

Kum-Kum Bhavnani, ed., *Feminism and Race* (Oxford: Oxford University Press, 2000).

Barbara Christian, *Black Feminist Criticism: Perspectives on Black Women Writers* (New York: Pergamon Press, 1985).

Sandra Gunning, *Race, Rape, and Lynching: The Red Record of American Literature, 1890–1912* (New York: Oxford University Press, 1996).

bell hooks, *Feminist Theory: From Margin to Center* (Boston: South End Press, 1984).

Deborah E. McDowell, *"The Changing Same": Black Women's Literature, Criticism, and Theory* (Bloomington: Indiana University Press, 1985).

Winston Napier, ed., *African American Literary Theory: A Reader* (New York: New York University Press, 2000).

Morag Shiach, ed., *Feminism and Cultural Studies* (New York: Oxford University Press, 1999).

Valerie Smith, *Not Just Race, Not Just Gender: Black Feminist Readings* (New York: Routledge, 1998).

NOTES

1. See Sara Evans, *Personal Politics: The Roots of Women's Liberation in the Civil Rights Movement and the New Left* (New York: Vintage, 1980), pp. 24–5.
2. On this subject, see, for example, Christie Farnham, "Sapphire? The Issue of Dominance in the Slave Family, 1830–1865," in Carol Groneman and Mary Beth Norton, eds., *"To Toil the Livelong Day": American Women at Work, 1780–1980* (Ithaca: Cornell University Press, 1987), pp. 68–83; Angela Davis, "Reflections on the Black Woman's Role in the Community of Slaves," *The Black Scholar* (November–December 1981), pp. 3–15 (reprinted from 3:4, December 1971).
3. Toni Morrison, *Beloved* (New York: New American Library, 1987), p. 162.
4. See, among other sources, Lorenzo Johnston Greene, *The Negro in Colonial New England* (New York: Columbia University Press, 1944; reprinted with an introduction by Benjamin Quarles, New York: Atheneum, 1969), pp. 314–15. The historical record is thin, but David Roper's biographical pamphlet does a creditable job of separating documented fact from circulating fiction. See David R. Roper, *Lucy Terry Prince: Singer of History* (Deerfield, MA: Pocumtuck Valley Memorial Association, 1997).
5. Marilyn Richardson, ed., *Maria W. Stewart, America's First Black Woman Political Writer* (Bloomington: Indiana University Press, 1987).
6. Quoted in Kenneth M. Stamp, *The Peculiar Institution: Slavery in the Ante-Bellum South* (New York: Knopf, 1956), p. 352.
7. William Wells Brown's 1853 novel *Clotel; or, The President's Daughter* predates *Our Nig* by six years, but it was published in London. However, *Our Nig's* status as the first published novel by an African American woman has been challenged recently by the recovery and authentification, also by Gates, of *The Bondwoman's Narrative*, believed to have been written during the 1850s by a black woman named Hannah Crafts.
8. Harriet E. Wilson, *Our Nig; or, Sketches from the Life of a Free Black*, edited and with an introduction and notes by Henry Louis Gates, Jr. (New York: Vintage, 1983), p. xii.

9. Frances Smith Foster, "Resisting *Incidents*," in Deborah M. Garfield and Rafia Safar, eds., *Harriet Jacobs and "Incidents in the Life of a Slave Girl"* (New York: Cambridge University Press, 1996), pp. 61–2.

10. Frances E. W. Harper, "The Two Offers," anthologized in Ann Allen Shockley, ed., *Afro-American Women Writers, 1746–1933: An Anthology and Critical Guide* (New York: New American Library, 1989), p. 65. "The Two Offers" was originally serialized in *The Anglo-African* in 1859.

11. Jane Rhodes, *Mary Ann Shadd Cary: The Black Press and Protest in the Nineteenth Century* (Bloomington: Indiana University Press, 1998), pp. xiv–xv.

12. Ann Allen Shockley, "The Black Lesbian in American Literature: An Overview," in Barbara Smith, ed., *Home Girls: A Black Feminist Anthology* (New York: Kitchen Table-Women of Color Press, 1983), p. 83.

13. Carolyn Sylvander, *Jessie Redmond Fauset, Black American Writer* (Troy, NY: Whitson, 1981), p. 5.

14. Elizabeth Ammons, *Conflicting Stories: American Women Writers at the Turn into the Twentieth Century* (New York: Oxford University Press, 1991), p. 23.

15. See Eleanor Flexner, *Century of Struggle: The Woman's Rights Movement in the United States*, rev. edn. (Cambridge, MA: Harvard University Press, 1975), p. 147.

16. Elizabeth V. Spelman, *Inessential Woman: Problems of Exclusion in Feminist Thought* (Boston: Beacon Press, 1988), p. 13.

17. See Matilda Joslyn Gage's account in Elizabeth Cady Stanton, Susan B. Anthony, and M. J. Gage, eds., *History of Women's Suffrage*, 6 vols. (Rochester, NY: Fowler and Wells, 1881), I, p. 116. See also Bert James Lowenberg and Ruth Bogin, eds., *Black Women in Nineteenth-Century American Life* (University Park: Pennsylvania State University Press, 1976), pp. 235–6; and Jacqueline Bernard, *Journey Toward Freedom: The Story of Sojourner Truth* (New York: Norton, 1976; reprinted with an introduction by Nell Painter, New York: The Feminist Press, 1990), pp. 163–7.

18. Phyllis Marynick Palmer, "White Women/Black Women: The Dualism of Female Identity and Experience in the United States," *Feminist Studies* 9:1 (Spring 1983), p. 152.

19. Jean Fagan Yellin, *Women and Sisters: The Antislavery Feminists in American Culture* (New Haven: Yale University Press, 1989), 79–80.

20. Elaine Showalter, "The Feminist Critical Revolution," introduction to Showalter, ed., *The New Feminist Criticism* (New York: Pantheon Books, 1985), p. 5.

21. Deborah E. McDowell, "New Directions for Black Feminist Criticism," in *Showalter, New Feminist Criticism*, p. 186.

22. Toni Cade [Bambara], ed., *The Black Woman: An Anthology* (New York: New American Library, 1970), p. 7.

23. Evans, *Personal Politics*, p. 83. In her chapter on gender discrimination within the Student Non-violent Coordinating Committee (SNCC), Evans calls Black Power a "Catalyst for Feminism" and credits strong black women with being the first to challenge the sexism within the movement – challenges to male authority that served as role models for white women.

24. Hazel Carby, "'Woman' Era: Rethinking Black Feminist Theory," chapter 1 in her book *Reconstructing Womanhood: The Emergence of the Afro-American Woman Novelist* (New York: Oxford University Press, 1987), pp. 9–10.
25. Claudia Tate, ed., *Black Women Writers at Work* (New York: Continuum, 1986), p. 121.
26. Mary Helen Washington, ed., *Invented Lives: Narratives of Black Women, 1860–1960* (Garden City, NY: Anchor, 1987), pp. xvii–xviii.
27. Barbara Smith, "Toward a Black Feminist Criticism," reprinted in Smith, *The Truth That Never Hurts: Writings on Race, Gender, and Freedom* (New Brunswick: Rutgers University Press, 1998), pp. 10–11.
28. See in particular McDowell's essay "New Directions for Black Feminist Criticism" and Hazel Carby's opening chapter in *Reconstructing Black Womanhood*, pp. 3–19.
29. Pauline Hopkins, *Contending Forces: A Romance Illustrative of Negro Life North and South* (Boston: Colored Co-operative Publishing House, 1900), pp. 13–14; reprinted with an introduction by Richard Yarborough (New York: Oxford University Press in conjunction with the Schomburg Library, 1988). Emphasis in the original.
30. In the early 1990s, more than a hundred years after *Iola Leroy* first appeared, Frances Smith Foster recovered and brought back into print three long-lost novels by Frances Harper, all of which were originally serialized in the *Christian Recorder*, the journal of the African Methodist Episcopal Church. Through years of painstaking research and detective work, Foster managed to piece together most of the texts of each of the lost novels: *Minnie's Sacrifice*, which was serialized in twenty installments between March 20 and September 25, 1869; *Sowing and Reaping*, which ran from August 1876 to February 1877; and *Trial and Triumph*, which appeared between October of 1888 and February of 1889. See Frances Smith Foster, ed., *Minnie's Sacrifice, Sowing and Reaping, Trial and Triumph: Three Rediscovered Novels by Frances E. W. Harper* (Boston: Beacon Press, 1994. Recent evidence suggests that Kelley may not have been black.
31. Houston A. Baker, Jr., *Workings of the Spirit: The Poetics of Afro-American Women's Writing* (Chicago: University of Chicago Press, 1991), p. 32.
32. Henry Louis Gates, Jr., foreword to *The Schomburg Library of Nineteenth-Century Black Women Writers* (New York: Oxford University Press, 1988), p. xix.
33. Sherley Anne Williams, foreword to *Their Eyes Were Watching God* (Bloomington: University of Illinois Press, 1978), p. vii.
34. For example, Alice Walker, who was so instrumental in reclaiming *Their Eyes Were Watching God* from obscurity, condemned Hurston's later work as "reactionary, static, shockingly misguided and timid." This is particularly true of *Seraph on the Suwanee*, Walker maintains, "which is not even about black people, which is no crime, but *is* about white people for whom it is impossible to care, which is." In his definitive literary history, *The Afro-American Novel and Its Tradition*, Bernard Bell asserts that Hurston's focus on white characters places *Seraph* outside the scope of his study, suggesting that black writers can focus only on black characters. See Alice Walker, "Zora Neale Hurston:

A Cautionary Tale and a Partisan View," in Walker, *In Search of Our Mothers' Gardens* (New York: Harcourt Brace Jovanovich, 1984); and Bernard Bell, *The Afro-American Novel and Its Tradition* (Amherst, MA: University of Massachusetts Press, 1987).

35. See Barbara Christian's essay "The Race for Theory" and Michael Awkward's rebuttal "Appropriative Gestures: Theory and Afro-American Literary Criticism," both in Linda Kauffman, ed., *Gender and Theory: Dialogues on Feminist Criticism* (Oxford and New York: Blackwell, 1989), pp. 225–46.

36. On this last point, see in particular Susan Gubar, "What Ails Feminist Criticism?," in Gubar, *Critical Condition: Feminism at the Turn of the Century* (New York: Columbia University Press, 2000).

2

GERALDINE HENG

Pleasure, resistance, and a feminist aesthetics of reading

"At the dances I was one of the most untiring and gayest . . . a cousin of Sasha, a
young boy, took me aside. With a grave face . . . he whispered to me that it did not
behoove an agitator to dance. Certainly not with such reckless abandon . . . My
frivolity would only hurt the Cause.
I grew furious at . . . the boy . . . I did not believe that a Cause which stood for a
beautiful ideal . . . should demand the denial of life and joy . . . [it] could not expect
me to become a nun and . . . the movement should not be turned into a cloister."
–Emma Goldman, *Living My Life* (1934)[1]

For medieval literary studies today, perhaps the most satisfying demand of
a feminist aesthetics of reading is the dance of negotiating a delicate balance
between resisting and acquiescing to what we read, when we read a medieval text: a dance which acknowledges that agency rests both in the text and
in ourselves, in deriving the meaning we find when we read. Because
medievalists work with texts written more than half a millennium ago, in
historical contexts and social conditions almost unimaginable today, any
other kind of trafficking feels a little suspect to us. If we are merely belliger-
ent with a text, treating it with mistrust (as in a "hermeneutics of suspicion") and noting its "symptoms" (in a "symptomatic reading") in order to
critique it for its ideology ("*ideologie-kritik*") and impose our own preferred
meaning by forcing the text to say what we would wish, the relationship
forged between the text and ourselves, we tend to feel, is not an adequate or
satisfying one. Committed to feminist principles and ideals, feminist medievalists invariably require a critical performance that respects the integrity
of the text, and its place in history, by acknowledging the delicate choreography of meaning-making in which the feminist reader and the medieval text
both participate, each possessing specific kinds of authority and knowledge,
in the moment of reading. Our dance, of course, has steps and turns in
common with *all* feminist readings of literature, of whatever literary period,
and so is offered here as an allegory of feminist reading and readers that
points to the example of others in feminist literary theory.

What results, for feminists, in that dance of meaning-making, is often
an aesthetics of contingency that emerges in the act of reading. Pleasures
and politics jostle together, from moment to moment, in the play of how

meaning materializes, and it might not be clear, in every instant, whether the text or the reader is the immediate authority for the meaning accrued. A spectrum of feminist readings has collected in medieval studies, each choreographing its negotiation of texts in its own patterns and ways, with the balance of tension and emphasis falling differently, depending on the particular reader, text, and circumstances. Although it is impossible in a short essay like this to suggest the variety that exists, I will sketch a few representative moments, with the understanding that the vast majority not mentioned are nonetheless also invoked, and then offer my own semi-resisting, semi-acquiescing feminist reading of a medieval text.

In the beginning was resistance and inventiveness: or, when canons were critiqued, reshuffled, and revised

Many feminist medievalists began simply as "resisting readers" who practiced the hermeneutics of suspicion on canonical texts – those "great works" whose genius was identified in dead white male traditions established in elite academies in Europe, England, and the United States a century or more or less ago – and vigorously specified the antifeminism or misogyny in *The Canterbury Tales*, Arthurian romances, or the Old French *roman de la Rose*, where the aesthetic conventions that had dominated literary criticism before feminism's arrival had once found only cause for celebration. Strategies of resistance displaced traditional aesthetic conventions assuming that texts (and genres) conditioned their own reception, while readers were to cooperate by preparing themselves suitably to receive the genius of the great works. Feminists, sensitive to gendered models in all practices – including aesthetic relations posited on active, dominant texts, and pliant, receptive readers – sought instead a *political aesthetics*, and found pleasure and beauty in resistance, judgement, and critique of whatever the great works were thought to deliver.

At the same time, those readers who continued to find pleasure in works that the fathers of medieval literary studies had canonized, despite the rampant textual misogyny now obvious to all, struggled with their persistent love for texts whose dominant discourses had been exposed, resisted, and critiqued: what, then, to do with the delight one still derives from these works, where is that pleasure coming from, and is such pleasure always necessarily suspect? Unexpectedly, strategies that called for reading a text's "symptoms," its "unconscious" or "unsaid," came to the rescue, as did an energetic impulse to read the subtexts, potential texts, residual texts, or emergent texts that could be said to exist within, under, behind, alongside, or interleaved with the dominant masculinist text that advertised itself with blazing self-regard. These new readings sometimes focused squarely on women characters (however marginal) or feminized figurations (however spectral), while putting aside the age-old imperative to focus primarily on what the male characters were doing in the foreground.[2]

Some volumes, like Joan Ferrante's *Woman as Image in Medieval Literature, From the Twelfth Century to Dante*, Jane Chance's *Woman as Hero in Old English Literature*, and Sheila Fisher and Janet E. Halley's edited *Seeking the Woman in Late Medieval and Renaissance Writings*, declared their intent in their very titles. Not only was reading "in the margins" eminently intuitive work for medievalists accustomed to scanning marginalia in manuscripts (where, often, more interesting things were happening than in the "main" text), but feminist medievalists schooled in poststructuralist and psychoanalytic theory as graduate students also found exciting feminine narratives cunningly secreted in their favorite literary works. (My own "Feminine Knots and the Other *Sir Gawain and the Green Knight*" and "A Woman Wants: The Lady, *Gawain*, and the Forms of Seduction" were among such examples of triumphal feminist readings of feminine texts.)

Another strategy – most memorably exemplified for medievalists in English by Carolyn Dinshaw's *Chaucer's Sexual Poetics* – was to declare that the seemingly antifeminist canonical author was, in fact, a feminist after all (or was sympathetic to principles we would recognize as feminist), or might be claimed as a feminist author once distinguished from some of his narrators, characters, and plots, and identified with other features in his texts. Recognition, in the critical theory of the 1970s and 1980s, that different author-constructs could make up the figure of each author (just as many texts could inhabit each work) spawned a poststructuralist Chaucer along with a feminist one; a queer Chaucer and a "postcolonial" Chaucer (or at least queer and "postcolonial" Chaucerian texts) followed in the next decade and a half.

But if for some feminist readers different schemas of "symptomatic reading" shared the consequence of retaining a critical canon, for others, guilt-free pleasures and politics were more readily available by asserting counter-canons of medieval women's writing. The *lais* and fables of the romancer Marie de France and the brilliant, provocative letters of Heloise, in the twelfth century; the theologized mystical revelations of the contemplative, Julian of Norwich, in the fourteenth; the allegorical, epistolary, educative, and polemical writings of the feisty and productive professional author, Christine de Pisan, in the fourteenth and fifteenth centuries; and the self-consciously performative biography dictated by Margery Kempe to her scribe in the fifteenth century, were among the many women's texts rediscovered and affirmed as central, not marginal, to medieval literary culture, and lodged within the established traditional canon by the determined efforts of feminist critics and scholars.

If feminist responses to such texts written by women seemed characterized by a tacit relaxation of vigilance – women's texts seemed to elicit not reading resistance, but fantasies of recognition and sympathetic identification that threatened to turn a feminist reader back into a cooperative recipient of a text's meaning – the textual erotics of receiving another woman's words did not so much revive an older aesthetics, postulated on passive or submissive readers, as demand, instead, new aesthetic formulations that challenged readers. Writing by medieval women often has affective styles, cultural priorities and values, modes of authority, narrative trajectories, and other features that differ from conventions established by male authorship. They are often *difficult to read*, if your tastes and expectations have been conditioned by the traditional canon. In order adequately to read a woman's work, it seemed, a reader had to undergo a self-reeducation in history and aesthetics, recover an archeology of women's lives, labor, spirituality, relations, and communities, and devise a feminist poetics that answered specifically to these texts. Some advocates of a women's canon felt that women's writing subverted and transgressed the aesthetic coordinates of the old canon, calling into question the status of even critical canons. As readers accustomed themselves to women's writing and to the issues, styles, and challenges they presented, notions of how texts mark gender in expressing subjectivity, desire, and subject positions *stylistically* as well as discursively arose and were debated.

One consequence was the complexification of older ideas as to what constituted female and male authorship in all its forms. Female authors – and not only feminine texts – were detected in male authorial signatures, texts, and traditions, sometimes in eclipsed or occulted fashion, but sometimes cited in ways that could be read, were one practiced in such detection and reading. Jennifer Summit's *Lost Property: The Woman Writer and English Literary History, 1380–1589*, is a fine recent example of this readerly development. In the spirit of the feminist adage that Anonymous was a woman, unsigned texts – always in great abundance in medieval literature – that were female-voiced, or articulated female points of view, also offered opportunities to discuss gender authorship speculatively and instigated the study of female audiences and literary patrons (though invariably, questions were posed about gender mimicry, impersonation, and appropriation by male authors seeking to speak as women and for women in unsigned texts).

Anonymously authored, female-voiced Anglo-Saxon lyrics (such as "The Wife's Lament" or "Wulf and Eadwacer") that express a woman's

perspective or locate a female persona seemed ineluctably to urge a recon-
sideration of traditional assumptions that authors, when anonymous, had
to be male, despite the admittedly low rates of female literacy in the
medieval period. (What was understood to constitute "literacy" was now
also revised for medieval contexts.) Odd features were found in unsigned
texts that might have been read to, or by, women, and could thus have been
shaped, commissioned, or otherwise influenced by women ("authored" in
the broadest sense), if not actually set down on the page by female hands.
(One unsigned Middle English romance, for instance, depicts a female
protagonist needing to stop in the course of her journey to answer a call
of nature – an interlude not often detected in texts with male signatures.)

Virtually all the reading strategies devised by feminists from the 1970s
onward continue to be deployed, with variations, and have been adapted for
use in the first decade of the new millennium. *The Cambridge Companion
to Medieval Women's Writing* (2003), edited by Carolyn Dinshaw and
David Wallace, indicates at a glance the lively range of reading strategies
now in force: the editors note that Roberta Krueger's contribution to the
volume finds Marie de France's texts "using a female voice that interrupts
masculine traditions," while Sarah McNamer discusses "the women who
may have written lyrics and romances" without leaving their names. Karma
Lochrie's chapter in the volume taps a vein of feminist queer readings,
emerging from the later 1990s, that consider "what happens between
female subjects . . . 'she and she,'" while Alcuin Blamires reminds readers
that church preaching was historically not a "masculine monopoly."[3]

If meaning and value, politics and pleasure, in *all* medieval texts are
understood today to be fluid and contested, more amenable to being accessed *differently*, thanks to feminist readers, perhaps queer feminist readings and so-called "postcolonial" feminist readings acknowledge most
explicitly an aesthetics and politics of desire that engages with the reconfigured relationship between reader and text. Dinshaw's *Getting Medieval:
Sexualities and Communities, Pre- and Postmodern* acknowledges the contemporary feminist's desire to make "entities past and present touch" when
it reads, for instance, the "unassimilable queerness" of Margery Kempe's
biography as a usable past that produces analogues, say, for understanding
US Republican projects to defund the National Endowments for the
Arts and the Humanities in the late 1990s. My own *Empire of Magic:
Medieval Romance and the Politics of Cultural Fantasy* attempts contextual
formulations of "race," "nation," and "empire" within the medieval period –
archeologizing constructs that are central to ethnic, Third World, and postcolonial studies today – and reads the traumatic phenomenon of September
11, 2001, as the materialization of the medieval political past in our time.

Questions of the past's precise relation to the present are, of course, questions of reading and feminist aesthetics in which the reader's desire and the urgent demands challenging her twenty-first-century society encounter what is there in the premodern text, speaking itself, demanding to be heard; and the variety of ways in which that textual "there" is heard and remains vital and alive for readers today recapitulates the history of feminist literary theory and its engagements with texts.

Making women of the world: or, how a thirteenth-century guide for incarcerated women helped to create an inquisitional culture and its new subjects

Some time around the beginning of the thirteenth century in Europe, I argue in *Empire of Magic*, historical shifts occurred that formed a crucible for the emergence of discourses of race and nation. These new conditions would result in racemaking and the expulsion of Jews from several countries, beginning with late thirteenth-century England; formulate a discourse on color and see the ascension of whiteness to centrality as a definitional construct of European Christian identity; and elicit newly imagined bonds of community (in societies otherwise riven by numerous internal divides) that would issue in nascent medieval nations by the fourteenth century.[4] Crucial to the shifts that took hold from approximately the late twelfth century onward is a new recognition and codification of difference in medieval Europe; before this time, scholars agree, a general tolerance of variety in human life and practices is discernible. In the *durée* I call the "long thirteenth century," however, differences began to be identified (and were devised) in order to be taxonomized, ruled over, and ordered into hierarchies – in canon law, legislation, and institutions – inserted into systems of power/knowledge for purposes of manipulation.

The Latin Church set an example of how a large social grouping that is internally divided and heterogenous might establish the umbra of a unified community: by, among other things, developing instruments that consolidated structures of governmentality through close attention to, and careful specification of, what is inside and outside itself. Feminist readers – attuned to strategies of exclusion and difference-making in institutions of patriarchal power and authority – are particularly well-positioned, as we will see, to grasp the significance of premodern practices that resulted in the exemplary emergence of race and persecutory mechanisms. In 1215 the Fourth Lateran Council, presided over by Pope Innocent III, issued seventy canons – laws binding churchmen and laity throughout the lands of Europe and Latin Christendom – that massively expanded the ambit of church interests and control (more than triple the canons issued by Lateran I, and more than double those issued by any council of the previous century). As a medieval technique of social control, "canon law," as one scholar puts it, effectively "covers most areas of life."[5] The canons of the Fourth Lateran Council ruled over everything from marriage, the sacraments, and the governance of clergy and parishes, to the payment of tithes, taxes and the making of contracts, to conditions of appearance and dress for racial and religious minorities living within Christian borders (including the wearing of an infamous self-distinguishing badge by Jews and Muslims). In the first half of the century, mendicant orders of friars – Dominicans and Franciscans – were established and functioned as the church's mobile agents-in-the-field who disseminated and policed doctrinal and ideological conformity through religious courts, missionizing, and conversion.

As a grasp of the precise relationship between the individual and the group, and between the interior and exterior of individual and social bodies, was refined, the century witnessed the rise of torture and inquisition as instruments of interrogation and evidence, along with the persecution of homosexuals, Jews, and heretics. The crusade – that military arm of the Latin Church mobilizing armies from all over Europe against the Muslim "infidel" since 1096 – was for the first time turned against *internal* members of the Christian faithful. In 1204 the Fourth Crusade captured and eviscerated Greek Christian Constantinople, theoretically ending the century-and-a-half-long schism between the Greek and Latin Churches; from 1208 to 1229 the Latin Church inaugurated the bloody, relentless persecution and massacre of heretical Albigensian Christians in southern France under the rubric of crusade. The drive toward totalization, regulation, and control is discernible also in intellectual and cultural work: the century oversaw a systematization of philosophy in the procedures of scholasticism and compilations of *summae*, witnessed the rise of universities as centers of knowledge and ideological reproduction, and saw the aggregation of literature into all-encompassing encyclopedia-like narratives (such as the Old French Vulgate Cycle of prose Arthurian romances).

In medieval England the examples, ideas, models, and instrumentalities that took hold in this period conditioned a matrix conducive to nationalizing impulses, with clear historical consequences. Instruments like torture and inquisitional trials had little purchase in England – but the recognition and codification of difference and the scrutiny of English communal life and identity began a scant three years after Lateran IV, when, in 1218, English Jews were forced to wear the notorious badge that identified them as outside the English community, even as they inhabited the same towns and borders as English Christians. Crown initiatives, legislation, and

Church dictates thereafter continually experimented with defining and re-defining the changing place, meaning, and role of the minority community of Jews in England, until the Jews were finally expelled *en masse* in 1290. Across almost a century, this public spectacle disclosed the process by which an England riven by internal differences – competing languages, cultures, ethnicities, regional and urban stratifications, and class/caste divides – slowly calibrated an understanding of how an overarching English collective identity might be imagined and posited, across innumerable heterogeneities, by the systematic manipulation of racial-religious differences identified with a minority group of internal outsiders.

For English Christians themselves, the thirteenth-century proliferation, in England, of such cultural matter as confessional manuals, guides on how to scrutinize conscience and root out sin, and poetry and prose on the close surveillance and disciplining of the interior self, provocatively suggest that inquisitional culture in England assumed markedly *interior* forms.[6] Self-surveillance and methodical self-interrogation to identify and root out deviance, reinforced by stipulations of penance, mortifications of the body and soul, and other modes of scrupulous self-disciplining, would eradicate internal waywardness and construct subjectivities at home in the homogeneity that an inquisitional culture demanded. All practices that demonstrate how older subjectivities can be analyzed and taken apart, and reconstituted differently, to produce new, more appropriate subjects and subjectivities, are, moreover, resources that are ultimately useful over the long haul of nation formation.[7]

To consider some of the forces at work in this period, and show how a feminist reading of a literary text written for women – even women in seclusion – can enable us to see the structures of power and social dynamics at play across an era and its culture, we now turn to the specific example of a famous popular text, the *Ancrene Wisse*.[8] The "Anchoresses' Guide" is a study initially directed at women in permanent voluntary enclosure in small cells called anchorholds, which were often attached to churches in towns or cities, to enact the religious ascetic ideal of solitary contemplation. The *Wisse* was written in the first third or half of the thirteenth century (no earlier than 1216 or 1221, if it was written by an Augustinian monk, or no earlier than 1236, if written by a Dominican friar),[9] a century in which 198 anchorites were distributed over the counties of England at 175 sites, with 123 of these being identified as female (and only 37 as male): more than twice the number of anchoresses identified in the twelfth century, and more than in any other century to follow.[10]

Originally written in English, for three well-born anchoresses, this popu-lar text soon came to address a larger social audience; indeed, Part 5 of the treatise's eight parts, on "Confession," proclaims that its message is aimed at "everyone alike" ("alle men iliche").[11] Ann Warren's *Anchorites and their Patrons in Medieval England* observes that "all of the major works [written for anchorites] were expected to reach a much larger audience" (p. 103), with the Middle English works in particular, including *Ancrene Wisse*, being considered major literary triumphs, a "literature [that] represents almost an embarrassment of riches . . . that the heights of the vernacular prose literary tradition in medieval England were reached in writings for anchorites is of major significance" (pp. 103–4).

Unlike confessional manuals – also plentiful in this period and equally adept at showing how to ferret out the secret connivings of the self – a literary treatise like *Ancrene Wisse* was not narrowly aimed at confessors authorized by the Church to hear and weed out sinful deviancies. Moreover, though the text has an eye to a general audience, the addressees of *Ancrene Wisse* in the first instance – anchoresses – were historical actors who wonderfully allegorized the ineradicable intimacy between an individual and society at large, and the close connection between the interior and exterior of persons and lived spaces. An anchoress was literally a walled-in recluse separated off from society in a prison-like cell far more solitary than the "cloister" lamented by Emma Goldman in my epigraph, but the attachment of many an anchorhold to a church also meant, contradictorily, that a vital intersection with societal life was symbolically (and pragmatically) delivered. Warren quotes a late thirteenth-century anchorite, Walter, who rumbles: "what is a house of enclosure if not a street corner since all of every age and sex have constant recourse to the church" (p. 110). *Ancrene Wisse* itself, in admonishing self-restraint from idle chatter, complains that each anchoress has "an old woman to feed her ears" with gossip and news, so that there is a saying, "From mill and from market, from smithy and from anchor house news ("tidings") are brought to one" (p. 48).

Anchorites sometimes performed duties as schoolteachers "in an age when few were literate and such resources not likely to be squandered" (Warren, *Anchorites and Their Patrons*, p. 112), while an anchorhold might serve as "an ideal place to store precious goods, money, and papers in an era when there were no banks and few places for the safekeeping of valuables" (p. 111). The spiritual capital and respect accruing to anchoritism, moreover – the "rise in status" that accompanied "the religious life (in all its manifestations)" – meant that anchorites' "visions were interpreted to clarify the future. Some anchorites were active as patrons . . . using their influence . . . aiding . . . in lawsuits. Some were in touch with the currents of their day: Loretta of Hackington [former Countess of Leicester] supported the mendicants when they first arrived in England in the early thirteenth century . . . Westminster anchorites advised kings" (pp. 110–11).[12] Ironically, the collective forces of the world pervade the walled-in dimensions of the anchorhold, which becomes a repository for the world's interests; the recluse, consigned to solitude in order to focus inward, finds herself solicited by the pull of an outside whose forces impinge fully on her inner life, demonstrating eloquently that a boundary meant to separate inside from outside also brings into connective relationship what it theoretically separates and holds apart.

Although an anchoress might seem today a quaint historical player of little importance, the contest for her soul, her consciousness, and her subjectivity in the thirteenth century makes her over into a touchstone and symbol for her culture and society in ways entirely familiar to feminists, who are deeply conscious of the multitudinous means by which women are made responsible for the burden of symbolization in society. In the thirteenth century, Warren notes, quoting Mary Byrne, "the English anchoress replaced the nun as the model of chastity and virtue" in "Latin didactic literature praising perfect feminine behavior" (p. 104 n.25).[13] Such celebration of perfection in women – the simultaneous praise and coercion of select women, for select, preferred modes of feminine behavior – neatly encapsulates the dilemma that confronts the feminist medievalist, as she attempts to negotiate a fair, sensitive, and historically appropriate response in her dance of reading: a reading that must balance a sensitivity to women's lives as they were necessarily lived and constructed, in historical and literary contexts, with due resistance to the coercive will-to-power that the dominant culture sought to muster and enforce.

Directed at the reclusive life, *Ancrene Wisse* is oddly neither an aid to contemplation and meditative progress, nor a mystical treatise, but a manual of watchful self-custody fixated on danger and threat, struggle and upheaval, and the unquiet, unruly roiling of body and interior consciousness that must be vigilantly and incessantly policed.[14] Marked off into eight parts by ornamental or colored initials, and by themes, the short, last segment is devoted to external rules of conduct, whereas Parts 2, 3, and 4, on the "Senses," the "Inward Feelings," and "Temptations" concentrate attention on regimenting the interior self and its bodily sense envelope, which are rendered as coterminous spaces of danger. Together with Part 5, on "Confession," and Part 6, on "Penance," four-fifths of the text are thus directed to cautionary, admonitory, or punitive/penitential aims, though interwoven into the painstaking description of snares, lures, and traps depicted as lying in wait for the individual are wonderfully narrated stories and anecdotes, bibilical precepts and patristic quotations, promises and allegories of divine rewards and consolations, eloquent, speaking images, coaxing and coercion, skilful warnings and provocative reticence, resonant reminders, and sonorous repetitions.

To impose order and systematicity, in the manner of scholastic procedure, the text schematically generates internally differentiated taxonomies of particulars grouped by the theme under discussion, whether the focus is the seven deadly sins or the requisites of confession. "Temptations," for instance – the longest and most fulsome segment, as many have noted – begins by specifying the existence of "outer (external)" and "inner (internal)" temptations ("uttre" and "inre" [p. 93]), with each being further subdivided twofold ("twauelt" [p. 99]). The outer temptations are taken up and described, followed by the inner, which are subdivided into temptations fleshly and spiritual ("fleschlich & gastelich" [p. 99]). Inner temptations are constituted by the seven deadly sins and "their foul offspring," each of which is allegorized by an animal whose bestiality is elaborated in evocative vignettes of human sinfulness, each offspring-sin also being named, numbered, and expatiated on, and the overall enumeration proceeding methodically and accumulating a disquisition of substantial length, a procedure of elaboration often found in penitential literature of the thirteenth century.

After the paced description and subdescriptions of the seven sins and their pernicious offspring follow further internal divisions of outer and inner temptations into "temptations slight and hidden," "temptations slight and manifest," "temptations strong and hidden," and "temptations strong and manifest" ("Fondunge liht & derne. Fondunge liht & openlich. Fondunge strong & derne. Fondunge strong & openlich" [p. 114]). But if temptations are numerous (and indeed, we are told, it is impossible that the thousandth part of them be named), there are also categories of comfort against temptation (nine kinds, and three reasons are offered for the ninth consolation), remedies and cures of seven kinds (including four kinds of helpful thoughts and three steps of patience) that include parables and reminders from the life of Christ with which to counter the lures of the seven deadly sins, and that are as methodically specified and laid out as the sins themselves.

The detailed process of classification and illustration, repeated through the text and representative of thirteenth-century penitential literature, suggests the active presence of nets woven and spread out to catch the anchoress in meshes both of peril and of consolation, and represents the anchorhold as the site of titanic forces of struggle and contestation: a crossroads where all interests converge to focus on the female subject who is seen as having to struggle through a strenuous, continuing process of being made and remade, from the moment of subjective death that occurs with her entry into the anchorhold. That entry, whose formal ceremonies sometimes included the celebration of a requiem mass for the (symbolically) dead person to be enclosed therein, is ritually completed when the door of the enclosure is sealed and the inhabitant permanently walled within. Part 2 of *Ancrene Wisse*, on the Senses, thus renders the anchoress as an individual whose life has ended, who is now annointed and buried in her enclosure, and asks, "what is the anchor house but her grave?" ("hwet is ancre hus bute hire burinesse?" [p. 58]). Part 5, on Confession, subsequently enshrines the death and rebirth of the individual as a *repeating* institutional process – as the *regular erasure and remaking of her subjectivity* – by showing how confession functions as a key practice of erasure that destroys an older, unwanted subjectivity, in order that a new, desired subjectivity might be periodically set in place.[15]

The conditions for successfully dismantling and erasing the traces of an old subjectivity are set down. Recognition of wrong and accusation that direct bitterness and wrath toward the old self; a chastened, penitent submissiveness ("sorrow"); unconcealed, plain ("naked") admission; a commitment to totalized ("whole") recollection of the past; shamefaced, self-abnegating humility; and frequency of practice are among the many requisite imperatives for breaking down old recalcitrances. Truthfulness, hopefulness, and steadfastness are also desirable, and confession must be voluntary and willing, without undue delay, but judiciously pondered and considered: sixteen parts ("sixtene stuch" [p. 156]), are identified, in all, as necessary to the process, each part being meticulously elaborated with explanations, illustrations, and exhortations.[16]

The comprehensive surveillance of the self accomplished, if even a fraction of the sixteen named components is successfully managed in some combination by the confessing individual, would be the envy of any professional interrogator today, whether officers of intelligence agencies or courtroom attorneys. Indeed, the former Kremlin's or current CIA's interrogators would not be as surgically, relentlessly comprehensive: *Ancrene Wisse* specifies that *every sin from childhood onward* (p. 161), however slight or insignicant, must be included in the self-examination and confession, and relates a frightening cautionary tale of a holy man's near-damnation because of a minuscule near-omission of a trivial childhood incident (p. 162).[17] The thoroughness with which the text as a manual for self-inquisition lays bare the structures by which a total surveillance of the interior self can be accomplished, and the secrets of individual consciousness brought to light and bared, is an extraordinary exhibition of analytic power and persuasional force: not least because the text conditions the individual to *internalize* self-inquisition and self-accusation.[18] Explicitly, *Ancrene Wisse*

declares, this segment is directed to "all people alike" (p. 175), and its
strictures are in many ways conventional to confessional literature of the
thirteenth century, a literature that, as scholars of varied persuasions have
noted, enforces "medieval techniques of control" (Tentler, "*Summa* for
Confessors," p. 137).

Part 6, on Penance – which studies the role of pain and suffering in
affecting subjectivity – follows on the heels of self-inquisition and confession. We are told that to preserve conditions of purity, two things ("twa
þinges"), again of outer and inner kinds, are required, but it is the description of the outer this time that arrests attention, with its vivid evocation of
the sensory envelope and the body in pain: pain through mortification of the
flesh with fasts, vigils, scourgings ("disceplines" [p. 188]), harsh garments, a
hard bed, sickness, and massive labors ("muchele swinkes" [p. 188]). The
religious imperative here is straightforward – a direct imitation and reproduction of Christ's suffering – but the spiritual imperative windingly argues,
in a section pitting the ancient medical practitioners Hippocrates and Galen
on bodily health against God and the disciples on the soul's health, that the
wellbeing of the body means the harm of the soul, whereas the body's injury
and torment would ensure the soul's wellbeing and protection from temptation (p. 189). Although the medieval spiritual logic here might seem
foreign to the modern reader, the psychology of its reasoning is unexcep-
tionably sound, and the psychological principles in force here are still
applied today.

Modern studies of the body in pain suggest that pain by its nature over
time or with due intensity breaks down subjectivity, disrupts the flow of
inner consciousness, and unhinges the coherence of the self: it reduces
consciousness to one focus – the source and experience of pain. So effectively does pain fragment inner integrity and concentrate attention obses-
sively, shutting out other stimuli and demands, that little remains – for
wrongdoing or deviancy, or agency of other kinds. Pain undoes agency
and the impression of being an agent. As the thirteenth century discovers,
pain, then, has many uses. Applied by inquisitors and external agents as
torture, it can, in good time, amass an evidentiary system of proofs and
lessons to guard against future deviancies of many kinds. Applied voluntar-
ily to oneself, it has a prophylactic function in warding off internal deviancies and supports confession by breaking down the individual subject. Seen
in this light, the body in pain is one of the consolations of the thirteenth
century, a remedy to temptation, and a safeguard against sin.

Moreover, lest we imagine that only minor discomfort, not pain, is
intended in penitential self-discipline, *Ancrene Wisse*'s segment on Penance
holds up an example to its audience: the infamous case of one penitent who

wears both a hairshirt and a heavy shirt of chainmail together on his body, bound hard with broad, thick bands of iron around his waist, thighs, and arms, so that the sweat caused is agony to endure. In addition, the man fasts (denies the body food), keeps vigil (denies the body sleep), and labors (subjects the body to hard labor), and yet asks to be taught something more with which he might torment his body (p. 195). Such a regimen, enjoined as desirable,[19] if applied as an institutional method of discipline today by external agents would fit readily into any codified proscription against torture. As an early example of how consciousness and subjectivity can be managed, and directed toward desired ends, its effectiveness is probably not in question.

The psychological astuteness of *Ancrene Wisse*, and its grasp of physiology and what the body can be made to bear, and with what outcomes, precedes the slick knowhow of modern manuals and practices of interrogation by about seven hundred years; yet as an example, in the West, of literature that shows how to discover, identify, manage, contain, and discipline differences, *Ancrene Wisse* – more wide-ranging, intelligent, and aesthetically fine than others of its kind – can scarcely be bettered. That women are the first addressees of *Ancrene Wisse*, but that the text quickly finds itself generalizing from reclusive female anchorites to a wider social audience at large, more than coincidentally articulates a long historical tradition of recognizing women as simultaneously essential and liminal within society: seen as marginal in some ways, but always seen as central whenever society requires touchstones for calibration, or figures for exercising crucial symbolic functions.

Precisely because *Ancrene Wisse* represents its addressees as women at risk (anchoresses, the text repeatedly notes, by virtue of their high aspirations are especially vulnerable to testing and trial), the text thematizes women as a prime field of contest in the production of appropriate kinds of individual subjects and subjectivities in the emerging order of the world in the thirteenth century. Anchoresses represent society at its best, *and also* at its most contested and pliable, and in conditions of continual remaking. Moreover, the private investigations established by the text for women in seclusion – procedures involving self-questioning, answer, performance, and trial – share fundamental features with sensational public trial procedures for notoriously public female figures like the late medieval Joan of Arc, heretics, and witches: women who are also at risk, liminal, and crucially symbolic, with unruly internal lives.[20] Furthermore – though this is not the place to elaborate the argument – the culture of interrogation and scrutiny in which *Ancrene Wisse* participates, and that creates female subjects in conformity to precise specifications, is also the culture of racial investigation and interrogation that conduces to race-making, and the entry of groups of people into race, in the Middle Ages.

A feminist reading of *Ancrene Wisse,* such as the one I have presented here, which is both acquiescent to the text's logic and resistant to the text's driving impulse to discipline and contain, thus shows how feminist theorizations of difference, subject-formation, and a historicized politics of location offer strategies by which *an entire culture in transition* might be grasped. A feminist reading of this kind, for instance, registers the text's anxious admission of the sheer contestability of Christian interiors – up for grabs, mutable, in danger, and subject to necessary, periodic remaking – and offers insight into a key driving impulse, in thirteenth-century social projects, to rule over human groups by marking exterior differences precisely to *end* the possibility of remaking and contesting identity: to fix, determine, and immobilize into hierarchy by battening on outer forms of difference discovered and devised through regimes of inspection coterminous with inner scrutinies of the soul. For my own projects and interests, feminist theorizations of premodern cultures can revise current theoretical axioms on the genealogy of racism and nation-formation in the West, axioms which assume that races and nations of an identifiably determinate kind do not arise before the Enlightenment (or at earliest before the Renaissance), and makes possible the archeological recovery of a cultural crucible and historical period that the West, with its emphasis on modernity and postmodernity, has forgotten, at a cost.

As September 11, 2001 has demonstrated, long after the West had consigned its Middle Ages to the status of dim cultural unconscious, non-Western Mediterranean mentalities remained fully mindful of medieval history, never forgetting the encounters of Christianity, Islam, and Judaism in the crucible of violent historical transformation in medieval crusades, pogroms, expulsions, counter-crusades and jihad. In part because of that Western forgetfulness, definitions of race have also been practiced in the West, since 9/11, that peculiarly return our historical moment – whose international culture, like the thirteenth century's, is massively in transition – back to medieval hypotheses – especially in the palpable confusion that exercises cultural essentialisms as determinants of racial identity today, when Arabs, Muslims, Middle Easterners, Arabic speakers, Semites in general, and South Asians are willy-nilly identified as target groups of potential aggressors, "terrorists." Medieval ways of understanding human groups, and of ordering and manipulating human differences, in answer to force demands, have returned with new, contemporary, force. Modes of interrogation that align the interior and exterior of individuals, and understand the relationship of individuals to groups, in historically marked, particular ways, have been researched and practiced again, with depressingly familiar results. And at the intersection of competing discourses stands once again the figure of woman, forced to bear a host of critical symbolic burdens: a gendered figure whose appearance in a veil can signify feudalized (that is, medieval) space, culture, and time, to Western mentalities, and, simultaneously, whose appearance in battle fatigues can signify imperial ambitions and imperial futures to Middle Eastern mentalities suspicious of the West.

What has this to do with feminist theorization, resistant readers, feminist political aesthetics, and a thirteenth-century penitential manual called the *Ancrene Wisse*? In the light of crucial strategies through which to understand the meaning of the past for our own time and urgencies, the answer is: everything.

Further reading

Alcuin Blamires, *The Case for Women in Medieval Culture* (Oxford: Clarendon Press, 1997).

E. Jane Burns, *Bodytalk: When Women Speak in Old French Literature* (Philadelphia: University of Pennsylvania Press, 1993).

Jane Chance, *Woman as Hero in Old English Literature* (Syracuse, NY: Syracuse University Press, 1986).

Carolyn Dinshaw, *Chaucer's Sexual Poetics* (Madison: University of Wisconsin Press, 1989).

Getting Medieval: Sexualities and Communities, Pre- and Postmodern (Durham: Duke University Press, 1999).

Carolyn Dinshaw and David Wallace, *The Cambridge Companion to Medieval Women's Writing* (Cambridge: Cambridge University Press, 2003).

Joan Ferrante, *Woman as Image in Medieval Literature, From the Twelfth Century to Dante* (New York: Columbia University Press, 1975).

Sheila Fisher and Janet E. Halley, eds., *Seeking the Woman in Late Medieval and Renaissance Writings: Essays in Feminist Contextual Criticism* (Knoxville: University of Tennessee Press, 1989).

Elaine Tuttle Hansen, *Chaucer and the Fictions of Gender* (Berkeley: University of California Press, 1992).

Geraldine Heng, "Feminine Knots and the Other *Sir Gawain and the Green Knight*," *PMLA* May (1991), pp. 500–14.

"A Woman Wants: The Lady, *Gawain*, and the Forms of Seduction," *Yale Journal of Criticism*, 5:3 (1992), pp. 101–34.

Empire of Magic: Medieval Romance and the Politics of Cultural Fantasy (New York: Columbia University Press, 2003).

Anne L. Klinck and Ann Marie Rasmussen, *Medieval Woman's Song: Cross-cultural Approaches* (Philadelphia: University of Pennsylvania Press, 2002).

Roberta Krueger, *Women Readers and the Ideology of Gender in Old French Verse Romance* (Cambridge: Cambridge University Press, 1993).

Clare A. Lees and Gillian R. Overing, *Double Agents: Women and Clerical Culture in Anglo-Saxon England* (Philadelphia: University of Pennsylvania Press, 2001).

The Medieval Feminist Index. www.haverford.edu/library/reference/mschaus/mfi/mfi.html

Barbara Newman, *From Virile Woman to WomanChrist: Studies in Medieval Religion and Literature* (Philadelphia: University of Pennsylvania Press, 1985).

Nancy Partner, ed., *Studying Medieval Women: Sex, Gender, Feminism* (Cambridge, MA: Medieval Academy of America, 1993).

Elizabeth Robertson, *Early English Devotional Prose and the Female Audience* (Knoxville: University of Tennessee Press, 1990).

Jennifer Summit, *Lost Property: The Woman Writer and English Literary History, 1380–1589* (Chicago: University of Chicago Press, 2000).

NOTES

1. Emma Goldman, *Living My Life* (New York: Knopf, 1934), p. 56.
2. When male characters were noticed, feminist scholars sometimes found – as did Caroline Bynum of historical actors (*Jesus as Mother: Studies in the Spirituality of the High Middle Ages* [Berkeley: University of California Press, 1982]) and Elaine Tuttle Hansen of literary characters ("The Feminization of Men in Chaucer's *Legend of Good Women*," in Sheila Fisher and Janet E. Halley, eds., *Seeking the Woman in Late Medieval and Renaissance Writings: Essays in Feminist Contextual Criticism* [Knoxville: University of Tennessee Press, 1989] – that the male characters were acting like women.
3. All references are to the editors' introduction, Carolyn Dinshaw and David Wallace, eds., *The Cambridge Companion to Medieval Women's Writing* (Cambridge: Cambridge University Press, 2003), pp. 1–10. *The Medieval Feminist Index*, archiving the Society for Medieval Feminist Scholarship's bibliographies and books reviewed in the Society's periodical (originally called *The Medieval Feminist Newsletter* but renamed *The Medieval Feminist Forum*), is invaluable, and can be accessed at: www.haverford.edu/library/reference/mschaus/mfi/mfi.html. Although it is impossible to cite the full range of feminist studies, a small representative sample of the variety of feminist reading strategies sketched above is offered in the list of suggested further reading, and the *Index* can be consulted for a fuller range.
4. For a full discussion of Jews in thirteenth-century England, and of the role played by Jews, "Saracens" (Muslims), and questions of "race-religion" in the English nationalist imaginary of the period, see Chapter 2 of my *Empire of Magic: Medieval Romance and the Politics of Cultural Fantasy* (New York: Columbia University Press, 2003). The introduction and Chapter 4 conceptualize "race" in the Middle Ages, consider racial articulation with religion, and discuss the uses of color in the consolidation of medieval European Christian identity.
5. Thomas N. Tentler, "The *Summa* for Confessors as an Instrument of Social Control," in Charles Trinkaus and Heiko A. Oberman, eds., *The Pursuit of Holiness in Late Medieval and Renaissance Religion* (Leiden: E. J. Brill, 1974), p. 117. The Council decrees, Jeremy Tambling notes, strengthened the dominance of the church and "entailed a level of power which insinuated itself

GERALDINE HENG

into the heart of secular life." See Tambling, *Confession: Sexuality, Sin, the Subject* (Manchester: Manchester University Press, 1990), p. 38.

6. Although Canon 21 of the Fourth Lateran Council made annual confession mandatory for Christians everywhere, only in England, as Mary Flowers Braswell observes, was "confession . . . required three times a year, rather than only once". See Braswell, *The Medieval Sinner: Characterization and Confession in the Literature of the English Middle Ages* (Rutherford: Fairleigh Dickinson University Press, 1983), p. 15.

7. R. I. Moore tracks the rise of a culture of governmentality, surveillance, and punishment in his *The Formation of a Persecuting Society: Power and Deviance in Western Europe 950–1250* (Oxford: Blackwell, 1987); while John Boswell's *Christianity, Social Tolerance, and Homosexuality: Gay People in Western Europe from the Beginning of the Christian Era to the Fourteenth Century* (Chicago: University of Chicago Press, 1980) follows the shift from a relative tolerance of sexual variety and homoerotic acts to the entrenching of persecution. On the role of the mendicant orders in generating and intensifying anti-Semitism in the thirteenth century, see Jeremy Cohen, *The Friars and the Jews: The Evolution of Medieval Anti-Judaism* (Ithaca: Cornell University Press, 1982). Sophia Menache's "Faith, Myth, and Politics: the Stereotype of the Jews and Their Expulsion from England and France," *The Jewish Quarterly Review* 75:4 (1985), pp. 351–74, links the Jewish expulsion from England to nationalizing impulses in the thirteenth century. A. C. Spearing's study on voyeurism, *The Medieval Poet as Voyeur: Looking and Listening in Medieval Love-Narratives* (Cambridge: Cambridge University Press, 1993) points to a medieval regime of sight that arguably participates in tendencies of surveillance, as does Karma Lochrie's *Covert Operations: The Medieval Uses of Secrecy* (Philadelphia: University of Pennsylvania Press, 1999). A rich vein of emergent scholarship in medieval studies now discusses England as a medieval nation, though understanding varies on how to define a "nation." Representative scholarship includes Thorlac Turville-Petre, *England the Nation: Language, Literature, and National Identity, 1290–1340* (Oxford: Clarendon Press, 1996); Claus Bjørn, Alexander Grant, and Keith J. Stringer, eds., *Nations, Nationalism and Patriotism in the European Past* (Copenhagen: Academic Press, 1994); and Simon Forde, Lesley Johnson, and Alan V. Murray, eds., *Concepts of National Identity in the Middle Ages* (Leeds: Leeds Texts and Monographs New Series 4, 1995).

8. I refer to *Ancrene Wisse*, "the Anchoresses' Guide," the name given in the Corpus manuscript, MS Corpus Christi College Cambridge 402, rather than the older editorial title, *Ancren(e) Riwle*, "the Anchoresses' Rule," because the treatise is more accurately a guide – a support – than a Rule, which suggests monastic and conventual rules that lay down commands rather than guidance. Eight manuscripts in Middle English survive, which attests to the text's popularity (the majority of medieval manuscripts, of course, do not survive; the use of the English vernacular, rather than the more scholarly Latin, also argues for dispersal among nonelite audiences not schooled in Latin, including audiences of women), five from the thirteenth century; there are also two French and four Latin manuscripts from after the thirteenth century.

9. Augustinian responsibility for the text is the default argument, and is magisterially represented by E. J. Dobson, *The Origins of Ancrene Wisse* (Oxford:

70

Clarendon Press, 1976), who argues against the possibility of Dominican authorship dismissively (see, for example, pp. 14–54). More recent scholarship has reinserted Dominican responsibility: see, for example, Bella Millet, "The Origins of *Ancrene Wisse:* New Answers, New Questions," *Medium Aevum* 61 (1992), pp. 206–28.

10. Ann Warren, *Anchorites and Their Patrons in Medieval England* (Berkeley: University of California Press, 1985), Appendix 1. Warren's data suggest that 780 anchorites existed on some 600 sites between 1100 and 1539, when Henry VIII ended English anchoritism.

11. All references are to the Corpus Christi manuscript edited by J. R. R. Tolkien, *Ancrene Wisse: Edited from MS Corpus Christi College Cambridge 402* (London: Oxford University Press, 1962), Early English Text Society No. 249, p. 175.

12. "Anchoresses usually had maidservants. The author of *Ancrene Wisse* regards two, an inside one and an outside one, as appropriate and envisages, naturally, a fair amount of converse between mistress and servants." (See Hugh White, trans., *Ancrene Wisse: Guide for Anchoresses* London: Penguin, 1993), p. xv. Nor were anchoresses exclusively solitary recluses: "There was a view that complete isolation was spiritually dangerous; two 'solitaries' together safeguarded one other's spiritual being" (p. 203 n.29).

13. On religious women in contemplative life in the period, see also Sharon K. Elkins, *Holy Women of Twelfth-Century England* (Chapel Hill: University of North Carolina Press, 1988), especially Chapter 2, on the eremitic life, and Chapter 8, on abbeys and anchorholds. On eremitism and monasticism in general, see Henrietta Leyser, *Hermits and the New Monasticism* (New York: St. Martin's Press, 1984).

14. Other medieval English narratives on self-custody, religious exemplars, and cautionary devotional advice directed at women can be sampled in Bella Millet and Jocelyn Wogan-Browne eds., *Medieval English Prose for Women: Selections from the Katherine Group and Ancrene Wisse* (Oxford: Clarendon Press, 1990). Preceding the fully fledged consciousness of alarming perils, and the constant vigilance enjoined on anchoresses in the literature of the thirteenth century, were twelfth-century hints, as Warren muses: "In the twelfth century there was much overt mystical writing. Yet when it came time to direct a work to anchorites, or at least to female anchorites, the tone is penitential and only minimally mystical" (*Anchorites and Their Patrons*, p. 1154 n.50). In the fourteenth and fifteenth centuries, a shift occurs, Warren notes, as the tone of anchoritic literature finally inclines toward a focus on quietude, joy, and contemplation: "in marked contrast to [the] early literature, the works of the second half of the fourteenth century . . . lead the anchorite toward mystical union with God in explicit and joyous terms . . . The goal of the contemplative life is stated and embraced . . . The shift of emphasis in the literary tradition – the expectation that the anchorite will be a contemplative as well as a penitential ascetic – is paralleled in the episcopal registers and the royal rolls of the fifteenth century" (p. 115); "at the onset of the fifteenth century a new word appears . . . That word is *contemplative*" (p. 119).

15. Tambling, who cites the *OED*'s eighth definition of "confession" as "a tomb in which a martyr or confessor is buried," or a crypt "in which the relics are kept," reflects on how appropriate it is that one dictionary meaning of "confession

should be a tomb . . . marking out how confession always has the attempt to bury and terminate a life through its narration" (*Confession*, p. 36).

16. Compare Aquinas's exhortation that confession should be "simple, humble, pure, faithful, and frequent, unadorned, discreet, willing, ashamed, strong and reproachful, and showing readiness to obey" (Tambling, *Confession*, p. 40). Although the Corpus Christi manuscript specifies sixteen vital elements to confession, it in fact elaborates seventeen (p. 170), which leads some translators to insert an addition to the list from another manuscript of the *Wisse* from the same period (the second quarter of the thirteenth century), MS Cotton Nero. A. 14, British Museum. Half a century ago, Dom Gerard Sitwell noted the close resemblance of Parts 4 and 5, on Temptation and Confession, to the *Summae Confessorum* – confessional manuals evincing a similar psychology and "teaching technique" – and suggested that *Ancrene Wisse*'s "chapter on confession might be taken as itself making a contribution to this particular type of literature." (See M. B. Salu, trans., *The Ancrene Riwle* (London: Burns and Oates, 1955), p. xxi. Alexandra Barrett more recently notes that "it is now a scholarly commonplace that *AW* shows the firm imprint of penitential literature"("The Five Wits in *Ancrene Wisse*," *Medium Aevum* 56 [1987], pp. 12–24).

17. Significance, Jerry Root observes, lies not in the categories of sin, but in sin's "seemingly endless proliferation" that "expands the discursive space of confession to nearly unlimited horizons": so that, ultimately, "the space of confession knows no bounds." See Root, *"Space to speke": The Confessional Subject in Medieval Literature* (New York: Peter Lang, 1997), p. 64.

18. If the text is attributable to the Dominicans, its procedures of self-inquisition are intelligible in other ways that link private to public contexts, since the Dominican order is closely identified in Europe with its role as roving inquisitor: "the Dominicans . . . were actively involved in the implementation of the programme of pastoral reform laid down by the Fourth Lateran Council in 1215 . . . Both the emphasis on confession in *Ancrene Wisse* and the author's tendency to look over the shoulder of his primary audience to a wider readership seem to reflect this" (Millet, "Origins of *Ancrene Wisse*," p. 216). Tambling, who dubs confession "the result of successful inquisition," suggests that confession is more useful than torture in "getting at the truth held in the soul" (*Confession*, p. 40).

19. This notable story in *Ancrene Wisse* is cited as an example of extreme fidelity to the medieval ideal of asceticism and suffering as expressions of religious piety, and speakingly exemplifies what David Wallace (in his public lecture, "Surinam: The Long History of Black and White," delivered at the University of Texas at Austin, on October 18, 2002) dubs "competitive abjection" in ascetic and penitential traditions featuring what he wonderfully calls "abjection envy."

20. Tambling follows D. W. Robertson in stressing that "the technique of asking for details of confession followed patterns of rhetoric appropriate for prosecutors in the law courts, derived from Cicero and Boethius" (*Confession*, p. 40). Linguistically, *Ancrene Wisse*'s Middle English "fondunge" does not distinguish between "temptations," "tests," and "trials" in its meaning. On the operations of confession in law as well as literature, see Peter Brooks's *Troubling Confessions: Speaking Guilt in Law and Literature* (Chicago: University of Chicago Press, 2000).

3

ELLEN ROONEY

The literary politics of feminist theory

Common sense assures us that feminist politics and feminist theory are intimately related. Any agitation on behalf of women's rights involves some sort of critique of the dominant order, some kind of "theory" of women's oppression in a patriarchal society. This is true even of feminist activisms that consciously present themselves as immediate expressions of women's experiences, emphatically privileging women's voices and committed to grass roots political action. It is necessary (though not sufficient) to observe that such a "presentation" of necessity involves a rhetoric, a strategy of representation and an argument, in which the model of direct action rooted in experience is set against other models and presented as the proper ground for authentic feminist activism. While all of this is true, when I suggest that any agitation on behalf of women's rights involves some theory of women's oppression, I mean something more essential or specific to feminism's project as such, to feminism as a way of thinking, writing, and acting.

The very possibility of any political action against patriarchy or masculinism requires an account of that masculinism's flaws, a dissent from the way in which it seeks to situate and dominate femininity. In the exposure of such a masculinist "narrative of femininity," stereotypes of woman and women appear as the effects of patriarchy, including, of course, of patriarchy's many stories. The disclosure of some such patriarchal narrative of femininity is the sine qua non of feminist agitation. The many works of feminist theory and polemic that have described the before and after of this moment of narrative disclosure have sometimes figured it as an epiphany, sometimes as a conversion, sometimes as a fall. Its myriad forms are a symptom of the varied modes of the feminine in social life, and it is inevitably connected to some counter-narrative, some resituating of women in a new, non-patriarchal space or practice, perhaps (though not always, as we shall see) in a new "femininity." Feminism thus always involves a "rewriting" of femininity or femininities, of the categories that define women as women.[1] Indeed, the *break* by which patriarchy is indicted – in order that it may be resisted – inevitably exposes "femininity" as ideology, that is, as a structure that we inhabit, one that we can study and thus critique, one that feminists desire to remake. Even the most apparently critically unself-conscious feminisms – including those that ferociously dismiss "theory" as speculative or distracting or even apolitical – narrate this break with the ideology of femininity, this tear in the *obviousness* of feminine subjectivity. In the process, what was once "common sense" – that we are women – emerges as a site for interrogation and political work. Simone de Beauvoir describes this movement in terms of the rejection of the naturalization of the category of woman: "One is not born, but rather becomes a woman." In the process of exposing the ideological work involved in becoming woman/women, theory and practice are intimately entwined *within* the domain of political action itself.

Even for those who are persuaded that theory is always already at work in all feminist practice, the step from a general argument or theory on behalf of feminism or women's liberation to a more narrowly focused feminist *literary* theory is not a trivial one. There are obvious differences between the kind of theoretical break that denaturalizes the subordination of women within the family, or that discloses the sexual myths of feminine passivity or normative heterosexuality, and the sort of theoretical work that focuses on literary canons, the relations between gender and genre, or the matter of a "feminine style." As we try to articulate these different theories, the location of many literary critical feminisms within the university is a complicating factor, insofar as this location gives much of what would be immediately recognizable as feminist literary theory an "academic" orientation. Another bit of common sense comes into play here, one that asserts that what we mean by the term "political" is to be taken literally and that it is obvious that interpretations of literary works are not "literally" political: such interpretations do not elect leaders, pass laws, rule on constitutional issues, or make state policy. As is often the case with insights that lay claim to common sense, this can be a difficult argument to oppose.

On the other hand, there are various ways to interpret this hierarchy of political forms. We must acknowledge that the very fact that feminist *literary* theory makes its home within the academy seems (in some contexts) reflexively to arouse suspicions that it is politically marginal at best, that is to say, that its concerns are "merely academic." (This has certainly been true in the United States.) At the same time, and despite the prevalence of such doubts, it is nonetheless still a commonsensical idea for many observers that the thoughts, analyses, and even the speculations of literary theorists concerned with questions of gender, sexual difference, or masculinist ideologies are closely connected to the political projects and organizations that address women's issues in the "real" world; indeed, more than merely plausible, this assumption has the status of something like a given.

Diana Fuss reflects on the stubbornness and the value of this view at the conclusion of her examination of the politics of feminist reading, "Reading Like a Feminist." Fuss has been analyzing debates about the grounds of feminist criticism, first, in terms of an "essentialist" view of women as a "class" fundamentally distinct from men and then in the light of the anti-essentialist critique of that view; she observes that certain terms come under harsh scrutiny in the course of these arguments, including such fundamental concepts for feminist theory as the self and experience. In the end, Fuss concludes that through all the sometimes bitter debates about the category and class "women" and its grounds, the notion of politics retains a special status, indeed, an *essential* place: "it is politics that is essential to feminism's many self-definitions. It is telling, I think, that anti-essentialists are willing to displace 'identity,' 'self,' 'experience,' and virtually every other self-evident category *except* politics. To the extent that it is difficult to imagine a *non-political* feminism, politics emerges as feminism's essence."[2] Fuss's observation registers the persistence of the view that a feminist reading practice or criticism will always be "political," however "tenaciously [politics] resists definition" (p. 111). In effect, she also argues that there may be no other category that unites the various and competing forms of feminist literary theory. "Politics is precisely the self-evident category in feminist discourse – that which is most irreducible and most indispensable . . . both the most transparent and the most elusive of terms" (p. 111). The oxymoron Fuss puts to work here – the "political" is a category both *transparent* and *elusive*, a darkness visible – is one that feminist literary studies continually confronts as it renews its political projects.

Yet, in our current historical moment – and not for the first time in the history of feminism or feminist literary theory – many troubling questions have been raised about the politics of feminist literary studies. While these questions are not entirely new, as we begin to consider their current forms we should recall that many of the earliest practitioners of feminist criticism were quite confident about the close relationship between politics and literary scholarship and about their own status as the intellectuals of a political movement. They often viewed themselves not only as literary critics who were part of a robust political campaign for women's rights, but as activists within the university, political agents in their own right, who would challenge not just the canons of their particular disciplines or the biases of their colleagues and intellectual predecessors, but the normal science of the university itself.[3] The transformation of the content of the university's curriculum was simultaneously to effect a reconfiguration of its forms and of many of the normative features of intellectual and institutional life. As Naomi Schor recalls, feminism's interrogation of institutional power in the academy expressed a "perhaps utopian longing for a different university, a university of differences."[4] Universities today do in fact differ in many ways from the universities the first feminist critics encountered, especially in national contexts where feminist literary studies has been embraced and broadly institutionalized, which we might take as a confirmation of some of the utopian hopes of the pioneers in the field. Ironically, however, some contemporary concerns about the politics of feminist literary studies are a direct result of the comfortable place that gender analysis now occupies within the university, the very success of the enterprise, as testified to in part by the existence of *The Cambridge Companion to Feminist Literary Theory*.

The full consequences of the difference that feminist critics have made remain unclear, particularly in terms of how feminist scholarship understands its own political tasks and powers. Insofar as some knowledge of feminist literary theory is often all but taken for granted in numerous literature departments, what difference does this new requirement make *politically*? On the other hand, to what degree must feminist criticism admit that it has been thoroughly assimilated to the university it once dreamed of reshaping, that is, to use a once pervasive phrase, "politically coopted"? What is the "proper" relation between intellectual work and political activity? Does feminist literary theory have a politics as such? If we seriously pursue the suggestion that the university is a site of political activity, do we have to ask not simply how feminist literary theory relates to the politics "out there," beyond the academy, but how specific projects *within* the academy achieve political effects? What do we mean when we say politics, and what does feminist literary theory have to do with it?

Kate Millett's *Sexual Politics* (1970) is an example of a US text from the confident period of the emergence of feminist literary studies, when the connections between literature, its critical reading, and a broad political movement were less tentative and apparently less fraught.[5] The terse title itself – no subtitle cautioning us that this book is about "literature, politics, and power," for example – reveals the author's confidence that her work on literature is political, indeed, directly political, a mode of politics. Of course, Millett was not a professional literary critic writing within an established scholarly genre, and she was politically active in the women's liberation movement, but such were the circumstances in which many early feminist critics first wrote. *Sexual Politics* was a bestseller (my paperback copy indicates 200,000 copies in print and features blurbs from reviews in the *New York Times* and *Time Magazine*, as well as *Cosmopolitan*). It was an undeniably eclectic volume devoted to topics as wide-ranging as psychoanalysis, the "official experimentation with the family" in Nazi Germany and Soviet Russia, and the meaning of "sexual revolution," as well as literature.[6] It did, however, begin life as a dissertation in the Department of English at Columbia University and contains extended readings of writers such as D. H. Lawrence, Henry Miller, and Jean Genet. Millett's introduction seems less concerned that her book's literary analyses may not be considered sufficiently political than that her political interpretations be acknowledged as criticism by an academy still wedded to the New Criticism and effusive, celebratory prose.

> It has been my conviction that the adventure of literary criticism is not restricted to a dutiful round of adulation, but is capable of seizing upon the larger insights which literature affords into the life it describes, or interprets, or even distorts. This essay, composed of equal parts literary and cultural criticism, is something of an anomaly, a hybrid, possibly a new mutation altogether. I have operated on the premise that there is room for a criticism which takes into account the larger cultural context in which literature is conceived and produced. Criticism which originates from literary history is too limited in scope to do this; criticism which originates in aesthetic considerations, "New Criticism," never wished to do so. (p. xii)

Millett's book was intended, and was widely received, as a polemic on behalf of a feminist sexual revolution. Indeed, among its blurbs, the cover boasts this self-description: "the landmark work that is breaking the tyranny of sexual roles." With such a direct power to intervene against "tyranny," to break the power of stereotypical sexual roles, as one of its attributes, it is clear that *Sexual Politics* was not perceived as hampered by its "field" of literary studies. A revolutionary feminist criticism was a central part of its *political* strategy.

The "mutation" represented by Millett's critical practice was its insistence that just as "sex has a frequently neglected political aspect," so does literature (p. xi).[7] This neglected political aspect of literature was one of feminist criticism's major themes. Millett's text exemplifies the explicitness with which many early feminist readers – within the academy and within the general culture of book reviewing and cultural criticism – conceived their literary critical projects as a mode of politics, literally as political action. We need not take such sanguine and confident pronouncements at face value, of course. The break with the tyranny of sexual roles that *Sexual Politics* promises is still very much in the making in many, many places. But the conviction that feminist critics and literary theorists embraced – that their work was in effect an arm of the then-burgeoning women's movement – was widely shared, including, most tellingly, by the vociferous opponents of any such innovation as "feminist literary theory."

It has been more than thirty years since the first gestures of feminist literary criticism emerged in academic circles. As the essays collected in this volume testify, it has since become a major critical component of literary studies in many university contexts. It may be difficult, from the perspective of the twenty-first century, even to recall how vehement, contemptuous, and dismissive the resistance to the claims of feminist criticism was in the early years of the project, when even to propose a dissertation on any but a handful of sanctioned women writers (Jane Austen or Emily Dickinson in the United States) was to court scandal. To reconsider the content of our literary canon, to reevaluate the aesthetic achievement of women writers, indeed, to question our own aesthetic values and criteria and investigate the play of sexual difference and sexism across literary texts from all periods, by men and by women – all these proposals were initially met with ridicule and deep-seated hostility. This resistance was unmistakably political, mounting an intellectual defense of the cultural prerogatives of patriarchy. This involved shoring up the reproduction of ideologies of masculine superiority and domination and of gender stereotypes (found in literature and quite prominently in literary criticism and theory); it also required a more immediate (theoretical and practical) defense of the critical modes, concepts and canons cherished by the professoriate (largely, though not entirely, male) then firmly in control of literary studies and its precincts, in the university and in the public sphere.

The emergence of feminist literary studies was thus confirmed as directly and obviously political in the eyes of its earliest practitioners in part because the hostility it generated was so fiercely political. No one involved on either side of these early battles would have called them "merely academic" or trivialized them as being of little consequence to the "real world." The early years of feminist criticism were also a period in which feminists (or women of whatever political disposition) within university literature departments were often an exceedingly small group, frequently seeking alliances in other departments (and helping to found interdisciplinary women's studies programs), generally without allies in arguments about reforming the curriculum or hiring new faculty. The word "embattled" appears repeatedly in the recollections of many feminist scholars from that period, and their opponents frequently trumpeted their complementary (if less appropriate) sense of being besieged. Those who disdained "the literature of women's liberation," as Harold Bloom called it, never doubted that there was such a thing and that feminist critics were guilty of perpetrating it against all aesthetic and even ethical criteria, putting what they described as "Western Civilization" itself at risk. The tireless polemicists of (what eventually became) the "culture wars" in the US academy were always eager to denounce the political effects and biases of what they called "victimization studies," listing feminist scholarship prominently in their catalogues of sins against the tradition.[8]

These polemics were fired by the mainstream critics' conviction that their own intellectual work was politically neutral. This view was entrenched and hegemonic in the US academy in the 1970s and 1980s, when feminist criticism first emerged and established itself there. This "ethic," as it flatteringly viewed itself, was difficult to expose as an alibi or cover story for a particular set of political views, not least because it so effectively protected those scholars who benefited from the status quo from recognizing that their own work was *actively producing* unequal, distorted, and unjust arrangements of knowledge and power, rather than simply reflecting home truths about the nature of literature and relations between the sexes. The idea that knowledge could be purely objective, isolated from consciously advocated and unconsciously lived values, was in this respect precisely an "ideology," one with consequences within the university and beyond. As Louis Althusser observed at the time (1970), ideology is never so powerful as when it is unconscious of its own ideological status, never so effective as when it claims merely to be "common sense."[9]

The obviousness of common sense, which Althusser warns against, does not, however, thrive only among those (antifeminist) scholars who insist on the neutrality and "innocence" of their interpretations and deride the notion that they, too, perform a kind of politics when they read. There are also feminist readers for whom the politics of reading is solely a matter of debunking other people's ideologies, not a question of proposing their own equally "ideological" problematics. Millett's critical propositions – that both sexuality and literature have "neglected" political aspects – were radical in their assertion of an *unacknowledged* politics at work in the private sphere of sexual relations and the privatized field of literary interpretation. Althusser's theory of ideology was radical both for its claim that ideology was a determining as well as determined feature of the social formation (not merely a "superstructure," an effect) and for its insistence that ideology not be thought primarily in terms of consciously held beliefs, dogmas, and programs. He argued that we must approach ideology in terms of our unconscious and therefore *unacknowledged* assumptions about the world as such, and, in particular, in terms of our assumption of (in the sense of our "taking on," our assuming the place of) subjectivity, of our own status as subjects in the world, subjects enabled by ideology. Althusser rejects the view that ideology is pure mystification, the lies of "priests and despots," manipulative falsehoods imposed upon the mass of the population by a ruling clique of "cynical men" (p. 163). Rather, he argues that ideology is a permanent feature of social life; it is transhistorical; and it affects all subjects as subjects, not only those of the ruling classes. Ideology is inescapable insofar as we are subjects; it can no longer be our political goal simply to strip the ideological blinders from our eyes and see the world as it is. As Althusser observes: "this is to recognize the effective presence of a new reality: *ideology*" (p. 133).

In the light of this theory of ideology – which sees it as a "reality," a reality that is essential to the formation of subjectivity and to our experience of ourselves as subjects – it is easy to see that an entrenched ideology of common sense might play a role within feminist debates about the politics of feminist literary theory. I began this essay with an uncontroversial observation: "common sense assures us that feminist politics and feminist theory are intimately related." The strong version of this claim asserts that the academic pursuit of feminist literary criticism is an effect of the political movements for women's liberation, an outgrowth of political activism. This view is a commonplace, if not a cliché. As an argument (though it can hardly bear the elaboration of actual argument, so obvious is its grounding in the "real"), it suggests that the *intellectual* work of revising traditional canons, critiquing the "phallic" criticism that erected them, debunking sexist ideology within literature, and tracing the contours of women's writing, is all explicable as a "reflection" of the *concrete political* work carried on elsewhere, in the streets, in women's organizations, in legislatures, and in the courts. From this perspective, feminist literary studies and feminist literary theories are quite simply the product of feminist politics, its progeny. The continuity between them appears indubitable; it goes without saying.

And yet, as I have pointed out, almost from the moment that feminist literary studies began to establish itself as a formidable player in academic criticism – that is, from the moment it might be said to have attained intellectual (and thus political) *power* beyond the circle of its first adherents – feminists began to question just what such a victory might mean, especially in terms of feminist criticism's political effects. These questions can take two forms, one turning primarily toward the university and the pressures it brings to bear on feminist scholars, the other primarily toward the state of current women's movements and their relation to academic feminism. Anxieties about academic success are palpable in many of these questions; "success" is potent enough, it seems, to threaten the inherent tendency of literary and academic feminisms properly to reflect their origins. Susan Gubar has recently given new voice to these doubts:

Have we feminists changed higher education or has it changed us? Do we retain our visionary hopefulness about the mission of feminism in colleges and universities, its capacity to transform traditional ways of knowing? Or have we begun to feel integrated into an academic system with its own ossified, frequently painful or pointless procedures? Has our incorporation into the professoriate required us to exhibit the selfishness and factionalism inculcated by careerist jockeying?[10]

The fear that feminism is now sufficiently mainstream to constitute an opportunity for careerism is one of the more "academic" forms of concern about the political effects of success.[11] Gubar's questions are concerned both with a feminism that is not one, an "assimilated" (*Critical Condition*, p. 104) feminist criticism that is merely a token in a quite different game, the game of career advancement, and with a feminism that is domesticated, not necessarily by sheer "selfishness" or lack of feminist intent, but by a capitulation to or too easy rapprochement with the structures of university life and institutional habit, by forms of complicity with the academy.

In her recent *Feminism Without Borders*, Chandra Mohanty also derides the careerism of certain feminisms within the university, "whereby the boundaries of the academy stand in for the entire world and feminism becomes a way to advance academic careers rather than a call for fundamental and collective social and economic transformation."[12] She reads this retreat to the boundaries of the university as a symptom of a "predominantly class-based gap between a vital women's movement and feminist theorizing in the U. S. academy" (p. 6). While putting into question any easy assumption about solidarity between the broader struggle for women's rights and the intellectual projects of academic feminist theory (she is not speaking here directly about literary studies), Mohanty stresses that this tangled question must consider the current state of women's political struggles, both in individual countries and locales and viewed from a global perspective. Whether from the point of view of the critiques of the women's movement that have been made by many feminists (and by some who refuse that title), or from the point of view that asserts that we are historically and politically in a postfeminist moment, the dynamics of feminist struggle have changed in the past thirty-odd years. Mohanty addresses these dynamics from the perspective of an antiracist feminism working in a global context where capitalism seems able to override all its former antagonists. She sees the "naturalization of capitalist values" as having a "profound influence in engendering a neoliberal, consumerist (protocapitalist) feminism concerned with 'women's advancement' up the corporate and nation-state ladder." This "protocapitalist or 'free-market' feminism" is "symptomatic of the 'Americanization' of definitions of feminism – the unstated assumption that

U. S. corporate culture is the norm and ideal that feminists around the world strive for" (p. 6), and its effects are felt across feminist organizations and theorizing far beyond the confines of university literature programs.

The challenges presented by "free-market feminism" are rather different from those confronting a powerful feminist literary theory in danger of becoming just one interpretative paradigm among others. Mohanty's invocation of the global context of feminist movements and the impact of a hegemonic US corporate culture on those movements introduces another question. Rather than asking if feminist (literary) theory has been depoliticized by "merely academic" politics, she directs attention to political conflicts among feminisms that have their basis in women's divergent interests and their perceptions and representations of those interests. Of course, one way to comprehend the debates about the politics of feminist literary theories or the relation between politics within literary studies and political struggles located elsewhere is simply to extend the metaphor of reflection we have just considered. Insofar as feminisms beyond the university emerge in a dizzying array of forms – socialist feminisms and radical feminisms and postcolonial feminisms, black feminisms and cultural feminisms and lesbian feminisms, Asian American feminisms and "free market" feminisms, Chicana feminisms and UN feminisms, Islamic and Jewish and "lipstick" feminisms, and the entire range of cross-connections among these and many other possibilities – so literary critical feminisms can be said to reflect or reproduce these "larger" divisions. In the field of feminist movements, there is no "feminism unmodified," as Catherine MacKinnon imagined it. Indeed, as many feminist thinkers, from bell hooks and Denise Riley to Elizabeth Spelman and Gayatri Spivak (and others) have argued, the very fantasy of a feminism defined only by the category of women or even by gender (common in the United States and the North more generally) has been silently normed by whiteness, heterosexuality, and middle-class status. As such, it often represents a very legible political class and its particular political program, one that hardly represents "women" as such; indeed, this feminist politics was enabled by the very form of uninterrogated "common sense" – this time vis à vis a universal "woman" projected out of very particular women's experiences – that protected certain masculinist literary critics from seeing the political interests at work in their allegedly universal "literary values."[13]

This recognition of the impossibility of speaking "for women" or "as a woman" without a simultaneous acknowledgement of the "intersectional" quality of every female subject's location means that feminist movements must orient themselves otherwise than in relation to any unified or universal category of woman. The political fragmentation of "feminism" signals the contradictions among women and, perhaps more precisely, among feminists. In speaking about the responsibilities of a "global feminism," Spivak has observed: "It seems to me that if one is talking about the prime task [of feminism], since there is no discursive continuity among women, the prime task is situational anti-sexism and the recognition of the heterogeneity of the field, instead of positing some kind of women's subject, women's figure."[14] Feminist literary theory might seem to move in the wake of this insight about feminist movements generally, miming the heterogeneity and contradictions of the social field and thus reinscribing its alliances and its divisions.

From this point of view, the politics of feminist literary theory are the politics of feminism at large. The divisions within feminist criticism are as intractable as the political divisions among feminists across nations, races, sexualities, and the international division of labor because they mirror those divisions, and their resolution is primarily a matter that will be settled elsewhere; social contradictions are not "solved" in theoretical practice of any kind and certainly not in theories that privilege attention to literary (or other cultural) works. In the insistent metaphor of certain materialisms, feminist movements in the "real world" are the ground of feminist theories, their determining context, and their referent.[15]

But what would the politics of feminist literary theory look like if we questioned the mirror relation that the commonplace asserts, interrogating the idea that intellectual work faithfully reflects practices elsewhere? This is not to say that there is no possible relation here, only that we should examine its forms and that they may only rarely be a matter of reflection or mirroring and often be remarkably remote from such mimetic logics. Might we find a relative autonomy in the practice of feminist literary theories that extends to their political consequences and stakes? Could there be an uneven development in the political work of academic feminists that would help us to think about the relation of theory to practice, and perhaps to think of theory as practice in terms that go beyond comforting slogans? Or, if we arrive at that end, will we have merely driven ourselves into a cul de sac, an elite, protected circle in which theory becomes its own reward and its own end, but is hopelessly cut off from political power and responsibility? Will we be in a position to think again about politics, to ask how feminist literary theory itself might help us to revise our assumptions about the relationship between politics and literature, between politics and theory, between literature or literariness and the "real"?

Barbara Johnson has pointed out that "the profound political intervention of feminism has indeed been not simply to enact radical politics but to redefine the very nature of what is deemed political – to take politics down from its male incarnation as a change-seeking interest in what is not nearest to hand, and to bring it into the daily historical texture of the relations between the sexes."[16] The reference is obviously to the expanding consequences of the insight that the personal is the political, but Johnson also suggests that the reach of the political is still (and always) to be disclosed. What if "common sense" conceals as much as it reveals, especially in its assertions about the nature of real politics or the meaning of the literal? What if the difference of opinion on the question of the politics of feminist literary theory is a matter having precisely to do with one's conception of "common sense" itself?

Ann Snitow is one of a number of feminist theorists who have described "a common divide [that] keeps forming in both feminist thought and action between the need to build the identity 'woman' and give it solid political meaning and the need to tear down the very category 'woman' and dismantle its all-too-solid history."[17] She captures this theoretical oscillation in the construction of the feminist subject's relation to "woman" in the following narrative of her own early feminism:

> In the early days of this wave of the women's movement, I sat in a weekly consciousness raising group with my friend A. We compared notes recently: What did you think was happening? How did you think our lives were going to change? A. said she had felt, "Now I can be a woman; it's no longer so humiliating. I can stop fantasizing that secretly I am a man, as I used to, before I had children. Now I can value what was once my shame." Her answer amazed me. Sitting in the same meetings during those years, my thoughts were roughly the reverse: "Now I don't have to be a woman any more. I need never become a mother. Being a woman has always been humiliating, but I used to assume there was no exit. Now the very idea 'woman' is up for grabs. 'Woman' is my slave name; feminism will give me freedom to seek some other identity altogether." ("A Gender Diary," p. 9)

Rather than find this contradiction between perceptions, motives, and theorizations paralyzing or disheartening, Snitow argues that feminism is inherently, permanently, and productively caught in the contradiction between women and feminism, in the necessary failure of feminism (or feminisms) ever adequately to represent or coincide with women, and thus in the repeated inscription of the problem of representing feminism and what it will do.

As Spivak has brilliantly argued, the problem of representation – in the double sense of a proxy and a portrait, a speaking for and a "'re-presentation,' as in art or philosophy"[18] – is a permanent problem for feminist politics and feminist thought. Any "feminist" subject engaging in situational antisexism must devise strategies for representing "women," "identity," "desire," "interest," and "politics." This is to say that identities – even those in which we feel most at home, which seem most transparent to us, and including the self-identity or unity of our "own interests," "our desires" – are a function of language, of modes of address, and of representational forces that are never entirely in the control of a speaking subject. Identity and difference – including feminist identities and the differences among them – have very little to do with what is obvious to common sense, with the already-known, or with the untenable view that in a certain political and experiential frame "there is no representation, no signifier . . . theory is a relay of practice (thus laying problems of theoretical practice to rest); and the oppressed can know and speak for themselves" (Spivak, *Crtique of Post Colonial Reason*, p. 264).

Snitow's sympathies are with those who would "deconstruct" woman, but she demonstrates that the division she announces is not one of stark opposites, but fragile positionings, subject to change. The contradiction between "being woman" and "not having to be woman" is thus not one that feminist theory or feminist movement can hope easily to solve, to think through. Rather, it is one that keeps forming in new contexts, as our "common sense" about the "real" is revised and subjectivity and experience itself come under the pressure of representation. As Denise Riley concludes in her powerful account of this definitive contradiction, "*Am I That Name?*": "feminism must be agile enough to say, 'Now we will be "women" – but now we will be persons, not these 'women.'" It must also be lucid enough to acknowledge that the fact that "the 'women' is indeterminate and impossible is no cause for lament. It is what makes feminism."[19]

I have put both the "real" and "common sense" in quotation marks in the preceding pages; the opposition Snitow outlines allows us to approach these powerful terms directly. In the contradictory feminist views of woman that she describes, common sense emerges to defend the strategy of "building the identity woman." Indeed, the political argument for this position represents itself as standing for political pragmatism, for "realism" in the nonliterary sense, and against the political irresponsibility of those theorists who see experience itself as the product of discourse. The claim is straightforward: without the categories (and identities) of woman and women, the fight for women's rights is incoherent. The urgent need to act in the "real" world, where illiteracy, poverty, and violent subordination still plague many women, precludes any "deconstruction" of women as a social group or as an existential category. Feminism contests the *meaning* of femininity and women's place in society; it cannot take seriously Kristeva's (in)famous assertion that "woman does not exist." Without the grounding provided by the category woman, it is not possible to pursue any political program whatsoever, within in the academy or elsewhere. The alternative – "to tear down the 'identity' woman" or "to seek some other identity altogether "– is not an alternative politics. It is a retreat from the political as such.

Not surprisingly, this argument has many variants. Some feminists insist that what is lost with the category of women is any possibility of thinking systematically about women's oppression. If feminism is an emancipatory movement, it cannot abandon the normative ground that an insistence on the constructed nature of subjectivity and of women "as a class" cedes. From this perspective, the category of women is essential to a necessary totalization of the social whole that is patriarchy; it cannot be allowed to dissolve in the play of differences among women that an emphasis on signification or representation seems to demand. In this view, women as a category is also fundamental to any effort to think about what Rosemary Hennessy calls "the material relation between the discursive (feminist critique) and the nondiscursive (women's lives)."[20] Materialism is here firmly on the side of the "real" or the nondiscursive; an insistence on "women" as representation or "woman" as discourse presents real hazards. "Women's lives" and the material conditions in which they obviously struggle threaten to vanish, washed away in a rush of signifiers. This kind of materialism (there are others) indicts the feminist theory it opposes – busily tearing down "woman" and her all-too-solid history – as irresponsible, politically quietistic or, pointedly, "academic," and it promises to restore this wayward speculation – dematerializing, idealizing, ahistorical – to a properly political path. (Feminist literary theorists may be particularly singled out for this critique insofar as they are professionally interested in questions of language, representation, and subjectivity in ways that are available to feminist academics in other fields (history, anthropology, or sociology), but not as strongly endorsed by disciplinary assumptions.)

How can the feminist compelled to tear down the identity "woman" refute the claim that she thereby abandons the real world of politics? How has feminist literary theory responded to such a critique? Barbara Johnson challenges the use of the word "real" to signify that which theories of representation privileging the workings of language cannot grasp. She notes that academics themselves often level this accusation, whether as a self-criticism or to indict a colleague: "nothing indeed could be more commonplace than to hear academics speak of the 'real world' as something lying outside their own sphere of operations" (Johnson, *A World of Difference*, p. 3). Recounting an anecdote that "depicts a typical view of the relations between academic 'theory' and the 'real world'" by pointing to lawyers' commonplaces about the irrelevance of theory and the mystique they attach to getting out "'in the real world,' 'on the firing line,' and 'in the trenches,'" Johnson observes that "implicit in the figurative language of this 'mystique' is the assumption that violence is more real than safety, the physical more real than the intellectual, war more real than school. So ordinary are these assumptions that I was recently startled to come across . . . a reference to 'the "real world," as the G. I.'s used to say'" (p. 3). The example of the soldier for whom the forms of army life and the battlefield are opposed to the "real world" illuminates the function of this epithet. "Suddenly it became clear to me that the 'real world' was constantly being put in quotation marks, always being defined as where 'we' are not . . . Yet these differing perceptions of the real are nothing other than perceptions of the boundaries of institutions. Whether one is in the university or in the army, the real world seems to be the world outside the institutions" (p. 3). This trick of representation and perception, in Johnson's view, distracts us, by the "assumption of unreality," from the "*real* articulations of power" in the institutions where we do the bulk of our concrete work (p. 3).

Johnson's example of the soldier for whom ordinary life away from the trenches is the "real" highlights the process – ideological, rhetorical, and representational – by which the real becomes common sense, an identity we cannot do without, and the literal site of politics, elsewhere. Her *political* response is to insist that reading this process is no less concrete, real, or consequential than other political activities and, indeed, forms an essential part of politics in the largest sense. Later in the same volume, Johnson reverses the terms by which identity, the real, and political effects are ranged against difference, textuality, and undecidability, the aporia of language: "it is often said, in literary-theoretical circles, that to focus on undecidability is to be apolitical. Everything I have read about the abortion controversy in its recent form in the United States leads me to suspect that, on the contrary, the undecidable is the political. There is politics precisely because there is undecidability. And there is also poetry" (p. 194).

Many feminist literary critics have taken this path through representation and language, through what Spivak, after Derrida, calls "the blank part of the text," to disclose the political in their work. A stark formulation of this theoretical shift is found in Parveen Adams's "A Note on the Distinction between Sexual Division and Sexual Differences." Adams insists that feminist analysis cannot break entirely with masculinist ideology so long as it advances a theory of representation in which representations copy reality. This is because reality is "always already apparently structured by sexual division, by an already antagonistic relation between two social groups." This investment in the a priori of sexual division means that

> the complicated and contradictory way in which sexual difference is generated
> in various discursive and social practices is always reduced to an effect of that

always existent sexual division . . . [thus] what has to be explained is how reality functions to effect the continuation of *its* already given divisions. (The different ways in which sexual differences are produced is actually denied as a political fact in this position.) In terms of *sexual differences* . . . what has to be grasped is, precisely, the *production* of sexual differences through systems of representation; *the work of representation produces differences that cannot be known in advance* (my emphases).[21]

Adams reasserts the "political fact" that systems of representation produce sexual differences, differences that are not a reflection of already existing, static, and knowable sexual divisions, masculine and feminine, differences *that cannot be known in advance*, that must be read and reread as they emerge.

Recalling Millett's concept of literature, we can see that Adams's account of representation takes a significant step forward. Millett contends that literature "describes, or interprets, or even distorts" life. Adams insists that political insight – and radical change – require us to take the measure of the way in which "life" emerges from "literature." Representation produces the differences, including sexual difference, that we then call (and indeed live as) "life;" representation makes those differences "real," if by real we mean determining, concrete, consequential, affecting, violent. Rather than measuring the distortion of a representation against what we call life – itself only available to us as another representation – Adams would have us disclose the work of representation in "worlding the world" (Spivak), in giving life itself a shape that appears, to our common sense, simply to *be* the real.

This shift in the relation between what we call representation and what we call real is captured in Nancy Armstrong's essay here, "What feminism did to novel studies." Armstrong traces the process by which feminist novel critics began to see femininity as a sign, a concept that accrues meaning from its relation to (and difference from) masculinity. With this move, she argues, novel critics "assaulted the foundational premise of feminist literary theory – that the gender differences appearing in fiction arose out of biological differences, a division of labor that accommodates those differences, or a bias that limits the possibilities of one gender." Feminist readers of the novel stopped tracking the ways in which novels distorted or reflected their social contexts or the biological differences between the sexes; they began instead to uncover the strategies by which novels *produced* forms of femininity (and masculinity, as well), both for their characters and for the concrete subjects, women and men, who read them. As Armstrong suggests, "if . . . the entire apparatus of gender precedes the fact of the body itself, then there is no such thing as a body that is not inscribed by the culture into which it is born. Once granted such priority over their historical context, novels no longer lack historical substance, but can serve as primary documents for a new kind of history."

One example of this new history is Armstrong's *Desire and Domestic Fiction*, subtitled *A Political History of the Novel*. When literature (and other cultural artifacts) are read this way, the political acquires new dimensions. Rather than residing in a space determined by social and economic factors at work elsewhere and being measured by their reflection of preexisting "contexts," literary texts are directly, substantively historical, an active force in the formation of sexual differences, as well as differences of race, sexuality, and nation, and in the meaning of politics as such. The politics of literature are literally the politics of agency and subordination, of the forms of subjectivity that are ceded power and those that are assigned "subjection" in the sense of "a subjected being, who submits to a higher authority, and is therefore stripped of all freedom except that of freely accepting his submission" (Althusser, "Ideology," p. 182). This new politics of literature differs from those Millett proposed, but one result is very much the same. Literary texts are directly political, their most fundamental operations historically determining as well as determined; they function both in the task "building women" *and* the project to "dismantle" them. This is not to say that the deconstruction of the identity woman is a task to be pursued solely within the confines of texts (at least, not within texts in our commonsense understanding of them as written documents). But it literally cannot take place without steady attention to texts, their rhetorics, and their narratives; they are an irreducible political force in the social field.

This concept of representation – as *productive* of differences rather than as *reflecting* predetermined differences – has radical consequences for the reading of nonliterary texts. In closing, I would like to point to another feminist reading that proceeds from the same assumptions – that language is productive of differences, including sexual differences, and that feminist critics must intervene textually *in order* to intervene politically. My example is an essay by the feminist critic and theorist Sharon Marcus. The topic of her essay is rape.

Marcus's article appears in an anthology addressing the politics of theory, edited by Judith Butler and Joan Scott.[22] She is a literary scholar working primarily on nineteenth-century English and French literature. But "Fighting Bodies, Fighting Words: A Theory and Politics of Rape Prevention," as its subtitle announces, is not literary criticism, at least not in an obvious way. The essay is not about nineteenth-century novels or other literary works. But if it is not literary at first glance, this is because Marcus questions the limits of literary studies, specifically our tendency to limit literary studies by presuming that they cannot intervene beyond a finite, elite sphere. With this presumption, we in effect unwittingly contain their political effects; we depoliticize them, even as we seek political results. Marcus pushes the limits of literary arguments in ways that expand the politics of feminist literary theory: her essay literally concerns rape, not "representations of rape," but the violent crime of sexual assault. Yet this characterization is not absolutely correct, for the word "literal" confuses the very issue Marcus hopes to clarify. She is indeed concerned with "representations of rape," but she calls commonsense understandings of the incompatibility between the literal and the figural into question; indeed, she demonstrates that this mystified distinction enables rape and that overturning it can help women to prevent rape. Her interest in representations, then, is not in how they reflect or distort the reality of rape. Rather, Marcus argues that representations *produce* the reality of rape – in interpretation and in the world. She proposes strategies to interrupt these representations and rewrite their figures in order to stop real rapes.

Marcus begins with the theoretical tension we have been considering: "some recent arguments about the incompatibility of poststructuralist theory and feminist politics designate rape and the raped woman's body as symbols of the real" ("Fighting Bodies," p. 385). Citing one of many critiques of poststructuralism's supposed relativism, she observes that such attacks posit three claims: "that rape is real; that to be real means to be fixed, determinate, and transparent to understanding; and that feminist politics must understand rape as one of the real, clear facts of women's lives" (p. 385). Attacks on poststructuralism's privileging of language accuse it of failing to address the reality of sexual violence, but Marcus notes that many of feminism's most effective interventions against rape originate in the insight that "rape is a question of language, interpretation and subjectivity" (p. 387).

> Feminist thinkers have asked: Whose words count in a rape trial? Whose "no" can never mean "no"? How do rape trials condone men's misinterpretations of women's words? How do rape trials consolidate men's subjective accounts into objective "norms of truth" and deprive women's subjective accounts of cognitive value? Feminists have also insisted on the importance of *naming* rape as violence and of collectively narrating stories of rape. (p. 387)

Marcus concedes that some theorists asking these questions persist in opposing the real (of violence) to the unreality of (mere) language, but she argues that their interpretative practice, "their emphasis on *recounting* rape[,] suggests that in their view actions and experiences cannot be said to exist in politically real and useful ways until they are perceptible and representable" (p. 387). The moment of representation cannot be elided or transcended, particularly if one hopes to achieve political results.

Marcus goes beyond this symptomatic reading of the way in which feminist theorists attack the problem of rape, however. She argues that a disturbing feature of even the most powerful feminist interventions against sexual violence is their tendency to assume that rape is inevitable; feminist theory and activism focus almost exclusively on the aftermath of rape, on legal reforms, on punishment, on counseling for victims.[23] Marcus ties this peculiar fatalism to a predispositoin to assume "violence as a self-explanatory first cause and [to] endo[w] it with an invulnerable and terrifying facticity which stymies our ability to challenge and demystify rape." As a counter-measure, she argues, we must realize that "rape is a language and use this insight to imagine women as neither already raped nor inherently rapable" (p. 387). She is quick to point out that "the statement that rape is a linguistic fact should not be taken to mean that such linguistic forms actually rape women" (p. 389). But she then powerfully discloses the multiple languages of rape, the place of actual speech itself in sexual violence; the "rape script" that prepares men and women for violent encounters in which violent female resistance is unimaginable; the narratives and institutions (to recall Johnson's term) that "solicit women to position [themselves] as endangered, violable, and fearful" (p. 390); the misguided (if well-intended) metaphors by which verbal threats are collapsed into sexual assault, with the consequence that the "rape has always already occurred" from the moment the rapist presents it as possibility. All of these factors are radically reconceived once we see their linguistic forms and their reality as one.

"Masculine power and feminine powerlessness neither simply precede nor cause rape; rape is one of culture's many modes of feminizing women. A rapist chooses his target because he recognizes her to be a woman, but a rapist also strives to imprint the gender identity 'feminine victim' on his target. A rape act thus imposes as well as presupposes misogynist inequalities; rape is not only scripted – it also scripts" (p. 391). Marcus's insight that rape is a language breaks with the rape script (its inevitability, its sheer facticity); it exposes the way in which that script and its physical inscription produce sexual difference and sexualized bodies, including the sexualized difference between the rapist and the rape victim. The scripts and narratives of rape render its status as "the real" commonsensical and its pervasiveness a mere fact of life, shaping the bodies of men and women, their capacity to fight and to be wounded, and their conceptions and their lived experiences of vulnerability and invulnerabilty. Marcus's attack on this script calls upon us literally to engender bodies differently, to rewrite these scripts, narratives, and institutions, thus to enable the female body to be born into a discourse that figures it as potent. "In the place of a tremulous female body or the female self as an immobilized cavity, we can begin to imagine the female body as subject to change, as a potential object of fear and agent of violence" (p. 400). To produce this sexual difference, whose final shape cannot be known in advance, is to move into a territory not figured in the rape script and its narrative, to refuse to grant violence the immunity it tries to claim from representation, to tear down the commonsense "reality" that engenders sexual violence and to build another.

Feminist literary theory's place in this perpetual undoing and rebuilding is not at the margins. Its intervention does not corrode political commitment or insight, but enacts a "persistent critique," in Spivak's phrase, of the work of representation in our experience of the real. Its readings disclose degrees of unfreedom, exclusions, and negations, across the often harsh terrain where any feminist politics must still proceed and in every practice of representation, including its own. I began this essay with the commonsense view that feminist theory and feminist politics are intimates. At its conclusion, I will venture to say that this intimacy endures; we have only lost its innocence.

Further reading

Michèle Barrett and Anne Phillips, eds., *Destabilizing Theory: Contemporary Feminist Debates* (Stanford: Stanford University Press, 1992).

Judith Butler and Joan Scott, eds., *Feminists Theorize the Political* (New York and London: Routledge, 1992).

Jane Gallop, *Anecdotal Theory* (Durham: Duke University Press, 2003).

Rosemary Hennessy and Chrys Ingraham, eds., *Materialist Feminism: A Reader in Class, Difference and Women's Lives* (New York and London: Routledge, 1997).

Trinh T. Minh-ha, *Woman, Native, Other: Writing Postcoloniality and Feminism* (Bloomington: Indiana University Press, 1989).

Chandra Talpade Mohanty, *Feminism Without Borders: Decolonizing Theory, Practicing Solidarity* (Durham: Duke University Press, 2003).

Cherríe Moraga, *Loving in the War Years: lo que nunca pasó por sus labios* (Boston: South End Press, 1983).

Judith Newton and Deborah Rosenfelt, eds., *Feminist Criticism and Social Change: Sex, Class and Race in Literature and Culture* (London: Methuen, 1985).

Denise Riley, *The Words of Selves: Identification, Solidarity, Irony* (Stanford: Stanford University Press, 2000).

Chela Sandoval, *Methodology of the Oppressed* (Minneapolis: University of Minnesota Press, 2000).

Hortense Spillers, *Black, White and in Color: Essays on American Literature and Culture* (Chicago: University of Chicago Press, 2003).

Gayatri Chakravorty Spivak, *A Critique of Postcolonial Reason: Toward a History of the Vanishing Present* (Cambridge, MA: Harvard University Press, 1999).

NOTES

1. These efforts involve a parallel rewriting or, at least, disordering of narratives of masculinities. What was implict in early feminist texts is now a major theme of feminist and queer theory scholars. The shift in many US universities from "women's studies" to "gender studies" programs is a symptom of this development.
2. Diana Fuss, "Reading Like a Feminist," in Naomi Schor and Elizabeth Weed, eds., *The Essential Difference* (Bloomington: Indiana University Press, 1994), p. 112.
3. See Dale Spender, ed., *Men's Studies Modified: The Impact of Feminism on the Academic Disciplines* (Oxford: Pergamon Press, 1981); Ellen Carol DuBois, Gail Paradise Kelly, Elizabeth Lapovsky Kennedy, Carolyn W. Korsmeyer, and Lillian S. Robinson, *Feminist Scholarship: Kindling in the Groves of Academe* (Urbana: University of Illinois Press, 1987); and Ellen Messer-Davidow, *Disciplining Feminism* (Durham: Duke University Press, 2002).
4. See Naomi Schor, "The Righting of French Studies," in Schor, *Bad Objects: Essays Popular and Unpopular* (Durham: Duke University Press, 1995), p. 72.
5. See Gayle Greene and Coppélia Kahn, eds., *Changing Subjects: The Making of Feminist Literary Criticism* (London: Routledge, 1993). I insert the qualification "apparently" to avoid the implication that in an Edenic (and so irretrievably lost) past the politics of feminist criticism was not a topic of debate. Generally, the past was not a kinder, gentler time when things were as they ought to be. In considering the example of the United States, I would offer three observations about the history of conflict among feminist critics: (1) in the early years of feminist criticism's institutionalization, scholars argued ferociously, but felt strongly bound to "the Movement"; (2) the status of "theory" as such was a topic of debate inside and outside the university; (3) while a politics of intellectual labor was pursued, quarrels about the nature of those politics abounded. See Alice Echols, *Daring to Be Bad: Radical Feminism in America, 1967–1975* (Minneapolis: University of Minnesota Press, 1989); and Katie King, *Theory in Its Feminist Travels: Conversations in U. S. Women's Movements* (Bloomington: Indiana University Press, 1994).
6. See Kate Millett, *Sexual Politics* (New York: Doubleday, 1970), pp. 176–89 and *passim*, 157–76, and 62ff.
7. Millett's comment about neglect dates her text; today the claim that sex has any aspect that is *not* somehow political is the provocative stance. Indeed, the Bush administration, seeking to justify its cancellation of an annual gay pride event held by Justice Department employees, recently announced that the President "does not believe we should be politicizing people's sexual orientation" (*New York Times*, June 7, 2003, p. A7.).
8. Rita Felski argues that such attacks persist into the late 1990s and have not entirely faded away. See Felski, *Literature After Feminism* (Chicago: University of Chicago Press, 2003), pp. 1–22.
9. See Louis Althusser, "Ideology and Ideological State Apparatuses," in Althusser, *Lenin and Philosophy and Other Essays*, trans. Ben Brewster (New York: Monthly Review Press, 1971), pp. 127–86, for ideology as unconscious and

the way in which ideological "subjects 'work by themselves'" (p. 181); and "From *Capital* to Marx's Philosophy," in Louis Althusser and Etienne Balibar, *Reading Capital* (London: Verso, 1970), pp. 11–70, for the critique of the "myth of innocent reading" (p. 14).

10. Susan Gubar, *Critical Condition: Feminism at the Turn of the Century* (New York: Columbia University Press. 2000), p. 104. See my introduction to this volume for a more detailed discussion of Lillian Robinson's essay, "Feminist Criticism: How Do We Know When We've Won?"

11. See my introduction for Lillian Robinson's response to the mainstreaming of feminist arguments and research topics in the 1980s.

12. Chandra Talpade Mohanty, *Feminism Without Borders: Decolonizing Theory, Practicing Solidarity* (Durham: Duke University Press, 2003), p. 6. Jennifer Wicke's "Celebrity Material: Materialist Feminism and the Culture of Celebrity," *SAQ* 93:4 (1994), pp. 751–78, argues that the "academic feminism/movement feminism divide is no longer relevant or compelling" in the US context because "there is no movement feminism in the United States." Feminist politics exist, but they are organized along wholly different lines: "Noting the absence of movement politics should not be construed as either criticism or exhortation, but simply as an observation that may help to explain the void that celebrity feminism partially fills" (pp. 752–3).

13. See Catherine MacKinnon, *Feminism Unmodified: Discourses on Life and Law* (Cambridge, MA: Harvard University Press, 1987). For the countervailing view, see bell hooks, *Feminist Theory: From Margin to Center* (Boston: South End Press, 1984); Denise Riley, *"Am I That Name?" Feminism and the Category of "Women" in History* (Minneapolis: University of Minnesota Prass, 1988); Elizabeth Spelman, *Inessential Woman: Problems of Exclusion in Feminist Theory* (Boston: Beacon Press, 1989); and Gayatri Spivak, *In Other Worlds: Essays in Cultural Politics* (New York: Methuen, 1987).

14. Gayatri Chakravorty Spivak, "The Problem of Cultural Self-Representation," in Sarah Harasym, ed., *The Postcolonial Critic: Interviews, Strategies, Dialogues* (New York: Routledge, 1990), p. 58.

15. Materialism is a contested term in feminist theory, describing work ranging from socialist feminisms of the 1970s to the "materialist" inquiry of Judith Butler's *Bodies That Matter: On the Discursive Limits of "Sex"* (New York: Routledge, 1993). See Toril Moi and Janice Radway, eds., "Materialist Feminism," a special issue of *SAQ* 93 (1994); and Teresa L. Ebert, *Ludic Feminism and After: Postmodernism, Desire, and Labor in Late Capitalism* (Ann Arbor: University of Michigan Press), 1996.

16. *Barbara Johnson A World of Difference* (Baltimore: The Johns Hopkins University Press, 1987), p. 31.

17. See Ann Snitow, "A Gender Diary," in Marianne Hirsch and Evelyn Fox Keller, eds., *Conflicts in Feminism* (New York: Routledge, 1990), p. 9.

18. *Gayatri Chakravorty Spivak, A Critique of Postcolonial Reason* (Cambridge, MA: Harvard University Press, 1999, p. 256).

19. Riley, *"Am I That Name?"* pp. 113–14.

20. *Rosemary Hennessy, Materialist Feminism and the Politics of Discourse* (New York: Routledge, 1993), p. 3.
21. Parveen Adams and Elizabeth Cowie, eds., *The Woman in Question* (Cambridge, MA: MIT Press, 1990), p. 103.
22. Judith Butler and Joan W. Scott, eds., *Feminists Theorize the Political* (New York and London: Routledge, 1992), pp. 385–403.
23. One counter-example would be the "Take Back the Night" marches once popular in various cities and on many US campuses.

PART 2

In feminism's wake: genre, period, form

4

NANCY ARMSTRONG

What feminism did to novel studies

Until the 1980s, when feminism emerged as a major force in novel studies, scholars and critics by and large read novels novelistically. In saying that we read novelistically, I refer to a process by which the critic identifies some kind of lack in the protagonist – a lack that someone or something else must supply. Once the protagonist is supplied with the missing ingredient – for example, Robinson Crusoe with land, Tom Jones with a patrimony, and Edward Waverley with English identity – that protagonist can overcome the obstacle that keeps him from improving his position in life and achieve recognition within the community whose order and vigor he consequently repairs and renews. His lack at once defines the magic ingredient that enables self-fulfillment along with social empowerment and creates the basis of identification for readers who feel that lack and wish to see it fulfilled. Feminist literary theory made a swift and telling intervention in this way of reading British fiction, when it persuaded a whole generation of readers to consider what female protagonists lacked rather than their male counterparts. During the 1980s this way of reading changed not only the novels read and taught in classrooms but also the imagined relationship between individual and nation that compels the identification of reader with protagonist. Feminist critics began to read Daniel Defoe's *Moll Flanders* in place of his *Robinson Crusoe*, Samuel Richardson's *Pamela* for Henry Fielding's *Tom Jones*, and Jane Austen's *Emma* rather than Walter Scott's *Waverley*.

Novel criticism acknowledged the success of these new reading practices during the 1990s, when it focused considerable attention on sentimental fiction as the imaginary seedbed of a more inclusive nation, class mobility, and aesthetic innovation. In the years following that success, few critics of the novel have reflected on the fact that feminism adapted a very traditional – that is, masculine – notion of lack to think about the status of women and the gendered division of labor, not to mention the historical role played by both the category of the feminine and the people who occupy it. Nor did they ask if feminism's intervention might have changed how readers construe the missing ingredient that ensures the fulfillment of self in society. I would like to take a step in that direction here.

Feminist critics most often identify the lack in terms of "agency," by which they mean the political authority to effect some change, however local and temporary. But such critics rarely seek a remedy for this lack in terms of either wealth or political power. Instead, they posit literacy as the precondition for achieving such power and therefore the key to female agency. Novels from Defoe's to those of Virginia Woolf indicate that an author-heroine must appear rational, consistent, durable, and personally resourceful before she can overcome some form of gender bias, do what that bias would not let her do, and achieve recognition within the community that appears progressive for letting her extend the limits of acceptable feminine behavior. Working within the paradox that one must first appear to have power before one can hope to exercise it, the first feminists taught a generation of readers to substitute a lack of "voice," or what we might call cultural power, for a lack of economic or political agency, as if the one form of power could be equated with the other. On the assumption that the relationship between feminism and modern fiction has choreographed all the major theoretical debates in the field of novel studies for the past two decades, I hope to show how feminist literary theory has transformed not only the field of novel studies, but our notion of what it means to have access to political power as well. In conclusion, I will suggest that through all these changes those of us who work in the field of novel studies not only persist in reading novelistically, but by doing so also limit the way we imagine our relation to society.

What is "the" novel?

It is fair to say that, until 1979, generations of readers asked and answered this question without significantly disturbing the canon of British fiction as it had been established at the turn of the nineteenth century by Mrs. Barbauld and Walter Scott.[1] With the publication of Elaine Showalter's *A Literature of Their Own* and Sandra Gilbert and Susan Gubar's *The Madwoman in the Attic*, everything changed.[2] Joined by Carolyn Heilbrun, Nina Auerbach, Nina Baym, Annette Kolodny, and others, these critics swiftly turned masculinist models of literary production to the purpose of identifying "a separate tradition" of women's writing. In one of the more influential gestures of this kind, Gilbert and Gubar drew on Harold Bloom's quasi-psychoanalytic concept of "the anxiety of influence" to describe the double bind in which the culture that gave rise to the novel placed the woman novelist. Bloom imagined literary history as the product of oedipal rivalries which one author felt toward the giants of previous ages who seemed to dwarf those who came after them. Gilbert and Gubar set about to challenge Bloom, when they saw the female novelist as a daughter brimming with both talent and resentment toward Bloom's rebellious son: all those women who wrote fiction could not readily think of themselves as supplanting a male author in a masculine tradition of letters. According to the oedipal dynamic loosely borrowed from Freud, daughters never want to supplant their fathers but instead compete with other women for his affection. To win such a competition they cannot very well rebel against tradition but instead must submit to it.

Women novelists, it was argued, put their genius to work devising new and ingenious ways to express their outrage at the position in which their gender placed them, while still submitting to the masculine rules of the novel genre. In the words of Gilbert and Gubar:

> By projecting their rebellious impulses . . . into mad or monstrous women, female authors dramatize their own . . . desire both to accept the strictures of patriarchal society and to reject them. What this means, however, is that the madwoman in literature by women is . . . in some sense the author's double, an image of her own anxiety and rage.[3]

Because of the limits that her culture placed on women novelists, according to Gilbert and Gubar, Charlotte Brontë had to rein Jane Eyre in. She created the mad Bertha Mason to act out the rage that neither she nor her heroine could express. Supported by her degenerate counterpart, the figure of a woman lacking the means of verbal expression and yet incapable of self-restraint moved to center stage as the heroine of feminist criticism. To calculate the impact of this figure on Victorian Studies, one need only tally up the sheer number of literary critical studies that use the prohibitions placed on their self-expression to justify unruliness on the part of women in the fiction of that period. The idea that fiction secretly endorsed rebellion against an oppressive father, husband, culture, and literary mode became so attractive that critics looked for signs of rebellion even in heroines who seem compliant to a fault, and they found its indirect expression in the most unlikely places: for example, the hysterical solitude of Charlotte Brontë's Lucy Snowe (*Villette*), the sacrificial boat trip of George Eliot's Maggie Tulliver (*The Mill on the Floss*), and the suicidal wanderings of Charles Dickens's Lady Dedlock (*Bleak House*). According to the feminist readers, women became aggressive, whether against themselves or against another, only when barred access to those legitimate means of self-expression readily available to men. Thus women compensated at the level of culture – by acting out, speaking forthrightly, or writing in ways critical of masculine authority – for what they lacked in social and political terms. How did the relocation of lack from male to female protagonist change our critical understanding of the novel as a genre?

The male protagonist's lack was, paradoxically, also an excess. Along with a lack of wealth and position, Robinson Crusoe, for example, has an excess of acquisitive energy and the skills required to convert raw nature into property. Midway through the eighteenth century, Tom Jones's lack of legitimacy goes hand in glove with an irrepressible good nature and sexual energy, qualities perfectly appropriate to a son of the landowning classes, once his birth is legitimated. The minute Tom arrives at a social position that can accommodate his excess, all signs of lack simply vanish; the novel has achieved its political objective.

It is relatively easy to identify the excess that catapults the male out of one social position and into another that strikes the reader as more appropriate for the individual in question. But what happens when a female has certain features in excess of her social position? That excess, whatever form it may take – an inclination for adventure, intellectual precocity, forthright speech, all manner of noncompliance – automatically puts her in violation of the principle that women are naturally subordinate to men, thereby jeopardizing her appeal for men, the very appeal on which a woman's hopes for upward mobility rested. When the lack is relocated from male to female protagonist, then, the result is two impossible choices, or what we call a double bind. If a woman, the protagonist of fiction could either remain in a servile position and retain her charm or elevate her economic position and sacrifice the very helplessness and submission that made her attractive to men. Such is the very bind in which Gilbert and Gubar place Charlotte Brontë by way of explaining the limits she put on her heroine. Mary Poovey supported this hypothesis in *The Proper Lady and the Woman Writer*, which discussed the historical predicament of late eighteenth and early nineteenth-century women writers.[4]

Fiction became a far more complex and interesting phenomenon when seen through the lens of feminist ideology. Rather than lavish attention on the formal strategies by which novels distributed economic and political rewards to men for certain acts of aggression, critics such as Poovey focused on the formal means by which fiction rewarded a verbally audacious woman by joining her to a husband of wealth and position. The heroine of sensibility had to challenge the norms of her culture without becoming unforgivably tasteless. Indeed, men had to find her audacity appealing. Feminists came to regard Richardson's *Clarissa* as exactly that: a sustained performance of verbal insubordination designed to appeal both to men whose authority was beyond question and to readers who could identify their interests with those of a heroine who used words to overturn such authority.[5] Austen's fiction could also be described in just such terms, as could novels by Emily and Charlotte Brontë, Eliot, and Woolf. Under the influence of psychoanalysis, feminists began to show how women authors used words to expand the interior world of the subject, and female consciousness became host to subversive possibilities that anticipated and, in some cases, challenged the work of Freud.[6] The constraints placed on women writers, their lack of experience in the public sphere, became, in other words, the means of achieving psychological expansion and subtlety.

How and when did the novel begin?

First published in the 1950s, Ian Watt's The *Rise of the Novel* was relatively ignored until the 1980s, when it inspired a flurry of corrective responses known as the "the origins of the novel" debate.[7] Watt more or less assumed that fiction was a permutation of the journalistic writing that marked the revolution in print culture, a revolution that transformed literature from the vehicle of aristocratic values to a democratically accessible public sphere, the means of amusement and information for a class of people engaged in commerce and trade. With their prosperity, so, too, grew their cultural importance and the kinds of writing that catered to their desire for upward mobility. During the 1980s a number of critical studies suddenly appeared to persuade us that novels began as criminal confessions, Puritan autobiographies, or political writing of various kinds and only gradually came to be recognized for what they were – ingenious imitations or fanciful displacements of the original. Each such point of origin for the novel made sense so long as one assumed that novelists responded to a demand for fiction from pretty much the same class of people that Watt had imagined: highly individualistic Protestant men who felt that they lacked not only a social position corresponding to each man's individual merit but also the kind of literature that catered to the fantasy of a society based on individual merit. This assumption remained firmly in place until feminism entered the debate over the novel's origins.

Given that the novel gained currency as a genre as it allowed readers to imagine a new relationship between individual and state, a relationship in which the individual acquired a social position equivalent to his worth in wit, drive, integrity, and perseverance; given as well that more than half the novels written during the eighteenth century were written by women, why assume that the first modern individual was male or that the novel was created by and for men? At some point during the mid-1980s, I asked this question. Once I had done so, there was no turning back. I discovered a sudden rise during the eighteenth century in the number of books written and published for the expressed purpose of telling women how to be women. Conduct books, they were called. In contrast with earlier conduct books, those appearing in the eighteenth century, alongside novels by such authors as Defoe, Richardson, and Austen, prescribed a distinctively modern brand of femininity that I called "the domestic woman." It was the novel's job, I reasoned, to rewrite this woman as a category that women would want to occupy and men to wed and be with but not occupy. Having developed the formal strategies for infusing this supposedly powerless woman with desire, moreover, it was the novel's job to reproduce and update that figure in response to historical changes. The purpose was to convince readers – often by offering semi-salacious but lethal alternatives – that the household she managed and the affectionate relationships she maintained were magic ingredients capable of compensating for whatever it was that one lacked.[8] What does the history of the novel look like, once we identify female conduct books and marriage manuals as its starting point?

Terry Lovell has argued that the novel began as a rather debased commercial form readily available to women authors and then rose to the status of literature during the age of realism, when women no longer dominated the scene as authors. As Lovell has also pointed out, literary pursuits of all kinds nevertheless retained a feminine gender that made them available not only to women authors but also to women readers as an important part of their polite education.[9] A cursory look at what people read in the way of novels makes it rather clear that where other kinds of fiction bent to the winds of fashion, the domestic novel has indeed enjoyed a steady publication history for almost three hundred years. Once we see the tradition of nineteenth-century fiction in this light, it becomes rather puzzling that for so many years literary criticism thought it reasonable to hold up the male *Bildungsroman* as the best example of the species. Any number of subgenres can be pulled into the model of domestic fiction and read in feminist terms, including the industrial novel, the female *Bildungsroman*, the detective novel, the colonial adventure novel, and the gothic romance. Even such novels as *Robinson Crusoe*, *Waverley*, Dickens's *Dombey and Son*, and most of Hardy can be read as novels whose protagonists either qualify as heads of a modern household – or face dire consequences for failing to do so. Having established this continuity from Richardson to Woolf, feminists could see important differences between, for example, the narratives of Aphra Behn, Eliza Haywood, and Delarivier Manley,[10] novels of sensibility,[11] and the dialectic of sentimentalism and sensationalism that informs so much of fiction from the late eighteenth century on.[12]

Once we replace the male *Bildungsroman* with the domestic novel as the dominant form of British fiction, however, we have to ask why. Why exalt the feminine side of the equation, when women were so lacking in economic and political terms? My own response to this question was to argue that women did in fact have considerable power, not only in writing fiction but also in assuming a place at the center of a modern household.[13] This position may have lacked economic independence and failed to qualify women for the vote until rather late in the modern period, but their lack of these traditionally masculine forms of power gave them power nevertheless – call it cultural power, the power over sexual morality, child-rearing, courtship rituals, the care of the body, and household consumption. These prerogatives were in no way natural to women. Indeed, women acquired this distinctively feminine authority in fiction that divided British culture into masculine and feminine domains, a great deal of which was written by women. Their lack in political terms was their cultural gain.

The great gender inversion

The conflict within feminism between Anglo-American essentialism and several brands of poststructuralism imported from France is an old story that enters the picture here. Once feminist literary theory had cut the tie between gender and nature and redefined gender as a product of cultural history, the stage was set for a complete reversal of the essentialist priorities established by the first generation of feminist literary critics. Those influenced by the deconstruction of Jacques Derrida, Paul de Man, and French feminists could argue, as Barbara Johnson did, that the undervaluing of women is the consequence of "the transfer of personhood to rhetorical entities" that allows male theorists, as well as male authors, "to claim a form of universality which can be said to inhere in language itself."[14] The fact that we all, male and female, become personifications by virtue of this transfer, does not explain why the self-resistance and uncertainty that results would allow someone like de Man to achieve "such authority and visibility, while the self-resistance and uncertainty of *women* has been part of what has insured their lack of authority and invisibility."[15] To answer the question of why the act of writing itself overcomes a lack in the case of male authors and produces one in the case of women, Naomi Schor focused "on the place and function of the detail since the mid-eighteenth century." In surveying this field, she observed that the history of this aspect of writing is not only associated with women but indicative of what they lack: that history is "bounded on the one side by the *ornamental*, with its traditional connotations of effeminacy and decadence, and on the other, by the *everyday*, whose 'prosiness' is rooted in the domestic sphere of social life presided over by women."[16]

Those concerned with how the categories of gender came to dominate both representation and world represented, drew, paradoxically, on the cultural historical assumptions of Michel Foucault. Although completely unconcerned with gender, Foucault operated on the principle that the only true cultural history is the history of categories that classify people and determine their places and thus their possibilities for interaction in a vast differential system that periodically reorganizes life, as its categories migrate, blend, and divide internally. Feminists used this notion of history, as I did, to explain how the categories of masculine and feminine coalesced out of earlier cultural materials as a means of displacing the value of blood and inherited wealth with that of intrinsic capacities for reason and sympathy. Such novels as Richardson's *Pamela*, Austen's *Pride and Prejudice*, Emily Brontë's *Wuthering Heights*, Charlotte Brontë's *Jane Eyre*, and many others recapitulate this historical process before delivering up the ideal household it holds forth as a carrot to the reader through several hundred pages. The cultural transformation of a world divided between aristocracy and populace into a world divided between men and women came first. Only when they believed in a world so divided could literate people inhabit those categories, marry, throw parties, spend their money, and reproduce themselves in both children and novels accordingly. Once they believed in a world so divided, furthermore, women could expand the limits of their domain and devise ways of participating in the intellectual and political life of their nation.[17]

The process of eroding the premise that feminist literary theory existed to compensate for women's lack of money and position by giving them a voice arrived at a turning point in Judith Butler's *Gender Trouble*.[18] Drawing on the later work of Jacques Lacan, Butler turns the acquisition of feminine identity into a negative process: regardless of one's biological sex, a person begins as a mix of possibilities and acquires a gender as that individual sheds either feminine qualities (and becomes masculine) or masculine qualities (and becomes feminine). What one lacks, in other words, gives one an identity. This is no simple once-only event, Butler maintains, but a process that we are condemned to repeat over an entire lifetime. More concerned with the fictional identities that we perform than with how fiction per se figures into this process, Butler's breakthrough work nevertheless had a profound effect on novel studies. Rather than consider how a protagonist grows or develops, literary critics could start looking for elements that repeat themselves and the precise form of lack produced by the necessary failure to perform exact repetitions. Let us consider what this second generation of feminist thought – heavily influenced by French poststructuralism – did to the reading practices established by Gilbert and Gubar.

When feminists began to regard femininity as a concept or condition that acquires meaning by virtue of its lack of masculinity, they assaulted the foundational premise of feminist literary theory that the gender differences appearing in fiction arose out of biological differences, a division of labor that accommodates those differences, or a bias that limits the possibilities of one gender for the benefit of the other. This was especially true of those feminists who worked on the novel. Rather than read the qualities, possibilities, and limitations that fiction assigns to women as a reflection, or effect, of their actual lack of economic and political authority, feminists influenced by poststructuralism read fiction as one, if not the major, cause of women's confinement to the household and forms of service associated with motherhood. If, for example, as deconstruction suggests, masculinity is textually dependent on its lack of femininity, then it follows that a man should feel threatened by women who exercise masculine forms of power or by men who flaunt signs of femininity.[19] Their excess is his lack. Hence the hostile reaction to the politically assertive feminists of the 1860s and 1870s,[20] as well as to "the new woman" who emerged at the end of the nineteenth century.[21] If, further, the entire apparatus of gender precedes the fact of the body itself, then there is no such thing as a body that is not inscribed by the culture into which it is born. Once granted such priority over their historical context, novels no longer lack historical substance but can serve as primary documents for a new kind of history.

Culture rising

When reading a novel, we like to think that it imitates life, and so we "get lost" in the story of a fictive protagonist. But if writing has the priority over being and determines our identity to the degree that poststructuralism suggests it does, then we ourselves are narratives featuring protagonists who overcome a lack and find or fail to find a gratifying place within the given social order. This is why we tend to read novels novelistically and consider some of them true to life. Literary criticism has long been accustomed to think of novels as effects, or responses to such historical events as the shift from Tory to Whig, the rise of the professional classes, the decline of empire, the Great Wars, the Great Depression, immigration from the colonies, or globalization. Novels respond to and register these changes, much as the household must adjust to changes in the national economy or women deal with the changing fortunes of men. But if literate members of modern culture do in fact think of themselves as novels, and have for at least two centuries, then novels must influence events. This is a question of domain. Where politics dominate culture – for example, in early twentieth-century Germany[22] or some postindependence-colonies[23] – history is a masculine affair, and nations appear to be driven by the desire to compensate for a lack of wealth and position, a fear of the feminine. When, on the other hand, culture gains the upper hand over politics, it infuses politics with the liberal morality of modern fiction. As Lauren Berlant explains, the public sphere becomes "intimate," elections hinge on the issue of which candidate lacks the qualities of a good father, and nations send people to die in battle if convinced that the middle-class household is under siege.[24] In this situation we find that "voice" indeed becomes a form of "agency," as much as, if not more than, wealth or position.

Up to this point, I have not included the American novel in this account of what feminism did to novel studies, and it is here that I must do so. In many respects, the two stories run parallel, not only because *critics of* American literature tend to be housed in English departments, but also because there was so much conversation across the Atlantic between British and US feminists. In the United States, however, writing fiction – indeed, writing itself – is even more closely associated with nationmaking than in Britain, and culture is therefore less distinguishable from politics. Among American-ists, Ann Douglas must be acknowledged for using the term "feminization"[25] to identify an alternative tradition to that inaugurated by the Puritan Fathers and extending through the transcendentalists to the novels of Nathaniel Hawthorne, Herman Melville, Mark Twain, and Henry James. The novels in this alternative tradition, as exemplified by Harriet Beecher Stowe's *Uncle Tom's Cabin*, were popular rather than literary, sentimental rather than political. Douglas succeeded in shifting what she saw as the lack *of* an indigenous tradition of American literature into a lack *within* the indigenous tradition, a substitution of culture for politics.

It took almost as many years for feminists to revise this argument as it took them to dislodge the assumption that the origins of the British novel were masculine. This second generation of feminists tried to compensate for the lack Douglas had created. Instead of betraying the metaphysical values of our founding fathers, according to Jane Tompkins, the rise of women novelists effected an emotional and spiritual transformation of a politically divided culture.[26] Coming at the same problem from a different angle, Cathy Davidson found the fiction written by, for, and about women superior in its realism to the canonical American literature of the period. "The private and nonfictional commentaries of the time," she explains, "suggest a contiguity between the sociology of the early American family and the plots of the sentimental novel."[27] Amy Kaplan added a vital link in the chain of an alternative tradition of American literature in her study of late nineteenth-century realism, a tradition, as she reads it, to which such women writers as Charlotte Perkins Gilman and Edith Wharton made perhaps the most interesting contributions.[28]

Curiously enough, the traditional theory of American literature as something that seventeenth-century British emigrants brought over to the New World on a boat could never account for the fiction produced in America during the eighteenth and early nineteenth centuries. The masculine tradition of reading American literature skipped ahead from the Puritan Fathers to the novels of James Fenimore Cooper, leaving critics to forage in the gap between 1720 and 1820 for examples of serious literature. It was not until the 1990s that a new generation of critics took up the project of converting what had been a lack of literature and a lapse in the national tradition into an era of great literary productivity. According to the new generation of critics, the eighteenth century saw the rise of sensibility in novels derived from the British model and infused with the American conviction that individuals shall be judged on certain qualities of free subjectivity.[29] Shirley Samuels, Julia Stern, and Elizabeth Barnes each set about to challenge the assumption that the new national culture was a masculine tradition.[30] Intrigued by the similarities between this argument and the feminist success in derailing the debate over the origins of the British novel, Leonard Tennenhouse and I attempted to effect a similar revision of the prevailing theory that American literature began with the Puritan Fathers.[31]

Why assume that Anglo-American culture – especially the novel – flowed only one way, from Europe to North America? Is it not just as possible that something happened to English literature when reproduced in the colonies that subsequently changed the way things were done back in Britain? During the very period when novels were enthralling the British readership, colonial authors were writing accounts of English women captured by Native Americans and exporting them back across the Atlantic, where they fueled an appetite for more. No doubt because these narratives were often written by women in a form that resembled Richardson's epistolary fiction, Tennenhouse and I noticed an uncanny resemblance between these protracted accounts of the solitary anguish of women taken by heathen savages and the emotional rollercoaster recounted by heroines of sensibility captive to the machinations of British libertines. We observed, moreover, that some of these American captivity narratives predated their sentimental English counterparts by a number of decades, suggesting that not only may the English novel have originated in colonial America but consequently the American novel as well.

Once one thinks of American fiction as beginning with the captivity narratives of the late seventeenth century, we end up with a very different picture of the tradition. Such novels as William Hill Brown's *Power of Sympathy*, Hannah Webster Foster's *The Coquette*, and Susanna Rowson's *Charlotte Temple* shed their anomalous character and constitute a direct line from the earliest colonial captivity narratives to the sentimental fiction of the nineteenth century. Indeed, as in the case of the British novel, any number of those authors who were once the spine of a purely masculine tradition could now be folded into a far more continuous and comprehensive tradition that tried and, in some cases, notably failed to imagine the nation in familial terms. Hawthorne's *The Scarlet Letter* and *The House of Seven Gables* belong to such a tradition, as do Melville's *Moby Dick* and *Pierre*, Edgar Allan Poe's *The Fall of the House of Usher*, and most of Henry James. With this radical change in the gendered and generic principle that identifies the mainstream or canon of American fiction, we can observe culture gaining ascendancy over the political and economic domains as the magical ingredient that a protagonist must acquire in order to achieve a gratifying position within the social order. Indeed, we might regard such novels as Theodore Dreiser's *Sister Carrie* and Wharton's *House of Mirth* as narratives that dialectically perform the ascendancy of culture over traditionally masculine forms of authority. In this respect, the relationship between feminism and American fiction follows much the same course as the relationship between feminism and British fiction: from the rhetoric of exclusion, to the identification of a separate minority tradition, to the displacement and subsumption of the dominant tradition.

The scramble for cultural capital

To address the dilemma in which feminism now finds itself, I must call attention to feminism's preoccupation with race in American fiction[32] and a similar concern with class in British fiction.[33] Beginning with Gilbert and Gubar, feminists have accentuated the contrast between Brontë's Jane Eyre and her haughty rival, Blanche Ingram, and, at the same time, denied the radical discontinuity between Brontë's heroine and Bertha Mason, the madwoman in the attic. There is more than a little irony in this identification in that *both* Blanche and Bertha come from the landowning class and participate in an exchange of women that preserves the exclusivity and conserves the wealth of that class. We might regard this impulse to expand the category of women down the social ladder as an expression of feminism's wish to expand its base. Moreover, one can observe this same wish at work suppressing racial differences in the American novel. Just as Jane Eyre serves feminists who work on British fiction,[34] Stowe's *Uncle Tom's Cabin* offers a privileged site for expanding the basis of feminist identification in American fiction, as feminists find in the relation between Eva and Topsy or Topsy and Aunt Ophelia some kind of affiliation between white women and black. The compulsion to expand the category of "woman" in either one direction or the other is a legacy that continues into my own generation of feminism, which assumes that gender is a class or racial formation. Indeed, it has become a critical commonplace to say that fiction naturalizes class and racial differences by holding forth a class-specific definition of woman, a normative model – the "Angel in the House" in England and "the cult of true womanhood" in the United States – in relation to which the women of other groups are invariably found to be lacking. In the words of Madhu Dubey, "the presence that defines black feminine characters in the novel as deficient is represented not by the black man but by the white woman."[35]

Harriet Jacobs's *Incidents in the Life of a Slave Girl* displaced *Uncle Tom's Cabin* as the central American text in the feminist canon as black feminism used it to identify the implicitly racist limits that white feminism placed on the category "woman." Hazel Carby points out how Jacobs's autobiographical narrative rejects "conventional feminine qualities of sub-mission and passivity" when the protagonist confronts the inevitability of rape, and endorses a "spirit of defiance" that characterizes all her encoun-ters with her master.[36] Saidiya Hartman contends that redefining in positive terms what was a deficiency according to the white feminine standard is not all that easy. Hartman shows that Jacobs must portray her life as a slave in terms that simultaneously acknowledge the difference between her situation and that of the white heroine and combat the cultural logic that found her lacking according to that standard: "The feat of *Incidents* is not simply its representation of the normativity of sexual violence but also the endeavor to actualize something 'akin to freedom' in this context, even if it affords little more than having a love whom one is thankful not to despise."[37]

Looking at the fiction of nineteenth-century England, Cora Kaplan makes a strikingly similar observation concerning class: "class meaning organizes and orders the split representation of women as good and bad."[38] Dealing with working-class fiction of the early twentieth century, Pamela Fox builds on Kaplan's argument to account for the fact that women of different classes responded differently to the split representation of women. Fox explains that "it was predominantly middle-class women who felt the daily strictures of (and protested against) romantic codes of behavior. Working-class women were typically denied access to those codes by their own cultural experience." As a result, "in autobiographical writing by working-class women at this time, susceptibility to romance ideology is associated with guilt, danger, and a sense of thrill, as well as outright contempt."[39] In working-class fiction the ideal woman of mainstream Victorian fiction lost whatever foothold in nature she might have had and was exposed – whether poignantly or ironically – as a fantasy of womanhood, a type rigidly circumscribed by the class whose interests she represented.

Feminism shifted the object of literary critical analysis from the author's sex to the gender of the text itself and the cultural domain in which that text offered compensation for the lack of political authority. In so doing, paradoxically, feminism made it possible for various groups other than feminism to appropriate that lack as their own. During the 1990s lesbian and gay people, black women, Asian Americans, and Chicanos/Chicanas, to mention a few, began to say about feminism much the same thing that Barbara Johnson said about the Yale critics, namely that "the transfer of personhood to rhetorical entities" allows feminist theorists "to claim a form of universality which can be said to inhere in language itself" (*World of Difference*, p. 45). The fact that we all, male and female, become personifications by virtue of this transfer does not explain why the self-resistance and uncertainty that results would allow a Barbara Johnson or a Judith Butler to achieve "such authority and visibility, while the self-resistance and uncertainty" of gay men and people of color had been "part of what has insured their lack of authority and invisibility" (p. 45). Gayatri Spivak equates the personification of the individual writing with Jane Eyre's complicity in the "soul-making" process that ensures the universal status of the modern Western individual and suppresses the very existence of subordinated populations as subjects; like Bertha Mason, the subaltern subject can't "speak."[40]

Berthold Schoene updates Johnson's use of "personification" when he refers to the process by which we acquire an identity in language as "impersonation." This is his way of insisting that writing as a male is not the naturally powerful stroke that feminism makes it out to be but the performance of a rhetorical feat rather more like than different from feminism's. "Individual impersonations of masculinity," he explains, are "precarious, tragically unstable and ultimately detrimental identity constructs that, instead of conducing to a man's quest for autonomous self-authentication, rigidly circumscribe it."[41] Rey Chow takes both these arguments a step further in denouncing feminist approaches "for which the emergence of 'woman' is the originary, Edenic event, while any attempt to challenge it . . . will have to be construed as a rude assault on the identity of an innocent victim."[42] She takes those feminists to task who feel betrayed by the rising generation who criticized feminism on the same grounds that Johnson criticized the Yale critics.

In Chow's estimation such old guard feminists consider the category "woman" closed and see their job as defending that category against assaults that expose its limitations from without (postcolonial feminism) or shatter its unity from within (racially or ethnically based feminisms). Rather than a resentful feminism, she wants a feminism that understands "the fundamentally open, indeed unfinishable, story of the emergence of 'woman' in the midst of unequal multiethnic representational practices" (*The Protestant Ethnic*, p. 182). To weigh in on the side of such openness is not the same thing as forecasting successive adjustments of the category "woman" to include more and more differences among women, as if any such abstraction did not require some form of exclusion to define itself. Quite the contrary: feminism has ushered in an age of openness, in which the admission of new groups within the category "woman" allows an internal shattering of that category that preserves the minority status of those gaining membership within it. Wendy Brown puts it bluntly: "Just when polite liberal (not to mention correct leftist) discourse ceased speaking of us as dykes, faggots, colored girls, or natives, we began speaking of ourselves that way."[43] So why do groups hold onto categories that they claim lack power, if what they want is empowerment? Why not become as one with the universally human, the "we" without any qualifier?

Romancing the lack

When feminism made its initial move and exposed the fact that the literary tradition, as defined by the British and US academies, excluded a great deal of fiction, specifically that authored by women, few knew that much more was at stake than the cultural capital of women academics. Feminist literary theory was indeed an instrumental part of what would become a successful twenty-year effort to increase the proportion of women in the academy, and move them up the ranks from the relatively menial positions they had once occupied disproportionately in British and US universities. Whether academic feminists felt all that much genuine affiliation with women in general, they couched their particular interest in terms of the general interest – "woman." In order to generalize its constituency, feminism adopted another rhetorical feature that would determine the nature and limitation of its success. I have throughout this essay referred to a "lack" – whether in women, in writing, or in the feminine domain. I explained how feminism first turned women's lack of economic and political control over their lives outward, so that a lack of masculine prerogative within the self, the book, or the household became a surfeit of bullying power in the other, dominant party. I also showed how feminism, in so constituting its oppressor, characteristically transformed this lack of political, or masculine, agency into a surfeit of agency at the level of voice: "*Speak* I must," Jane Eyre exclaims, sending tremors of pleasure – that of resentment unbound – through generations of readers: "I had been trodden on severely and *must* turn: but how? What strength had I to dart retaliation at my antagonist? I gathered my energies and launched them in this blunt sentence."[44]

With this powerful combination of rhetorical features – the acknowledgement of a lack produced in the self by an overpowering other, a lack that consequently justifies excess on the part of the victim in the form of speech – feminism sealed its own fate. To separate itself from the form of power – as reflected, for example, in the masculine canon of fiction, the criteria for literariness, and the imperial "we" of the literary critical establishment – feminism defined itself as lacking precisely those things. Paradoxically, however, and perhaps to its complete surprise, feminism did in fact compensate in large part for a lack of economic and political power by 1) appropriating the form of the novel as the basis of a literary domain equivalent to the social domain of the household; 2) arguing that within that domain, culture led to money and power, not the other way around; and 3) subsuming within the feminine the masculine canon and practice of reading British and American fiction. I should add that this dialectical relation of feminism to the tradition of reading within the field of novel studies reproduced itself outside novel studies in relation to poetry and drama. The study of fiction, once regarded as an area of literary study with little prestige, consequently came to occupy the center of British and American literary studies.

If what feminism did to the field of literary studies exemplifies the relation of minority to dominant cultures, we could reasonably look forward to a moment when the periphery – as represented by ethnic, diasporic, and postcolonial studies – would displace the liberal middle-class core of literary studies. But feminism is, I believe, more accurately understood as the exception as well as the catalyst and model for a succession of such displacements. In assuming centrality over the field of novel studies, after all, feminism not only succeeded in transforming that field, it also transformed the kind of power that it took to dominate it. As a result, culture came to speak as powerfully as, if not even more so than, money or established position. Moreover, in the effort to devalue a literary tradition that insisted that domination by ruling-class men was natural, desirable, necessary, and right, feminism insisted that culture spoke most powerfully when it spoke from the periphery.

By relocating cultural power to the periphery and opposing it to economic and political power, feminism extricated itself from the double bind that forced a woman to appeal to masculine forms of authority in order to register her objections to those same forms of authority. In so doing, however, feminism eluded the grip of one double bind only to place itself squarely within another. Feminism discovered that ceding the position of outsider to other excluded groups was virtually the same as relinquishing the foundational category ("woman") that had authorized the "voice" of white middle-class women. At almost the same time, however, feminism also discovered that if one claims the position of outsider in the wake of a successful assault on the universality of the white male subject, one risks going the way of that subject.[45] Cultural authority does not remain "decentered" for very long, if at all; it invariably forms new centers. By capturing such authority specifically on behalf of disenfranchised voices, feminism simultaneously seized authority from women's traditional lack of economic and political power and handed over that power to groups who lacked the means to represent themselves. Thus, either way, the future of feminism lies in the appropriation of its signature rhetorical strategies by those groups who will continue to revise the tradition of the novel, including the tradition now constituted by feminism.

Further reading

Nancy Armstrong, "Why Daughters Die: The Racial Logic of American Sentimentalism," *Yale Journal of Criticism* 7:2 (1994), pp. 1–24.
  Fiction in the Age of Photography: The Legacy of British Realism (Cambridge, MA: Harvard University Press, 2000).
Michel Foucault, *The History of Sexuality*, 3 vols., trans. Robert Hurley, *Volume I: The Will to Knowledge* (New York: Pantheon Books, 1978).
Kate Flint, *The Woman Reader 1837–1914* (Oxford: Oxford University Press, 1993).
Sharon Marcus, *Apartment Stories: City and Home in Nineteenth-Century Paris and London* (Berkeley: University of California Press, 1999).
Anne McLintock, *Imperial Leather: Race, Gender and Sexuality in the Colonial Context* (New York: Routledge, 1995).
D. A. Miller, *The Novel and the Police* (Berkeley: University of California Press, 1988).

NOTES

1. Homer Obed Brown, *Institutions of the English Novel: From Defoe to Scott* (Philadelphia: University of Pennsylvania Press, 1997), pp. 171–201.
2. Sandra Gilbert and Susan Gubar, *The Madwoman in the Attic: The Woman Writer and the Nineteenth Century Literary Imagination* (New Haven: Yale University Press, 1979); and Elaine Showalter, *A Literature of Their Own* (Princeton: Princeton University Press, 1977).
3. Gilbert and Gubar, *Mad woman in the Attic*, p. 78.

4. Mary Poovey, *The Proper Lady and the Woman Writer: Ideology as Style in the Works of Mary Wollstonecraft, Mary Shelley, and Jane Austen* (Chicago: University of Chicago Press, 1984).

5. In "Going Farther: Literary Theory and the Passage to Cultural Criticism," *Works and Days* 3:1 (1985), pp. 51–72, Ellen Rooney explains how the crossover from traditional textuality to cultural politics – specifically a feminist cultural politics – irreversibly changed the way that the rape of Clarissa could be read.

6. See Shoshana Felman, *Literature and Psychoanalysis: The Question of Reading, Otherwise* (Baltimore: The Johns Hopkins University Press, 1982); and Naomi Schor, *Breaking the Chain: Women, Theory, and French Realist Fiction* (New York: Columbia University Press, 1985).

7. Ian Watt, *The Rise of the Novel: Studies in Defoe, Richardson and Fielding* (Harmondsworth: Pelican, 1972).

8. Nancy Armstrong, *Desire and Domestic Fiction: A Political History of the Novel* (New York: Oxford University Press, 1987).

9. Terry Lovell, *Consuming Fiction* (London: Verso, 1987).

10. See Catherine Gallagher, *Nobody's Story: The Vanishing Acts of Women Writers in the Marketplace, 1670–1820* (Berkeley: University of California Press, 1994).

11. See Janet Todd, *Sensibility: An Introduction* (London: Methuen, 1986); and Claudia Johnson, *Equivocal Beings: Politics, Gender, and Sentimentality in the 1790s* (Chicago: University of Chicago Press, 1995).

12. See Ann Cvetkovich, *Mixed Feelings: Feminism, Mass Culture, and Victorian Sensationalism* (New Brunswick: Rutgers University Press, 1992); and George E. Haggerty, *Unnatural Affections: Women and Fiction in the Late Eighteenth Century* (Bloomington: University of Indiana Press, 1998).

13. Armstrong, *Desire and Domestic Fiction*.

14. Barbara Johnson, *A World of Difference* (Baltimore: The Johns Hopkins University Press, 1987), p. 45.

15. Ibid., p. 45.

16. Naomi Schor, *Reading in Detail: Aesthetics and the Feminine* (London: Methuen, 1987), p. 4.

17. See Deirdre David, *Intellectual Women and Victorian Patriarchy* (Ithaca: Cornell University Press, 1987); and *Rule Britannia: Women, Empire, and Victorian Writing* (Ithaca: Cornell University Press, 1996).

18. Judith Butler, *Gender Trouble: Feminism and the Subversion of Identity* (New York and London: Routledge, 1990).

19. See Eve Kosofsky Sedgwick, *Between Men: English Literature and Male Homosocial Desire* (New York: Columbia University Press, 1985).

20. See Elaine Showalter, *The Female Malady: Women, Madness, and English Culture, 1830–1980* (New York: Penguin, 1987); and Denise Riley, *"Am I That Name?": Feminism and the Category of "Women" in History* (Minneapolis: Minnesota University Press, 1988).

21. See Ann Ardis, *New Women, New Novels: Feminism and Early Modernism* (New Brunswick: Rutgers University Press, 1990); and Sally Ledger, *The New Woman: Fiction and Feminism at the Fin de Siècle* (Manchester: Manchester University Press, 1997.

22. See Laura Frost, *Sex Drives: Fantasies of Fascism in Literary Modernism* (Ithaca: Cornell University Press, 2002).

23. See Rey Chow, "The Politics of Admittance: Female Sexual Agency, Miscegenation, and the Formation of Community in Franz Fanon," in Chow, *Ethics after Idealism: Theory – Culture – Ethnicity – Reading* (Bloomington and Indianapolis: Indiana University Press, 1998).

24. Lauren Berlant, *The Queen of America Goes to Washington City: Essays on Sex and Citizenship* (Durham: Duke University Press, 1997).

25. Ann Douglas, *The Feminization of American Culture* (New York: Avon Books, 1977).

26. Jane Tompkins, *Sensational Designs: The Cultural Work of American Fiction, 1790–1860* (New York: Oxford University Press, 1985).

27. Cathy N. Davidson, *Revolution and the Word: The Rise of the Novel in America* (New York: Oxford University Press, 1986), p. 122.

28. Amy Kaplan, *The Social Construction of American Realism* (Chicago: University of Chicago Press, 1988).

29. See Gillian Brown, *Domestic Individualism: Imagining Self in Nineteenth-Century America* (Berkeley: University of California Press, 1990).

30. Shirley Samuels, *The Culture of Sentiment: Race, Gender, and Sentimentality in Nineteenth-Century America* (New York: Oxford University Press, 1992); Julia Sterne, *The Plight of Feeling: Sympathy and Dissent in the Early American Novel* (Chicago: University of Chicago Press, 1997); and Elizabeth Barnes, *States of Sympathy: Seduction and Democracy in the American Novel* (New York: Columbia University Press, 1997).

31. Nancy Armstrong and Leonard Tennenhouse, *The Imaginary Puritan: Literature, Intellectual Labor, and the History of Personal Life* (Berkeley: University of California Press, 1992).

32. See Toni Morrison, *Playing in the Dark: Whiteness and the Literary Imagination* (New York: Vintage, 1992).

33. See Pam Morris, *Literature and Feminism: An Introduction* (Oxford: Blackwell, 1993).

34. Mary Poovey is especially good at explaining why the governess offered such a topos in her *Uneven Developments: The Ideological Work of Gender in Mid-Victorian England* (Chicago: University of Chicago Press, 1988).

35. Madhu Dubey, *Black Women Novelists and the Nationalist Aesthetic* (Bloomington: Indiana University Press, 1994), p. 39.

36. Hazel Carby, *Reconstructing Womanhood: The Emergence of the Afro-American Woman Novelist* (New York and Oxford: Oxford University Press, 1987), p. 56.

37. Saidiya V. Hartman, *Scenes of Subjections: Terrror, Slavery, and Self-Making in Nineteeneth-Century America* (New York: Oxford University Press, 1997), p. 105.

38. Cora Kaplan, *Sea Changes: Culture and Feminism* (London: Verso, 1986), p. 11.

39. Fox, Pamela, *Class Fictions: Shame and Resistance in the British Working-Class Novel, 1890–1945* (Durham: Duke University Press, 1994), p. 149.

40. Gayatri Chakravorty Spivak, "Three Women's Texts and a Critique of Imperialism." *Critical Inquiry* 12 (1985), pp. 243–61; and "Can the Subaltern Speak?," in Cary Nelson and Louis Grossberg, eds., *Marxism and the Interpretation of Culture* (Urbana: University of Illinois Press, 1988), pp. 271–313.

41. Berthold Schoene-Harwood, *Writing Men: Literary Masculinities from Frankenstein to the New Man* (Edinburgh: Edinburgh University Press, 2000), p. 4.
42. Rey Chow, *The Protestant Ethnic and the Spirit of Capitalism* (New York: Columbia University Press, 2002), p. 182.
43. Wendy Brown, *States of Injury: Power and Freedom in Late Modernity* (Princeton: Princeton University Press, 1995).
44. Charlotte Brontë, *Jane Eyre* (Oxford: Oxford University Press, 1975), p. 37.
45. Thus Rey Chow takes Susan Gubar to task: "Despite having become dominant, . . . white feminism as voiced by Gubar continues to position itself as a culture on the defense" (*The Protestant Ethnic*, p. 181).

5

LINDA ANDERSON

Autobiography and the feminist subject

"I am not fully known to myself, because part of what I am is the
enigmatic traces of others."
– Judith Butler, *Precarious Life* (2004)[1]

The subject of autobiography

Feminism has had an almost symbiotic relationship with autobiography,
which has often acted as the shadow and locus for its evolving debates
about the subject. However, autobiography has not always been completely
passive and has had questions of its own to ask of feminism, often to do
with specificity and the need to find room, inside or outside theory, for
difference and the disconcerting diversity of texts and writing subjects. If
we go back to the early stages of their relationship, we can see how in the
1960s and 1970s, as second-wave feminism flourished, autobiography
seemed to provide a privileged space for women to discover new forms
of subjectivity, both through the reading of autobiographical writing by
women, historical as well as contemporary, and through the production of
texts which explored the female subject in franker, less constricted or more
inventive ways. Later, however, as poststructuralist theory began to transform feminist thinking, autobiography became the site for major theoretical
debates about the subject. Toward the end of the 1970s, therefore, the notion
of a female selfhood which could be triumphantly liberated from its neglect
or repression under patriarchy and made visible through writing was put into
question by psychoanalytic and poststructuralist thinking which instead
insisted that the subject did not preexist the process of its formation within
language, and that all identities, including gendered identities, are never fully
realized but instead a story of repeated failures to achieve fullness or closure.[2]

While many critics contended that out of this poststructuralist critique of
identities came the possibility of new representational spaces, the bleakest
outcome for the female subject was that she was now doubly alienated:
occupying a place of "alterity and non presence"[3] within a symbolic which
is seen as phallocentric, she could now never hope to capture the full
position of the subject which had dissolved before her eyes, as it were, into
a phantasm. For Nancy Miller, writing in 1986, this "crisis of the subject,"

already established as an orthodoxy, seemed to obey a peculiarly masculine political imperative, and to be badly timed for women, depriving them of an important historical stage in their relation to subjecthood. "Because women have not had the same historical relation of identity to origin, institution, production that men have had, they have not, I think, (collectively) felt burdened by too much Self, Ego, Cogito, etc."[4] What Miller wryly suggests is how theory – in the powerful context in which she is writing, the US academy – can coopt that very difference it is the bearer of, for its own political goals. Elizabeth Weed similarly noted, in a reflective moment at the end of the same decade in which Miller was writing, that there was a tendency for US reworkings of poststructuralism to emphasize its "discursive production as 'academic' theory (philosophical, linguistic, etc.) at the expense of its political resonance."[5] How can feminism intervene into the deployment of poststructuralist discourse for its own ends? Can there be a feminist politics without a stable female subject to refer to? Is there a way of positioning oneself as a subject as a tactic, strategy, or pragmatic move without getting weighed down with the history of all that term's bias and exclusions?

These questions have in Elizabeth Weed's formulation "nagged at"[6] feminism since the mid-1980s onward, and have been matched by a similar tension within criticism of autobiography. Bella Brodski and Celeste Schenk in 1988 attempted to find a new place for their influential anthology of new critical approaches to women's autobiography, *Life/Lines*, between the two countervailing critical forces of essentialism and a poststructuralism conceived of in purely textual terms. Thus they contended that "the critical and political stance of *Life/Lines* is to maintain female specificity and articulate female subjectivity without either falling back into the essentialism that has plagued both American feminist criticism and *écriture feminine* in France or retreating into a pure textuality that consigns woman – in a new mode to be sure – to an unrecoverable absence."[7] Diane Elam, in 1994, siding more unequivocally with postructuralism, contended, along with Paul de Man, that autobiography is an "impossible" genre since "experience" can never be directly represented and all autobiographies produce fictions or figures in place of the self-knowledge they seek.[8] Women's autobiography has thus to be read as a "strategic necessity at a particular time, rather than an end in itself." Elam is thinking of the inadequacy of the "traditional structure of autobiography," which has as its goal "the self-realization of the subject," and its inability to represent the complex questions opened up around the female subject at this time.[9] However, her reference to a "strategic" use of autobiography could also suggest something else: not a limitation but a possibility of new rhetorical spaces for the subject, a refusal to foreclose the meanings of autobiography before we begin to assess them. Using autobiography to mark the limits of theory, while it runs the danger of denying autobiography's own implication in theory, also indicates the way that theory's hold on its own terms may be fragile, and that there is an ongoing excess or complexity which autobiography may help to name. Shoshana Felman, in her book *What Does a Woman Want?: Reading and Sexual Difference*, noting how autobiography and theory have sometimes mingled within the same text, argues that each may act as a form of resistance to the other, unsettling the claims to truth of both. In Virginia Woolf's *A Room of One's Own*, autobiography is "summoned . . . as a *resistance to theory* and to its claim to be a statement and not merely an utterance," while the turn to theory, in this text and in other key texts such as Simone de Beauvoir's *The Second Sex* and Adrienne Rich's "When We Dead Awaken: Writing as Revision" suggests the "impossibility of a direct access to the female autobiographer."[10]

While it is Felman's point that the female autobiographer may only be able to represent her autobiography as "missing" – as inhabiting a gap between discourses – the force of her autobiographical intervention as "speech act" or strategy is profoundly unsettling. In this essay I want to explore the ways that autobiography has provided not just a useful testing ground for feminist theories, but also productive space for different notions of the female subject to emerge, one which can register the plurality of subjects – and perhaps just as crucially – the plurality of reasons for the use of the self as a form of writing. As Reginia Gagnier has pertinently remarked, "all autobiographical moves . . . are 'interested'"[11] or, elsewhere, there is a "pragmatics of self-representation" which supersedes questions of truth.[12] What – or who – calls the subject into being could be, according to this view, just as significant as how the subject has been cast and recast in theory.

Feminist confessions

Thinking back to those earlier decades again, we can see that what feminism was initially looking to autobiography to provide was a textual model of "consciousness-raising," writing that would enable that same movement between the personal and the political, between personal revelation and collective recognition, that women's groups were also seen as facilitating. As Rita Felski has pointed out, feminist autobiographical writing often took the form of confession at this time, offering to its readership an intimate and frequently painful experience which was also seen as part of a progressive revelation to the self and others of women's fate under patriarchy and the need for change.[13] This writing then aimed to provide recognitions for the reader, not so much of the uniqueness of the writer, as of what binds the writer and reader together in their communal identity as women. "Whoever thinks this is all, *one* woman who wrestled with her shame, *one* unique herstory separate from all the others has not understood," Anja Meulenbelt writes at the end of her "political life story," *The Shame is Over*.[14] By asserting in this way another communal dimension, a meaning beyond the personal, the act of self-exposure takes on a political justification, and could be seen as deriving its necessity not from individual desire but from a painful quest for truths, hidden by society, which could be reclaimed and made available for others. In her autobiography, *Taking it Like a Woman*, Anne Oakley is articulate about what drives her own particular act of authorship:

> This book is about my life, but it is also about others – for it would be arrogant to suppose I'm unique; I'm not. In those passages in the book where I write about myself I have no drive salaciously to exhibit a purely private history. On the contrary, this has been a most painful and difficult book to write, and it goes against the grain of a basically shy and retiring nature to see myself in print in this way. The book has taken far longer to write than any other book I have written, because, I think, the chief obstacle to describing oneself as an individual located in a particular manner in a particular culture is the need not to be honest with oneself, to conceal the person one is from oneself and, indeed, from everybody else. But I have persevered in this task precisely because I know I am living and writing about something which is recognizable to others.[15]

This passage, strongly self-justificatory, also helps to illustrate Felski's analysis of how women's confessional discourse can become implicated in those structures of power it is attempting to separate itself from; of how, striving for an authentic selfhood, it can also reveal the subject's dependence on the same cultural and ideological systems it had seemingly rejected or overcome. Here Oakley's ambivalence around her "exhibitionism" for which she must find some "higher" meaning, also reveals how difficult it is to escape the shame of self-exposure, that anxiety of authorship, which has attended so many women writers. Paradoxically, Oakley here succeeds in situating herself only in terms of a statement of apology or self-denial. De Man, writing about Rousseau's *Confessions*, has demonstrated how shame and confession inevitably go together, each producing the other in an endless, repetitive round. Shame is not assuaged but rather amplified by confession, which then leads to further performances of feeling.[16] The confessional mode, therefore, though risky in what it appears to reveal and in how it pushes the subject beyond customary boundaries, could nevertheless also be seen as regressive for women, coopting them back into a familiar dynamic where their acts of self-assertion can be allowed to exist socially or psychologically only if contained within a rhetoric of self-abasement and denial.

This paradox, whereby an impulse toward emancipation seems to double back on itself, converging with culturally conservative forces, seems also to undermine the attempt to make personal knowledge the basis for more generalized, political insights into women's lives. Wendy Brown, writing about the complexities of censorship and silencing, has noted that one of the consequences of confessional discourse is that, instead of providing a way of articulating experience which is also "true" for others, breaking a silence or exposing social taboos or injuries, it tends to monopolize the space, preempting the possibility of other different or emergent voices. Brown points to the tendency for the story of the greatest suffering to become the true story within feminism, disenfranchising others whose experience, though belonging to the same "category" or "group," is not so obviously traumatizing. There is, she argues, a "norm-making process in traditions of breaking silence" that can work against its own avowed political purpose, by ironically silencing "the very persons these traditions mean to empower." Provocatively, she asks us to consider the political meaning of silence, and its status, not as the opposite of speech, but as itself carrying modalities of meaning, which are "as varied as the modalities of speech." What if, she asks, incessant speech "not only overwhelms the experience of others, but overwhelms alternative (unutterable, traumatized, fragmentary, or inassimilable) zones of one's own experience." What if silence provides other, more varied possibilities, to the sufferer?[17]

One of the contexts in which Brown's caveats seem particularly relevant is that of confessional discourse about sexual abuse. When women began to speak publicly about their experiences of sexual abuse in the 1970s onward, they were breaking the silence around a previously taboo area, refusing to remain "in denial." As one therapist wrote, out of her experiences with adult survivors of childhood sexual abuse: "Refraining from denial is an act of courage for these survivors. They had to choose quite literally between being alienated from themselves and reality or being alienated from family members who still denied abuse. Each of them eventually chose reality and themselves, often at the cost of family ridicule or ostracism."[18]

Yet, however personally significant or politically important these stories were in shifting the public and professional perception of abuse, they could also, as Janice Haaken has argued, serve a unifying function, eliding other "disunifying differences" between women.[19] Judith Hermann, as she records in her book *Trauma and Recovery*, for instance, saw it as a necessary part of therapeutic practice, when working with a survivors' group, to focus on "the shared experience of trauma in the past, not on interpersonal difficulties in the present."[20] For Haaken, the trauma model also had a defensive role, warding off or helping to "contain" political conflicts within feminism and permitting "political mobilization around the least controversial issue within feminism: child sexual abuse." Like Brown, therefore, Haaken is aware of the potential for silencing within this dynamic of speaking out, and argues for the "cultural space" for a variety of different stories and ways of reading them.[21]

To use one's experience as representative, in the way that Oakley, Meulenbelt, and other feminist autobiographers have done, is to attempt to assert its political meaning, to seek to offer a more general means of reflection on the experience and construction of female subjectivity. The questions elided or overlooked in such a conception of feminist autobiography were, of course, who is being represented and who excluded or silenced, and these became the key questions for feminism in the 1980s, as feminist theory itself began to be seen as the product of a Western universalizing agenda and both the political and the ethical basis of "speaking for others" was called into question. In 1986 Miller, as we have seen, could refer to women "collectively," though her use of parentheses suggests a certain uneasiness or tension about where this word belongs within her discourse. By 1991 she is reflecting on the crisis over "representativity" – both "speaking *as* and speaking *for*" – which makes any gesture toward a female collectivity problematic.[22] Similarly, Rich, whose earlier work had been based on the political relevance of her own experience as a woman and a woman writer, was by 1986 deeply caught up in the "morality of pronouns"[23] and the difficulty of finding a politically adequate form of address:

> The difficulty of saying I – a phrase from the East German novelist Christa Wolf. But once having said it, as we realize the necessity to go further, isn't there a difficulty of saying "we"? You cannot speak for me. I cannot speak of us. Two thoughts: there is no collective movement that speaks for each of us all the way through. And so even ordinary pronouns become a political problem.[24]

Can there be a stance, Rich asks, which is politically and ethically responsible, which does not negate, ignore, or appropriate others? Can linguistic codes be made to mesh with political imperatives?

Significantly, the pronoun that is missing from Rich's meditation on the "political problem" of pronouns is "you." It is this pronoun, and the political and ethical importance of the "I's" relation to it, that Judith Butler has explored recently in her attempt to redirect our thinking about personal and political responsibility. For Butler, the context of her questions is a theory of the subject which has seemingly undermined the subject's ground of agency and accountability, the poststructuralist subject which has seemed so threatening to a certain idea of politics. What Butler argues, however, is that we are ethically implicated in the lives of others precisely to the extent that we cannot control language, and cannot achieve unity and mastery over ourselves. For her, the "you" is a necessary condition of "I" since there can be no account of myself which exists outside the structure of an address, which exists outside the norms of language, even if the addressee remains "implicit and unnamed, anonymous and unspecified." Moreover, if I address "you," I must also have been addressed in my turn, brought into language, and now be able to tell my story only through norms of narrative which remain both external and disorientating. "In a sense," Butler writes, "my account of myself is never fully mine, and is never fully for me."[25] This failure or lack of knowledge can create an ethical relation to the Other. There is never a fully satisfactory account, one which finally captures the subject. By the same token, the Other remains outside full knowingness, and in that way also lives on as Other. "What might it mean to make an ethic of the unwilled?," Butler asks. And what might it mean, instead of defending the autonomy of the subject, to prize its "difficult and intractable, even sometimes unbearable, relationality"?[26]

These are profound questions, and they go beyond a view of the subject's "relationality" which allows the subject to define itself through others and yet remain the same. Within critical writing about autobiography, there has been an important body of work which has looked to "relationality" as the defining difference between men's and women's autobiographical writing. Mary Mason's ground breaking essay in 1980 took four diverse historical examples – Julian of Norwich, Margery Kempe, Margaret Cavendish, and Anne Bradstreet – and found that what united them was the way the "self-discovery of female identity" was bound up with the simultaneous identification of some 'other'.[27] Although the relationship could take different forms, from a mystical dialogue with a divine other to a generalized sense of communal belonging, what was "more or less constant" was the "evolution and delineation of an identity by way of alterity."[28] Mason believed that her examples signaled an important alternative tradition within autobiography which has tended otherwise to get lost in the endless replaying of "the Western obsession with the self."[29] Susan Stanford Friedman has voiced a similar idea, seeing the notion of a "separate and unique selfhood," enshrined within autobiographical tradition, as producing a critical bias which leads to the marginalization of texts by women. Women's autobiographical writing, according to Friedman, directly reflects crucial differences about women's sense of self. The problem with "individualistic paradigms", then, is that they "do not take into account the central role collective consciousness of self plays in the lives of women and minorities.

They do not recognize the significance of interpersonal relationships and community in women's self-definition, nor do they explain the ongoing identification of the daughter with the mother."[30] Women's autobiographical writing, according to Friedman, requires an approach which can recognize and validate these social and psychological differences.

However committed both these approaches seem to be to establishing an alternative to the hegemonic "individualistic" model for autobiography, they ironically collude with it, having produced a version of female selfhood which is "essentially" different, and thus, in effect, a mirror image, which helps to sustain the masculine subject in his place. In effect, the story of gender becomes the overarching story, obliterating the "real" historical narrative of women's lives. No other story can be told, therefore, than the story that has already been laid down, a story which must endlessly organize itself around the same dynamic. Neither, significantly, do these approaches allow for the disruptive effect of other voices in relation to the autonomous subject, whether these be the others occluded by virtue of race, gender, or class, against whom nevertheless the self is defined, or a network of visible relations which the subject, even at the height of its self-preoccupation, cannot make disappear. Miller has drawn attention to the way "others" have played a vital role in the autobiographies of men, which, once it is noticed, should make us "revise the canonical view of male autobiographical identity altogether."[31] One of her examples is Saint Augustine, whose *Confessions* have often been read as establishing a narrative paradigm for the autonomous subject. Miller draws our attention to the way Augustine's mother plays a vital role in the text. Although Augustine moves to a place "beyond" her, after her death, she cannot be erased, even though critics have tended to overlook her, taking Augustine's final position of "mastery" as the "truth" of the whole text.

That the unified subject is an impossibility, always haunted by others, anxiously defending against its own uncertainty and ruin, is, of course, Butler's argument. One can tell one's story only by becoming disoriented, by routing oneself through something that is not oneself.[32] That this bears upon the "dream" of autonomy, of a certain kind of "sovereign subject," is clear, but it is also worth briefly returning, with these ideas in mind, to those feminist autobiographies we looked at previously, which offer a trajectory of self-discovery, of the progressive revelation of the "truth" of the self. As we have seen, the idea of a selfhood which is also representative, through which women readers can recognize themselves, was central to these narratives. This overarching ideological intent, however, should not make us lose sight of how far the subjects in these texts suffer a profound disorientation. If feminism, as it was understood at this time, offered to shore up the subject, provide a collective narrative, these autobiographies rather seem to look to the future for a recognition that still has to happen: "I need her just as much as she needs me, but she doesn't know it yet . . . Myself, but no longer who I am."[33] As Butler suggestively remarks: "I cannot muster the 'we' except by finding the way in which I am tied to 'you.'" And that relation, impossible to fix or reify as "relationality," also undoes the subject, makes her other. "We are not only constituted by our relations," as Butler states; we are also "dispossessed by them as well."[34]

Material subjects

In her important essay "Under Western Eyes: Feminist Scholarship and Colonial Discourses," written more than ten years ago, Chandra Mohanty drew attention to two projects which must be addressed simultaneously by feminism: one is "the internal critique of hegemonic Western feminisms"; the other is "the formulations of autonomous, geographically, historically, and culturally grounded feminist concerns and strategies."[35] Her essay, coming under the first of those headings, is an eloquent deconstruction of how Western feminist discourses have produced a singular, homogenized "third world woman", arbitrarily constructing an image which effectively subsumes "the material and historical heterogeneities of the lives of women in the third world."[36] Trying to include third world "difference" within one political framework, as Mohanty points out, has the effect of replicating the imperialistic gesture whereby third world "otherness" is used to sustain the first world as the norm or privileged vantage point: "Without the overdetermined discourse that creates the third world, there would be no (singular and privileged) first world."[37]

Autobiographical writing by non-Western women has undoubtedly contributed to the project of realizing the heterogeneity of women's lives, that second project outlined by Mohanty. Representing "ethnic diversity," within collections of writing on autobiography, became an earnest aim from *Life/Lines* onward, though, since diversity has no limits, the desire for inclusivity was also bound to founder on its own impossibility: "Asian women's autobiographies, despite our strenuous efforts to include them, remain underrepresented in our collection."[38] The setting up of specific categories of "difference," in this case Asian women's autobiographies, runs the risk of seeming to extend a norm, already established, and to gesture toward some ideal of completion. It returns us to the full implications of Mohanty's first project, and the compelling need to undertake a critique of Western theoretical perspectives which will help to release the critical potential of multiple subjects, no longer stabilized under descriptive categories. Gayatri Spivak has challenged us to perceive how the

"subjective structure" of autobiography can easily become the object of someone else's knowledge, turning autobiographical subject, within an ethnographic framework, into "native informant." "The person who knows has
all of the problems of selfhood. The person who is known, somehow seems not
to have a problematic self."[39] How can we get away from a model which seems
to identify some women in terms of their "experience" or locus while reserving
the "problems of selfhood" for others, typically Western, white, and middle
class? What reading and interpretative strategies are needed to understand,
instead of the unified subject, a fractured, plural subject whose location is
mobile, never settled through simple designation? In what ways does the genre
of autobiography itself need to be understood differently for "difference" to be
understood?

Sidonie Smith and Julia Watson have suggested that the proliferation of
alternative words for women's autobiography – from life-writing to personal narrative – itself marks "a shift away from an uncritical Western
understanding of the subject of autobiography."[40] For Doris Sommer, her
choice of the term *testimonios* (testimonials) for Latin American women's
writing arises precisely out of a need to mark their differences from the
genre of autobiography, which has historically privileged the "extraordinary individual." The testimonials to which she is referring, though written
in the first person, have a "plural subject."[41] By that she does not mean that
the singular becomes plural by replacing or subsuming the group, but
because the singular is part of the whole, an extension of the collective.
Moreover, the reader is never invited to identify with the speaker; it is not a
"we" which includes her, but one that asserts its difference from the reader.
The writing is a response to political emergency and is in some ways
"impersonal," part of a strategy to "win political ground" by recording
the popular struggle. Sommer, for instance, quotes from Domitila Barrios's
testimony *Let Me Speak! Testimony of Domitila, a Woman of the Bolivian
Mines*, where she asserts with particular clarity the need for the kind of
political "evidence" that testimonial writing can provide: "And there
should be testimony. That's been our mistake, not to write everything down
that happens . . . like the testimonies that we had in the union, or on the
miners' radio stations . . . all of that would have been useful to us."[42]
Sommer sees this writing as offering a form of resistance to Western discourse, using the "autobiographical pose" for different ends: "It is . . . a
reminder that life continues at the margins of Western discourse, and
continues to disturb and challenge it."[43] However, she also casts some
doubt on her own conclusions by pondering whether in the end the difference is not a matter of how we read: autobiography could recuperate
identities to its own paradigmatic history or it could provide a space of

excess and resistance, depending on how we interpret it. It might be possible, therefore, to think of all autobiographies as testimonials if singularity were viewed as an assertion merely, an illusion of "standing *in* for others as opposed to standing *up* among them."[44]

In her reading of Sommer's essay, Elspeth Probyn has drawn out another, slightly different implication from these testimonial writings from that arrived at by Sommer. What emerges from Sommer's material for Probyn is less a new way of thinking about the formation of a "plural subject" than a sense of the immediacy of the texts and the way they place the self within a precise time and place. Probyn is wary of a tendency she finds within Sommer's essay of moving toward more abstract conclusions about "communities of women"; this, she argues, may have more to do with our own longings than with what these texts tell us, which is always specific, to do with a concrete historical and geographical situation. The use of the self may properly be seen in this writing as "tactical" or strategic; the stakes of writing are raised in a context where such writing is both urgent and dangerous: "These women need to tell of themselves (to help others) as they need to avoid making that self into a locus (thus inviting retaliation against themselves). The self here, because of specific historical reasons, takes on the tactical logic of guerrilla warfare."[45] For Probyn, the act of writing these documents has a purpose. They arise from a situation which they, at the same time, comment on. They are "conjunctural" documents, where person and situation are imbricated in each other, each illuminating the other.[46]

In order further to illuminate her argument about uses of the self, which, while employing the autobiographical mode, shift our attention away from autobiography as a genre or "unifying discourse" and the subject, whether individually or communally, as its exclusive focus,[47] Probyn turns from testimonial writing to an important autobiographical text by Carolyn Steedman, *Landscape for a Good Woman*.[48] Steedman is primarily interested in how the dominant discourses, narrative and theoretical, marginalize the specificities of class. Drawing for their construction on the objects and experiences of the bourgeois household which they nevertheless present as "neutral," these discourses, Steedman argues, cannot "work" for other histories, literally cannot make sense of other lives. For Steedman, this is graphically represented in a meeting between the Victorian social commentator Henry Mayhew and an eight-year-old girl selling watercress in the streets of London. According to Steedman, Mayhew is confounded by a narrative where work is the child's identity, and where the "things" she describes – "pieces of fur, the bunches of cress, the scrubbed floor" – do not seem to have the same meaning or metaphorical resonance they would have in canonical (middle-class) narratives. As a result, he cannot really *see* her or hear what she is saying.[49] Steedman uses moments or images from her own life which similarly challenge culturally powerful discourses. One such is a memory of her father picking bluebells and then being caught and humiliated by the forestkeeper. This memory, Steedman suggests, does not accord with the theory of patriarchy which puts the father at the center of the family and culture. In adulthood she reflects on the childhood experience, wondering "how the myth works when a father is rendered vulnerable by social relations, when a position in a household is not supported by recognition of social status and power outside it."[50]

For Steedman, her autobiographical memories are not so much moments which contribute to the representation of her as an individual as "interpretive devices," ways of interrogating the "truth" of theory.[51] The memory allows reflection on a social configuration, without reifying or generalizing the individual self. For Probyn, Steedman's work puts into practice a notion of the self as a "point of view" which can allow new insight into "the construction of particular conjunctural social moments."[52] Images and memories within the autobiography relate to material situations and objects but they are also inflected through systems of discourse and imbued with the feelings – the hopes and disappointments – of real people. As such they serve as a bridge, or "historical structure of feeling."[53] Probyn's argument relates to the place of the detail and how it must be viewed differently, not as a particular example or evidential content for a larger system, but as a "point of view" which allows us to raise questions about new facts that it has itself brought to light. Clearly, this could also give autobiography a particularly important epistemological role. Rather than "constructing a self," autobiography could now be seen as providing, through material images, a point of view which allows new ways of interrogating social reality. According to Probyn, what we can take from Steedman is "a way of using the self, of putting the self to work in order to 'cut into the real.'" In this version of autobiography and the use to which we as readers can put it, as Probyn demonstrates, the self can be both an "object of inquiry" and a means of understanding "where and how it is lodged within the social formation."[54]

Probyn's understanding of the subject in terms of a speaking position which both arises from and comments on the social does not mean that she simply equates discursive and material locations. There is no "proper" place to speak from and no summative speaking of the self, only endless attempts to map the conjuncture of discourse and materiality that the subject makes possible.[55] In later work she has returned to the idea of location and the necessity to think about both the specificity of this and the complex layering of space, which makes "belonging" anywhere not a static concept, but a matter of moving between different, though possibly overlapping, sites.[56]

Paul Gilroy has proposed, from a slightly different point of view, the special value of the term "diaspora" in making us rethink the idea of belonging and interrupting the "ontologization of place." According to Gilroy, diaspora "disrupts the fundamental power of territory to determine identity by breaking the simple series of explanatory links between place, location and consciousness."[57] For Gilroy, remembrance and commemoration, which he distinguishes from the idea of a spontaneous common memory that simply unites subjects, take on a special significance as a way of registering the mobility of the subject, and its contingent linkage with locations and identities. Gilroy is, of course, trying to provide a positive way of mobilizing theoretically what is also felt by many as a cruel wrenching away from the possibility of stable identity.

At the end of her memoir *In Search of Fatima: A Palestinian Story*, Ghada Karmi, having fulfilled her desire to return geographically to the place of her childhood, has to confront her alienation: "There was nothing here to which I could attach my longing for home . . . No homeland, no reference point, only a fragile, displaced and misfit Arab family in England to take on those crucial roles."[58] However, the memoir as a whole has produced an identity out of multiple locations and the movement, often created by memory and longing, between them. Moreover, the subject, as point of view, in Probyn's terms, allows an interrogation of social reality – in particular England from the 1950s onward – with new "facts," formed by her particular situation. Her description of the outsiders' misperception of English codes of politeness as genuine feeling might be one example of how her memoir creates a different perspective or meaning through its conjunction of discourses and experience.[59]

A consideration of material locations has taken us away from the idea of testimony with which this section began, and it is with further brief consideration of the idea of testimony that I want to end this essay. As we have seen, Probyn found Sommer's emphasis on community within Latin American women's testimonials too abstract, and chose to argue instead for the importance of their particularity. However, overlooked so far in Sommer's discussion of community is her important consideration of the role of the reader or witness, who, since many of the narratives she is citing are oral – which means that their written form involves a recording of them by others – is often addressed with immediacy as "you." This testimonial relationship, for Sommers, is not one of identity: reader and writer remain distinctive, neither able to imagine taking the other's place. However, the "interpersonal rhetoric" of testimony, according to Sommer, its appeal to a "you," spreads possible identifications through the text, perhaps even corrupting the ideal of cultural coherence that the speaker or narrator seeks to defend.[60]

Felman has defined testimony as a speech act which addresses what cannot be presented as a "completed statement" or "totalizable account" of events. It is here that the importance of witnessing also resides. For testimony will also depend on the listening of others to bear witness to what it cannot directly represent or fully understand.[61] In this way it could be thought of as a collaborative project, exceeding what can be owned or comprehended by the individual, addressing not only others' capacity for understanding, but their vulnerability as well. In the comparison she draws between autobiography and testimony in *What Does A Woman Want?*, Felman has written about how we cannot presume in advance what a text has to tell us. Rather, we as readers bear witness to a "a literary process of surprise, to the way in which the Other (and the story of the Other) has addressed us by surprising us."[62] If connecting autobiography with testimony has the effect of foregrounding an ethical dimension, a political seriousness, it also has the effect of drawing attention to it as a mode of communication, an encounter which could involve and, indeed, surprise us. In this way autobiography could have much to teach us not only about others but also about what we have yet to know about ourselves.

Further reading

Linda Anderson, *Women and Autobiography in the Twentieth Century*, (Hemel Hempstead: Prentice Hall, 1997).

Tess Cosslett et al., eds., *Feminism and Autobiography: Texts Theories, Methods* (London: Routledge, 2000).

Leigh Gilmore, *Autobiographics: A Feminist Theory of Women's Self-Representation* (Ithaca and London: Cornell University Press, 1994).

Nawar Al-Hassan Gooley, *Reading Arab Women's Autobiographies* (Austin: University of Texas Press, 2003).

Nicola King, *Narrative, Identity, Memory: Remembering the Self* (Edinburgh: Edinburgh University Press, 2000).

Laura Marcus, *Auto/biographical Discourses* (Manchester: Manchester University Press, 1994).

Nancy Miller, *Getting Personal* (London and New York: Routledge, 1991).

Sidonie Smith, *Subjectivity, Identity and the Body: Women's Autobiographical Practices in the Twentieth Century* (Indiana University Press: Bloomington, 1993).

Sidonie Smith and Julia Watson, eds., *De/Colonizing the Subject: The Politics of Gender in Women's Autobiography* (University of Minnesota Press: Minneapolis, 1992).

Victoria Stewart, *Women's Autobiography: War and Trauma* (Basingstoke: Palgrave Macmillan, 2003).

Julia Swindells, ed., *The Uses of Autobiography* (London: Taylor and Francis, 1995).

Anne Whitehead, *Trauma Fiction* (Edinburgh: Edinburgh University Press, 2004).

NOTES

1. Judith Butler, *Precarious Life: The Powers of Mourning and Violence* (London and New York: Verso, 2004), p. 46.
2. See Julia Kristeva's definition of the "subject in process" in "A Question of Subjectivity: An Interview" in Mary Eagleton, ed., *Feminist Literary Theory: A Reader* (Blackwell, Oxford, 1986), pp. 351–3 (p. 351).
3. Domna Stanton, "Autogynography: Is the Subject Different?," in Stanton, *The Female Autograph* (New York: New York Literary Forum, 1984), p. 16.
4. Nancy Miller, "Changing the Subject: Authorship, Writing and the Reader," in Miller, *Subject to Change: Reading Feminist Writing* (New York: Columbia University press, 1988), pp. 102–21. 106.
5. Elizabeth Weed, "Introduction: Terms of Reference," in Weed, ed., *Coming to Terms: Feminism, Theory, Politics* (New York: Routledge, 1989), pp. ix–xxxi, xi.
6. Ibid., p. xiii.
7. "Introduction" in Bella Brodski and Celeste Schenck, eds., *Life/Lines: Theorizing Women's Autobiography* (Ithaca and London: Cornell University Press, 1988), p. 14.
8. See my discussion of Paul de Man in my *Autobiography* (London: Routledge, 2001), pp. 12–16.
9. Diane Elam, *Feminism and Deconstruction: Ms. en Abyme* (London and New York: Routledge, 1984) p. 65.
10. Shoshana Felman, *What Does A Woman Want?: Reading and Sexual Difference* (Baltimore and London: The Johns Hopkins University press, 1993), p. 142.
11. Reginia Cagnier, "The Literary Standard, Working-Class Autobiography, and Gender," in Sidonie Smith and Julia Watson, eds., *Women, Autobiography, Theory* (Wisconsin: University of Wisconsin Press, 1998), p. 266.
12. Reginia Cagnier, *Subjectivities: A History of Self-Representation in Britain, 1832–1920* (Oxford: Oxford University Press, 1991), p. 4.
13. Rita Felski, *Beyond Feminist Aesthetics* (Cambridge, MA: Harvard University Press, 1989), pp. 91–6.
14. Anja Meulenbelt, *The Shame is Over* (London: The Women's Press, 1980), p. 275.
15. *Anne Oakley, Taking It Like A Woman* (London: Jonathan Cape, 1984), pp. 2–3.
16. Paul de Man, *Allegories of Reading: Figural Language in Rousseau, Nietzsche, Rilke and Proust* (New Haven and London: Yale University Press, 1979), p. 286.
17. Wendy Brown, "Freedom's Silences", in Robert C. Post. ed., *Censorship and Silencing: Practices of Cultural Regulation* (Los Angeles: Getty Research Institute for the History of Art and the Humanities, 1998), pp. 320–1.
18. Linda T. Stanford, *Strong at the Broken Places: Overcoming the Trauma of Childhood Abuse* (London: Virago, 1991), p. 40.

19. Janice Haaken, "The Recovery of Memory, Fantasy and Desire in Women's Trauma Stories: Feminist Approaches to Sexual Abuse", in Haaken, *Women. Autobiography, Theory* (Madison: University of Wisconsin Press, 1998) p. 358.

20. Judith Hermann, *Trauma and Recovery* (New York: Basic Books, 1992), p. 223, quoted in Haaken, *Women, Autobiography, Theory*, p. 356.

21. Haaken, *Women, Autobiography, Theory*, p. 359.

22. Nancy Miller, *Getting Personal* (London and New York: Routledge, 1991), p. 20.

23. Adriana Caverero, *Relating Narratives: Storytelling and Selfhood*, trans. Paul A. Kottman (New York: Routledge, 2000), pp. 90–1, quoted in Judith Butler, "Giving An Account of Oneself", *Diacritics* 31:4 (2001), pp. 22–40 (p. 24).

24. Adrienne Rich, "Notes Towards a Politics of Location", in Rich, *Of Blood, Bread and Poetry: Selected Prose, 1979–1985* (London: Virago, 1987), p. 224.

25. Judith Butler, "Giving An Account of Oneself", *Diacritics* 31:19 (2001), pp. 22–40 (p. 26).

26. Ibid., p. 39.

27. Mary Mason, "The Other Voice: Autobiographies of Women Writers," in Brodski and Scherik, eds., *Life/Lines*, p. 22.

28. Ibid., p. 41.

29. Ibid., p. 44.

30. Susan Stanford Friedman, "Women's Autobiographical Selves: Theory and Practice," in Shari Benstock, ed., *The Private Self: Theory and Practice of Women's Autobiographical Writings*, (Chapel Hill: University of North Carolina Press, 1988), p. 56.

31. Nancy Miller, "Representing Others: Gender and the Subject of Autobiography," *differences* 6:1 (Spring 1994), pp. 1–27 (p. 5).

32. Butler, "Giving An Account of Oneself," p. 28.

33. Meulenbelt, *The Shame is Over*, p. 256.

34. *Butler, Precarious Life*, p. 49.

35. Chandra Mohanty, Ann Russo, and Lourdes Torres, eds., *Third World Women and the Politics of Feminism* (Bloomington: Indiana University Press, 1991), p. 51.

36. Ibid., p. 53.

37. Ibid., p. 74.

38. Brodski, and Schenck, eds., *Life/Lines*, p. 13.

39. Gayatri Spivak, "Questions of Multiculturalism," in Sarah Harasym, ed., *The Postcolonial Critic: Interviews, Strategies, Dialogues*, (New York: Routledge, 1990), p. 66.

40. Smith and Watson, eds., *Women, Autobiography, Theory*, p. 29.

41. Doris Sommer, " 'Not Just a Personal Story': Women's *Testimonios* and the Plural Self," in Brodski and Scherik, eds., *Life/Lines*, p. 107.

42. Ibid., p. 109.

43. Ibid., p. 111.

44. Ibid., p. 112.

45. Elspeth Probyn, *Sexing the Self: Gendered Positions in Cultural Studies* (London and New York: Routledge, 1993), p. 99.

46. Ibid., p. 100.

47. Ibid., p. 101.

48. Carolyn Steedman, *Landscape for a Good Woman* (London: Virago, 1986).
49. Ibid., pp. 128–39. See also the discussion of this episode in Trev Lynn Broughton and Linda Anderson, eds., *Women's Lives/Women's Times: New Essays on Autobiography* (New York: State University of New York Press, 1997), pp. 4–5.
50. Steedman, *Landscape*, p. 72.
51. Ibid., p. 28.
52. Probyn, *Sexing the Self*, p. 101.
53. Ibid., p. 102.
54. Ibid., p. 105.
55. Ibid., p. 106.
56. Elspeth Probyn, *Outside Belongings* (London and New York: Routledge, 1996), pp. 10–11.
57. Paul Gilroy, *Against Race: Imagining Political Culture Beyond the Color Line* (Cambridge, MA: The Belknap Press of Harvard University Press, 2000), p. 123.
58. Ghada Karmi, *in Search of Fatima: A Palestinian Story* (London and New York: Verso, 2002), p. 445.
59. Ibid., pp. 248–50.
60. Sommer, "'Not Just a Personal Story,'" p. 118.
61. Shoshana Felman and Dori Laub, *Testimony: Crisis of Witnessing in Literature, Psychoanalysis and History* (New York and London: Routledge, 1992), p. 5.
62. Felman, *What Does A Woman Want?*, p. 133.

6

KATHERINE MULLIN

Modernisms and feminisms

This essay investigates the tangled and often contradictory relationship between two notoriously complex ideological forms. Just as there are many feminisms, so there are many modernisms. A range of diverse, even incompatible aesthetic practices are commonly labeled modernist, including Futurism, Symbolism, Imagism, Vorticism, Expressionism, and Surrealism. Attempts to define modernism, then, are often made with the broadest of brushstrokes. Modernism can be characterized as a set of "multiple revolts against traditional realism and romanticism."[1] Its preoccupations might include a commitment to paradox and ambiguity, a tendency toward aesthetic self-consciousness, an interest in techniques of montage and juxtaposition, or a fascination with the demise of the integrated individual personality.[2] Or modernism can simply be labeled an art of crisis, a term Michael Levenson finds to be inevitably central in discussions of this turbulent cultural moment.[3] Studies of literary modernism tend to focus on the period 1890 to 1930 as the years when a new kind of writing emerged, one characterized by new aesthetic codes, unprecedented experimentations with literary form, and radical transformations in social, philosophical, and cultural themes.

This common definition of modernism as the art of a specific historical period in one sense evades the difficulties of defining the movement in other ways. Yet, importantly, it also emphasizes its historical coincidence with feminism. The period 1890 to 1930 was simultaneously a time of increasing feminist agitation, as women in various countries entered higher education and the workplace in unprecedented numbers, campaigned for the vote, and placed issues of sexuality and gender firmly on the political agenda. Literary culture was highly conscious of the rise of this "New Woman" – educated, emancipated, independent, outspoken, feminist – and the crisis in sexual politics that she personified. The closing decade of the nineteenth century saw the increasing feminization of the literary marketplace, as more than a hundred novels representing the "New Woman" and challenging the conventional Victorian marriage plot were published.[4] The aesthetic radicalism of modernism thus came into being alongside the political radicalism of this "first wave" of feminism. How did modernism respond to feminism, and what kind of a place were women able to find within this new literary movement?

As Jane Eldridge Miller and others have noted, the explicitly feminist "New Women" novelists of the 1890s – George Egerton, Rhoda Broughton, Sarah Grand, Grant Allen, Olive Schreiner, and others – were not easily incorporated into the modernist project.[5] Instead, this brand of feminism was more commonly constructed as one of the ideologies that modernist practitioners should react *against*. In 1904 William Courtenay's *The Feminine Note in Fiction* attacked the "New Woman" novel about gender relations and "sex problems" for "failing to realise the neutrality of the artistic mind."[6] He proposed a new "virile" standard of aesthetic value, and his association of artistic merit with masculinity would be frequently repeated in the various manifestos by which an emerging modernist sensibility tried to define itself. In February 1909 the first of several such declarations appeared in the form of F. T. Marinetti's first Futurist Manifesto. Marinetti immediately connects aesthetic radicalism with the battle of the sexes: "We will destroy the museums, libraries, academies of every kind, will fight moralism, feminism, every opportunist cowardice."[7] Lest the point be missed, he again insists upon the heroic masculinity of the Futurist project: "We will glorify war – the world's only hygiene – militarism, patriotism, the destructive gestures of freedom bringers, beautiful ideas worth dying for, and scorn for women."[8]

Marinetti's vision of a modernism emphatically gendered male became part of a discernible trend. Wyndham Lewis's short-lived Vorticist journal *Blast* similarly invited readers to "BLAST years 1837 – 1900 / Blast . . . RHETORIC OF EUNUCH AND STYLIST / SENTIMENTAL HYGIENICS."[9] Like Marinetti's Manifesto, *Blast* associated the new modernist age with virility and potency, the Victorian era with effeminacy and sentimentality. This emphasis on modernism as masculine is threaded through several other avant-garde little magazines of the period. The US journal *The Little Review*, which published Lewis, James Joyce, Ezra Pound, and others, gendered itself through its tagline "For virile readers only."[10] Its British sister-paper *The Egoist* started life as *The Freewoman* in 1912, subtitled "*A weekly feminist review*", yet within a year the title was softened to *The New Freewoman: A weekly humanist review*. The title shift was, however, not enough to reflect the journal's purpose as both a feminist forum for discussions of sexuality and gender roles, and the arena where male modernists such as Joyce and T.S. Eliot might make their debut. As the paper

increasingly attracted a readership of both genders, a group of men involved
with the journal began to challenge its sexual politics. In December 1913
Pound and his modernist colleagues Richard Aldington, Huntley Carter,
and Reginald Wright-Kauffman wrote to *The New Freewoman*'s editor, the
feminist dissident Dora Marsden:

> We venture to suggest to you that the present title of the paper causes it to be
> confounded with organs devoted solely to the advocacy of an unimportant
> reform in an obsolete political institution. We therefore ask with great respect
> that you should consider the advisability of adopting another title which
> will mark your paper as an organ for individuals of both sexes and the
> individualist principle in every department of life.[11]

The "unimportant reform" was, of course, women's suffrage, still five years
away from achievement in the United Kingdom, yet Marsden conceded the
change. Her concession allowed Pound to take a post as the journal's
literary editor, and transform it into a modernist literary periodical.[12]

For Rachel Blau DuPlessis, the transformation of *The New Freewoman*
into *The Egoist* in December 1913 is a "symbolic moment" marking "the
equivocal relationship of 'high' Modernism to feminisms and to gender
issues."[13] The moment can be read as a parable of modernism's aggressive
and pointed erasure of feminism, even when the merit of the cause – votes
for women – should have been clear. Some recent feminist studies have
argued that the parable is compounded by a longstanding critical focus on
modernism as exclusively male. "Modernism as we were taught it at mid-
century was . . . unconsciously gendered masculine," claims Bonnie Kime
Scott at the start of her anthology of female modernist writing, *The Gender
of Modernism*.[14] Scott's study positions itself as a corrective to Hugh
Kenner's *The Pound Era*, which presented modernism as an almost entirely
male literary movement orchestrated by one presiding genius.[15] *The Gender
of Modernism* can be placed alongside other valuable feminist reappraisals
of modernism during the 1980s and 1990s. Shari Benstock's *Women of
the Left Bank* explores the work of women writers living in Paris between
1900 and 1940, reminding us of the importance of writers such as H. D.,
Gertrude Stein, Djuna Barnes, Rebecca West, and the publisher Sylvia
Beach.[16] Gillian Hanscombe's and Virginia L. Smyer's *Writing for
their Lives* continues Benstock's project, investigating the contributions of
Dorothy Richardson, Bryher, Mina Loy and Amy Lowell to modernism.[17]
Cheryl Wall's *Women of the Harlem Renaissance* similarly draws atten-
tion to an implicitly masculinist African American modernist canon through
her investigation of the work of Jessie Redmon Fauset, Nella Larsen,
Zora Neale Hurston, and other black women writers.[18] Yet feminist

reassessments of modernism cannot ignore what Andreas Huyssen calls "the powerful masculinist and misogynist current within the trajectory of modernism."[19] Despite recent feminist scholarship, the popular perception continues to see modernism as male. Most people, as Janet Wolff observes, would find it difficult to think quickly of women modernist writers, with the possible exception of Virginia Woolf.[20]

We might pause here to consider how modernism became so closely associated with masculinity. As we have seen, manifestos and definitions of modernism tend to present the movement as virile and manly, in contrast to the feminine flabbiness of nineteenth-century writing, and, in particular, the "social problem" writings of the "New Women" novelists. This definition of modernism as male can be traced back to the social conditions of the modernist period, which offered men and women very different experiences of what it meant to be a modernist. If we turn back to Marinetti's 1909 Futurist Manifesto, we can immediately see how modernity is associated with warfare. Marinetti proposes to "destroy the museums, libraries, academies of every kind" and "glorify war," while he also intends to "fight feminism" and promote "scorn for women." In one respect, Marinetti's manifesto seems uncannily prescient, since the Great War of 1914–18 is both crucial to the development of modernism and a cultural phenomenon that was largely, though not entirely, male. Women did not fight in the trenches. They did not, with a few exceptions, experience the ubiquitous closeness of death. They were not traumatized in the same way by the experience of machine warfare or shell shock. And, as Benstock and others have argued, postwar trauma was crucial to the foundation of modernism.[21] One of modernism's foundational texts, Eliot's *The Waste Land* (1922), was in part written during the closing months of the war. On one level, it testifies to his grief over the death of male friends in the trenches. Images of buried corpses threatening to surface, crowds of the undead surging over London Bridge, and the trench-like "rats alley / Where the dead men lost their bones," all speak eloquently of war.[22] D. H. Lawrence's *Lady Chatterley's Lover* (1928) and Woolf's *Mrs Dalloway* (1925) each feature men scarred by their wartime experiences. Clifford Chatterley bears the physical signs of warfare, as his injuries make him impotent and wheelchair-bound, while Septimus Smith's shell-shocked visions of his dead comrade Evans precipitate his suicide. War, and the male bonding it produced, was both an almost exclusively masculine experience and integral to modernism.

For many British women, the Great War marked a point when an increasingly radicalized and militant campaign for female suffrage was suspended in order to allow women to devote their attentions to the war effort. The suspension of suffragette campaigns in 1914 was widely seen as the sacrifice of a lesser struggle for a greater. The military parallel was explicit in the medals for service and bravery bestowed by the Women's Social and Political Union on women who had suffered imprisonment and hunger strikes for the cause. It was tacitly validated when the vote for women over thirty was granted in the United Kingdom in 1918, followed by the granting of women's suffrage in the United States two years later, gestures interpreted by many as rewards for women's service in wartime.

If male modernist sensibilities were dominated and shaped by the Great War, then many of their female counterparts found an alternative formative experience through the suffrage campaigns in Britain and the United States and through an affiliated interest in feminist issues. The crusade for the vote was but one aspect of a broader climate of feminist inquiry and challenge. During the first decades of the twentieth century, the nature of sexuality, marriage, and motherhood was fiercely debated. Influential polemics such as Christabel Pankhurst's *The Great Scourge and How to End It* (1913) blamed the double standard of sexual morality for an epidemic of venereal disease, while Cicily Hamilton's bestselling *Marriage as a Trade* (1909) argued that the cultural insistence on marriage as a woman's destiny seriously hampered her intellectual development. These and affiliated issues were, meanwhile, the topic of debate among feminist societies such as the Freewoman discussion circle, which met fortnightly in Bloomsbury to explore topics including homosexuality, "free unions" (cohabitation outside marriage), and wages for motherhood. For many women, the political agitation and intellectual debates precipitated by the campaign for the vote offered formative experiences of gender bonding that arguably paralleled male experiences of war.[23]

Importantly, women's political activism and debate during the first decades of the modernist period together offer a strong illustration of the feminist credo that the personal is political. Feminist arguments for the vote often stressed how enfranchisement would enable women to attend more efficiently to those issues and duties which were gendered female – the care of children, the custodianship of sexual morality, the guardianship of the home.[24] Feminist insistence that the vote would not necessarily remove women from their proper sphere was colorfully exemplified in a series of postcards showing leading suffragists engaged in domestic tasks, captioned "Mrs Snow Makes Pastry," "Miss Agnes Leonard Cleans the Stove," and "Mrs Despard Knits a Comforter."[25] As this kind of propaganda suggests, for many committed feminists the Victorian ideology of separate spheres, with the public life of politics and work for the male, and the private life of home and children for the female, still pertained. This division becomes particularly apparent when we turn to men's and women's very different experiences of the city, that insistent location of much modernist writing.

As many critics have observed, modernism is in one sense a literature of the city, whether that city be the London of Eliot or Woolf, the Paris of Lewis or Barnes or the Dublin of Joyce.[26] Urban experience is characterized by isolation within the crowd, by a concomitant sense of anonymity and alienation, and by both the dangers of crime and the exhilarations of urban diversity and adventure. The art historian Griselda Pollock notes how the stroller "symbolizes the privilege or freedom to move about the public arenas of the city observing but never interacting, consuming the sights through a controlling but rarely acknowledged gaze."[27] Yet while men might stroll anonymously and unmolested through urban space, women often occupied a more conspicuous and therefore more unstable position. Some public spaces – bars, cafés, clubs, even public lavatories – were, at the turn of the twentieth century, were perceived to be out of bounds to "respectable" middle-class women. Woolf's genteel Pargiter sisters find that

> [f]or any of them to walk to the West End even by day was out of the question. Bond Street was as impassable, save with their mother, as any swamp alive with crocodiles. The Burlington Arcade was nothing but a fever-stricken den as far as they were concerned. To be seen alone in Piccadilly was equivalent to walking up Abercorn Terrace in a dressing gown carrying a bath sponge.[28]

As Woolf eloquently outlines, women's access to the city was heavily circumscribed. Women of her class who wished to explore the metropolis were forced to devise reasons or pretexts for doing so, ranging from shopping, as Rachel Bowlby and Erika Rappaport have recently shown, to urban philanthropy, as Judith Walkowitz has explored.[29] Mere strolling in the paradigmatic urban space of modernist writing was, for many women, a compromised and compromising pleasure.

In these contexts, a male modernist insistence on the "virility" of this new form of artistic practice is more easily understood. Set in the city and haunted by the trauma of a recent war, one dominant strand of modernism flourished among self-consciously male coteries.[30] Pound, among others, zealously fought to maintain the exclusivity of the modernist brotherhood. Not satisfied with accomplishing *The New Freewoman*'s transformation into *The Egoist*, he also took pains to exclude women from the other modernist journals he was connected with. In a remark echoing his earlier comments on *The New Freewoman*, Pound argued that "No woman should be allowed to write for *The Little Review*," adding that such a ban "would be a risk. It would cause outcry, boycott etc. But most of the ills of the American little magazines are (or were) due to women."[31] Women were, however, tolerated on the periphery of this strand of "virile " modernism, where they dispro-portionately appear as editors, publishers, patrons and the hostesses of literary salons. *The Little Review* was founded and edited by Margaret Anderson and Jane Heap, first in Chicago and later in New York. *The Egoist* was run by Dora Marsden and Harriet Shaw Weaver, the latter an unassum-ing heiress who divided her wealth between subsidising her journal, the British Communist Party, and Joyce. Other women facilitators of modernism include Sylvia Beach and Adrienne Monnier, proprietors of the Paris-based Shakespeare and Co. bookshop and publishing house.[32] Natalie Barney, Nancy Cunard, and Peggy Guggenheim were three wealthy female patrons of modernism who supported writers financially and through their literary salons.[33] "Throughout my life, women have been my most active helpers," acknowledged a grateful Joyce.[34] That such women are frequently termed the "midwives of modernism" speaks volubly of the sexual politics of the amanuensis role.

If we turn to women practitioners of modernism, we discover how many women writers deliberately evaded the role of "helper" and instead sought to invent a modernism of their own. The term echoes the phrase coined by Woolf, whose theoretical writings return time and again to the problem of intellectual and artistic freedom for women writers. Woolf's seminal essay *A Room of One's Own* (1928) explores women's exclusion from literary culture, noting how would-be women writers were turned away from libraries, refused access to the major universities, and denied the cultural space and material resources necessary to creative life. While Woolf suggests at one point in her essay that all great writing is androgynous, she also argues for a separate literary tradition of women's writing in response to these circumstances. Women's writing, she suggests, is an art of exclusion: "if one is a woman one is often surprised by a sudden splitting off of consciousness, say in walking down Whitehall, when from being the natural inheritor of that civilisation, she becomes, on the contrary, outside of it, alien and critical."[35] *A Room of One's Own* develops Woolf's thought from earlier in her career that women's writing was a genre of its own:

> It is probable, however, that both in life and in art the values of a woman are not the values of a man. Thus, when a woman comes to write . . . she will find that she is perpetually wishing to alter the established values – to make serious what appears insignificant to a man, and trivial what is to him important.[36]

For Woolf, women's writing was radically distinct from the writing of men because it related to an occluded and marginalized female experience.

Crucially, not only content but also *form* was subject to these gender differences. Deriding "the sentence made by men" as heavy and ponderous, Woolf argues that the woman writer must alter the sentence "until it takes the natural shape of her thought without crushing or distorting it."[37] For Woolf, the innovations of modernist literary practice could readily be adapted for feminist purposes. She singled out her fellow modernist Dorothy Richardson for special praise:

> She has invented, or if she has not invented, developed and applied to her own use, a sentence which we might call the psychological sentence of the feminine gender. It is of a more elastic fibre than the old, capable of stretching to the extreme, of suspending the frailest particles, of enveloping the vaguest shapes.[38]

Turning to a passage from the first volume of Richardson's novel sequence *Pilgrimage, Pointed Roofs* (1915), we can see what Woolf meant:

> The organ was playing "The Wearin' o' The Green". It had begun that tune during the last term at school, in the summer. It made her think of rounders in the hot school garden, singing-classes in the large green room, all the class shouting "Gather roses while ye may", hot afternoons in the shady north room, the sound of turning pages, the hum of the garden beyond the sun-blinds, meetings in the sixth form study . . . Lilla, with her black hair and the specks of bright amber in the brown of her eyes, talking about free-will.[39]

As Woolf observes, Richardson's account of her heroine Miriam Henderson's thought processes echoes in its use of clauses and ellipses the sequential network of Miriam's memories of school. Woolf's position at the center of the female modernist canon is unsurprising, given her lifelong commitment to exploring the theoretical issues behind women's participation in a vehemently masculine literary culture. Her belief that women's writing differed from men's in both its content and its form can be traced in the writings of both Richardson and Woolf's other female modernist peers.

We shall turn first to Woolf's claim that the woman writer will choose a different type of literary content; she will wish "to make serious what appears insignificant to a man, and trivial what is to him important." The belief that the subjects of women's writing are "trivial" is one that can be easily traced in the examples of "virile" modernist discourse given above, whether it be Marinetti's claim that modernist art is analogous to the serious male business of warfare, or Pound's dismissal of the campaign for female suffrage as "an unimportant reform in an obsolete political institution." As Andreas Huyssen has shown, an important aspect of this ideology gendered modernist high culture as masculine, as opposed to a feminized *mass*

culture. Women were implicitly situated as both the consumers and producers of pulp, of "insubstantial" and evanescent popular literature and
culture, whereas the male modernist, in contrast, emerges as objective,
ironic, in control of his aesthetic means; in other words, the practitioner
of serious and durable art forms.[40] Woolf's defense of "the trivial" as an
appropriate subject for women writers responds to this argument by
opening up the question of what might be a fit topic for modernism. In
her own literary practice, and in the work of other women modernists, we
can see a sustained focus on a "female" world that explores with seriousness
what might otherwise be damned as trivial.

If we turn to modernist representations of domestic space, we can perceive a self-conscious awareness in writers of both genders that the world of
family, home, love, marriage, and romance has traditionally been labeled a
female world. For Lawrence, domesticity is presented as suffocation, as
interior space threatens to overwhelm Paul Morel in *Sons and Lovers*
(1913) or Constance Chatterley in *Lady Chatterley's Lover*. The outdoors,
the natural world, offers an escape route from that constriction. *The Waste
Land* also dismisses domesticity as cloying and oppressive, most notably in
Eliot's description of the typist's squalid bedsit, where she lays underwear
out to dry and serves up tinned food. Joseph Conrad's *The Secret Agent*
(1907) sees the home as the site of violence, as the seemingly submissive wife,
daughter, and sister Winnie turns murderer, then flees into the dark under-
world of London to escape the consequences of her crime. These examples
together suggest a male modernist discomfort with, or even repulsion from, a
domain culturally inscribed as female. Such negative male representations of
domestic space, so frequently contrasted with their exhilarated depictions of
the city, offer an intriguing comparison with the portrayal of domesticity by
their female counterparts.

Woolf's own commitment to a feminist representation of "the trivial" can
be seen in the centrality of domestic women within her work. Although her
alertness to the dangers of the traditionally "trivial" female sphere of home
and family was vigorously articulated in her 1931 essay "Killing the Angel
in the House," her love for her "angel" mother and her sporadic interest in
homemaking complicated any straightforward feminist repudiation of the
domestic role in her writing. Her depiction of the female private sphere is,
accordingly, highly ambivalent. In both *Mrs Dalloway* (1925) and *To
The Lighthouse* (1927), intellectual women and artists – Lily Briscoe, Miss
Kilman – are counterpointed with the figure of the perfect hostess – Mrs.
Ramsay or Clarissa Dalloway. Woolf celebrates the domestic woman as a
version of the artist, most notably when we see Clarissa choreograph her
party so meticulously, or Mrs. Ramsay admiring the aesthetic unity of the

boeuf en daube, or the fruitbowl of exquisitely arranged yellow pears and purple grapes. Her final novel, *Between the Acts* (1939), elaborates on this figure of the hostess-artist in the character of Miss LaTrobe, who, against the looming backdrop of encroaching war, finds an outlet for her artistic sensibilities in the apparent provincial banality of a village pageant.

Woolf's ambivalent focus on domestic life, female, interior space, and a subject matter that might be negatively classed as trivially feminine can also be traced in the work of other women modernists. May Sinclair turns to the domestic sphere to interrogate the institutions of marriage and the family in *Mary Oliver* (1919) and *The Life and Death of Harriet Frean* (1922), novels which fused a quotidian subject with a highly experimental narrative style. Gertrude Stein's fascination with domesticity is exemplified both in *The Autobiography of Alice B. Toklas* (1932), an experimental novel masquerading as the life-writing of her domestic partner, and in *Tender Buttons* (1913), where ordinary household objects – a carafe, a tumbler, tables, chairs, eggs, coffee, or sugar – are the obliquely glimpsed subjects of Stein's linguistic innovations:

A NEW CUP AND SAUCER
Enthusiastically hurting a clouded yellow bud and saucer, enthusiastically so is the bite in the ribbon.[41]

Subtitled *Objects, Food, Rooms, Tender Buttons* is a highly experimental text that attempts to make us see familiar objects differently. Here, a yellow cup and saucer, perhaps with a ribboned pattern around the rim, is loaded with "clouded" and dim meanings – enthusiasm and pain.

The sense, however, that domestic life, love affairs, or motherhood were somehow inappropriate subjects for modernist experimentation influenced the critical receptions of several other women writers. Jean Rhys's novels of female objectification, romantic betrayal, and emotional withdrawal were praised for their "instinct for form" by Ford Madox Ford, but frequently criticized for their "sordid" subject matter – women living alone in squalid bedsits, trading sexual favors for subsistence.[42] Similarly, Eliot paid Katherine Mansfield's work the backhanded compliment of praising "the skill with which the author has handled perfectly the *minimum* material," the "slightness" of both her content and her chosen form, the short story, making her writing "what I believe would be called feminine."[43] Mansfield's stories about unhappy marriages or young women in sexual danger were seen, by Eliot and others, to be "delicate" and "feminine," but insufficiently rigorous or serious to be included within the high modernist canon. The experimentalism of Loy's *Love Songs* was in a similarly uneasy conflict with the intimacy of her subject matter, her "feminine" exploration of the nature and need for sexual love. In poems such as "Parturition," Loy connected the creative process to childbirth:

> I am the centre
> Of a circle of pain
> Exceeding its boundaries in every direction
> The business of the bland sun
> Has no affair with me.[44]

"Parturition" flaunted the femininity of Loy's poetic persona in ways which self-consciously challenged the butch swagger of much modernist poetic theory.

These are but a few necessarily brief indications of the ways in which women modernists took what Woolf classes as "the trivial" for their subjects, and how the perceived "femininity" of their content often distracted attention from the stylistic innovations of their work. In the closing section of this essay, we shall turn from content to form to explore the implications of Woolf's affiliated belief that women writers invented a distinctively feminine mode of writing with radical aesthetic potential. The idea that the modernist revolution in the arts offered exciting opportunities for women writers to escape from the ponderous masculinity of Victorian realism has been frequently articulated by a number of critics since Woolf. For Sandra Gilbert and Susan Gubar, modernist texts can be read as a direct product of contemporary feminism, for they argue that male modernism was an aggressive response to increasingly vocal feminist demands for political, cultural, and creative autonomy.[45] The French feminists of the 1970s and 1980s, led by Julia Kristeva, Luce Irigaray and Hélène Cixous, also argue for modernism's radical feminist potential by suggesting that women writers use avant-garde linguistic forms to escape the confines of patriarchal language.[46] Similarly, Alice Jardine has suggested that modernism allows the "putting of women into discourse," permitting women writers to take unprecedented control of the means of writing.[47] These disparate claims for the centrality of women to modernism's formal practices may sit uneasily alongside the unabashedly misogynist statements of many male modernists discussed earlier. Yet if we look at the experiments with literary form carried out by many women modernists, we can see how some women did indeed seem to be undaunted by their male colleagues' discouragement, instead seeing in modernism the opportunity for creative liberation.

Woolf singled out Richardson for special praise, commending her invention of what "we might call the psychological sentence of the feminine gender." Yet Richardson was only one of many female modernists engaged in the unpicking and remaking of what could be defined as a literary text. One of the most radical was Stein, who, as we have seen, repeatedly focused on the familiar world of women. Stein's innovation, however, lay in her wish to do for language what Picasso and his fellow Cubists were attempting in painting when they tried to represent an object from several different angles simultaneously on the same canvas. Stein's writing similarly attempts to defamiliarize the everyday by using a muted "palette" of a few key words and phrases. Her long experimental novel *The Making of Americans* (1925) was subtitled *Being a History of a Family's Progress* and, just as she attempted to make us look afresh at a cup and saucer in *Tender Buttons*, so in *The Making of Americans* she revised the domestic genre of the family saga:

> Yes we are very little children when we first begin to be ourselves grown men and women. We say then, yes we are children, but we know then, way inside us, we are not to ourselves real as children, we are grown to ourselves as young grown men and women. Nay, we never know ourselves as other than young and grown men and women.[48]

In this typical passage, a limited vocabulary and rhythmic repetitions present the oft-discussed question of the relationship between childhood and adulthood from a range of different perspectives. It thereby attempts to make the familiar strange, loading it with accumulated and silted layers of meaning.

Stein's technique of linguistic accretion stands in sharp contrast to the stripped-down style of another innovative female stylist, the poet Hilda Doolittle, named "H. D., Imagiste" by her sometime fiancé and collaborator, Ezra Pound. The Imagist school of poetry was promoted by Pound, Eliot and T. E. Hulme and flourished from 1909 until 1917. Imagist poets were reacting against a poetic tradition they perceived to be rigid, overblown, and unoriginal. They proposed an alternative form of poetry that relied instead on calm, clear, pure, and intensely visual images, which might be apprehended in an instant. H. D. was central to this new form of free verse. Her poetry, with its simple images, helped to shape both the theory and the practice of Imagism. Her poem "Never More Will the Wind" is an eloquently streamlined depiction of grief and loss:

> The snow is melted,
> The snow is gone,
> And you are flown:
>
> Like a bird out of our hand,
> Like a light out of our heart,
> You are gone.[49]

H. D.'s work was published not only in coterie little magazines such as *The Little Review* and *The Egoist*, but also in the 1914 volume *Des Imagistes: An Anthology* and in five subsequent Imagist collections during the 1910s. As Richard Aldington, then literary editor of *The Egoist*, put it, "H. D. *was* Imagism."[50] Called "the perfect Imagist" by her peers, H. D. formulated by example the poetic movement that influenced Pound, Eliot, and others. Like Stein, H. D. was at the forefront of modernism's innovations in form.

Woolf, Richardson, Stein, and H. D. are, of course, just four examples of women writers who contributed to the aesthetic innovations that characterize modernism as a literary movement. A list of other women writers who were integral to the development of modernism might include Djuna Barnes, Willa Cather, Zora Neale Hurston, Anna Kavan, Nella Larsen, Mina Loy, Marianne Moore, Laura Riding, Christina Stead, Sylvia Townsend Warner, Antonia White, and Anna Wickham. This list is certainly not exhaustive. Recent studies have also newly appraised women writers of the period who are less obviously "experimental" than those given here, yet who nonetheless might arguably be classed as modernist, such as Elizabeth Bowen, Radclyffe Hall, Molly Keane, and Rosamund Lehmann.[51] It would be impossible to survey here the diverse and complex contributions of so many very different women writers to the modernist project. The wealth of names can only stand as an indication of the richness of the field of modernist writing by women.

One strand of modernism, we have seen, deliberately presented itself as a men's club, whose members, bonded together by the largely masculine experience of war, set about forging a radical new aesthetics appropriate to a turbulent new century. This form of modernism is seen to be dominated by the triumvirate of Pound, Eliot, and Joyce, and animated by the brash polemics of Futurism, Vorticism, and other self-consciously masculine manifestos. Yet, as Scott observes, "in settling for a small set of white male Modernists and a limited number of texts and genres, we may have paused upon a conservative, anxious, male strain of Modernism, however valuable and lasting those texts."[52] An alliance between modernism and feminism might initially seem an unpromising one, but the historical contingency connecting experimental literary practice and an increasingly vocal campaign for female suffrage and a new sexual politics is only the most obvious point of contact between the two. The wide range of modernist writing by women shows that many women either evaded or were undaunted by misogynist proscriptions. Instead, they found modernism's focus on stylistic innovation to be liberating, offering a new kind of writing in which to articulate a new kind of female experience. Gender often becomes the subtext and the subject of female-authored modernisms, from Woolf pondering over the feminine sentences of Richardson, to Stein making domesticity new, rich, and strange. Stephen Dedalus, the quasi-autobiographical protagonist of Joyce's *A Portrait of the Artist as a Young Man*, ends that novel with a famous plea for artistic inspiration: "Old father, old artificer, stand me now and ever in good stead."[53] Turning from Joyce and his male peers to the women writers working alongside him, we find modernist aesthetic practices gendered rather differently.

Further reading

Ann L. Ardis, *New Women, New Novels: feminism and Early Modernism* (New Brunswick: Rutgers University Press, 1990).

Shari Benstock, *Women of the Left Bank: Paris 1900–1940* (London: Virago, 1987).

Rachel Bowlby, *Just Looking: Consumer Culture in Dreiser, Gissing and Zola* (London: Methuen, 1985).

Suzanne Clark, *Sentimental Modernism: Women Writers and the Revolution of the Word* (Bloomington: Indiana University Press, 1991).

Bruce Clarke, *Dora Marsden and Early Modernism* (Ann Arbor: University of Michigan Press, 1996).

Marianne DeKoven, *Rich and Strange: Gender, History, Modernism* (Princeton: Princeton University Press, 1991).

Sandra M. Gilbert and Susan Gubar, *No Man's Land: The Place of the Woman Writer in the Twentieth Century* (New Haven: Yale University Press, 1988).

Gillian Hanscombe and Virginia L. Smyers, *Writing for Their Lives: The Modernist Women 1910–1940* (London: The Women's Press, 1987).

Andreas Huyssen, *After the Great Divide: Modernism, Mass Culture, Postmodernism* (London: Macmillan, 1988).

Jane Eldridge Miller, *Feminism, Modernism and the Edwardian Novel* (London: Virago, 1994).

Erika Rappaport, *Shopping for Pleasure: Women in the Making of London's West End* (Princeton: Princeton University Press, 2000).

Bonnie Kime Scott, ed., *The Gender of Modernism*: critical anthology (Bloomington: Indiana University Press, 1990).

Cheryl Wall, *Women of the Harlem Renaissance* (Bloomington: Indiana University Press, 1995).

NOTES

1. Eugene Lunn, *Marxism and Modernism: An Historical Study of Lukács, Brecht, Benjamin and Adorno* (London: Verso, 1985), p. 34.

2. Ibid., pp. 34–7.

3. Michael Levenson, 'Introduction' to *The Cambridge Companion to Modernism* (Cambridge: Cambridge University Press, 1999), p. 4.

4. Ann L. Ardis, *New Women, New Novels: Feminism and Early Modernism* (New Brunswick: Rutgers University Press, 1990), p. 3.
5. See Jane Eldridge Miller, *Feminism, Modernism and the Edwardian Novel* (London: Virago, 1994); and Ardis, *New Women, New Novels*.
6. William Courtenay, *The Feminine Note in Fiction* (London: Chapman and Hall, 1904), p. 27.
7. F. T. Marinetti, "Manifesto of Futurism," first published in *Le Figaro*, February 20, 1909, trans. Eugen Weber, reprinted in Eugen Weber, ed., *Movements, Currents, Trends: Aspects of European Thought in the Nineteenth and Twentieth Centuries* (Lexington, MA: Heath, 1992), p. 265.
8. Ibid., p. 267.
9. *Blast* Issue One, June 20, 1914, p. 19.
10. *The Little Review*, June 1918, p. 1.
11. Letter quoted in Jane Lidderdale and Mary Nicholson, *Dear Miss Weaver: Harriet Shaw Weaver 1876–1961* (London: Faber and Faber, 1970), p. 66.
12. For a full discussion of the complexities of the title change, see Bruce Clarke, *Dora Marsden and Early Modernism* (Ann Arbor: University of Michigan Press, 1996), pp. 129–32.
13. Rachel Blau DuPlessis, *The Pink Guitar: Writing as Feminist Practice* (London: Routledge, 1990), pp. 44–5. By the term "'high' Modernism," DuPlessis refers to the period from around 1910 to 1930, when writers such as Pound, Joyce, Eliot, Proust, Woolf, Stein, Stevens, Kafka, and Rilke radically redefined what literature could be and do.
14. Bonnie Kime Scott, ed., *The Gender of Modernism: A Critical Anthology* (Bloomington: Indiana University Press, 1990), p. 2.
15. Hugh Kenner, *The Pound Era* (Berkeley: University of California Press, 1951).
16. Shari Benstock, *Women of the Left Bank: Paris 1900–1940* (London: Virago, 1987).
17. Gillian Hanscombe and Virginia L. Smyers, *Writing for Their Lives: The Modernist Women 1910–1940* (London: The Women's Press, 1987).
18. Cheryl Wall, *Women of the Harlem Renaissance* (Chicago: Indiana University Press, 1995).
19. Andreas Huyssen, "Mass Culture as Woman: Modernism's Other," in Huyssen, *After the Great Divide: Modernism, Mass Culture, Postmodernism* (London: Macmillan, 1988), p. 49.
20. Janet Wolff, *Feminine Sentences: Essays on Women and Culture* (London: Polity Press, 1990), p. 54.
21. See Benstock, *Women of the Left Bank*, p. 36, and, more recently, Sarah Cole, *Modernism, Male Friendship and the First World War* (Cambridge: Cambridge University Press, 2003).
22. T. S. Eliot, *The Waste Land*, section 2, "A Game of Chess," II.150–1, in Eliot, *Selected Poems* (London: Faber and Faber, 1985).
23. See Lucy Bland, *Banishing the Beast: English Feminism and Sexual Morality 1885–1914* (London: Penguin, 1995) for a compelling account of gender debates closely affiliated to the suffrage campaigns. For more on the suffrage campaigns themselves, see Lisa Tickner, *The Spectacle of Women: Imagery of the Suffrage Campaign* (London: Chatto and Windus, 1989).

24. For the "femininity" of some suffrage discourse, see Bland, *Banishing the Beast*, pp. 1–45, and Tickner, *Spectacle of Women*, pp. 145–60.
25. Tickner, *Spectacle of Women*, p. 73.
26. This point has been made repeatedly by Raymond Williams. See his *The Country and the City in the Modern Novel* (Oxford: Oxford University Press, 1985).
27. Griselda Pollock, *Vision and Difference: Femininity, Feminism, and Histories of Art* (London and New York: Routledge, 1988), p. 67.
28. Virginia Woolf, *The Pargiters* (New York: Harcourt Brace, 1977), p. 37. For more on women's relationship to the city, see Deborah Epstein Nord, "The Urban Peripatetic: Spectator, Streetwalker, Woman Writer," *Nineteenth Century Literature* 46:3 (December 1991), pp. 351–75.
29. See Rachel Bowlby, *Just Looking: Consumer Culture in Dreiser, Gissing and Zola* (London: Methuen, 1985); Erika Rappaport, *Shopping for Pleasure: Women in the Making of London's West End* (Princeton: Princeton University Press, 2000); Judith Walkowitz, *City of Dreadful Delight: Narratives of Sexual Danger in Late Victorian London* (London: Virago, 1998).
30. See Wayne Koestenbaum, *Double Talk: The Erotics of Male Literary Collaboration* (London: Routledge, 1989); and Laurence Rainey, *Institutions of Modernism: Literary Elites and Public Culture* (New Haven: Yale University Press, 1999).
31. Pound quoted in Steven Watson, *Strange Bedfellows: The First American Avant-Garde* (New York: Abbeville Press, 1991), p. 385.
32. For accounts of these women's roles in nurturing modernism, see Margaret Anderson, *My Thirty Years War* (New York: Covici, Friede, 1930); Sylvia Beach, *Shakespeare and Company* (Lincoln: University of Nebraska Press, 1991); and Lidderdale and Nicholson, *Dear Miss Weaver*.
33. See Benstock, *Women of the Left Bank*, for more about the culture of the literary salon in modernism.
34. Richard Ellmann, *James Joyce* (Oxford: Oxford University Press, 1983), p. 634.
35. Virginia Woolf, *A Room of One's Own* (New York: Harcourt, Brace and Jovanovitch, 1957), p. 101.
36. Virginia Woolf, "Women and Fiction," in Michèle Barrett, ed., *Virginia Woolf: Women and Writing* (London: The Women's Press, 1979), p. 49.
37. Ibid., p. 48.
38. Virginia Woolf, "Dorothy Richardson," in Barrett, ed., *Virginia Woolf*, p. 191.
39. Dorothy Richardson, *Pilgrimage I: Pointed Roofs* (London: Virago, 1992), p. 2.
40. Huyssen, "Mass Culture as Woman."
41. Gertrude Stein, *Tender Buttons: Objects, Food, Rooms* (Los Angeles: Sun and Moon Press, 1991), p. 20.
42. Ford Madox Ford, preface to Jean Rhys, *The Left Bank and Other Stories* (New York: Books for Libraries, 1970), pp. 24–5.
43. T. S. Eliot, *After Strange Gods: A Primer of Modern Heresy* (London: Faber and Faber, 1934), pp. 35–6.
44. Mina Loy, "Parturition," in Loy, *The Lost Lunar Baedeker*, ed. Roger Conover (Manchester: Carcanet, 1997), p. 4.
45. Sandra M. Gilbert and Susan Gubar, *No Man's Land: The Place of the Woman Writer in the Twentieth Century, Volume 1: The War of the Words* (New Haven: Yale University Press, 1988).

46. See Julia Kristeva, *Revolution in Poetic Language* (New York: Columbia University Press, 1984); Luce Irigaray, *Speculum of the Other Woman*, trans. Gillian C. Gill (Ithaca: Cornell University Press, 1985); and Hélène Cixous, "The Laugh of the Medusa", *The Hélène Cixous Reader*, ed. Susan Sellers (New York: Routledge, 1994), pp. 33–50.

47. Alice Jardine, "Opaque Texts and Transparent Contexts: The Political Difference of Julia Kristeva," in Nancy Miller, ed., *The Poetics of Gender* (New York: Columbia University Press, 1986), p. 105.

48. Gertrude Stein, *The Making of Americans: Being a History of a Family's Progress* (Chicago: Dalkey Archive Press, 1995), p. 5.

49. H. D., "Never More Will the Wind," in H. D., *Hymen* (London: The Egoist Press, 1921), p. 9.

50. Richard Aldington, *Life for Life's Sake* (London: Cassell, 1968), p. 124.

51. See in particular Maud Ellmann, *Elizabeth Bowen: The Shadow Across the Page* (Edinburgh: Edinburgh University Press, 2003); and Suzanne Clark, *Sentimental Modernism: Women Writers and the Revolution of the Word* (Bloomington: Indiana University Press, 1991).

52. Scott, *Gender of Modernism*, p. 16.

53. James Joyce, *A Portrait of the Artist as a Young Man* (London: Penguin, 1973), p. 253.

7

KARI WEIL

French feminism's *écriture féminine*

What came to be called French feminism in the United States is principally identified with a group of women writers who achieved prominence in France in the 1970s and 1980s. Although they did not think of themselves as a group, these women promoted an exciting, new approach to thinking about women, their bodies, and their desires, which changed both the shape and the locus of feminist thinking within the US academy. Because of French feminism's emphasis on language as both the ultimate tool of women's oppression and a potential means for subverting, if not escaping that oppression, it made literary studies the leading discipline in the growing field of women's studies. Its grounding in contemporary, intellectual thought brought a heady and difficult field of French theory to the foreground of feminist literary thinking, thus directing its focus away from historical and experiential research. What made French feminism so popular, some would say, had to do with the traditional seductiveness of things French and the inferiority complex experienced by US women in relation to the sophisticated style of their continental sisters. Seduction was clearly part of it – these were texts which, for all their intellectualism, talked about desire and the body, about women's erogenous zones and the possibilities of unleashing their libidinal force in writing. For French feminists, women's desire is what is most oppressed and repressed by patriarchy, and what most needs to find expression – an all but impossible task since, according to them, language is itself patriarchal. "*Jouissance,*" the French word for orgasm or for a pleasure so intense that it is at once of the body and outside it, became a fashionable term of literary theory for an intensity which, like woman's pleasure, is outside language.

And yet, many asked, how could pleasure be considered part of a feminist practice? Had not women's erotic body, her vulnerability to seduction by countless rakes, been precisely the stuff of literature that feminists wanted to contest and rewrite through the discovery of an alternative tradition – one in which women were the agents of creation, not just its sexual objects?

And why the emphasis on the body in the first place? Had it not been, in part, because of patriarchal associations of woman with the physical and natural realm that women's participation in intellectual life and cultural production had been disparaged, if not forbidden?

These questions take us already into some of the complicated issues involved in French feminism and the shifts it brought about in literary analysis. Feminist literary criticism had focused largely either on revealing the blindness and misogyny of patriarchal representations of women, or on discovering an alternative female-authored tradition. After the advent of French feminism, the focus was neither on the status of women as producers of literature, nor on the representation of women's experience in literature, but rather on the production of the "feminine" in literature. Work influenced by French feminism focused on the way that notions of woman and femininity are constructed and valorized in and through literature regarded as a system of signs governed by a logic of difference and divorced from any real reference to men and women. Masculinity and femininity both derive their meanings, and, more importantly, their values, in opposition to each other, but that opposition is produced through a repression of particular qualities on one side and their projection onto the other. Hence the understanding of masculinity as powerful, reasonable, and essentially of the mind is derived from the definition of femininity as vulnerable, emotional, and essentially of the body. She is the negative of what he wants to be. The purpose of examining such oppositions is not only to reveal the symbolic denigration of "the feminine." It is also to reveal the illusions on which the oppositions themselves, and the hierarchies they establish, are constructed: hierarchies of mind over body, reason over emotion, power over vulnerability.

By raising issues of desire and the body, French feminism finds deception at the base of the great, Western intellectual traditions which presume to derive Truth from the mind as separate from the body. In fact, the body or matter must be seen as contributing the very condition for thought. Indeed, just as the very highly theoretical and intellectually demanding focus of their address to the body would seem to render invalid any simple judgment of woman *as* body, so the analyses of French feminists work to demonstrate the fundamental inseparability and interdependence of concepts of mind and body, reason and emotion, and, ultimately, masculinity and femininity.

French feminism, then, or at least the particular subset of French feminism which was most influential in the United States, worked largely on the symbolic realm of existence as a source of psychical oppression and strove to invent ways of challenging those meanings. The slogan "No Revolution Without a Disruption of the Symbolic" brought criticisms from feminist activists who denounced French feminism's divorce from the real, social struggles of women, as well as from feminist critics who advocated the reading of female authored works. For many, however, they seemed to be getting at something deeper, something more foundational to woman's oppression under patriarchy. On one level, with their irreverent stance toward the traditional tools and hierarchies of academic analysis, French feminists offered to US feminism a means to safeguard feminist analysis from becoming just another critical method alongside the others. On a second level, because French feminists called attention to the inadequacies both of our language and of all systems of thought to address the question of "woman," they called for a revolution in theory in which women would be the principal actors and authors, a revolution in which the traditional divide between theory and practice would be effaced in the act of writing. In its US context, furthermore, the French feminist treatment of the so-called question of "woman" would undergo its own critical reevaluation to become an inquiry into the relation between the category of the feminine and the variety of ways in which women actually lived.

Contexts: de Beauvoir to Derrida; from and against

As a subset of the wider Women's Liberation Movement (MLF) which was born in France in the late 1960s, French feminism grew under the influence of three primary forces: the massive work of Simone de Beauvoir on woman's "condition," the assault on humanism waged by the new intellectual currents of postwar thought, and finally, the political atmosphere of May '68. While de Beauvoir rejected the term feminist, *The Second Sex*, published in 1949, was a landmark text for bringing the sexed body to the forefront of literary, political, and philosophical thought. Even though many of the feminists who followed her tended later to turn their backs on her, she was in many respects their intellectual mother. "Mother," it should be stressed, is a role that de Beauvoir deliberately distanced herself from, both in her life (she never had children) and in her thought, believing that it was primarily because of their identification with the maternal function that women were confined to a domestic role and prohibited from transcending their bodies and nature to become fully human. Women are rendered "the sex," "the other" of man, the center of the universe. "For him she is sex . . . She is defined and differentiated with reference to man and not he with reference to her; she is the incidental, the inessential as opposed to the essential. He is the Subject, he is the Absolute – she is the Other."[1]

The Second Sex focuses largely on the way women have been made into man's other and so robbed of their own ability to define themselves. In particular, the second volume describes the way "one is not born but becomes a woman" through changes wrought on women's bodies – changes which prepare them ultimately for maternity. Women have passively accepted the meanings men have imposed on them, but need not do so. De Beauvoir calls upon literary works by both men and women to document, on the one hand, the myths and fears of women perpetuated by male authors. Woman may represent poetry, she may be love, but above all, de Beauvoir shows, she is Nature to man's consciousness, the bodily other who either assures through opposition, or threatens by temptation, his intellectual and spiritual activity, hence his transcendence.[2] On the other hand, women's texts are used to represent women's experience of their bodies – the pain, disgust, and ultimately shame they sense from their bodily changes and functions, the way that women, too, come to regard their bodies as alienating, "something other than herself" (de Beauvoir, *The Second Sex*, p. 29).

De Beauvoir's emphasis on the material and psychological forces behind women's oppression, and her use of literature to politicize sex and make known the inequities of the sexual divide made *The Second Sex* an essential text for international feminism of the 1960s.[3] There is little questioning of whether language can ever give a transparent and truthful representation of experience. De Beauvoir's unquestioning acceptance of the patriarchal values which denigrate the body, femininity, and hence maternity will be troubling to later generations of feminists and to the French feminists in particular. "The 'feminine woman,'" she writes in her conclusion, "in making herself prey, tries to reduce man, also, to her carnal passivity . . . But the 'modern woman' accepts masculine values: she prides herself on thinking, taking action, working, creating, on the same terms as men" (p. 718). In other words, the "modern woman" is and will be one who says: "I too can be a man." She accepts the masculine as the norm for "authentic" humanity, a norm she, too, can incarnate, but only if she denies the difference of her feminine body and all that it may imply.[4]

French feminists rejected de Beauvoir's faith in agency (over the body as over language), and her espousal of patriarchal standards and values. They reversed her disdain for woman's body and made an empowering affirmation of its particularities, and, above all, its desires. They reversed, also, her apparent trust in the possibility of controlling and creating one's identity. This apparent rejection of agency would be criticized by other feminists as disempowering, as their affirmation of the body would be criticized as essentializing. How is it possible to envision a feminine difference which will not fall prey to othering and thereby confirm the definitions of femininity created by patriarchy? How is it possible to celebrate the body and woman's desires in the language of theory?

Almost twenty years after *The Second Sex* appeared, France experienced an unprecedented revolution – more ideological than political – which produced a "culture of protest" out of which a varied but forceful woman's movement would emerge.[5] May '68 began as a revolt against a dated educational system then became a more general movement against the bureaucratization of French life and institutions which, consequently, had no regard for individual needs and turned out carbon-copy humans capable only of following a routinized life: *"métro-bureau-dodo"* ("subway-work-sleep"). While '68 offered little in the way of a political agenda and so had only limited political effects, what it did was demonstrate that personal life was also a matter of politics, and this link between the personal and political would greatly influence the development of the women's movement. Politics was no longer considered simply the practice of parties and government, but a matter of how one lived one's everyday life, what it could be and what it could mean. As Claire Duchen explains:

> the anti-authority and anti-hierarchy basis of these new political ideas greatly influenced the way that the MLF was to operate. The way that women experienced the events, however, took them away from the mixed organizations with which they had been involved, and led to the formulation of the concept of sexual politics, which, as an examination of sexual and social relations deriving from a gendered social hierarchy, did not yet exist.
>
> (Duchen, *Feminism in France*, p. 7)

May '68 was formative both positively and negatively for the women's movement, for in their attempts to share in the anti-authoritarian stance, women came face to face with their subservience to the men in the movement who regarded them more as secretaries and caretakers rather than comrades in arms and ideas. It became increasingly clear to these women that a separate revolution would be necessary – one with "a completely different theory of oppression and exploitation, which placed gender squarely in the centre of their analysis" (p. 8).

What came to be known in the United States as French feminism represents only a small portion of the varied thinking within the MLF. As Claire Moses has argued, the particular interest of US critics in a handful of feminist theorists – Cixous, Irigaray, Kristeva – over and against the many concerns of the women's movement in general betrayed a bias – a literary/theoretical bias – on the part of the US academics responsible for importing their texts. Those such as Carolyn Burke and Elaine Marks who were initially responsible for introducing the texts of French feminism were themselves literary critics working in French. But what Moses terms "the engagement with discourses, the disinterest in events" was part of a larger turn in intellectual life which was itself imported from France.[6] The term "discourse", referring to the way one puts events or experience into language, regardless of the experience itself (if indeed there is an experience outside language) became a widespread critical term through the work of Michel Foucault. But much before Foucault, French philosophical thought was witnessing an antihumanist turn to language as what writes us, misrepresents us, imprisons us even, despite our efforts and beliefs to the contrary. In particular, the writings of Jacques Derrida and Jacques Lacan would provide a major influence on French feminists' methods of inquiry and critique; they who would eventually take the masters' tools to tear down these structures and reveal their patriarchal bias.

To summarize briefly, both Derrida and Lacan challenged the humanistic vision of the world advanced by phenomenology and existentialism whereby the subject is conceived of not only as agent (of choice, action in the world), but also as master/origin of meaning: the meaning of his self and the meaning or knowledge that he produces concerning the world around him. Poststructuralist psychoanalysis would undermine such notions of self-mastery by showing how even our unconscious is written for us. Lacan's rereadings of Freud emphasize what is only implicit in Freud, that subject-ivity is formed in and through language. The child's ability to establish the separateness from the mother that is necessary for subjectivity coincides with what Lacan will call his/her "entry into" language – emphasizing the fact that language precedes us. We are not only the active users of language, but because we can never invent it anew, we are also subjected to its terms and limitations – language writes us, too. For feminists, this perspective reveals how we are also born into patriarchy since language is its primary tool of subjection, writing even our unconscious. While alienation is at the crux of Lacanian subjectivity, women would appear to be doubly alienated from the means of self-knowledge.

Derridean deconstruction, which shifts the focus from subjects to the texts they write, waged a final assault on the logic of identity by replacing the very notion of identity with that of difference, or *"différance."* Written in French with an "a" to make it a verbal noun, *différance* emphasizes the illusory status of identity that is always being deferred – either spatially or temporally. To put it another way, identity is only negative – not this, not that, and it can never be absolute since it is always relational to something outside of itself. Derrida builds on the logic of difference to subvert what he calls the "logocentric" foundations of Western, metaphysical thought, its faith in a single origin of truth and meaning, or in a consciousness that can say "I am that I am" without reference to anything outside itself. Above all a strategy for critical reading, deconstruction examines these first things, these originary meanings such as man or truth or reason and it demonstrates how each defines itself through its difference from what it is not: woman (or animal), falsehood, emotion; and how that difference is turned, moreover, into a hierarchical opposition: man over woman, truth over falsehood. Here, of course, is where deconstruction begins to have specific value for feminism. If man can be defined only in reference to woman (or vice versa), then the definition of woman inhabits or is part of the definition of man. The differences which are constructed between entities in order to hierarchize between them mask differences within entities. As identities, masculine and feminine are political constructions, not innate essences.

In very different ways, the writings of Lacan and Derrida demonstrated how the meaning of the feminine is subordinated as they also point to the illusory logic that sustains such subordination. Each, that is, offers the possibility for subverting not only what Derrida calls logocentrism but also phallo-logocentrism: the false reasoning and/or false images by which man has asserted his primacy and power over women. At the same time, however, Lacan and Derrida created stumbling blocks for French feminists. Derridean *différance* has made it all but impossible to consider any difference as foundational – including sexual difference. Hence the idea of a specifically feminine language or desire is untenable within his philosophy. Lacan will go even further, granting that the feminine or woman has been excluded from knowledge, thereby making fun of any who might try to find her and speak for her:

> There is woman only as excluded by the nature of things which is the nature of words, and it has to be said that if there is one thing they themselves are complaining about enough at the moment, it is well and truly that – only they don't know what they are saying, which is all the difference between them and me.[7]

For all his deflation of phallic mastery, Lacan perpetuates the Freudian tradition of considering male subject formation as the norm for all subjectivity; a norm by whose standards female subjects are always regarded as lesser than or lacking. Finally, even as they may mock patriarchal rule, Lacanian theories seem to point to the inevitability of patriarchy and thus render futile any feminist attempts to undermine or change it.

For these reasons, French feminist theory has turned the reading strategies of their masters against them, revealing the phallocentrism of Lacan's and Derrida's own writings and also revealing, thereby, their potential conflict with feminist aims. Consequently, what was initially the most provocative notion of French feminism, at least for literary theory, that of *"écriture féminine,"* or "feminine writing," must be seen to be both built upon and turned against the philosophies of Derrida and Lacan. The term *"écriture"* itself is one that Derrida uses to correspond to the notion of *différance* and refers to a process of textual production in which meaning is never fully present, never totalizable, but, rather, always deferred or in process. What, then, can a feminine writing be, especially if femininity itself is void of identity? As we turn to the notion of "feminine writing" we begin to see the difficult line which French feminists tread, wanting, on the one hand, not to collude with a system of thought which has constructed identities such as femininity only to subordinate them, and on the other hand, to discover or, at least, imagine a different "feminine" which has been heretofore oppressed and unspoken because it is unspeakable within patriarchal language.

Is it French, is it feminist, is it theory?

In its promotion of a paradoxical writing practice, can we call French feminism a theory? It would appear that theory, like French and like femininsm, is a term not easily assumed. French feminism is hardly French, except perhaps in its constructed opposition to Anglo-American feminism.[8] Only one of the four principal proponents was a French native, Monique Wittig (and she subsequently moved to the United States); Hélène Cixous was born in Algeria, Luce Irigaray in Belgium, and Julia Kristeva in Bulgaria. On the other hand, these women came to writing in Paris in the late 1960s and early 1970s. Wittig was primarily a writer of fiction. Cixous had been trained as a literary scholar. Irigaray had trained in the Freudian school of Lacan but was expelled after the publication of the book which was her doctoral thesis, *Speculum of the Other Woman*. Kristeva went to Paris to train as a linguist and literary scholar and was active in a group responsible for producing the avant-garde literary magazine, *Tel Quel*. She also trained as a psychoanalyst and, like Irigaray, carries on a private practice.

Grouped by Americans as feminists, that label has not always been claimed by these women. What can feminism mean when woman is said not to exist? Wittig's essays, for instance, focus on the "category of sex" as a political construct of heterosexual society, designed to keep women as reproducers of the species and heterosexuality. Kristeva, more steeped in the Derridean philosophy of *différance* writes that *"woman as such* does not exist . . . it's useless to cling to our belief in the latest community except to obtain the right to abortion and the pill."[9] From this, it follows that a feminist practice can only be negative, at odds with what already exists so that we may say "'that's not it.'"[10] Wittig's novel *Les Guérrillères* (1968) represents a moment of this negativity in fictional form when women reject their bodies as a potential source of identity: "They say they must now stop exalting the vulva. They say that they must break the last bond that binds them to a dead culture."[11] The novel is structured around the invention of a new narrator, not the unmarked and universal "it" but a feminure and plural *"elles,"* a group of women united not by their essence but by their struggle. So, too, Wittig's feminist writing practice cannot be defined through women, but through a struggle against woman's patriarchal inscription.

With regard to the theoretical implications of such a practice, Wittig's confidence is closer to de Beauvoir than to Cixous or Irigaray. Wittig is most explicit about her debt to de Beauvoir, a debt which is evident in her ultimate faith in the neutrality of language and reason. Hence her linguistic experimentation, her play with symbols, pronouns, and even typography carves a special place for aesthetic practice, but this does not carry over into her theoretical essays. As Judith Butler writes: "for Wittig, language is an instrument or tool that is in no way misogynist in its structures, but only in its applications."[12] The point, for Wittig, is to take conscious control of the tool, whether in theory or in literary practice and in so doing prove that even the so-called "particular" point of view of a woman can be universal, can speak for the absolute subject. "Language as a whole gives everyone the same power of becoming an absolute subject through its exercise."[13] For Wittig, the absolute subject would also be the subject of theory.

For both de Beauvoir and Wittig, then, the linguistic subject is a rational subject who would usurp theory: "I believe we have not reached the end of what Reason can do for us."[14] For Cixous, Irigaray, and Kristeva, however, language, understood through Lacan and Derrida, is also that which splits the subject, subjecting it to structures of thought and expression outside its control and beyond its reason. Hence there can be no "absolute subject" and no theoretical subject either for man or for woman. Indeed, from their perspectives, theory itself is understood to be a phallic, if not fallacious position of those who presume to be, in Kristeva's terms, "masters of their speech." Mastery is achieved by excluding or even destroying what they cannot know or understand. In an essay entitled "Any Theory of the 'Subject' has Always Been Appropriated by the 'Masculine,'" Irigaray concurs that "Man's home has indeed become these/his theoretical elaborations." She identifies theoretical speculation with the mirror image of the speculum and specularity to suggest that "man only asks (himself) questions that he can already answer."[15]

Ecriture féminine, then, must not be a theoretical practice but rather, as Kristeva writes, must "call into question the very posture of this mastery"

(*NFF*, p. 65). It is an activity which disables any clear separation of inside and outside, subject and object, such that one cannot know whether one is mastering or being mastered. The subject does not write, "it writes," claims Cixous, referring to the ambiguous relation of subject and object in a writing practice controlled by unconscious drives. Hence, she claims, there can be no theory outside the practice itself: "it is impossible to *define* a feminine practice of writing . . . for this practice can never be theorized, enclosed, coded – which does not mean that it doesn't exist. But it will always surpass the discourse that regulates the phallocentric system" (*NFF*, p. 253).

Ecriture: *poetry or pathology*

Neither theory nor theorizable, *écriture féminine* is conceived of as a future, if not utopian practice. "I shall speak about women's writing: about *what it will do*," Cixous writes in her so-called manifesto, "The Laugh of the Medusa"(*NFF*, p. 245). Women must write their bodies, write their desires and so unleash their power. Despite denouncing theory, Cixous does not hesitate to describe and theorize a writing of and through the body which will liberate the "immense resources of the unconscious", "realize the decensored relation of woman to her sexuality," to her pleasure and thereby "confirm women in a place other than that which is reserved for her in the symbolic."[16] Indeed, she goes so far as to offer as example of such a writing the language of "those wonderful hysterics" who "subjected" Freud to their "passionate body-words, haunting him with their inaudible thundering."[17] "It is you Dora," she writes, invoking Freud's hysterical patient of that name, "who cannot be tamed, the poetic body, the true 'mistress' of the Signifier." Cixous's gleeful interpretation of Dora as heroine, representative of "the one who resists the system"(*NBW*, p. 154), points, simultaneously, to the precarious status of such a writing which hovers on the edge of protest and uninterpretable silence, of resistance and pathology, if not of poetry and theory. Indeed, Cixous's positing of the hysteric as successful rebel is criticized by her co-author, the anthropologist Catherine Clément: "The analysis I make of hysteria comes through my reflection on the place of deviants . . . They all occupy challenging positions foreseen by the social bodies, challenging functions within the scope of all cultures. That doesn't change the structures, however. On the contrary, it makes them more comfortable" (*NBW*, p. 155).

The limitations and possibilities of hysterical language will be taken to a most provocative end in the work of Irigaray where she connects hysteria not to a language of woman's own, but to mimicry. Hysterics have long been associated with imitation and especially imitation of traditional signs of femininity which might allow them to hide or disavow their unacceptable aggressive or erotic impulses. What other path than mimimcry is open to women, Irigaray asks, implying, thereby, that all women are, to some extent, hysterics. "How could she be anything but suggestible and hysterical when her sexual instincts have been castrated, her sexual feelings, representatives, and representations forbidden?" (*Speculum*, pp. 59–60). While the rhetorical question suggests that women have no way out, no other way to represent their desires because they have no language of their own, Irigaray also suggests that all is not lost in this performance: "hysterical miming will be the little girl's or woman's effort to save her sexuality from total repression and destruction" (p. 72). Indeed, she will go further, suggesting that a deliberate mimicry is a first phase of thwarting the traditional feminine role, by "convert[ing] a form of subordination into an affirmation" and affirming especially her otherness from that role.

> To play with mimesis is thus, for a woman, to try to recover the place of her exploitation by discourse, without allowing herself to be simply reduced to it. It means to resubmit herself – inasmuch as she is on the side of the "perceptible," of "matter" – to "ideas," in particular to ideas about herself, that are elaborated in/by a masculine logic, but so as to make "visible," by an effect of playful repetition, what was supposed to remain invisible: the cover-up of a possible operation of the feminine in language. It also means "to unveil" the fact that, if women are such good mimics, it is because they are not simply resorbed in this function. *They also remain elsewhere*: another case of the persistence of "matter," but also of "sexual pleasure".[18]

Mimicry, then, is not only a linguistic restriction, but also a strategy. It is Irigaray's principal strategy in *Speculum* for poking holes at phallologocentrism without presuming to stand outside of it. There, through a practice of citation of texts from Freud to Plato, Irigaray reverses the position and gender of speaking subject and spoken object – putting herself in the role of the philosopher pronouncing upon woman. She thereby calls attention to the logical blindspots of such pronouncements about femininity that her very stance negates. Mimicry, then, has subversive potential, but only as it also acknowledges women's imprisonment in a male language.

The pathological potential of *écriture féminine* is even more pronounced in its assimilation to what Kristeva calls the "semiotic" – a signifiying process understood, on the one hand, in relation to avant-garde poetics, and, on the other hand, through Lacanian theories of subject formation. Like Cixous, Kristeva shows great interest and faith in the power of certain avant-garde practices to produce ruptures in the symbolic, ruptures which may thus lead to changes in the very way the subject is produced. In the temporal terms of psychoanalytic subject formation, the semiotic is associated with the infant's bodily rhythms and instinctual drives, which will be repressed by so-called symbolic language. Even as this prelinguistic form of signification can only be known through symbolic language, it nevertheless has the power to "destroy the symbolic."[19] Thus, for Kristeva, the semiotic is the key to any change, any revolution in meaning. At the same time, however, Kristeva warns of dangers both for the psyche and for culture, since the drives are "always already ambiguous, simultaneously assimilating and destructive . . . the semiotized body [is] a place of permanent scission."[20] Hence Butler writes that Kristeva's theory is "self-defeating," since any sustained presence of the semiotic can lead to "psychosis and the breakdown of cultural life itself. Kristeva thus alternately posits and denies the semiotic as an emancipatory ideal."[21] From Cixous to Kristeva, therefore, the liberatory possibilities of writing a different desire seem increasingly undercut either by the power of symbolic language to force the repressed libido into a repetition of its own structures, or to cast its unleashed potential as pathological. At best, that different desire can be glimpsed at moments, or heard by a sympathetic ear, but it can never be fully articulated or represented.

The feminine: essence or difference

Thus far we have described the ambiguous status of this writing practice. But what of its relation to the feminine or, perhaps more importantly, to women? Even the term *"féminin"* in French contains an ambiguity and can be translated as either female or feminine. It can refer to sex and to gender; to what may be biological and innate, and to what is learned or acquired. Does a writing that is *"féminine"* come from the female body, or is it feminine only in its contestation of what is understood to be masculine and universal? The ambiguity of the term has led to the two major criticisms brought against *écriture féminine*: on the one hand, a charge of essentialism that denies the infinitely different, lived experiences of women; on the other, a modernist, rhetorical practice that risks doing away with women in its valorization of femininity. The latter case is reflected in Alice Jardine's examination of the way modernist thought has consistently coded as feminine that which has eluded its grasp, while at the same time neglecting women in the search to reincorporate that elusive space. Cixous and Kristeva pay tribute to such modernists as Kleist, Genet, and Artaud while similarly neglecting women writers. If male modernists, according to Cixous, inscribe "a proliferating, maternal femininity" (*NBW*, p. 84), what about female ones? Does a woman who writes/speaks as a woman or mother merely support the naturalization of sexed experience that modernist thinkers, feminists among them, have undertaken to subvert, and if so, how to speak of woman's femininity?

Irigaray suggests that as a kind of subversive writing, mimicry is only a first phase, to be followed by a more specific attempt at a *"parler-femme"* ("speaking (as) woman"). This would imply finding the means to express in language what the hysteric, for instance, can only express in pathological symptoms. The starting point for such expression is woman's discovery of her repressed desires and more specifically, her repressed pleasure or *jouissance*. The implication for Irigaray, as for Cixous, is that women's libido is not only repressed, but essentially different from man's. That difference, furthermore, gives rise to a different language. "A woman's body," Cixous writes in "The Laugh of the Medusa," "with its thousand and one thresholds of ardor – once, by smashing yokes and censors, she lets it articulate the profusion of meanings that run through it in every direction – will make the old single-grooved mother tongue reverberate with more than one language" (*NFF*, p. 256). Whereas Irigaray warns that "there is no simple manageable way to leap to the outside of phallogocentrism, *nor any possible way to situate oneself there, that would result from the simple fact of being a woman,*" she also writes that "woman's desire would not be expected to speak the same language as man's" (*This Sex*, pp. 162, 25). This is because, as she goes on to describe, women's pleasure functions according to a different, libidinal "economy" from the one where "whose is bigger?" has the most value. Indeed, even the question of "whose" does not funtion in the same way in this economy which, according to Irigaray, is foreign to the notion of property.

As the title of her later book, *This Sex Which is not One*, suggests, Irigaray designates the female sex as that which has no proper identity, nor proper form. Located in the in-between, as that which defies the borders between one and two, self and other, it is that which, in the male economy, would not count as sex. Whereas the male economy, especially as viewed through psychoanalysis, defines sexual identity around having or not having a penis, women's sexuality has no proper bodily part. "Woman has sex organs more or less everywhere" (*This Sex*, p. 28). Writing also of the "inanity of propriety," Cixous explains that woman is "capable of losing a part of herself without losing her integrity" (*NFF*, p. 259).

The promotion of feminine difference leads to experiments with prose that break normal syntax, effacing the borders between subject/verb or active/passive: "Text: my body . . . the rhythm that laughs you"(*NFF*, p. 252). Irigaray's "When Our Lips Speak Together," a lyrical meditation on the multiple organs – both oral and genital – through which woman expresses her desire renders the borders of identity a fluid exchange between self and other and effaces distinctions between singular and plural subjects: "Between our lips, yours and mine, several voices, several ways of speaking resound endlessly, back and forth. One is never separable from the other. You/I: we are always several at once." This deconstruction of singular identity leads, moreover, to an ethical imperative: "And how could one dominate the other? . . . one cannot be distinguished from the other; which does not mean that they are indistinct" (*This Sex*, p. 209).[22]

Kristeva also turns to motherhood as an ethical model, a "herethics," representing the ambiguity, the otherness within all subjectivity. Her own experimental prose is explicitly linked to the maternal through the semiotic – those bodily rhythms and pulses which create a signifying bond between mother and infant both in the womb and in the period after birth. Such are the drives which will be repressed by what Freud calls the oedipal phase, and what Lacan calls the symbolic – associated with the institution of the paternal law which forces the infant to give up his attachment to his mother and take his correct, independent, subject postion. Kristeva's focus on the semiotic is an atttempt to displace the Lacanian emphasis on the father's role in the production of language and to give prominence to the mother in organizing the drives into a presymbolic or pre-oedipal signifying system. Whereas certain aesthetic practices can allow for access to this expression, Kristeva argues that women can attain it "through the strange form of split symbolization (threshold of language and instinctual drive, of the 'symbolic' and the 'semiotic') of which the act of giving birth consists."[23] Contesting the Judeo-Christian repression of the mother's voice by speaking as mother in her essay "Stabat Mater," she represents this splitting through the splitting of the pages: the left side taken by the "impossible" language of the mother, the right by a scholarly discourse on motherhood. If the left side is impossible, it is because it is signification without a subject: "It happens, but I'm not there," as she explains in "Motherhood According to Bellini."[24] "No communication between individuals but connections between atoms, molecules, wisps of words, droplets of sentences."[25] Such communication can be recognized only in parts through a language that is foreign to it – that of the subject in the symbolic.

The focus on the maternal represents a decisive shift from de Beauvoir's denunciation of motherhood and resistance to any designation of feminine difference. Indeed, it is around the French feminist focus on the maternal that the loudest charges of essentialism have been raised by feminist critics.[26] Cixous's identification of feminine writing with mother's milk ("she writes with white ink," *NBW*, p. 95) or Irigaray's evocation of woman's speech as an exchange of fluid, "a flux that never congeals or solidifies" (*This Sex*, p. 215) appears to locate the essence of femininity and feminine writing in biology if not in a specific maternal experience which all women do not share. Kristeva's identification of maternal and semiotic, moreover, seems to reinscribe patriarchal definitions of the mother as other, outside culture, potentially psychotic, and in need of the paternal law to be spoken. What can the value of this focus on the maternal be for feminist theory?

In an effort to rethink the terms of the critique waged against French feminists, Naomi Schor writes that "the anti-essentialist aspect of their work is that which is most derivative, that is most Derridean. When Cixous and Irigaray cease to mime the master's voice and speak in their own voices, they speak a dialect of essentialese, the language of what they construe as feminine." Rather than condemn this as a slip, however, Schor suggests it would be "ultimately more interesting and more difficult to attempt to understand just how and why Cixous and Irigaray deconstruct and construct femininity at the same time."[27] This construction of identity in the face of its necessary deconstruction has led to one of the most important turns in recent feminist theory, that of reevaluating essentialism as a potential strategy.[28] Kristeva herself asserted early on that "we must use 'we are women' as an advertisement or slogan for our demands" (*NFF*, p. 137), an acknowledgment seconded by Toril Moi when she comments that "it still remains *politically* essential for feminists to defend women as women in order to counteract the patriarchal oppression that precisely despises women *as* women."[29]

But the strategic value of essentialism goes beyond strictly political gains, to the less immediate and less material effects of a change in the meanings of femininity and its associations. Most relevant in this regard is Margaret Whitford's evaluation of Irigaray as a "theorist of change, seeking to define the conditions under which change could take place." What Irigaray wants most to change is the dominance of the "male imaginary" over our culture, thereby "uncovering the female imaginary and bringing it into language."[30] "I am trying," Irigaray wtites, "to go back through the masculine imaginary, to interpret the way it has reduced us to silence, to muteness or mimicry, and I am attempting, from that starting point and at the same time, to (re) discover a possible space for the feminine imaginary" (*This Sex*, p. 164). That dominance, she argues, has been gained through a kind of matricide by which patriarchy has buried its connections to the feminine and to the body or matter. Patriarchal culture has repressed its own maternal origins and it has made it impossible for women to represent or imagine their own relation to the mother by refusing her difference from the male subject.

Antigone, not Oedipus, is the mythical figure Irigaray turns to in order to demonstrate the resulting genealogical impasse for women. Antigone can envision a future only through her brother. As a woman she has no future and identifies with her mother not in giving life, but in suicide. "She will cut off her breath . . . so that her brother, her mother's desire, may have eternal life. She never becomes a woman" (*Speculum*, p. 219).

The first step, then, is for woman to imagine her relation to her mother's body, in order to reverse the devaluation of her origins and her "imaginary" within culture . . . "imagine woman imagines . . . " (p. 133). As Whitford explains, Irigaray's imaginary is somewhere between the phenomenological notion of the imagination and the Lacanian "imaginary" – his term for the stage which precedes the symbolic.[31] Like the semiotic, the imaginary is associated with the mother, whose connection to the infant has not yet been broken by paternal law. Where the imaginary is presymbolic, the imagination is post; it depends on the symbolic to produce its images and narratives. Irigaray would like to make clear, moreover, that the imaginary, like the imagination, is sexed, "bearing the morphological marks" of either the male or female body. What this means, for Irigaray, is that neither imaginary can substitute for the other, neither is universal. Whereas both the phenomenological imagination and the Lacanian imaginary are associated with illusion or fiction as opposed to scientific truth, truth is not a critera for evaluation for Irigaray's imaginary. What is important is that the images with which we represent our desire be life-sustaining, and sustaining of an other, bodily, pleasure. "And what I wanted from you, Mother, was this: that in giving me life, you still remain alive."[32]

The "feminine" of *écriture féminine* must not be regarded as representing something which exists in the world, but as (re)productive, giving life to new possibilities for imagining and so living women's bodies and desires. Some have said that this feminine is not feminist enough, not sufficiently engaged with the world to effect change. Others would call it "postfeminist," referring to its refusal to embrace stable definitions of women and their interests which drive political agendas.[33] What is femin*ist* about French feminism? On the one hand, all four of the writers I have discussed reject the traditional feminist denigration of the body and of feminine pleasure. On the other hand, all also recognize the dangers of essentializing or homogenizing women's bodies under the oppressive conditions of patriarchy. French feminists also reject Marxist and liberal notions of agency and choice, instead relying on theorists who emphasize the unconscious, the split subject and the primacy of language. At the same time, these writers want to go beyond the playful deconstruction of the male tradition, and strive to write in such a way as to open up another space for female imagining and action. French feminists used *écriture* as a weapon not to represent the feminine but to create it through experimental poetics. By creating the feminine in their own work, they hoped to provoke women to participate in reimagining their lives and their world. Such a provocation has immense political and aesthetic possibilities that are still untapped today.

Further reading

Carolyn Burke, Naomi Schor, and Margaret Whitford, eds., *Engaging with Irigaray: Feminist Philosophy and Modern European Thought* (New York: Columbia University Press, 1994).

Hélène Cixous, *Coming to Writing and Other Essays*, ed. Deborah Jenson (Cambridge, MA: Harvard University Press, 1991).

Verena Andermatt Conley, *Hélène Cixous: Writing the Feminine* (Lincoln and London: University of Nebraska Press, 1984).

Christine Delphy, "The Invention of French Feminism: An Essential Move," *Yale French Studies* 87 (1995), pp. 166–97.

Nancy Fraser and Sandra Lee Bartky, eds., *Revaluing French Feminism* (Bloomington and Indianapolis: Indiana University Press, 1992).

Jane Gallop, *The Daughter's Seduction: Feminism and Psychoanalysis* (Ithaca: Cornell University Press, 1982).

Elizabeth Grosz, *Sexual Subversions: Three French Feminists* (Sydney: Allen and Unwin, 1989).

Alice Jardine, "Opaque Texts and Transparent Contexts: The Political Difference of Julia Kristeva," in Nancy Miller, ed., *The Poetics of Gender* (New York: Columbia University Press 1986).

Ann Rosalind Jones, "Writing the Body: Toward an Understanding of L'Ecriture Féminine," *Feminist Studies*: 2 (Summer, 1981), pp. 247–63.

Toril Moi, ed., *French Feminist Thought, A Reader* (Oxford and New York: Blackwell, 1987).

Kelly Oliver, ed., *The Portable Kristeva* (New York: Columbia University Press, 1997).

ed., *French Feminism Reader* (Lanham, MD: Rowman and Littlefield, 2000).

Gayatri Chakravorty Spivak, "French Feminism in an International Frame," *Yale French Studies* 62 (1981), pp. 154–84.

Margaret Whitford, ed., *The Irigaray Reader* (Cambridge: Blackwell, 1991).

NOTES

1. Simone de Beauvoir, *The Second Sex*, trans. H. M. Parshley (New York: Vintage, 1989), p. xxii.
2. Transcendence is a term that de Beauvoir takes from existential philosophy to refer to the means by which an individual justifies his or her existence by engaging in freely chosen projects.

3. On this point, see Toril Moi, *Sexual/Textual Politics: Feminist Literary Theory* (London: Methuen, 1985).

4. In existential philosophy the "authentic" individual is one who accepts his or her freedom of self-definition and who engages in projects which further that definition.

5. On the "culture of protest" and its relation to French feminism, see Claire Duchen, *Feminism in France: From May '68 to Mitterand* (London, Boston, and Henley: Routledge and Kegan Paul, 1986), p. 5 *passim*. Further references will be cited in parentheses in the text.

6. Claire Moses, "Made in America: 'French Feminism' in Academia," *Feminist Studies* 24:2 (Summer 1998), p. 284.

7. Jacques Lacan, "God and the *Jouissance* of the Woman," in ed. Juliet Mitchell and Jacqueline Rose, eds., *Feminine Sexuality* (New York: W. W. Norton & Co., 1985), p. 144.

8. On the construction of French feminism in opposition to Anglo-American feminism, see Moi's *Sexual/Textual Politics* and Moses's "Made in America."

9. Julia Kristeva, *About Chinese Women*, trans. Anita Barows (New York: Marion Boyars, 1986), p. 16.

10. Julia Kristeva, "Woman Can Never Be Defined," in Elaine Marks and Isabelle de Courtivron, eds., *New French Feminisms* (New York: Schocken Books, 1981), p. 137. Further references to this collection will be cited in parantheses in the text as *NFF*.

11. Monique Wittig, *Les Guérillères,* trans. David Le Vay (Boston: Beacon Press, 1969), p. 72.

12. Judith Butler, *Gender Trouble: Feminism and the Subversion of Identity* (New York and London: Routledge, 1990), p. 26.

13. See the chapter entitled, "The Point of View: Universal or Particular?," in Monique Wittig, *The Straight Mind and Other Essays* (Boston: Beacon Press, 1992).

14. Wittig, "Homo Sum," in *The Straight Mind*, p. 56.

15. Luce Irigaray, *Speculum of the Other Woman*, trans. Gillian C. Gill (Ithaca: Cornell University Press, 1985), p. 137.

16. The essay is appropriately placed in a section of *New French Feminisms* called "Utopias."

17. Hélène Cixous and Catherine Clément, *The Newly Born Woman*, trans. Betsy Wing (Minneapolis: University of Minnesota Press, 1975), p. 95. Further references will be cited in parentheses in the text as *NBW*.

18. Luce Irigaray, *This Sex Which Is Not One*, trans. Catherine Porter (Ithaca: Cornell University Press, 1985), p. 76.

19. Julia Kristeva, *Revolution in Poetic Language,* trans. Margaret Waller, in Toril Moi, ed., *The Kristeva Reader* (New York: Columbia University Press, 1986), p. 103.

20. Ibid., p. 95.

21. Butler, *Gender Trouble*, p. 80.

22. Ethics will be the central concern of Irigaray's 1984 text, *The Ethics of Sexual Difference*, translated in 1993.

23. Julia Kristeva, "Motherhood According to Bellini," *Desire in Language*, ed. Leon S. Roudiez (New York: Columbia University Press, 1980), p. 240.

24. Ibid., p. 237.

25. Kristeva, "Stabat Mater," in Moi, ed., *The Kristeva Reader,* p. 181.

26. See, for instance, Domna Stanton, "Difference on Trial: A Critique of the Maternal Metaphor in Cixous, Irigaray, and Kristeva" in Nancy Miller, ed., *The Poetics of Gender* (New York: Columbia University Press, 1986).

27. Naomi Schor, "Introducing Feminism," in Schor, *Paragraph 8* (Oxford: Oxford University Press, 1986), pp. 98–9.

28. Those most influential in this regard would include Diana Fuss, Naomi Schor, Gayatri Spivak, and Margaret Whitford. See Naomi Schor and Elizabeth Weed, *The Essential Difference* (Bloomington: Indiana University Press, 1994).

29. Moi, *Sexual/Textual Politics*, p. 13.

30. Margaret Whitford, "Luce Irigaray and the Female Imaginary: Speaking as a Woman," *Radical Philosophy* 43 (Summer, 1986), p. 3.

31. For a fuller explanation, see Whitford, "Luce Irigaray," pp. 3–4.

32. Luce Irigaray, "And One Doesn't Stir Without the Other," trans. Hélène Vivienne Wenzel, *Signs* 7:1 (Autumn, 1981), p. 67.

33. Sophia Phoca and Rebecca Wright, *Introducing Postfeminism* (New York: Totem Books, 1999).

8

NICKIANNE MOODY

Feminism and popular culture

The study of popular culture addresses both media texts and cultural practices. This ever-expanding area of scholarship includes film, science fiction, television, romance novels, popular music, magazines: all the seeming ephemera in the public domain that through its popularity remains in production and circulation or has attained a place in cultural memory. As a field that encompasses and interrogates the production, distribution, and interpretation of all popular media forms, this much-maligned discipline demands particularly stringent intellectual and methodological rigor. Feminist interventions in the field have been both inspiring and infuriating. For example, Germaine Greer's three and sixpence purchase of the two romance novels analyzed in *The Female Eunuch* does not actually misrepresent the genre, but her anecdotal discussion of their impact falls short of the systematic methodology expected in scholarly research in popular culture.[1]

Difficulties in studying popular culture arise from the scale of the mass media, its ephemeral nature, and the paradox of its apparent inconsequence. Feminist analysis of popular culture intensifies the debate over whether popular texts merely reflect society or act as part of the process of mediation in social life. The understanding that popular and mass media texts act as sites of cultural practice, which Greer acknowledges in her discussion, links popular culture directly to ways of thinking, feeling, and acting in the world. The status of these texts as shared cultural reference points that make visible ideologies, discourses, and values is a major topic of feminist analysis. Popular culture constitutes a space of exchange between dominant and subordinate cultures and provides a valuable area of study for those who hope to understand social change. The interest that feminist researchers have had in popular fiction, popular music, youth culture, and the experience of media in everyday life has contributed significantly to the development of both method and theory in this multidisciplinary field.

The development of cultural studies

Feminist popular culture studies are part of the broader field of cultural studies. Marxist thought has dominated the development of cultural studies and more particularly the study of popular culture in both the United States and Britain. Introducing their reader *Popular Culture: Production and Consumption* (2001), C. Lee Harrington and Denise Bielby[2] identify four approaches to research in this field. The two dominant traditions, British and US, develop in the mid-twentieth-century and use early social theory in order to consider contemporary cultural experience. British cultural studies is generally associated with the Centre for Contemporary Cultural Studies formed at the University of Birmingham in 1964. The Centre is aligned with the broad Marxist tradition, but it draws on a range of theoretical paradigms and traditions. One of its major contributions to the contemporary analysis of popular culture is the use researchers have made of the early twentieth-century Italian political theorist Antonio Gramsci. Gramsci proposed the concept of hegemony to understand the role of popular culture in establishing a political consensus, an arrangement whereby the subordinate class accepts the worldview of the dominant class as common sense. Gramsci's theory posits moments of resistance to the prevailing ideology of the dominant class, which lead to a struggle to remake the hegemony. The theory of hegemony conceives of popular culture as a decisive location for imagining radical change, though it is understood that popular texts will always, ultimately, work to reestablish the consensus they temporarily challenge. Seen from this perspective, consumers of popular culture need not be considered as passive. Rather, they are active participants in the creation of meaning, and their activity includes resistance to their subordination. This recognition of the unavoidable process of negotiation in the construction of any hegemony has been particularly useful to feminist researchers studying popular culture and its contribution to gender socialization.

On the other hand, during the 1970s US analyses of popular culture were influenced by theories developed in an alternative Marxist tradition. Max Horkheimer, director of the Institute of Social Research affiliated to the University of Frankfurt during its exile in the United States in the 1930s, was particularly interested in the production of the culture industry, rather than in the consumption and meaning of popular culture. In the 1940s Horkheimer and Theodor Adorno, another member of the Frankfurt school, examined the standardized production of culture for a homogenized audience. Their interest in production encouraged US researchers to develop methodologies that focused on interactions between those involved in the economic processes of contemporary cultural industries and the status of popular forms as commodities.[3]

The third, more consciously interdisciplinary approach that develops in the same period is primarily concerned with defending the legitimacy of studying popular culture. The championing of cultural studies is associated with the publication of the US *Journal of Popular Culture* in 1969 and the founding of the Department of Popular Culture at Bowling Green State University in Ohio, in 1972. Alongside these initiatives, the Popular Culture Association, established in 1970, acted as a forum through which researchers from different disciplines and international perspectives could study popular culture and establish a network through which to debate their findings. The necessarily interdisciplinary nature of this network – drawing together scholars from many established disciplines – continues to shape current scholarship in the field.

Finally, the fourth approach outlined by Harrington and Bielby emerges from a redefinition of cultural studies in Britain instigated by the Open University at Milton Keynes. in the late 1990s. An example of this new direction can be found in *Doing Cultural Studies: The Study of the Sony Walkman* (1997), where Paul du Gay[4] outlines "the circuit of culture" and the necessity of connecting the worlds of cultural production and consumption in order to understand the circulation of cultural meaning. Du Gay argues that if we want to understand the social, personal and political implications of cultural practices, we must expand our sites of inquiry from consumption and production to include identity, representation, and the relationship between different media forms. While demonstrating the complexity of the task of understanding popular culture, du Gay's study particularly highlights the theoretical (and resource) implications of scale involved when studying contemporary culture. Curiously, although feminist scholars have contributed a great deal to studies of identity and representation, the only discussion of female roles and identities in his project is a brief mention of how mothers have the potential to influence family spending. Du Gay's analysis fails to acknowledge the significance of Sony Walkman's 1980s advertising campaign, which represented liberated women as potential Sony consumers.

The analysis of popular culture

For a text to become genuinely popular and have significant collective meaning in complex social contexts, its appeal needs to be heterogeneous. It cannot, therefore, simply interpellate a single subject position; it *must* be accessible to multiple cultural identities. Popular texts are always polysemic, porous, and marked by significant interstices. They are open to contradictory readings and capable of articulating ambiguity or negotiating tensions in cultural values. This means that we must look at popular culture en masse and in detail, avoiding the temptation to dismiss it as simplistic. If we understand popular culture as a site of struggle and its study as the pursuit of *how* texts and practices generate meaning, then, concepts such as "masculine" and "feminine" appear unstable, not monolithic. We can see that they have to be continually remade and that popular cultural contributes to that process. Across historical moments, femininity will be made to mean in different ways, and those shifting meanings will be contested. The recognition of the destabilizing potential of this process of cultural exchange has ensured the appeal of the study of popular culture to feminist theorists. In the pages that follow, I offer a sampling of the scholarly work in which they have pursued that appeal and traced its social and political force.

Approaches and applications: gender ideology in popular fiction

In *Women's Oppression Today* (1988), Michèle Barrett discusses the mechanisms by which textual representations reproduce gender ideology through the use of different conventions. She identifies the common use of stereotyping, collusion, compensation, and recuperation. Stereotyped images are standardized, fixed by convention and common sense, which is difficult to dispute. They contribute to the process of collusion, whereby the audience tacitly agrees with received ideas in order to participate in or enjoy popular culture. Compensation is the process that maintains a discourse concerning the moral *value* of femininity, while recuperation negates challenges to dominant gender ideology that may emerge in the text.[5] These terms are useful for interpreting the complexly consensual nature of popular texts. Andrew Milner sees the attraction of studying popular culture as lying in its potential for subversion and the constant interplay between subordinate and dominant class positions evident in everyday interactions.[6] In this instance, it is the interrogation of and challenge to patriarchy that popular culture offers or denies that is of most significance.

Images of women

In her discussion of the relationship between feminism and research in popular culture, Joanne Hollows makes a distinction between two approaches to media texts that characterize early feminist work. She distinguishes these as the "images of women" readings and interpretations focused on "images for women."[7] The first position is concerned with how the media creates stereotypes and misrepresents the realities of women's lives and of social change, thus sustaining patriarchal images and values. The second approach is equally convinced of the direct effect of the media on its audiences, but introduces the concept of "women as images." Popular culture, especially Hollywood film, is argued to be produced for consumption by a male spectator, thus requiring women to collude with masculine desires, as they have no other subject position from which to engage with the narrative or filmic spectacle. Hollows sees the first approach as triggered by an interest in image and the representation of femininity originating in Betty Friedan's examination of the media in *The Feminine Mystique* (1971). The content analysis of these early studies demonstrated the extent of media stereotyping, but, as often happens in text-based approaches modeled on literary criticism, meaning was taken to be self-evident and the audience imagined as without recourse. Such analysis did (and still does) concentrate on the way the media misrepresents women and critiques damaging patriarchal imagery. This type of media analysis presents valid criticism, but it ignores the relationship between theory and experience that is so vital to current research in popular culture. The audience's lively engagement with (and sometimes contestation of) texts is overlooked.

Taking Gaye Tuchman's 1978 essay "The Symbolic Annihilation of Women by the Mass Media" as an example, Hollows argues that this approach assumes that the media has a direct, unified effect on its audience.[8] She identifies a shift in the 1970s, when feminist film critics suggested that analysis should focus upon "women as images." This change produced extremely important contributions to the analysis of popular film, culminating in Laura Mulvey's 1975 essay "Visual Pleasure and Narrative Cinema." In her analysis Mulvey appropriated psychoanalysis to explain how images of women were coded as objects of pleasure for the gaze of the male spectator. The essay made gender and spectatorship central concerns within feminist film criticism and validated the study of popular classical Hollywood film. As rich as this theoretical approach has been, it, too, fails to encompass the idea of an active audience that may reject or mediate any subject position.

Images for women

The study of images for women has a different agenda. Hollows emphasizes that it is motivated by an interest in legitimating the study of women's genres.[9] In this way feminist analysis could broaden its scope to include many areas of popular culture, including genre fiction. One of the main genres of popular fiction given serious consideration by feminist writing is the romance novel. Romance is a more complex formula to define than it may appear. Many different kinds of women's writing are grouped together under this category, and the range of the genre is further complicated by a high percentage of reprinting and recycling of earlier narratives. The most common area of feminist research in romance fiction is the Mills and Boon/ Harlequin series. These texts condense the romance formula by focusing on the heterosexual couple almost to the exclusion of women's other roles and relationships. The narratives tend to culminate in declarations of love and commitment and do not pursue the experience of the relationship beyond this point.[10] Although these novels are not necessarily homogeneous and do respond to changes in cultural climate, they are structured around a "narrative logic of romance."[11] They do, however, demonstrate how flexible patriarchal ideology has to be in order to maintain its credibility for new generations of women. Feminist researchers who have studied this ideological formation are often concerned with women's participation in maintaining patriarchy. This interest in the reproduction of ideology marks a point of convergence between feminist theories of popular culture and feminist literary studies.

High literary culture: reading and narrative strategies

Even as feminist popular cultural studies developed during the 1970s and 1980s, feminist literary scholars undertook to recover and celebrate a female literary tradition; this research, though concerned with "high culture," is relevant to examinations of women's popular cultural production. (Indeed, theorists from both fields have questioned the usefulness and clarity of the distinction between high and low.) Early examples of this literary analysis included Elaine Showalter's *A Literature of Their Own* (1978) and Ellen Moers's *Literary Women* (1977). These studies provided frameworks for understanding the narrative strategies employed by female authors who ventured into print during the nineteenth century and the process of women's collective reading experience in the period.

Subsequently, these models proved useful for analyzing contemporary work, allowing systematic examination of assumptions about women's cultural production. As Judith Newton observes, "In these novels, in particular, the very covertness of power, the nature and degree of its disguise are material tactics of the resisting weak, are social strategies for managing the most intense and compelling rebellions."[12] In order to explain the interconnection of this fiction and its function as a site of protest, Newton uses Raymond Williams's concept of a "structure of feeling"[13] to refer to an emerging development of consciousness that proposes alternative or

NICKIANNE MOODY

oppositional responses to dominant ideology.[14] Although her analysis is drawn from literary studies, Newton's aim is to understand the relationship between cultural contexts and how texts are read. She wants to consider "how ideologies governing middle class women intersect with and are interdependent upon more general ideologies which sustain and legitimate the power of the male bourgeoisie in relation to society as a whole."[15] Indeed, she is interested in examining how works of literary fiction function as popular culture in the way they articulate and circulate ideas, images, and values that support and resist oppressive ideology. As Dale Spender has noted, the connection between women's access to literacy and participation in commercial publishing during the eighteenth century cast them as a threat to a masculine literary heritage, and thus they have been excluded from it.[16]

Newton's discussion of power in nineteenth-century women's novels is framed by her account of the negative reaction she experienced from staff and students when she taught a course on women's literature from a feminist perspective at La Salle College in 1974. Such responses to literature courses helped to make the canon of popular culture a route to broadening scholarly discussion of feminism. Sarah Lefanu's[17] experience teaching feminism and science fiction for adult education classes in London was far more satisfying. Lefanu asks whether science fiction as a genre offers women writers the opportunity to consider politics within a more appropriate imaginative space. She finds evidence of the use of science fiction by women to narrativize social inquiry about patriarchy and also as a philosophical tool to explore feminist thought. Science fiction becomes a form through which feminist thought is both articulated and disseminated. Lefanu's analysis centers on texts such as Marge Piercy's *Woman on the Edge of Time*, Joanna Russ's *The Female Man*, and Suzy McKee Charnas's *Walk to the End of the World*. Feminist writers in the genre imagine and explore separatist communities, the exacerbation of women's oppression, the relationship between patriarchy and capitalism, women's roles, and the deconstruction of patriarchal language. Similar observations can be made of women writers and audiences who appropriated both the detective genre and the western during the 1980s and 1990s. This particular use of popular cultural forms by feminist writers and academics and writers has played a major role in introducing feminist theory to the curriculum outside women's studies. But in recent years the main concern of feminist analysis has been adolescent popular fiction.

Genre and adolescence

While accepting the possibility of resistant or subversive readings of the magazine *Jackie*, Angela McRobbie is concerned with how teen magazines construct adolescent femininity. She observes that the repetition of style, form, and content affirms a set of values about the biologically fixed career for women. The address of the magazine invites the reader to enter an intimate sorority, only to reveal that the narrative of romantic success is predicated on a contradictory competitiveness with other women.[18] The stories reach happy or sad conclusions determined by whether a girl remains single or becomes part of a heterosexual couple. The romantic idealization in these narratives contrasts with the accounts of relationships with boys discussed on the problem page, but adolescent romantic ideology is none-theless predicated on the moment of bliss, the essential successful moment in the feminine career. And yet, "the 'romantic moment' at its central 'core' cannot be reconciled with its promise for eternity" ("*Jackie*: An Ideology," p. 273). *Jackie* supplies the appropriate response for these disappointments through tips on fashion and make-up, confidence-building advice, and promoting the belief that both romance and being a girl are "fun" (p. 273).

McRobbie notes that *Jackie* is read rebelliously, specifically in opposition to school, which appears only within the problem pages; the admittedly nebulous social world of the stories is located in the flats and working lives of the older teenage characters. This indistinct environment provides neu-tral space, mundane locations that are transformed into the moments of a feminine career delimited by courtship, marriage, and motherhood. McRobbie indicates that the reading of *Jackie* may be a shared culture that will remain elusive to cultural researchers: "until we have a clear idea of just how girls 'read' *Jackie* and encounter its ideological force, our analysis remains one-sided" (p. 282). One of the points McRobbie makes concerns the magazine's compartmentalized and fragmented structure, which I think is significant to its potential to function as shared culture. This fragmenta-tion affords specific readers choices that prompt discussion. Moreover, its fashion features present choices and economic alternatives and, as the adventure of romance takes place in the potential world of employment, flat shares, and the city, it invites speculation as to the cultural meaning specific to any given group of readers. The quizzes, true-life confessions and dilemmas support this premise; they all seem to require discussion and debate to enhance their pleasure. Since *Jackie* represents an early stage in the feminine reading career and cannot resolve the romantic paradox through the culmination of the love affair in sex or marriage, it perpetuates the anticipation of choice and the prospect of freedom. Two interesting themes that McRobbie does not pursue, the refusal entirely to condone male infidelity and the acceptance of discovering that if a boy is not your type you should try again, might be relevant to discuss with this generation of readers. Before the magazine folded, it was possible to find within the safe confines of its Cathy and Claire problem page special extended narratives about mixed-race relationships, the anticipation of college, and the experience of working-class girls' lives, all of which intruded into considerations of the romantic ideal.

Given the pronounced age stratification characteristic of popular culture, the idea that *Jackie* constitutes the adolescent stage of the feminine reading career is extremely interesting. This model contrasts with the hobby and leisure magazines of the same period that were produced for men and boys and articulated very different identities and lifestyles. *Jackie*'s role in the feminine reading career was to overturn the license of adventure stories available for pre-adolescent girls. These adventure stories for a younger audience featured a group of girls whose activity was licensed because they acted for the good of the local community. *Jackie* met the need to replace this pre-teen authorized adventure with the ideology of romance. The ideology of romance needed to be introduced before the *Jackie* audience could move on to the more glamorous sexual world of glossy women's magazines, which would then in turn be replaced by reading matter focused on housekeeping. This progression of reading and socialization into roles, behaviors, and expectations is a part of a compensatory culture; McRobbie's reading identifies the significant reconfiguration that takes place as romance is replaced by consumerism as a defining adolescent ideal.

The key term in McRobbie's discussion of teenage popular culture is adolescence. In her essay "Femininity and Adolescence," Barbara Hudson bases her discussion on interviews with fifty teenage girls, local teachers, and social workers. She finds that "femininity and adolescence are *subversive* of one another" because adolescence is a "masculine" construct.[19] An inherent conflict emerges when the two are combined. Hudson uses the Foucauldian concept of discourse to locate teenage magazines within "the matrix of ideas, terminology and practices surrounding the area of social life at a particular time."[20] Through her interviews with participants in that social life, she can demonstrate that knowledge of femininity is drawn from ideology articulated as the attitudes and expectations of older people. This means that even when girls have experiential knowledge that contradicts the romantic ideals of fiction or other aspects of femininity that are discursively structured, they do not have the vocabulary to pursue alternative viewpoints and may be forced to return to the narrative evaluations of the feminine career.

Such studies of popular culture from feminist perspectives are typical of the small scale of ethnographic research. Ethnography, which sets out to describe everyday life, is by necessity narrow in its scope and has to be read in conjunction with many other sources. Its strength lies in its ability to detect and analyze cognitive dissonance, appreciating that what people say is not necessarily a sure guide to what they actually do. This approach allows researchers to consider the meaning of femininity, resistance to feminine socialization, and even the rejection of feminism through the practices and ideology of consumer culture that underpin postfeminism.

Popular music and popular television

Sara Douglas argues that the popular culture of the late 1950s and early 1960s made a significant contribution to its audience's participation in the women's movement in the later 1960s and the 1970s.[21] In particular, she identifies a new genre of music, "girl talk," that enabled expression for teenage girls chafing under patriarchal restrictions, though it did not necessarily dispute the validity of these constraining ideologies. The "girl talk" genre of popular music brought the contradictions of gender inequality and the double standard clearly to the surface of teenage female listeners' consciousnesses. As John Cawelti has noted, in the study of popular fiction, new genres act as narrative forms engaged with existing social interests and attitudes that "assist in the process of assimilating changes in values to traditional imaginative constructs."[22] He argues that they negotiate emergent tensions and ambiguities in values by providing narrative spaces designed to open up these conflicts and allow exploration of taboo areas.[23] Popular culture can accommodate multiple subject positions and allow for the consideration of alternative ways of living. Transferring this logic of cultural negotiation from popular fiction to popular music, Douglas argues that in the popular culture of the period femininity is rendered visible as a masquerade; more specifically, the pleasures of the "girl talk" musical genre provided the opportunity to try on for size different perspectives and reactions to adult gender roles. This process works precisely because popular culture does not have an essential meaning; it may be structured by a dominant discourse, but its pleasure lies in its polysemy and in the ways it can be shared. The contradictions of patriarchal logic and the Manichean divides between female representations can be readily discerned, challenged, and ridiculed, even while inviting empathy.

Douglas's detailed analysis of various forms of popular culture from the period, especially the fantastic narrative environments of *Bewitched* and *I Dream of Genie*, demonstrates this by outlining the cultural climate that immediately preceded second-wave feminism in the United States. It emphasizes the significance of media literacy and the everyday experience of the cultural practices associated with teenage narrative engagement that had an impact on lifestyle choice. Douglas argues that despite the overt ideological content of these programs (where witchcraft and magic are subsumed or used in the service of the domestic sphere), female audiences would respond to the character's potential for subversion. Recognizing that the characters' heavily gendered domestic position is a life choice, female audiences relate to the characters by acknowledging that, given similar magical powers, their own choices would be different. When second-wave feminism laid the social, economic, and political groundwork to make other choices available (albeit only to the white middle classes), many educated white middle-class women either chose to leave the domestic sphere or supported the right of others to do so.

Women's experience of film

In the light of this kind of possibility for resignifying popular culture, one of the most interesting feminist interventions in popular culture studies has been the contribution made by oral historians collecting the testimony given by women about their experience of media institutions such as the cinema, popular music, and the family holiday. In an adaptation of this perspective, Jackie Stacey's *Star Gazing* used questionnaires and letters to examine the cinemagoing experience, its influence on the meaning of Hollywood films, and the representation of female stars during the 1940s and 1950s.[24] Similarly, I have been interested in the redefinition of masculinity and femininity in British film during the same period. During the Second World War, film production was under the direction of the Ministry of Information, which viewed women as part of an audience that needed to be kept on side and supportive of the war effort. Film was considered a significant part of domestic propaganda because it was believed that it would reach less-educated groups, including women, children, and working-class men in reserved occupations. Analysts of popular film are intrigued by how this policy led to a relaxation in the rigid prewar British censorship regulations for filmmaking.[25] During this period the Ministry of Information employed cultural censorship that markedly changed the content, style, and message of British films made at this time, and *improved* their quality. The less restrictive approach as to what could now be represented enabled greater realism and forms of speculative fantasy that were problematic under the previously rigid regulatory code with its extensive list of what could not be represented. The films developed a collective public information style that was retained by filmmakers trained during this time, notably the director/producer team of Michael Relph and Basil Dearden. The frank, authoritarian realist style of this type of filmmaking formalized itself in the arrival during the postwar period of the British social problem film and a subgenre of films concerned with narratives about the health service and nursing.[26]

Both genres represented women as conforming to patriarchal ideas of service, femininity, and successful motherhood or alternatively meeting social disgrace and personal disaster as victims of these patriarchal standards. Films such as *Millions Like Us* (1943), *Brief Encounter* (1945), and *No Time for Tears* (1957) were extremely popular in their mediation of patriarchal discourse. The social problem film, which appears in the postwar period, continues to represent these ideologies. John Hill identifies the genre as structured by a distinct discourse that diffuses the idea of wider social problems by fixing them on personal dilemmas, most prominently blame for the failure represented by juvenile delinquency, a failure laid squarely on the mother and her role in the family home.[27] One of the films analyzed by Hill is *Sapphire* (1958) in which the detective formula is used to close down the possible areas of speculation. In the film the murder investigation starts with the discovery of a middle-class woman's body, but the plot reveals that the victim's racial transgression makes her in effect the perpetrator of the crime. The victim, who is murdered before the narrative is presented to the audience, does not have an opportunity to speak up for herself when the discovery of a red petticoat in her underwear drawer places her on the boundaries of respectability. The investigation confirms her transgression when it uncovers the denial of her mixed racial origins and her decision to pass as white. The premise of the film was publicized as an exposure of the ridiculousness of racial intolerance in Britain. However, it is her disruption of the pretensions of middle-class patriarchy for which Sapphire is consequently punished.

The chief suspects during the investigation are her white fiancé David, her prospective father-in-law, and an unidentified black dancing partner. In his interview with the police, David says that he knew Sapphire was pregnant and asserts that he was willing to marry her, forgoing his architecture scholarship and ending his father's aspirations for his career. The denouement of the film reveals that the murderer was in fact David's sister Mildred, thus narratively displacing racial hatred from the masculine sphere into the established conventions of female hysteria. This reading is supported by the suggestion that Mildred is separated from her husband and is therefore not safely contained by marriage. Her jealous response to Sapphire's confidence in David's love and his promise to marry her combines with Mildred's racism to push her over the edge into violence and a murder that is clearly coded as aberrant psychology. Femininity is thus pathologized, and the male family members absolved.

Sue Aspinall's examination of the earlier wartime women's films focuses on their response to films that considered the distinction between the uniqueness of a love affair and the more mundane nature of marriage. Aspinall argues that "the presentation of women in such a restrictive range of modes of being, as objects either of desire or contempt or idealization, must become particularly crucial when ways of living and being female are in transition."[28] Despite the variety of films made, there were few direct challenges to these existing modes of femininity except those implicit alternatives that audiences imagined to the decisions made by characters on screen. Unexpected meanings arose from *Sapphire*, just as they did in response to the repetitive playing out of conformity in US television in the same period that Douglas analyzed. When I interviewed older women who had seen *Sapphire* when they were teenagers, I met two who said that they went out and bought red petticoats in solidarity with Sapphire and the world of unlicensed sexuality and mutable identity depicted in the film. As Sapphire was exorcised from the film, they had to imagine the trajectory of her life and enjoyed the imaginative freedom they exercised in doing so. Through their actions and imaginings, both women clearly rejected the dominant ideology of the social problem discourse and adapted the text to their own cultural practice. Supporting Douglas's thesis concerning conformity, both women also went on to become part of the women's movement during the 1960s and 1970s.

Postfeminism

In another account of feminist interest in girls and women's magazines, McRobbie sees this kind of willingness to analyze and even revise popular culture as an important part of the development of academic feminist study.[29] The debate about postfeminism as carried out by critics such as Imelda Whelehan explores a wide range of film, television, popular music, and cultural practice. McRobbie enters a debate into what has now become a central issue in feminist considerations of popular culture: a conflict between the feminist beliefs of an older generation and their perception of the wayward delinquency of a postfeminist generation. In order to maintain and increase their sales, contemporary women's magazines need to respond to the cultural climate and to represent their female readers in ways that are pleasurable. The magazines have to engage with feminist themes and with issues that shape contemporary women's identities.[30]

McRobbie sees the main change in these magazines (*Just Seventeen* and *More!* are the ones she examines) as the freedom their editors have claimed to address female sexualities, which she argues has been won for them by the impact of feminism on the acceptability of women learning about their bodies and the choices to be made about them.[31] She compares the feminist agenda of the Boston Women's Health Collective and the frank sex education provided by the magazines. The teen magazines, at least overtly, are seen to meet the Collective's aims of sexual openness, and despite continued criticism from feminist writers, this aspect of their content is frequently defended. This content is also seen as appropriate in an era of AIDS and HIV when a "more explicitly sexual culture . . . is itself the production of government approved awareness and prevention programmes."[32]

Feminism has also been addressed – out of necessity – in Mills and Boon romantic fiction published since the beginning of the 1990s. Mills and Boon's *Temptation* series was launched for British readers in 1985 during the same period in which magazines for teenage girls also underwent their transition. This series incorporates relatively explicit and extramarital sex into the formula, allowing heroines to articulate and initiate sexual rather than only romantic desire. The series thus responded to a postfeminist sensibility and reconstructed romance for contemporary social mores. Within the new narrative structure, not only does the hero have to move beyond the ideological standard of nineteenth-century patriarchy, but more work is required from the heroine, who has to overcome the influence of her mother's damaging and "old-fashioned" feminism.[33] As the heroine in Linda Spencer's *Spring Fancy* announces: "I get it from my mother, whose main goal in life has been to succeed. And success to her is career. I find myself at times mirroring her – shall we call it middle class disdain for the careerless multitudes? And when I catch myself at it, I hate it."[34] The compromise that leads to marriage in this series is often the couple's negotiation of male insecurity represented as a response to the woman's successful career. Marriage is no longer necessary to license sexual relations and is more closely connected with parenting.[35]

Her analysis of the new magazines leads McRobbie to use the term "new sexualities" to characterize the shift evident in their narrative range. Romance ceases to be the young women's goal and is decisively replaced by "a much more assertive and 'fun-seeking' female subjectivity."[36] McRobbie does not use the 1990s term "girl power"; nevertheless, this is what is being discussed. Popular culture is sanctioning female behavior that eschews femininity as passive and submissive. The representation of female subjects as preoccupied by lust rather than romance is managed by a specific style of editorial, one that maintains the intimacy created for *Jackie* readers but is dramatically reconfigured. *Jackie* readers could discursively challenge adult authority through their affiliation with romance and the status this gave them. The new teenage magazines do not seek to attain adulthood through the world of romance; instead, they seek to prolong the childhood lack of responsibility. McRobbie's argument sees a complicity here that allows producers and readers "to bond together and line up together against the outside (adult) world!"[37] This means that although there is plenty of "common-sense feminism" evident in these magazines, politicized feminism itself is perceived as aligned with "regulation and adult authority."[38] The postmodern feminism of the magazines asserts the dominance of sex and shopping in women's lives and identity formation. Although this is at the heart of current feminist debate about the rebellious nature of postfeminist young women, McRobbie clearly argues that popular culture remains a space where the struggle between a disapproving older generation and the experience of young women in the twenty-first century can still take place as a debate.

Indeed, the debate about postfeminism uses popular cultural references almost exclusively. Postmodern practice, writing, and cultural analysis from this transitional period, which is fully aware of the intellectual tradition of feminism, is an important route to understanding cultural change. For example, Madonna's consistently controversial image, which rests on the makeover, her promotion of sexual expression, notable success in the music industry, and an antipatriarchal stance, has offered a collection of different responses to the negotiation of gendered experience. Whether or not women were fans during their childhood and adolescence, Madonna's provocation across her career sets up the same dualities and contradictions that are evident in other forms of popular culture produced for women.[39] Georges-Claude Guilbert sees Madonna's work as a perpetually evolving popular narrative, which has longevity because it takes on the status and function of myth.[40] The stories that surround her propose imaginary and continually shifting solutions to social contradictions. In his definition of myth, storytelling has the social function of organizing relationships between individuals by channeling negative and positive cultural concerns.[41] In this way Madonna is part of a process through which society can explore contemporary gender politics; she provides imaginative constructs that permit challenges, ideological conformity, *and* exploitation. Guilbert argues that Madonna is a response to "the anxieties of the public, she stages them, sings about them, acts them out and plays with them" (*Madonna*, p. 36).

In an article for *The Village Voice* quoted by Guilbert, Steve Anderson views Madonna as "a repository for all our ideas about fame, money, sex, feminism, popular culture, even death." (p. 148). Surveying the "excess, artifice, overstatement, sensuality and beautiful appearances" of her work (p. 189), Guilbert's analysis emphasizes two aspects that are significant to postfeminist commentary: humor and power clearly predicated on economic status. Financial security is a prevalent theme in women's popular culture, which frequently appears to undercut traditional feminism's idealism and raise the issue of what a feminist agenda comprises. At the time McRobbie reviews teenage magazines in the late 1990s, the analysis of commercial pop frequently sees a similarity between Madonna and the Spice Girls. For different generations, their "use of exuberance and humour" in different media performance makes evident "that feminism is not only for the serious and . . . focuses the issue of what constitutes a feminist agenda in the 1990s."[42]

Production and consumption have often been considered as gendered opposites. We know that this polarization is unstable and therefore liable to being remade in popular culture, and we can identify through its shifts how cultural change is being negotiated. Historically, production has been given positive, creative, and masculine connotations, while consumption is aligned with negative and passive femininity.[43] However, to understand consumption we need to consider how this cultural practice is made meaningful by consumers and how it contributes to active identity formation beyond this stereotyped valuation. Daniel Miller has considered how the act of shopping can be differentiated and how the meanings of objects or purchases are subject to change when they are recontextualized.[44] The new women's and girls' magazines privilege personal consumption over romance. Consumption is part of the construction of the "fun-seeking" feminine identity that McRobbie identifies and Madonna personifies. Moreover, current patterns of consumption are indicative of a cultural shift from modernism to postmodernism that is evident in the deliberate playfulness of the shopping experience. Fixed social identities, especially in terms of class and gender, are effaced, allowing the consumer to experiment with alternative plural or hybrid identities. Shopping in the colorful new magazine spreads affirms the acceptance of varieties of taste and style, consumer power, individual choice, and the collective experience of its readers. The debate about the positive and negative aspects of women's consumption of beauty and leisure products is just as polarized as the debate over the consumption of romance, and both demonstrate that popular culture is both a contentious site of struggle for meaning and identity and an active one.[45]

Chicklit fiction

Such debates provide a premise for the popular, academic, and cultural reception of chicklit fiction. There are forerunners of this publishing phenomenon, but Helen Fielding's *Bridget Jones's Diary* (1996) is the bestseller that convenes the genre. Bestsellers by definition attract a heterogeneous audience, and *Bridget Jones* makes its appeal to the generation of "girl power," to those who have experience of contemporary spinsterhood, and to an older generation. Written by a successful journalist in her late thirties, its ironic stance delivers its postfeminist protagonist over to the full humiliation expected of a romantic heroine, while offering the reader a subject position that can "allow us to identify with Bridget and celebrate our failings in a rather complacent act of self-indulgence."[46] This tone is also detectable in the ambiguity present in the depiction of MTV cartoon heroines, *Ally McBeal*, and the exploration of new sexualities and identity consumption that underpins *Sex and the City*.

An understanding of the forms of popular culture emphasizes that popular texts are just that because they are able to produce a range of meanings by leaving themselves open to interpretation, while containing the possibility of inclusion in a range of different cultural practices, both personal and collective. They can be absorbed, resisted, or appropriated, and they thus make a definite contribution to cultural change. Obviously, chicklit cannot simply be studied by an analysis of *Bridget Jones*. *Bridget Jones* is, like *Jackie*, part of an extensive body of popular fiction with a range of narratives, characters, values, and sexual mores that are only superficially homogeneous. In the same manner as women's magazines and women's films, the books that are sold in this category (rather than assigned there by academic consideration) present both orthodoxies and challenges to anxieties commonly held by women. It is certainly still possible to identify and debate the oppressive conventions that Barrett identified in earlier fiction for women: the use of stereotype, collusion, compensation, and recuperation. However, the ironic tone matching the style of contemporary women's magazines is often willing to ridicule and deconstruct these consensual techniques, preparing narrative space for the consideration of alternative imaginative constructs. Instead of the single heroine, chicklit envisages multiple points of connection occupied by women, which increasingly span several life stages and choices. The narrative resolutions, fantasies, and attitudes to feminism, the body, and gender politics can also be differentiated and hold surprises.

Feminism has made an effective contribution to the study of popular culture. However, its early tendency to castigate women's participation in popular culture as an interaction with harmful ideologies and its later concern with identifying deviant cultural forms has not broadened the area of research. Careful and consistent analysis of popular cultural forms in the context of ordinary consumption is still too rare. The perceived dangers of popular culture are too often placed in the foreground as academic and cultural reference points, as, for example, when youth culture is considered primarily as a threat. The recognition of popular culture as indicative of, and contributory to, cultural change deepens the understanding of literary and social contexts, while feminist popular culture studies remain a rich but problematic interdisciplinary area of study.

Further reading

Michèle Barrett, *Women's Oppression Today* (London: Verso, 1988).

Anne Beezer, Jean Grimshaw, and Martin Barker, "Methods for Cultural Studies Students" in D. Punter, ed., *Introduction to Contemporary Cultural Studies.* (London: Longman, 1986).

Boston Women's Health Collective, *Our Bodies, Our Selves* (New York: Simon and Schuster, 1973).

Elizabeth Frazer, "Teenage Girls Reading *Jackie*," *Media, Culture and Society* 9:4 (1987), pp. 407–25.

Angela McRobbie, "*Jackie* Magazine: Romantic Individualism and the Teenage Girl," in McRobbie, *Feminism and Youth Culture* (Basingstoke: Macmillan, 1991).

Ellen Moers, *Literary Women* (London: The Women's Press, 1978).

Laura Mulvey, "Visual Pleasure and Narrative Cinema," in C. Penley, ed., *Feminism and Film Theory* (London: Routledge, 1988).

Neil Nehring, *Popular Music, Gender and Postmodernism* (London: Sage, 1997).

Elaine Showalter, *A Literature of their Own.* (London: Virago, 1978).

Gaye Tuchman, "The Symbolic Annihilation of Women by the Mass Media," in G. Tuchman, A. K. Daniels, and J. Benet, eds., *Hearth and Home: Images of Women in the Mass Media* (Oxford: Oxford University Press, 1978).

Sheila Whiteley, *Sexing the Groove: Popular Music and Gender* (Routledge, 1997).

NOTES

1. Germaine Greer, *The Female Eunuch* (London: Paladin, 1970).
2. C. Lee Harrington and Denise D. Bielby, *Popular Culture, Production and Consumption* (Oxford: Blackwell, 2001).
3. Ibid., p. 4–5.
4. Paul du Gay, Stuart Hall, Linda Janes, Hugh Mackay, and Keith Negus, *Doing Cultural Studies: The Story of the Sony Walkman* (London: Sage, 1997).
5. Andrew Milner, *Contemporary Cultural Theory: An Introduction* (London: UCL Press, 1994), p. 116.
6. Ibid., p. 131.
7. Joanne Hollows, *Feminism, Femininity and Popular Culture* (Manchester: Manchester University Press, 2000), p. 38.
8. Ibid., p. 24.
9. Ibid., p. 38.
10. Nickianne Moody, "Mills and Boon's *Temptations*: Sex and the Single Couple in the 1990s," in L. Pearce and G. Wisker, eds., *Fatal Attractions* (London: Pluto Press, 1998).

11. Janice Radway, *Reading the Romance: Women, Patriarchy and Popular Literature* (Chapel Hill: University of North Carolina Press, 1984).
12. Judith Newton, *Women, Power and Subversion* (London: Methuen, 1981), p. 13.
13. Raymond Williams, *Marxism and Literature* (Oxford: Oxford University Press, 1977), p. 131–2.
14. Newton, *Women, Power and Subversion, p. 11.*
15. Ibid., p. 13.
16. Dale Spender, *Mothers of the Novel* (London: Pandora, 1986), p. 76.
17. Sarah Lefanu, *In the Chinks of the World Machine* (London: The Women's Press, 1988).
18. Angela McRobbie, "*Jackie*: An Ideology of Adolescent Femininity," in B. Waites, T. Bennett, T. and G. Martin, eds., *Popular Culture Past and Present* (London: Croom Helm, 1981), p. 265. Further references will be cited in parentheses in the text.
19. Barbara Hudson, "Femininity and Adolescence," in Angela McRobbie and Mica Nava, eds., *Gender and Generation* (Basingstoke: Macmillan, 1984), p. 31.
20. Ibid., p. 31.
21. Sara Douglas, *Where the Girls Are* (New York: Three Rivers Press, 1995).
22. John Cawelti, *Adventure, Mystery and Romance* (Chicago: University of Chicago Press, 1976) p. 36.
23. Ibid., p. 35.
24. Jackie Stacey, *Star Gazing: Hollywood Cinema and Female Spectatorship* (London: Routledge, 1994).
25. Nicholas Pronay and Jeremy Croft, "British Film Censorship and Propaganda During World War Two," in J. Curran and V. Porter, eds., *British Cinema History* (London: Weidenfeld and Nicolson, 1983), p. 150.
26. Julia Hallam, *Nursing the Image* (London: Routledge, 2000).
27. John Hill, "The British Social Problem Film: *Violent Playground* and *Sapphire*," *Screen* 26:1, pp. 34–48.
28. Sue Aspinall, "Women's Realism and Reality in British Films 1943–53," in James Curran and Vincent Porter, eds., *British Cinema History* (London: Weidenfeld and Nicolson, 1983), p. 290.
29. Angela McRobbie, "*More!* New Sexualities in Girl's and Women's Magazines," in J. Curran, D. Morley, and V. Walkerdine, eds., *Cultural Studies and Communications* (London: Edward Arnold, 1996).
30. Ibid., p. 191.
31. A. McRobbie, "*More!* New Sexualities in Girls' and Women's Magazines," in McRobbie, (ed.), *Back to Reality? Social Experience and Cultural Studies* (Manchester: Manchester University Press, 1997), p. 202.
32. Ibid., p. 199.
33. Moody, "Mills and Boon's *Temptations*," p. 149.
34. Linda Spencer, *Spring Fancy* (Richmond: Mills and Boon, 1985), p. 170.
35. Moody, "Mills and Boon's *Temptations*," p. 150.
36. McRobbie, "*More!* New Sexualities Magazines," in McRobbie, (ed.) *Back to Reality?*, p. 198.
37. Ibid., p. 200.

38. Georges-Claude Guilbert, *Madonna as Postmodern Myth* (New York: McFarland and Co., 2002), p. 3. Further references will be cited in parentheses in the text.

39. Ibid., p. 187.

40. Ibid., p. 7.

41. Sheila Whiteley, *Women and Popular Music: Sexuality, Identity and Subjectivity* (London: Routledge, 2000), p. 225.

42. Hollows, *Feminism, Femininity and Popular Culture*, p. 115.

43. Daniel Miller, *Material Culture and Mass Consumption* (Oxford: Blackwell, 1994).

44. Hollows, *Feminism, Femininity and Popular Culture*, p. 132.

45. Imelda Whelehan, *Overloaded* (London: The Women's Press, 2000), p. 138.

46. Cawelti, *Adventure, Mystery and Romance*, p. 35.

PART 3

Feminist theories in play

9

REY CHOW

Poststructuralism: theory as critical self-consciousness

Any discussion of poststructuralism will need to revisit, however briefly, the intellectual event known as structuralism. According to Michel Foucault, structuralism is about problematizing – or denaturalizing – the centrality of the human subject: "[D]uring the mid-sixties," he said in an interview, "an entire series of intellectual figures were defined as 'structuralists' who had conducted completely different kinds of investigations, but having one point in common: the need to oppose that set of philosophical elaborations, considerations, and analyses centered essentially on the theoretical affirmation of the 'primacy of the subject.'"[1] Foucault's remark was made with the privilege of hindsight, and what remains important to our discussion is how the structuralist method accomplishes this task that he summarizes so succinctly.

The problem of the subject is enunciated in structuralism by way of the investigation of the age-old philosophical question, meaning. To perform its tasks, structuralism specializes in isolating and articulating the synchronic organizational relations that underlie, that give coherence to, observable phenomena. To cite two common examples from linguistics and anthropology: speakers of a particular language are often able to use it fluently without being entirely conscious of the rules that inform their utterances; similarly, peoples living within particular kinship arrangements can conduct their social relations without being entirely conscious of the rules that define their customs. Structuralism, in seeking to explain how languages, kinship systems, and other such collective behaviors work, aims methodologically at uncovering the logic that holds them together despite their superficially fragmentary appearances, that makes them function systematically, as it were. To borrow the words of Michael Lane, who has provided an illuminating critical discussion of the terms in question: "*A structure is a set of any elements between which, or between certain sub-sets of which, relations are defined*";[2] accordingly, structuralism is "a method whose primary intention is to permit the investigator to go beyond a pure description of what he

perceives or experiences (*le vécu*), in the direction of the quality of rationality which underlies the social phenomena in which he is concerned."[3]
Because, as Lane describes it, structuralism is ultimately concerned
with relations that may be formalized and apprehended as a whole or a
totality, its methodological scope, ideally speaking, includes all human
social phenomena. Insofar as they are constituted and mediated by languages (that is, shared sets of rules or codes), meanings that are traditionally
studied in the humanities (such as linguistics, literature, and history) and the
arts (music, painting, choreography, etc.), as well as in the social sciences
(such as anthropology, economics, psychology, sociology), should all be
available for structuralist examination.

While the work of Ferdinand de Saussure on linguistics is generally recognized as a founding instance of the structuralist method, other scholars (as
well as Roman Jakobson and Noam Chomsky in linguistics) have also been
noted for their contributions in different disciplines – Vladimir Propp's work
on the morphology of folktales, Claude Lévi-Strauss's work in anthropology,
Roland Barthes's and Julia Kristeva's work in literary studies, and Jacques
Lacan's work in psychoanalysis, to mention just a few. Although controversial, the key advantage of the structuralist method is the alternative it offers to
the old-fashioned, historicist, or causal models of scholarly inquiry (such as,
for instance, comparative grammar and etymology) through its then-novel
manner of defining, indeed devising, the "objects" under study. Rather than
simple historical continuity (and thus the various chronological stages undergone by a particular phenomenon), structuralism emphasizes relations – that
is, differences or differentials – as the principal hinge by which meanings
should be grasped; accordingly, these meanings are deducible from, yet not
reducible to, the actual phenomena themselves. In other words, whereas the
historicist or causal methods of inquiry more or less assume the presence of
such phenomena as the most critical data for investigation, for structuralism,
the most critical data are understood to be beyond the immediately perceptible activity or social event. What is immediately perceptible becomes, on
the contrary, an incomplete, precisely because empirically present, object, the
meaning of which can be accessed only through a scientific process of relating
the parts to the (invisible) whole.

For a seminal thinker and anthropologist such as Lévi-Strauss, the fundamental mechanism of structural relations is the binary opposition, to which
social and cultural phenomena may be reduced. Again, Lane provides a
helpful description of this conceptual model: "The structuralist method,
then, is a means whereby social reality may be expressed as binary oppositions, each element, whether it be an event in a myth, an item of behaviour
or the naming and classification of natural phenomena, being given its value

in society by its relative position in a matrix of oppositions, their mediations and resolutions."[4] In the case of Lévi-Strauss, who is interested in the particularity of diverse cultural groups, this tendency to seek out, indeed to believe in, underlying structures that are the same across cultures is, to say the least, self-contradictory.

For subsequent generations of thinkers, older structuralists' euphoria about the attainability and universality of structures as such became increasingly untenable. Such euphoria was punctured, most famously, in the early work of Jacques Derrida. For Derrida, the structuralist concentration on structure is tantamount to an endorsement of the philosophical habit of privileging a fixed center or origin in the production of meaning. This center, he writes, has different names throughout the centuries, including essence, existence, consciousness, conscience, God, man, and so forth, but its function is always a transcendent one:

> The function of this center was not only to orient, balance, and organize the structure – one cannot in fact conceive of an unorganized structure – but above all to make sure that the organizing principle of the structure would limit what we might call the *freeplay* of the structure . . . [T]he center also closes off the freeplay it opens up and makes possible.[5]

The paradox about the center is that while it often appears to be within a particular structure of signification, it simultaneously occupies an exterior position that allows it to operate and control the structure from a primordial vantage point, in such a manner as to be free of the palpable materiality – that is, the actual physical and temporal processes – of structuration.

The line of critical work that Derrida inaugurated, with classics such as "Structure, Sign, and Play in the Discourses of the Human Sciences," *Of Grammatology*, and essays in the collections *Writing and Difference* and *Speech and Phenomena*, can be read as a series of attempts to obstruct the euphoric flight from the materiality of structuration and, simultaneously, to restore such materiality to the very act of signification, in particular linguistic and textual signification. With Derrida's remarkable interventions, it no longer makes sense to talk only about structures because structures themselves will now need to be understood as illusory impressions that have resulted temporarily from the often idealist and ideological halting of the process of structuration. In the case of binary oppositions, specifically, such a halting can be explained as follows: despite the appearance of structural relativity, usually one of the two terms in a relation of difference is given epistemological precedence and used as the criterion to determine the value of the other in a hierarchical fashion. By the term *post*structuralism, then, scholars refer to this theoretical move, introduced by Derrida, of problematizing the belief in the be-all and end-all of structures (as meaning-generators, developers, and accountants) and to the multiple varieties of universalism-critiques that follow in its wake. The *OED*'s definition of "poststructuralism" is useful here for a clarification of the emergence and current usage of the term: "An extension and critique of structuralism, especially as used in critical textual analysis, which rejects structuralist claims to objectivity and comprehensiveness, typically emphasizing instead the instability and plurality of meaning, and frequently using the techniques of deconstruction to reveal unquestioned assumptions and inconsistencies in literary and philosophical language."

To put it somewhat differently, poststructuralism may be described as a philosophical and theoretical effort to radicalize (the meaning of) meaning as conventionally derived from various stable forms of *identities*, including the text, history, and thought, as well as the subject itself. Identities are now redefined as what result from, rather than what give rise to, differential relations. While poststructuralism officially emerged in debates dating back to the 1960s – see the essays in the classic collection *The Structuralist Controversy*, for instance – the term as it is used today is often less concerned with this early history and its many French-language players than with the wide-ranging effects of poststructuralism as a form of critical practice – the conceptual transformations it has wrought, the paths of critical reading it has inaugurated, and the institutional and cultural problems it has left unresolved. When discussing the features and impact of poststructuralism, scholars most commonly emphasize its contribution to a definition of meaning as shifting rather than stable and unified, and its challenge to assumptions of naturalness in signification. For instance, Raman Selden, Peter Widdowson, and Peter Brooker write that poststructuralism "has discovered the essentially *unstable* nature of signification."[6] Chris Beasley writes that poststructuralists "are . . . inclined to destabilize [the] perception of a static structure and place more emphasis on the contextual fluidity and ongoing production of meaning, whether referring to language, communication systems or other aspects of cultural and social life," and "to stress the shifting, fragmented complexity of meaning (and relatedly of power), rather than a notion of its centralized order."[7] Kathleen Gormly writes that poststructuralism "involves a relentless questioning of ideologies and concepts that appear to be 'natural,' 'stable,' and 'known.'"[8]

Bracketing referentiality: poststructuralism's inward turn

The crucial contribution made by poststructuralism, then, is the questioning of the absoluteness of any determinant of meaning, a questioning that in poststructuralist language is sometimes referred to as the bracketing, or deliberate suspension, of referentiality. Just why is this such a crucial contribution? Why is referentiality such a dangerous kind of slippage, for poststructuralists, at least? Using the terms provided by Derrida, we may say that referentiality, insofar as it provides the illusion that some external reality exists prior to the act of signification, has always been the privileged term in relation to the latter: imagined as the original and authentic something that directs and controls signification while itself remaining unhindered and unchanged by signification, referentiality is perhaps the most commonplace manifestation of the paradoxical functioning of the center and hence the most tenacious part of the metaphysics of presence. Thus whereas in its aim to achieve scientific objectivity structuralism is still preoccupied with structure, poststructuralism, following Derrida, renders even the concern with structure suspect. Such a concern, it warns, is precisely an instance of ideological stoppage of the chain of signification: structure itself is none other than an ultimate kind of referentiality. By contrast, poststructuralism reminds us that the chain of signification will always continue to shift and defer, and produce differences, regardless of the conscious motivation or intention of those who happen to be actors.

Understandably, this stubborn resistance to referentiality, this drastic rooting-out of (the belief in) any extrasystemic determinant in the production of meaning (be that determinant in the form of subject, object, consciousness, or perception), remains to this day poststructuralism's most controversial, because indeed most radical, intervention. As I have indicated elsewhere, it is possible to see this intervention as the writing of a special kind of alterity.[9] This alterity is derived from a methodical process of reinscribing the difference hitherto thought to exist between (two) entities as one that is already *within* entities. For instance, the difference between "man" and "woman" may be shown as a split (difference) within man or masculinity, a split that is then projected outward and given body as "woman"; alternatively, the difference between "non-Jew" and "Jew," again, may be shown as a repressed, unwanted part (difference) within the anti-Semitic non-Jew, who then externalizes it by labeling it "Jew." In both cases, "woman" and "Jew" seem to be differences/identities existing external to "man" and "non-Jew," but, for poststructuralists, it is more accurate to argue that they are in fact markers of an internal dislocation or alienness, that the names "woman" and "Jew" simply objectify/externalize an earlier rupture that is immanent to "man" and "non-Jew" themselves. To deconstruct a binary opposition, thus, is not to destroy all the values and differences attached to it. Rather, it is to take apart, to rewind in slow motion, the process of differentiation that was already at work in constituting the binary opposition in the first place and that, nonetheless, has been suppressed in order for the binary opposition to stand (belatedly, in the more readily perceptible form of an external or spatial difference, a difference between entities).

This move to reinscribe difference and otherness *from the interior of an ongoing state of affairs* – a move that is parasitic by definition, its mechanism being the reversal and displacement of what is always already established and accepted as the norm – suggests that poststructuralism does not and cannot have any positive agenda of its own to speak of. Terry Eagleton's diatribes offer a glimpse of some of the most oft-repeated criticisms of poststructuralism's essential emptiness and apparent political evasiveness. Poststructuralism, as Eagleton puts it sarcastically, "allows you to drive a coach and horses through everybody else's beliefs while not saddling you with the inconvenience of having to adopt any yourself."[10] The point of poststructuralism, one may counter, is precisely that *all* beliefs need to be deconstructed as unconscious bearers of some residual metaphysics. But do we not have to consider supplementary questions such as: Whose beliefs? At what point in time and place? Under what circumstances are such beliefs pursued, and under what circumstances should they be attacked – and with what consequences? Where the subject involved is a socially marginalized group, which may have the political need to adhere to certain goals or beliefs (such as religion, nationalism, different kinds of human rights, etc.), poststructuralism's tendency to reject externally observable difference (say, in the form of longstanding practices of discrimination) and bracket referentiality (say, a belief in some larger agent to which such group clings) can easily turn into a political impediment, making it virtually impossible to advance the more urgent and practical agendas of improving the social conditions of the underprivileged or disenfranchised concerned.

Meanwhile, although the most frequent criticisms of poststructuralism tend to portray it as an apolitical, indeed nihilistic enterprise, indifferent to the real problems of the world, a more simple issue that accompanies the bracketing of referentiality remains elided. In what oftentimes amount to unending acts of (linguistic and textual) self-referentiality, the focus on the materiality of signification must be recognized as part and parcel of a politics of vigilance, one that rightly admonishes against any facile over-looking of signification as a transparent process. But what are the wider political implications of such intense acts of *self*-referentiality?

By bracketing referentiality, separating it from the signified, and redefining the signified as part of the chain of signification and an effect produced by the play of signifiers, poststructuralism has established an epistemological framework in which what is thought to lie "outside" can, indeed must, be continually recoded as what is inside. There is hence no outside to the text. Because of this, we could also argue, with due respect to Derrida, that the poststructuralism that specializes in textual vigilance really does not offer a way of thinking about any outside except by reinscribing it as part of an ongoing interior (chain) condition. This is not exactly the same as saying that such poststructuralism is a closed system of permutations; rather, it is simply that its mechanism of motility, which successfully rewrites referentiality as the illusory effect produced by the play of temporal differences, also tends to preclude any other way of getting at the outside than by directing it inward, ad infinitum.

To this extent, the mode of operation adhered to by those whose post-structuralist practice is primarily that of devout vigilance to the text may ultimately become indistinguishable from a kind of compulsion or inevitability (something akin to an inner or natural law, now ascribed to language and signification). This resurgence of what for lack of a better term is a kind of nature – in a method that otherwise astutely warns against any illusions of nature, origin, primordialness, authenticity, and so forth – appears to be an intricate methodological problem that merits much further discussion than has hitherto been forthcoming. If textually vigilant poststructuralism specializes in foregrounding the alterity that is inherent to, that is an inalienable part of, any act of signification, has it not by the same token essentialized such alterity (or its process of reinscription) in the form of an ultimate determinant – a ghostly double to the act of signification, indeed, but a lurking reference nevertheless?

If structuralism begins as an intellectual endeavor to challenge the naïve empiricism and historicism of certain scholarly methods (so that the object of study is to be found in relations that have to be theorized rather than straightforwardly in the empirically observable phenomena themselves), textually vigilant poststructuralism has, it may be argued, taken this laudably abstract initiative to an extreme whereby the only safeguard against the errors of historicism and empiricism is a form of critical practice that is increasingly opaque and impenetrable because compulsively "self-referential." This impasse at which an exclusive focus on the act of (textual) signification inevitably arrives (that is, one that begins with a refutation of nature-thinking in the name of the all-encompassing reach of the text, only then eventually to end up where the text itself, by virtue of its reiterated irrefutability, becomes nature) is perhaps what prompts some poststructuralists to pursue comparable theoretical questions in an alternative trajectory of inquiry, as suggested in the work of Foucault.

Knowledge/power: the alternative offered by Foucault

If, for Foucault, deposing the primacy of the subject was the one thing in common among scholars who were called "structuralist," the way he goes about deconstructing that ultimate reference, man, is interestingly distinct from Derrida's. Here Foucault's own poststructuralist method shares something similar with his approach to Freudian psychoanalysis. In the case of the latter, it is well known that Foucault critiques Freud for what he calls the "repressive hypothesis," namely, the widespread belief in the West, since the nineteenth century, in repression (together with liberation) as a key to the secret of human sexuality.[11] But if it throws into question the paradigm of lack and castration that is firmly lodged in the conventional narrative of sexual repression, Foucault's critique of Freudian psychoanalysis nonetheless acknowledges that it is an extraordinarily effective mode of knowledge production. Indeed, Foucault's own notion of discursive power is in part based on his understanding of how *talk* about sexual repression (as instigated by Freudian psychoanalysis) has activated an unprecedented proliferation of practices and discourses, leading thus to ever more obsessions with the topic.

Unlike Lacan, who takes Freud's discussion of sexuality in the direction of language and semiotics in order to explore the psychoanalytic subtleties of subjection-through-sexual-difference, Foucault takes that discussion instead in its practical historical manifestations. The perversions and abnormalities that Freud discusses as variants of a polymorphous sexuality, Foucault rewrites as the outcomes of modern Western society's controls over human populations through the implementation of specific mechanisms since the eighteenth century. (In particular, he discusses four types of institutional practices that together form "strategic unities" in enforcing "normal" sexuality: hysterization of women's bodies, pedagogization of children's sex, socialization of procreative behavior, and psychiatrization of perverse pleasure.[12]) Foucault's interest in the social regimentations and penalizations of sexual behaviors indicates that while his work proceeds fully in accordance with Freud's definitive argument that the sexual instinct is nonessentialist in character, he has chosen to sidestep that argument in order to focus, instead, on the efficient rationalizations of human sexuality in modern times through steady institutional surveillance. Rather than a matter of "instincts and their vicissitudes," which, as Freud's own elaborations demonstrate, require ever more efforts at categorization, subdivision, and *internal differentiation*, sexuality in Foucault's work is a vast, heterogeneous apparatus that includes legal, moral, scientific, architectural, philosophical, and administrative discourses, all of which are linked to the production of knowledge (and its accompanying subjectification) with ever-shifting boundaries and effects of inclusion and exclusion.

In a parallel manner, although his work may be seen as proceeding in step with the astute Derridean critique of anthropocentrism in Western history and philosophy, Foucault's approach to anthropocentrism and its truth claims is decidedly different. Whereas Derrida's work concentrates on the activity of language and signification in order to deconstruct it from within, Foucault pursues the institutions, procedures, disciplines – in other words, the complex networks of technologies in modern Western society – by which man comes to constitute himself as an object of knowledge in the first place. His work, from *The Birth of the Clinic* and *Madness and Civilization* to the famous, unfinished project of *The History of Sexuality*, may be seen as a consistent series of endeavors in this direction. The theme that fascinates him, he says in the interview cited above, is what he calls the "limit-experiences" – "Madness, death, sexuality, crime: these are the things that attract my attention most."[13]

Rather than focusing on the production of meaning in man's linguistic texts (in which man's agency is defined solely in terms of his word-using capacity, as a speaker, writer, or reader), what concerns Foucault is how man, like the stars, the plants, and the animals that have been objects of knowledge since ancient times, becomes likewise objectified – in fact, invented – in modernity, and how, in order for that to happen, he must be distinguished from those who are deemed not quite man enough. For Foucault, this contingent but violent process of boundary-marking (which gives us the figure of modern man as we know him) is what underwrites conceptions of the insane, the sick, the criminal, the child, the homosexual, etc., together with the respective practices by which these "others" are stigmatized and the institutions to which they are banished. In Foucault's hands, modern anthropocentrism is thus deconstructed as at once a way of thinking and an unmistakable politics, as Mary C. Rawlinson puts it: "The first effect of Foucault's strategy . . . is to make the horizon of our thought appear before us as an object: to expose the rules of knowledge, specific lines of authority, and mechanisms of effect."[14]

This shift to man's status as an object (rather than exclusively as a subject defined through language) enables a kind of theoretical inquiry that is post-structuralist in implication without having incessantly to bracket so-called referentiality and return to the internal workings of human signification. Instead, it becomes possible and even necessary to investigate a whole array of discourses – scientific, biological, medical, philosophical, literary, political, moral – with the effect that not only man's mind (or speech) but also his entire body (in all its mundane gestures, movements, and engagements) is shown to be subjugated to systemic means of regulation, training, enhancement, punishment, correction, and elimination. Foucault thus ushers in a corporeal semiotics in which bodies can be seen, as Bob Carter writes, "as texts bearing, and baring, the inscriptions of a thousand tiny techniques of subjectification."[15] As Lois McNay puts it: "This insistence on the body as an historically specific entity distinguishes Foucault's theory from those of other [poststructuralist] theorists, such as Derrida, where the body is a metaphorization of the more general philosophical problem of difference."[16]

As we learn, with Foucault, how we come to know and believe ourselves to be naturally "human," we are also confronted with the disturbing idea that truth (such as the truth about the kinds of souls and bodies that we are) is not only cognitively but also historically and politically produced: "humanity" as a type of knowledge, securely embedded in discourses such as medicine and psychiatry, for instance, as well as in education, family, and other types of social training, is inseparable from the institutional power networks in which it seeks to legitimize itself as the "norm" and "universal" truth. Rawlinson's analysis provides a pointed summary of Foucault's most influential contributions along these lines:

> Foucault disturbs and puts into question classical philosophical conceptions – of the universality of truth, of the necessity of regular procedures that dehistoricize and disindividuate the scientific knower; of the essential separability of the faculty of knowledge and the faculty of the will; of the conception of knowledge itself in terms of forms of representation and self-representation. A genealogical analysis of modern scientific medicine reveals that the epistemological and the political, knowledge and power, are ineluctably intertwined, so that truth is not so much discovered – as if it lay ready-made in an objective reality patiently awaiting the articulate voice of science – as produced according to regular and identifiable procedures that determine in any given historical situation what it is possible to say, who is authorized to speak, what can become an object of scientific inquiry, and how knowledge is to be tested, accumulated, and dispersed.[17]

As Joan Scott writes, from poststructuralism's theoretical insistence on the fluidity of meaning comes a type of scholarly work that centers not on what but on *how*, not on the meaning as a product but as an ongoing process. Although she is speaking about poststructuralism in general, Scott's words are particularly apt as a description of the questions and possible analyses that have been inspired by Foucault:

> Poststructuralists insist that words and texts have no fixed or intrinsic meanings, that there is no transparent or self-evident relationship between them and either ideas or things, no basic or ultimate correspondence between language

and the world. The questions that must be answered in such an analysis, then, are how, in what specific contexts, among which specific communities of people, and by what textual and social processes has meaning been acquired? More generally, the questions are: How do meanings change? How have some meanings emerged as normative and others been eclipsed or disappeared? What do these processes reveal about how power is constituted and operates?[18]

With Foucault, in other words, the most crucial intervention of poststructuralism – the challenge to referentiality as the absolute determinant of meaning – retains its resiliency and flexibility without becoming reified into an obsession with the interiority of linguistic signification. The instability of meaning, once acknowledged, is tactically converted into an attention to the symbiotic relationship between power and knowledge as such. From this it follows that even the bases of academic intellectual work, what is conventionally thought of as "neutral" and "disinterested," is now understood to require continual revamping, and that it is through such revamping that abstract thought will continue being relevant for society at large.

Poststructuralism and feminism: to be continued

The relationship between poststructuralism and feminism is a contentious one, not least because of a persistent divide – and an unfortunate binary opposition – between "theory" and "politics." For many feminists influenced by or sympathetic to issues repeatedly raised in Anglo-American empirical thinking, poststructuralism, with its insistence on the openness of the signification process and the relativity of all forms of identities, may come across as too abstract and indifferent to the actual inequality between men and women. For instance, calling attention to the existing disparity between social groups in matters such as the attainment of authorship, citizenship rights, and other privileges, some have voiced complaints about poststructuralism's theoretical ease with the dismantling of the subject.[19] Others charge that male poststructuralists' interest in pure difference at the expense of sexual difference may simply be another ruse of phallocentrism.[20]

Conversely, feminists predominantly sympathetic to poststructuralist theory tend to believe that Anglo-American feminist critical practice, despite its activist politics, is often too mired in patriarchal aesthetics to be able to address the dissident or revolutionary nuances of the text. In her bestseller *Sexual/Textual Politics*, for instance, Toril Moi, following the leads of women theorists writing in French such as Hélène Cixous, Luce Irigaray, and Julia Kristeva, chastises Anglo-American feminist critics for their methodological shortcomings and urges a (poststructuralist) feminist politics that is equally attentive to textuality and sexuality.[21]

This sense of incompatibility between poststructuralism and feminism, however, is not necessarily inevitable, for there are, arguably, important affinities between the two kinds of critical practices. While some feminists, following Derrida, combine poststructuralist textual vigilance and feminist queries in close readings of literary and philosophical texts, and go on to pursue the relevance of deconstruction for cross-cultural analyses, others take up the routes of intellectual inquiry introduced by Foucault and actively engage with social histories, marginalized group identities, cultural studies, and the history of ideas. (Derrida and Foucault should be taken at this juncture as shorthands for the two major poststructuralist trends I have outlined.) As Kathleen Gormly writes, although many feminists see post-structuralism as counter to their goals "because it represents theory as elitist, white, and male" and "divorced from the kind of tangible political action that impelled the feminist movement in the first place," at the same time "much of feminist criticism may be said to be 'poststructuralist' because of its interest in examining the assumptions upon which fixed notions of gender (for instance, that women and men are naturally different) are based, and in its desire to work toward transforming these assumptions."[22]

Indeed, it would perhaps not be inaccurate to conclude that the relationship between poststructuralism and feminism has been an uneasy but eminently fruitful collaboration, characterized now by feminists' (often justified) distrust of poststructuralism as still ideologically rooted in patriarchy and masculinism, now by the two practices' mutual interest in demolishing entrenched (and often conservative) habits of thinking. In the context of continuing debates about poststructuralism's germaneness for feminism, Joan Scott has provided one of the most persuasive arguments for how the two are closely connected. She points out that both proceed with a characteristic *critical self-consciousness*: "Poststructuralism and contemporary feminism are late-twentieth-century movements that share a certain self-conscious critical relationship to established philosophical and political traditions."[23] Speaking of her own experience with poststructuralism, Scott indicates that she "found a new way of analyzing constructions of meaning and relationships of power that called unitary, universal categories into question and historicized concepts otherwise treated as natural (such as man/woman) or absolute (such as equality or justice)."[24]

It is impossible to provide a comprehensive list of the scholarly works by feminists who have adopted various aspects of poststructuralism in their own critical practices, but for the reader's information I would like to conclude by mentioning a few strategic examples in various disciplines and subfields in the English-speaking academic world that have influenced my own thinking (full titles can be found in the guide to further reading): Nancy Armstrong on the agency of the middle-class domestic woman and her contributions to the rise of the English novel and the formation of modern Western culture; Judith Butler on the processes of our sexual identities' cultural formation and reiteration, as well as on the psychological moorings of social and institutional power; Teresa de Lauretis on feminism, psychoanalysis, and semiotics as mutually informing ways of understanding the politics of gender in film and modern literature; Naomi Schor on the detail as an ubiquitous, gendered problem in modern Western literature and aesthetics; Jenny Sharpe on the figure of the woman, across race and class, in the histories and writings of imperialism; Kaja Silverman on the subject in semiotics, on film, and on the philosophical underpinnings of visuality and spectatorship in Western modernity; Gayatri Chakravorty Spivak on the productive possibilities of juxtaposing poststructuralism, Marxism, and feminism, and their interlocking usefulness for any reading of the postcolonial non-Western as well as Western worlds; Robyn Wiegman on the evolving relationship between feminism and the discipline of women's studies in the larger context of the academic production of knowledge; Linda Williams on the positive, albeit fraught, relationship between feminist practices of spectatorship and pornographic filmmaking and reception.

These and many other feminist scholars' works have not only added new contents and forms of analysis to their respective disciplines and subfields; in many cases they have fundamentally revised the modes of inquiry that constitute the core of the latter. Although the complexity and sophistication of their works can be addressed only individually, it should be pointed out that collectively they represent something of an irreversible paradigm shift in the pursuit of humanistic knowledge in the contemporary Western world. These works not only make it impossible ever again to ignore the multifaceted roles played by women in all matters pertaining to cultural representation; they also increasingly call into question the absoluteness of currently accepted categories of knowledge, including those of sexual differentiation.

In addition to deconstructing the institutional power bases for the production of femininity involved in different genres and media, then, it has become necessary, as well, to challenge prevalent assumptions about terms such as "man" and "woman," to historicize how those assumptions became naturalized, and to explore what other kinds of knowledge – and "limit experiences," to use Foucault's phrase – have been delegitimized and silenced in the process. However difficult and conflictual the alliance between feminism and poststructuralism may have been, this energetic critical self-consciousness, as

Scott reminds us, is a positive consequence of major magnitude. It is an alliance that ought, in my view, to be continued.[25]

Further reading

Nancy Armstrong, *Desire and Domestic Fiction* (New York: Oxford University Press, 1987).

Judith Butler, *Gender Trouble: Feminism and the Subversion of Identity* (New York and London: Routledge, 1990).

Rosalind Coward and John Ellis, *Language and Materialism: Developments in Semiology and the Theory of the Subject* (London: Routledge and Kegan Paul, 1977).

Teresa De Lauretis, *Alice Doesn't: Feminism, Semiotics, Cinema* (Bloomington: Indiana University Press, 1984).

Jeremy Hawthorn, "Post-Structuralism," *A Glossary of Contemporary Literary Theory*, 4th edn. (London: Arnold, 2000).

Greig E. Henderson and Christopher Brown, "Poststructuralism," *Glossary of Contemporary Literary Theory*, March 31, 1997. University of Toronto. (www.library.utoronto.ca/utel.glossary/Poststructuralism.html. July 12 2002).

Naomi Schor, *Reading in Detail: Aesthetics and the Feminine* (New York: Methuen, 1987).

Jenny Sharpe, *Allegories of Empire: The Figure of the Woman in the Colonial Text* (Minneapolis: University of Minnesota Press, 1993).

Kaja Silverman, *The Subject of Semiotics* (New York: Oxford University Press, 1983).

The Threshold of the Visible World (New York: Routledge, 1996).

Gayatri Chakravorty Spivak, *In Other Worlds: Essays in Cultural Politics* (New York: Methuen, 1987).

Robyn Wiegman, *American Anatomies: Theorizing Race and Gender* (Durham: Duke University Press, 1995).

"Feminism, Institutionalism, and the Idiom of Failure," *Differences* 11: 3 (Fall 1999–2000), pp. 107–36.

Linda Williams, *Hard Core: Power, Pleasure, and the "Frenzy of the Visible"* (Berkeley and Los Angeles: University of California Press, 1989).

NOTES

1. Michel Foucault, "'But Structuralism Was Not a French Invention,'" in Foucault, *Remarks on Marx: Conversations with Duccio Trombadori*, trans. R. James Goldstein and James Cascaito (New York: Semiotext(e), 1991), pp. 85–6. Foucault reminds the audience that structuralism had actually begun in Eastern Europe as an intellectual reaction against the dogmatism of Stalinist Marxism before becoming an event in France in the 1960s.

2. Michael Lane, introduction to *Introduction to Structuralism*, ed. and intro. Michael Lane (New York: Basic Books, 1970), p. 24 (emphasis in the original).

3. Ibid., p. 31.

4. Ibid., p. 32.
5. Jacques Derrida, "Structure, Sign, and Play in the Discourse of the Human Sciences," (trans. from the French), in Richard Macksey and Eugenio Donato, eds., *The Structuralist Controversy: The Languages of Criticism and the Sciences of Man* (Baltimore: The Johns Hopkins University Press, 1970, 1972), pp. 247–48 (emphasis in the original).
6. Raman Selden, Peter Widdowson, and Peter Brooker, "Poststructuralist Theories," in *A Reader's Guide to Contemporary Literary Theory*, 4th edn. (London: Prentice Hall, 1997), p. 151 (emphasis in the original).
7. Chris Beasley, *What Is Feminism?: An Introduction to Feminist Theory* (Thousand Oaks, CA: Sage, 1999), p. 91.
8. Kathleen Gormly, "Poststructuralism," in Elizabeth Kowaleski-Wallace, ed., *Encyclopedia of Feminist Literary Theory* (New York: Garland Publishing, 1997), p. 318.
9. See Rey Chow, introduction to Chow, *Ethics after Idealism: Theory – Culture – Ethnicity – Reading* (Bloomington and Indianapolis: Indiana University Press, 1998); and Chow, "The Resistance of Theory; or, the Worth of Agony," in Jonathan Culler and Kevin Lamb, eds., *Just Being Difficult? Academic Writing in the Public Arena* (Stanford: Stanford University Press, 2003), pp. 95–105.
10. Terry Eagleton, *Literary Theory: An Introduction*, 2nd edn (Minneapolis: University of Minnesota Press, 1996), p. 125.
11. See Michel Foucault, *The History of Sexuality*, 3 vols., trans. Robert Hurley, *Volume I: The Will to Knowledge* (New York: Pantheon Books, 1978).
12. Ibid., pp. 104–5.
13. Foucault, *Remarks on Marx*, pp. 99–100.
14. Mary C. Rawlinson, "Foucault's Strategy: Knowledge, Power, and the Specificity of Truth," *The Journal of Medicine and Philosophy* 12 (1987), p. 379.
15. Bob Carter, "Rejecting Truthful Identities: Foucault, 'Race' and Politics," in Moya Lloyd and Andrew Thacker, eds., *The Impact of Michel Foucault on the Social Sciences and the Humanites* (London: Macmillan, 1997), pp. 130–1.
16. Lois McNay, *Foucault and Feminism: Power, Gender and the Self* (Boston: Northeastern University Press, 1992), p. 16.
17. Rawlinson, "Foucault's Strategy," p. 373.
18. Joan W. Scott, "Deconstructing Equality-Versus-Difference; or, the Uses of Poststructuralist Theory for Feminism," in Anne C. Herrmann and Abigail J. Stewart, eds., *Theorizing Feminism: Parallel Trends in the Humanities and Social Sciences*, 2nd edn. (Boulder, CO: Westview Press, 2001), p. 256. Scott's essay was originally published in *Feminist Studies*, 14: 1 (Spring 1988), pp. 33–50.
19. For a well-known account that criticizes poststructuralist theorists (such as Foucault and Roland Barthes) for indirectly delegitimizing the assertion of the subject in other contexts such as feminism, see Nancy K. Miller, "Changing the Subject: Authorship, Writing and the Reader," in Teresa de Lauretis, ed., *Feminist Studies/Critical Studies* (Bloomington: Indiana University Press, 1986), pp. 102–20.
20. See Naomi Schor, "Dreaming Dissymmetry: Barthes, Foucault, and Social Difference," in Alice Jardine and Paul Smith, eds., *Men in Feminism* (London: Methuen, 1987), p. 109.

21. Toril Moi, *Sexual/Textual Politics: Feminist Literary Theory* (London: Methuen, 1985).
22. Gormly, "Poststructuralism," p. 318.
23. Scott, "Deconstructing Equality-Versus-Difference," p. 255. See also the introduction to Judith Butler and Joan Scott, eds., *Feminists Theorize the Political* (New York and London: Routledge, 1992).
24. Ibid., pp. 254–5.
25. Many thanks to Dan Bautista for his helpful research assistance.

10

ROSEMARY MARANGOLY GEORGE

Feminists theorize colonial/postcolonial

Postcolonial feminist theory's project can be described as one of interrupting the discourses of postcolonial theory and of liberal Western feminism, while simultaneously refusing the singular "Third World Woman" as the object of study. From the early 1980s onward, postcolonial feminism in the West has been centrally concerned with the terms in which knowledge about non-Western women was produced, circulated, and utilized. In postcolonial literary analyses, issues of location, of representation, of "voicing" female subjecthood, and of the expansion of the literary canon emerged as important foci. As a critical approach, the postcolonial literary feminism that would radically alter the study of literature in the Western academy can be traced to a few key critical essays written in the early 1980s. In this essay I discuss a range of the most significant contributions to postcolonial literary feminism and situate them in relation to the work of numerous scholars in the fields of colonial and postcolonial studies and feminist literary scholarship. I will present Gayatri Chakravorty Spivak, a feminist and cultural theorist, born and educated in India and based in the United States as an exemplary critical figure; a discussion of the trajectory of her work will allow us to consider some of the major ideas in the field. Postcolonial feminist literary critics negotiate with a wide range of related discourses in order to revise the terms in which the location of the critic and of the literary subject are understood. Indeed, postcolonial feminist criticism contests the very location of literature itself.

Much of the theoretical energy of early postcolonial feminist scholarship focused on challenging Western feminist literary theory's investment in first world women's texts, in uninterrogated national literary traditions, and in a benevolent, ultimately patronizing, reception of third world women, in and out of literary texts. At the same time, postcolonial feminists scrutinized the gendered blind spots of the mostly masculinist postcolonial critique of relations of power in colonial contexts and newly independent states. Thus postcolonial feminist scholarship has as its characteristic markings: the fashioning of cautionary signposts, the disclosure of absences, an insistence on what cannot be represented in elite texts, an emphasis on the more than "purely literary," and the persistent embedding of gendered difference in a larger understanding of race, nationality, class, and caste. Despite the disciplining tone of many of the occasions for such scholarship, in the late 1990s and early 2000s, a postcolonial feminist approach harnesses the wisdom of many different critical strands; a coalitional scholarship, it is indebted even as it contributes to scholarship in a range of fields that extend feminist discourse beyond any simple notion of the literary or of gender.

I use the term "postcolonial" in this essay to refer to a critical framework in which literary and other texts can be read against the grain of the hegemonic discourse in a colonial or neocolonial context: this framework insists on recognizing, resisting, and overturning the strictures and structures of colonial relations of power. It takes its inspiration from and constantly refers to the intellectual work that contributed to the end of Europe's colonial occupation of the globe, from the mid-twentieth century to the present. But the postcolonial critical framework is more than a condensed theory of decolonization. Rather, it is a methodology especially invested in examining culture as an important site of conflicts, collaborations, and struggles between those in power and those subjected to power. While colonial control over far-flung empires was largely accomplished through use of force, the "superiority" of the colonizer was crucially reinforced through cultural "persuasion." British colonizers spread the secular scripture of English literature through the colonial education system as a means of establishing the "innate" superiority of British culture (and therefore of British rule) in the minds of the native elites. As Cheikh Hamidou Kane, the Senagalese writer, noted in his 1963 novel, *Ambiguous Adventure*: "The cannon compels the body, the school bewitches the soul."[1]

Anticolonial national struggles and postcolonial literary discourse developed an implicit conviction that cultural sites have the potential to change social and political reality. Indeed, the urgency to end colonial rule was often first publicly expressed in cultural texts. In the present, the term "postcolonial" is differently invoked by different practitioners. For the most part, however, this critical stance counters the usual relations of power between First and Third World locations in the linked arenas of economics, politics, and cultural production.

Like other scholars and cultural practitioners arguing from the margins in the 1980s and 1990s, postcolonial theorists in the West and elsewhere were engaged in the task of widening the range of literary texts and practices understood as worthy of scholarly attention, that is, as canonical. In order to achieve this goal, the role of literary texts in society had to be retheorized:

thus, for instance, Ngugi Wa Thiongo argued for two literary categories: the literature of oppression and the literature of struggle; he thus challenged the conventional practice of distinguishing among literary texts solely on the bases of form (*Writers in Politics*, 1981). Other scholars, for example, those working on testimonials or on transcribed oral texts, argued for a reevaluation of the *type* of texts considered worthy of analysis. Concurrently, postcolonial literary criticism finally put to rest the humanist notion that the best literary texts transcended politics by carrying within them the pearls of what would be *universally* acknowledged as wisdom. By disclosing, as Edward Said did in *Orientalism* (1978) and *Culture and Imperialism* (1992), that literary texts were shaped by and in turn shaped the ruling ideologies of their day, they demonstrated the logic of tracing both colonial and anticolonial ideologies through literature.[2] Postcolonial feminists intervened to insist that men and women experience aspects of colonialism and postcolonialism differently. Yet they also vigorously maintained that gender was not *invariably* a fundamental marker of difference. Postcolonial feminists have noted, for example, that European women in the colonial period wrote frequently about their "Eastern Sisters," but that there were very few instances in which alliances between women *as women* overcame the difference of race under a colonial system. As a result, gender must be understood as operating in tandem with the pressures of race, class, sexuality, and location.

In the late 1980s and 1990s, postcolonial theorists were very invested in reexamining colonial and "native" discourses from the nineteenth and early twentieth century, produced and circulated in Europe and in the colonies, especially those that constructed "modernity" in opposition to "traditional" or "native" customs. European texts repeatedly justified and explained colonial domination by reinforcing a series of hierarchized oppositions such as civilized/savage, modern/traditional, mature/childlike, and, most significantly, rational/irrational. Dipesh Chakrabarty's *Provincializing Europe* (2000) is an example of a postcolonial critical text that attempts to undo the central position that Europe has held as "the Universal" in non-European locations thanks to the legacy of these colonialist oppositions. While Europe in the late twentieth and early twenty-first century is clearly no longer the embodiment of the universal human, a certain Europe still occupies a central position in the scholarly imagination. Postcolonial criticism aims to "provincialize Europe" and to counter the hegemonic weight of an Enlightenment universalist world view by insisting on the humanity of colonized peoples and on the value of non-European thought and culture. Postcolonial feminists bring to this revisionary reading of center and periphery a keen sense of the gendered dynamics of knowledge production in colonial discourse and in the postcolonial critique of the same.

Arguably, one of the inaugural moments of postcolonial feminist literary criticism in the West was the publication of Spivak's "Three Women's Texts and a Critique of Imperialism" in the Fall 1985 issue of *Critical Inquiry*. In this short essay, Spivak forced a rethinking of the ways in which literary texts, especially those written by women, had been deployed in feminist arguments. Spivak brilliantly focuses on Charlotte Brontë's *Jane Eyre*, one of the "cult texts" of Western academic feminism; she argues that in the novel, as in twentieth-century feminist criticism, Jane Eyre and Bertha Mason Rochester become who they are – heroine and less than human, respectively – because of the politics of imperialism. Prior to Spivak's essay, the authoritative feminist critical analysis of *Jane Eyre* was the lynchpin chapter in Sandra Gilbert's and Susan Gubar's hugely successful *The Madwoman in the Attic* (1979). Despite titling their book after the experiences of *Jane Eyre*'s Creole Bertha, who is declared insane and locked in the attic of her husband Mr. Rochester's English country house, Gilbert and Gubar were quite oblivious to Bertha's significance, except insofar as she served as Jane's "dark double": Bertha would do for Jane what Jane could not herself do. Gilbert's and Gubar's reading of the novel brought to a crescendo the feminist celebration of Jane as the solitary heroine who begins life "without connections, beauty or fortune" and ends having acquired all three *and* the power to narrate her version of the story of her life. In these readings Jane's triumph is her transformation, seemingly through the power of her first-person narrative, from a timid, impoverished governess into a desirable woman the hero cannot live without. When the first-person narrator begins the last chapter of the novel with "Dear Reader, I married him," the immolation of Bertha and her leap to her death (the plot event that allows Jane finally to accept Mr. Rochester's marriage proposal) is quite easily forgotten in the celebratory conclusion to the romance plot.

"Three Women's Texts and a Critique of Imperialism" made the feminist argument exemplified by Gilbert's and Gubar's work completely untenable, by demonstrating how "the feminist individualist heroine of British fiction," the fully individual feminine subject that is the apotheosis of liberal feminism, comes into being through violence done to the Other. Spivak argues that this becoming of the subject /the individual is brought about not just by marriage and childbearing, but by "soul making" – a task that requires the violence done to the soulless, less than human Other. With much assistance from the Caribbean novelist Jean Rhys's *Wide Sargasso Sea* (1965), Spivak demonstrates that "so intimate a thing as personal and human identity might be determined by the politics of imperialism."[3] Using Rhys's narrative, which tells Bertha's version of the story of her marriage to Mr. Rochester, Spivak deftly demonstrates that "the active ideology of imperialism . . . provides the discursive field" for the Brontë novel. Following Spivak, we might ask: Where do Mr. Rochester's wealth and Jane's fortune come from? Why is Bertha initially considered an attractive match? And how is it that her legal rights as Mr. Rochester's wife are so easily disregarded by the narrative and the reader? The resulting discussion of the novel's imbrication in the global relations of domination established under British imperialism significantly alters our understanding of the gendered politics of fiction. If the study of eighteenth-century English novels and conduct books demonstrates, as Nancy Armstrong argues, that "the modern individual was first and foremost a female," in the wake of Spivak's essay postcolonial feminists argued that the nineteenth- and twentieth-century English woman of liberal feminism was first and foremost authorized by the economic, political, social, and cultural axioms of British imperialism.[4]

The 1990s saw the publication of many essays, special editions of journals, and books that reexamined the much-trammeled terrain of eighteenth- to twentieth-century British literary, legal, and other texts with a view to explicating the investment in Empire that had gone unnoticed in earlier scholarship. Of these projects, Lata Mani's analysis of the British colonial discussion of the custom of *sati* (spelt "suttee" in the colonial period) in nineteenth-century India illustrates colonial discourse's construction of "native custom and practice" as barbaric, thus rationalizing the imposition of a "civilizing" European colonial rule. But Mani also interrogates the patriarchal "native" representation of this custom in which newly widowed wives immolated themselves on their husbands' funeral pyres. As she shows, *sati* was not a practice followed all over the Indian subcontinent, nor was it the necessary fate of all widows in a particular caste or class. Rather, it was practiced sporadically in scattered incidents that were, however, scrupulously recorded by British observers. Mani's study discloses the use to which the burning widow (referred to as the *sati*) was put in simultaneously furthering the colonial project and protecting indigenous patriarchal power. Mani argues that the *satis* "become sites on which various versions of scripture/tradition/law are elaborated and contested"(p. 115).[5] She demonstrates that the elaborate narratives compiled by eyewitnesses contain no record of the widows' motivations, utterances, reasoning, or subjectivity, or even of their pain. In Mani's words: ". . . even reading against the grain of a discourse ostensibly about women, one learns so little about them . . . neither subject, nor object, but ground – such is the status of women in the discourse on *sati*" (p. 118). Despite the colonizers stated concern for the wellbeing of native women, the real purpose of this debate around the practice of *sati* was to reinforce the "necessity" of the regulatory presence of British colonial rule.

In her 1988 essay "Can the Subaltern Speak?," Spivak succinctly notes that the same nineteenth-century descriptions of *sati* (even after the abolition of this rite by William Bentinck in 1829), allow us to understand the way in which colonial rule presented itself: as "white men saving brown women from brown men." Against this colonialist reading of the anti-*sati* campaign, Spivak places the Indian nativist argument, which she condenses into the phrase, "the women actually wanted to die." She argues that "the two sentences go a long way to legitimize each other. One never encounters the testimony of the women's voice-consciousness. Such a testimony would not be ideology-transcendent or 'fully' subjective, of course, but it would have constituted the ingredients for producing a countersentence."[6] Spivak points to what will become a major preoccupation of postcolonial feminist writing: namely, if and how disenfranchised women can represent, speak, and act *for themselves*, despite oppressive conditions. Postcolonial feminism unflinchingly acknowledges that there are many obstacles in the path of securing such "voice-consciousness." Yet, despite the odds, postcolonial feminist discourse strives to create the space for this "countersentence" to be spoken by the "gendered subaltern."

The use of the term "subaltern" in this context has a particular history that bears repeating. In the early 1980s the Italian political theorist Antonio Gramsci's term "subaltern classes" (used by Gramsci to denote the oppressed) was taken up by an intellectual collective called the Subaltern Studies group at work on South Asian (specifically Indian) historiography.[7] The alterations in theory, methods, and objects of study that this collective brought to the fore reshaped the space in which feminist postcolonial criticism moved. And in turn, postcolonial feminists altered the gender dynamics of Subaltern Studies scholarship.

The objectives of the Subaltern Studies approach to historiography are set out in Ranajit Guha's preface to the first volume (1982) of the influential *Subaltern Studies* journal, now in its third decade of publication. Guha states the objectives of the group as the promotion of "a systematic and informed discussion of subaltern themes in the field of South Asian Studies" and the study of the "general attribute of subordination in South Asian Society whether this is expressed in terms of class, caste, age, gender and office or in any other way."[8] These historians rethought and rewrote Indian history in the light of their realization that the official *nationalist* history in the postcolonial period had not made a radical break from official *colonial* historiography. Every historical text in the postindependence period was written in direct relation to official Indian nationalism, and the nationalist narration of independence continued to be an elite history, presenting independence struggles as waged by a few charismatic leaders with many unquestioning followers. Prior to the Subaltern Studies intervention, Indian historians were generally unable to see the struggles of disenfranchised groups outside this elite history; when these struggles were noted, it was in terms of an entrenched national framework.

Subaltern Studies looks beneath and beyond this official history. For example, in *Event, Metaphor, Memory: Chauri Chaura 1922–1992*, Shahid Amin, a central participant in the collective, reexamines the infamous February 4, 1922 event in which rioting peasants burned down a police station and killed 22 Indian policemen (to the cry of "Victory to Mahatma Gandhi") in Chauri Chaura in north India.[9] This violent uprising was condemned by both the British and the Indian nationalists. (Gandhi temporarily halted his anti-British agitation in despair at the violence in Chauri Chaura.) Amin painstakingly records and analyzes both official and unofficial sources about the motivations and interests of the local, unknown peasant-actors behind this violent attack. In national and imperial memory, Chauri Chaura marks one of the lowest points of the independence struggle: the local concerns of the peasants of the region were erased in conventional historical accounts unless evoked to "serve the purpose of distinguishing authentic popular protest from 'crime.'"[10] As Ania Loomba has noted, the Subaltern Studies approach "shifts the crucial social divide from that between colonial and anticolonial to that between 'elite' and 'subaltern.'"[11] The arrival of national independence elevated certain groups to the status of "national elites" and, sadly, made very little difference to the opportunities and routes for advancement (agency, voice, self-representation) open to subaltern groups. Spivak describes these subaltern peoples as those who are left out of the relay race between empire and nation; these are historical actors to whom the baton is never passed.[12]

Postcolonial feminist scholars have exposed and rectified what has been identified as the one major flaw in the otherwise brilliant reworking of Indian history by the Subaltern Studies group: they propose a serious, multifaceted feminist consideration of gender within and outside of official histories. Thus Spivak's question, "can the subaltern speak?," while following the work of the Subaltern Studies collective, brings gender powerfully to bear on the enterprise. Leela Gandhi characterizes Spivak's query as "utterly unanswerable, half-serious and half-parodic," yet Gandhi begins her book-length discussion of postcolonial theory with the challenge this question poses to the "race and class blindness of the Western academy."[13] The import of Spivak's question lies in her insistence on bringing "gender blindness" (even within the scholarship of critical intellectuals) into the discussion of subalternity. Whether seeking the "low growl" of the bestial Bertha in *Jane Eyre* or the unintelligible cries of the *sati* from the colonial period and of disenfranchised women in the postcolonial era, the "impossible" task of giving voice to the gendered subaltern is a primary concern in postcolonial literary feminism. What is the purpose of the postcolonial feminist critic as she attempts to record the speaking voice, agency, and subject position of the subaltern figures for whom she clears a space in discourse? At her bleakest and most cautionary, Spivak considers such feminist scholarship as no more than "information retrieval" by the "native informant" (read non-Western feminist located in the West).[14]

Spivak presents the contemporary Bengali writer Mahasweta Devi's body of work as an outstanding example of an alternative mode of feminist scholarship/cultural production that *acts* as a political ally of the subaltern subjects it represents. Devi is not easily classifiable as *simply* an elite writer: in addition to her fiction writing, she is also a tireless activist and advocate for bringing the constitutional and legal rights due to all Indians to the most underprivileged communities in the country. Her fiction transforms literary language and theme by incorporating the classical literary language of high culture, official colonial/governmental language, English, Bengali, and regional dialects *and* by making subaltern subjects central to her fiction. In 1981, when Spivak published her translation of Devi's short story "Draupadi" in *Critical Inquiry*, she radically altered the usual assumptions about the kinds of literary texts considered worthy of analysis in the pages of academic journals. Spivak's foreword, with its gloss of the story and its discussion of the literary critic's role, was not directed at a comparative literature audience or to area specialists, but to the mainstream Western reader of literature and literary theory.

"Draupadi" represents a very different kind of literary text, a radically different female protagonist, and a revolutionary literary response to the violence of gang rape. In this story the female protagonist Draupadi is a tribal woman who is also a leader in the revolutionary Naxalbari agitation (a peasant and urban student movement in Bengal and other Indian states in the late 1960s and early 1970s). The story describes the normalized discourse through which state-sanctioned violence and torture is recorded in the bland phrase "killed in a police encounter." When Draupadi is captured and gang-raped by the police, her refusal to clean up, cover her ravaged body, and look decent after the rape, and her defiant insistence that Senanayak, the army officer in charge, acknowledge the damage done to her makes for a chilling conclusion to the story:

> She looks around and chooses the front of Senanayak's white bush shirt to spit a bloody gob at and says, There isn't a man here that I should be ashamed. I will not let you put my cloth on me. What more can you do? Come on, *counter* me – come on, *counter* me –?

> Draupadi pushes Senanayak with her two mangled breasts, and for the first time Senanayak is afraid to stand before an unarmed *target*, deeply afraid.
> [*Italicized words are in English in the original Bengali*][15]

Devi's protagonist is not the usual female subject of a "feminist" literary text. Draupadi is a subaltern woman with agency and with voice. Her "countersentence" is on record in this short story. *But what does it amount to?* The story makes clear that Draupadi will be killed – another statistic to be filed away and forgotten as the casualty of a "police encounter." This grim conclusion articulates the political dilemma of the elite postcolonial critic that Spivak captures in her wistful query "can the subaltern speak?" And when she does "speak," is she heard? Does she automatically acquire agency? And if she has agency, does she gain control of her life or, at least, as this story proposes, of a dignified death? How powerful is the "countersentence" spoken within the cultural text?

In her foreword to the story, Spivak inaugurates a new literary critique by seeing in Senanayak "the closest approximation to the first world scholar in search of the third world." She adds: "The approximation . . . relates to the author's careful presentation of Senanayak as a pluralist aesthete" (*In Other Worlds*, p. 179). Senanayak's specialist knowledge, his eagerness to track down Draupadi, the violence he authorizes, his pride in his skills, his villainy, make this a very uncomfortable parallel. What do we (elite First and Third World-based feminist postcolonial critics) do with this parallel? Spivak forces the critic to acknowledge her power as a reading subject, as a consumer of texts about subaltern women and men. The very acts of reading and writing about these texts, of making "them" into objects of study, enable "us" and give us currency in our academic setting. Devi and her readers (regardless of their locations) might be said to "bear witness" to the oppressive conditions in which the subalterns of our world live their lives. But postcolonial feminist criticism does not often allow itself the relative comfort of this interpretative framework (or alibi). The publication of this and other stories (often in translation) gives elite audiences a glimpse of the work (not all of it literary) that a leftist intellectual and activist for social justice like Devi does *elsewhere*. Spivak's feminist reading and Devi's fiction give cultural work its due importance, but both also point to the ways in which the reader and scholar are implicated in the violence of the story.

Postcolonial feminist criticism developed in this period in relation to other critical feminist projects as well. From the early 1960s onward, there was a powerful and multifaceted movement by US-based "women of color" (as they began to call themselves) for equal rights in all spheres of life. This struggle emerged from and alongside the feminist and civil rights movements of the 1960s–1970s, with women of color insisting on the double oppression they faced on account of their race and gender. As part of their resistance to racial and gendered prejudices, women of color in the United States also developed powerful critiques of mainstream white feminism for its race-related blind spots, and against the masculinist bias of nationalist struggles for racial uplift within their own communities. Like postcolonial theorists, these women were inspired by nationalist struggles in the third world. Thus women of color in the United States argued that they were also "third world women," despite the irony of their geographic location.

Two texts from the early 1980s consolidated theorizing from this position: the poetic and incisive *This Bridge Called My Back*, edited by Cherríe Moraga and Gloria Anzaldúa, with a foreword by Toni Cade Bambara (1981), and Chandra Mohanty's "Under Western Eyes: Feminist Scholarship and Colonial Discourses" (1984). These early texts, emblematic of this critical tradition, connected the US-based women of color critique (conventionally linked with US feminist and civil rights movements) with the then-burgeoning postcolonial feminist critique (whose arena was usually defined in the United States as "foreign," given its preoccupation with the contours of the erstwhile colonial spaces of Britain and her former colonies and the general amnesia about US imperialism).

Mohanty's "Under Western Eyes" was first published in 1984 in the academic journal *Boundary 2*, then republished in Teresa de Lauretis's influential anthology *Feminist Studies/Critical Studies* in 1986, then reprinted in *Feminist Review* in 1988 and again in 1991 in the immensely important *Third World Women and the Politics of Feminism*, edited by Mohanty, Russo, and Torres.[16] Very widely read, this essay engaged both women of color and postcolonial feminist concerns and soon became constitutive of both fields. In the essay Mohanty formulates a theoretically nuanced critique of the "discursive colonialism" toward "third world women" practiced by elite women, both in the geographic West and outside it. She maps the contours of privilege in feminist writing and the effects of such West-oriented feminism on the non-West. She pinpoints the effect of feminist analysis that constructs a singular and generic "third world woman" as the object of study. Third world women always function in such work as "a homogenous, powerless group . . . often located as the implicit victim of particular socioeconomic systems" (*Third World Women,* p. 57).

Mohanty's concern is that even as elite feminism intervenes in traditional disciplinary analysis, an "ethnocentric universalism is produced in western feminist analysis" and "a homogenous notion of the oppression of women is assumed, which, in turn, produces the image of an 'average third world woman'" – one who is studied most often in terms of her fertility (p. 56). Mohanty thus both names and challenges the objectification of women in the third world as perennial victims within scholarship on topics as seemingly disparate as economic development, male violence, familial systems, genital mutilation, and "the Islamic code." Marking the gap between the heterogeneous conditions in which women live their lives in the third world and the monolithic "third world woman" of elite feminist discourse, "Under Western Eyes" is a foundational text for all contemporary feminist endeavors, even those that are not readily identified as postcolonial. The cautions that Mohanty offers are now part of the "common sense" of the field. Yet, even as recently as 2001–2, the discussion of Afghan women in the mainstream US media provided many examples of the imperialist first world reading of third world women that Mohanty vociferously and painstakingly critiqued in an essay written more than twenty years ago!

Mohanty's essay, along with some of the writing produced in parallel discussions such as Denise Riley's *"Am I That Name?" Feminism and the Category of "Women" in History* (1988), Judith Butler's *Gender Trouble* (1990), and other work on this topic, began to disassemble one of feminist literary criticism's most revered and "natural" categories – that of "the woman" and, subsequently, of "the woman writer." A long-presumed, *automatic* unity based in gender was repeatedly challenged by these feminists, who were quick to point to the ways in which women were *multiply* constituted subjects. As Mohanty states: "by women as a category of analysis, I am referring to the crucial assumption that all of us of the same gender, across classes and cultures, are somehow socially constituted as a homogeneous group identified *prior to the process of analysis*" (p. 56, my emphasis). Yet "women" as a category of analysis has long been considered central to feminist theory and practice. What does it mean for feminist discourse and practice to give up the category of women as foundational? Postcolonial feminism had only to turn to anticolonial discourse to see the very special place it granted to women and to understand that this special status was to be firmly resisted.

Postcolonial feminists were especially astute in noting *and refusing* the exalted yet largely symbolic status allotted to women in many nationalist struggles. Indeed, gender symbolism in colonial and postindependence periods remains essentially unchanged: women were paradoxically both central (as symbolic figures) and marginal (in terms of actual changes in their material circumstances) to nationalist projects, just as they had been to colonial projects. Partha Chatterjee's influential essay on "The Nationalist Resolution of the Women's Question" in the Indian context best surveys the terrain in which such discussions of women as subjects and objects of discourse played out.[17] Chatterjee argues that nationalism resolved the women's question through the separation of the domain of culture into two spheres: the material and the spiritual. Colonialism, it was believed, had left the spiritual or private realm of culture untouched; this realm was embodied by the Indian woman. The spiritual sphere was thus a space in which the nation imagined itself as already free; cultural arenas were seen as not always in the same subordinate relation to the colonizers as economic or political arenas. What resulted from this nationalist reasoning was a firm association of women with the spiritual, cultural, and private realms. Indian nationalists deftly invoked prevalent patriarchal gender inequalities to resist colonial interference in the intimate reaches of "native" lives. As a consequence, reforming women's lives became a contentious arena of struggle between colonists and nationalists. Mrinalini Sinha's discussion of the age of consent (for marriage) debates in late nineteenth- and early twentieth-century British India provides a good illustration of the gendered dynamics of social reform.[18]

During independence struggles and immediately after, most nations were figured as female, and women were the ground on which national identity was erected. In Loomba's succinct reformulation of Benedict Anderson's argument: "If the nation is an imagined community, that imagining is profoundly gendered" (*Colonialism-postcolonialism*, p. 215). Postcolonial feminist scholars have argued that while women may make minimal gains when mobilized as symbols of the new nation, they are easily returned to the domestic or to a depoliticized private sphere when independence is achieved. As Deniz Kandiyoti notes: "the vagaries of nationalist discourse are reflected in changing portrayals of women as victims of social backwardness, icons of modernity, as boundary markers or privileged bearers of cultural authenticity."[19] In these symbolic sites, Kandiyoti argues, women's claims to "enfranchised citizenry" ("Identity and its Discontents," p. 378) are ultimately limited because they are "held hostage" to the needs of the nation and tenaciously subjected to patriarchal control in the familial sphere. That is, they are caught in the role of mother/daughter/wife in both familial *and* national discourse. This disposition does not go unchallenged, however. As Lila Abu-Lughod makes clear in her discussion of the Middle

East, "women themselves actively participate in these debates and social struggles, with feminism, defined in sometimes quite different ways, having become by now an inescapable term of reference."[20] Thus women in these locations are simultaneously participants in and hostages to nationalist projects – both empowered and undercut by the weight of their symbolic place.

As in the colonial era, in the postindependence period women are also the primary objects of reform and manipulation, especially under state-sanctioned modernization projects. Reforming/modernizing the lives of women in the Middle East, as Abu-Lughod demonstrates, is regulatory and emancipatory: modernity in the Middle East, she argues, introduces an era of the consolidation of the domestic as the proper arena for women within a new, heterosexual nuclear family model, with the man as head of household and the concomitant devaluation of women's homosocial networks. "The forms of feminism in the Middle East tied to modernity," she writes, "ushered in new forms of gendered subjection (in the double sense of subject positions for women and forms of domination) as well as new experiences and possibilities" (*Remaking Women*, p. 13).

Elite women's writing in these locations reflects the pride, ambivalence, and tension of embodying the locally defined ideal of womanhood. Popular literature by women in the newly independent nations expresses a desire to evolve into a female subject who is "free" from the many representations of proper womanhood that are abundantly produced in various nationalist texts, yet the contours of this desired self are defined by these representations. Thus in a range of texts, including *Changes: A Love Story* by the Ghanaian writer Ama Ata Aidoo, *Nervous Conditions* by the Zimbabwean writer Tsitsi Dangarembga, *Women of Sand and Myrrh* by the Lebanese writer Hanan al-Shaykh, and *That Long Silence* by the Indian writer Shashi Deshpande, frustration at the appropriation of the body, labor and intellect of the female subject by state, communal, or familial projects forms a central theme of the realist plot.[21] For the women in these fictional texts, belonging to, indeed, being the showpiece of a newly independent nation holds no guarantees.

Postcolonial literary criticism brings the world (through its literature and other cultural productions) into the arena of Western scholarship; understandably, this is not easy to "manage" since "the world" is a wide and varied space. While postcolonial theory may well be able to avoid the dangers of previous waves of Western knowledge production about the non-West, there is no avoiding the fact that the interests of the first world shape what is exported from the once colonized parts of the world, including cultural "products." Once brought to the attention of Western academia and the multinational publishing industry, the fiction and culture of the non-Western parts of the globe tend instantly to become "representative" of their geographic location. But are the texts chosen for explication by post-colonial scholars truly "representative" of national literatures, as is implicitly or explicitly claimed? Indeed, is literature the most representative cultural form in every context? Some might argue that in many countries in the developing world, where illiteracy is widespread, film, storytelling, music, or drama may be the cultural forms to study. The very attention paid to literary texts written in the languages of the former colonizers (often languages with contemporary global currency) produces divisions and inequalities on the home ground.

For example, consider the distortions that the Western valuation of literatures in English creates in the Indian literary scene, where an ongoing struggle is being waged between Indian writers in English and those writing in other Indian vernacular languages. This "conflict" was publicized in the United States by the provocative argument that Salman Rushdie made in 1997 in a special issue of the *New Yorker* on South Asian literature fifty years after Independence. Rushdie argued that, except for the work of the occasional writer such as Sadat Manto (Urdu), the best Indian writing since 1947 has been written in English, rather than in any of India's sixteen or so officially recognized regional languages, each with its own rich literary heritage.[22] Add to this arrogant assertion the undeniable fact that the Indian literature that has garnered the largest royalties, as well as international literary awards, has been written in English. More recently, the broad strokes of this battle were exposed by the exchanges between "IWE" (Indian writers in English) and writers in the vernaculars (regional languages) on the occasion of the first International Festival of Indian Literature (New Delhi, February 2002) showcased in recent issues of the Indian magazine *Outlook*. Regional writers of repute such as U.R. Ananthamurthy (Kannada), Dilip Chitre (Marathi), Sunil Gangopadhyay (Bengali), Balchandran Nimade (Marathi), Gurdial Singh (Punjabi), and Rajendra Yadav (Hindi) are quoted denouncing Indian writing in English as "second-rate," "artificial western flowers," "a third-rate serpent-and-rope trick," "removed from their own ethos," and "rootless."[23] Writers such as Shashi Deshpande (English) responded with astonishment and hurt at the hostility expressed by vernacular writers: "We belong to the same world you did, all of us were part of the ocean called Indian Literature . . . This is our home, as it is yours; we did not drop out of the skies when we started writing in English."[24]

While there is no single or simple explanation for such hostilities, postcolonial feminist theorizing has certainly had a role to play in elevating the literary over other cultural productions and, within the literary, in valorizing novels that need no or minimal translation into first world languages and expectations. For example, the frequency with which certain kinds of texts (such as the realist English, French, or Spanish- language narrative of gendered oppression written by a third world woman writer) are assigned in college-level survey courses or seminars on postcolonial literature no doubt fuels publishers' interest in just such fiction.

Feminists have increasingly argued that the location from which and about which one writes and reads is critical. While postcolonial feminist criticism places itself in opposition to all that is mainstream in the literary establishment of the West, when viewed from the non-Western world, US- and British-based postcolonial feminist critical theory is readily associated with other Western feminisms and postmodernisms. The poet Adrienne Rich coined the term "the politics of location" in the early 1980s when her travels outside the United States made her recognize the white privilege she enjoyed by virtue of her first world affiliations, race, and (US) citizenship.[25] Postcolonial feminist scholarship has assiduously elaborated on Rich's notion, and it has become a shorthand for a scrupulous awareness of one's relation and proximity to power. This awareness acts as a check on assuming the universality of one's position, for it relentlessly draws attention to the location from which any theorization is launched. Despite the relatively easy access between the West and non-West that the new modes of communication have established, the politics of location continue to be a crucial consideration for postcolonial feminists.

As the reader of this essay may have noted, the location and colonial relation that is central to postcolonial feminist theory and practice is the British colonial occupation of India and the postcolonial Indian state. This preponderance of work on the British and Indian context is not accidental: many major practitioners in the field of postcolonial studies, as recognized by the Western academy, are of Indian origin. Spivak, Homi Bhabha, Chandra Mohanty, Dipesh Chakrabarty, and other scholars (myself included) in the field were born in and had their early education in postindependence India, but work within the British and US academia. Also, significantly, nineteenth-century British India and twentieth-century postindependence India are the primary foci of the Subaltern Studies historians whose theorizations of how knowledge is produced and history is made are a major influence on postcolonial studies. One result is that the Indian context has become like the body on which a dress is fitted: a great deal of the "canon" of postcolonial critical writing emanates from the Indian location and therefore explicates or fits the Indian context best.

Over the past three decades, of course, feminist theorizing has been done in other postcolonial contexts, but these texts have not thus far become as central to the Western academic canon of postcolonial feminism as have the kind of "India-oriented" work described in this essay. Thus, for example, many scholars, such as Ifi Amadiume, Abena Busia, Carole Boyce Davis, Anne Adams Graves, Anthonia Kalu, Juliana Nfah-Abbemji, Obioma Nnaemeka, Filomena Chioma Steady, Florence Stratton, and others have written on African literary feminism. This work enlarges the scope of postcolonial feminism and revises India-centric theories in fruitful ways. Florence Stratton, for instance, in *Contemporary African Literature and the Politics of Gender*, argues that the most important feature of African women's writing is its ongoing dialogue with the fiction produced by African male writers.[26] Stratton is especially invested in refuting generalizing theories about African and postcolonial fiction based on the work of male writers that have been proffered by scholars such as Abdul JanMohammad and Fredric Jameson.[27] To elaborate on one such concern: Stratton demonstrates the ways in which African women writers and their concerns are erased within Jameson's characterization of *all* third world literature as "necessarily . . . national allegory . . . *so that the story of the private individual destiny is always an allegory of the embattled situation of the public third world culture and society.*"[28] Instead, Stratton demonstrates, African women writers exhibit "an antagonistic response to the 'national allegories' produced by some of their male counterparts – allegories which . . . encode gender definitions which operate to justify and maintain the status quo of women's exclusion from public life."[29] As the Senegalese writer Mariama Bâ states bluntly: "The nostalgic songs dedicated to African mothers which express the anxieties of men concerning Mother Africa are no longer enough for us."[30]

More recent work in feminist postcolonial literatures has also challenged the all too common tendency to read African and other postcolonial literary texts as sociological evidence of the everyday realities of the national context in which it was written. For example, Ayi Kwei Armah's *The Beautyful Ones are Not Yet Born: A Novel* (1968), written in the disappointing aftermath of the Ghanaian independence struggle, sees dirt and excrement everywhere, but this should be read in metaphorical terms, not as a depiction of everyday life. Armah's contemporary, Ama Ata Aidoo, who wrote *No Sweetness Here* (1969), a collection of short stories that takes its title from a phrase in *The Beautyful Ones*, is no less disappointed by the corruption and neocolonial patriarchal systems that independence fails to alter, but her choice of metaphors and other novelistic details is quite different from Armah's. Since their fiction was produced in Ghana right after independence, it is tempting to read Armah and Aidoo as straightforwardly mirroring nationalist sentiment. But, as Stratton makes clear, third world writers do not universally feel the burden of creating national allegories in their fiction; they focus on the many varied aspects of everyday life or of the imagination in their texts. Thus the literary criticism produced from the vantage position of postcolonial feminism insists on reading against the grain of formulaic analyses of third world literature.

As Stratton's work and that of other feminist scholars working in post-colonial societies remind us, it is important to recall that subjection to European colonialism and nationalism is not the only salient feature of societies that are nevertheless accurately described as postcolonial. The very terms "colonial discourse" and "postcolonial theory" may obscure the fact that these (once-colonized) parts of the world have long histories that go way back before European colonialism and, no doubt, long futures beyond it. Needless to add, there are also many feminisms and academic feminist theories in these locations that have only the slightest link with literary studies. For example, postcolonial feminist commentary has produced groundbreaking work on the ways in which the colonial and/or nationalist state has used gender and sexuality to its advantage and concurrently to the disadvantage of women whose lives are subject to such authority. Postco-lonial feminists have worked extensively on sexuality in these contexts in order to formulate a decolonized understanding of the relations of power and gender. Yet, as Jacqui Alexander has succinctly noted, even in feminist critiques that are cognizant of the importance of sexuality to institutional apparatuses, much work remains to be done "on elaborating the processes of heterosexualization at work within the state apparatus."[31]

Increasingly, postcolonial scholars within the Western academy have begun to theorize a "new" Diaspora Studies that considers the effects of mass migrations beyond the groups (Jews, Greeks, Armenian) to which the term "diaspora" was exclusively applied before the 1960s. As Western academia slowly opened up to scholarly articulations of diasporic experi-ences of travel and resettlement, of cultural production "on the road," as it were, of cross-continental links that endure over generations and of the differentiated, diasporic sense of belonging and citizenship in all locations, new issues relating to gender and sexuality in a cross-continental framework are elaborated upon by feminists. Diaspora Studies serves as an interesting site for feminist and other scholars, straddling as it does several geographic locations that are held in one framework. Thus an immigrant's view of the West is both linked to and distinguished from one or more parts of the non-Western world.

Forty years after women of color in the United States associated them-selves with "women in the third world," the changes in immigration law, the movement of capital and jobs, globalization, and other economic and political forces all call for reformulations of the relations between people who live in and move among different corners of the planet. For example, under the rubric of Diaspora Studies, one can study the long history of the transportation of "indentured labor" from China and South Asia to meet the demands of a plantation economy after the abolition of slavery in the nineteenth century. We might ponder how gendered, labor, sexual, and familial relations were reorganized in these circumstances. Moving to the current phase of globalization, we may ask who are the subalterns and elites in the new global economies. What was the impact of the changes in immigration law in 1965 on racial and class dynamics in the United States? Consider the full implications of the slogan "We Are Here Because You Were There" that is frequently used by black and Asian British subjects protesting about various aspects of race relations in the United Kingdom. How are citizenship, gender, sexuality, and familial dynamics reformulated in a diasporic context? How does the conventional understanding of nationality signify in the age of what Aihwa Ong has called "flexible citizenship" in her study of transnational Asians? Newly emerging feminist scholarship on these issues goes well beyond the "literary" and beyond a pristine understanding of gender as an isolated factor.

Also, other well-established areas of study – such as Asian Studies and Asian American or Latin American Studies – come into conversation with postcolonial studies under the aegis of diaspora. Asian American Studies over the past decade has moved well beyond a purely national understanding of its scope to study the effects of US imperialism in Asia, new immigration, and transnational labor arrangements that stretch from Asia to the United Kingdom and out into other geographies. Thus a novel such as Jessica Hagedorn's *Dogeaters* (1991), set in the Philippines in the Marcos era, can be classified both as postcolonial fiction (given its clear elaboration of the impact of US imperialism on the Philippines) and as a classic Asian American novel framed by the protagonist Rio's immigration to the United States. As the novel makes clear, the United States shapes Rio's everyday life well before she steps onto US shores. Increasingly, the foods, music, television channels, languages, and peoples of the Philippines are now visible and established in thriving Filipino American communities in the United States. There are many such local contact zones where third world meets first world and irreversibly mix the categories of "West" and "non-West." The so-called "mainstream" cultures of the West are now irreversibly colored by the contributions from their immigrant populations and thus by past and present imperial policies.

Returning our attention to postcolonial literary feminist criticism: literary critical feminist territorial boundaries are not as clear-cut in the twenty-first century as they were imagined to be even a decade ago. We are at the threshold of a new location, one that *approaches* what we might call "global literary studies" – a situation that calls for a radical rethinking of the claims we have become accustomed to making when we produce feminist and/or literary scholarship. We can no longer make claims about how literary texts function as cultural artifacts and as political tools without having to think hard about how such texts might play out in other locations. This is not to suggest glibly that today information and influence circulate easily among scholars working in different parts of the world, but rather to argue that we cannot proceed with our scholarly projects oblivious to how our work speaks to scholarship or readership in different locations. Writing to this enlarged audience alerts one to the kinds of theoretical and practical negotiations that will soon be required *as a matter of course* in the era of global literary studies. Many cultural practices (literary and nonliterary) are produced every day across the globe, and many theorists and intellectuals (whose names do not appear here) continue to reflect on and articulate the significance of such work. The challenge for postcolonial feminist scholarship within the Western academy is to look beyond this location and engage with literary texts and literary criticism produced elsewhere, but always with a clear understanding of the pitfalls of apprehending the world with the aid of the old imperial analytical tools supplied by our common history of colonialism.

Further reading

Leela Gandhi, *Postcolonial Theory: A Critical Introduction* (New York: Columbia University Press, 1998).

Ania Loomba, *Colonialism-Postcolonialism* (New York: Routledge, 1998).

Chandra Talpade Mohanty, Ann Russo, and Lourdes Torres, eds., *Third World Women and the Politics of Feminism* (Bloomington: Indiana University Press, 1991).

Edward Said, *Orientalism* (New York: Random House, 1993).

Culture and Imperialism (New York: Vintage, 1994).

Gayatri Chakravorty Spivak, *The Spivak Reader* eds. Donna Landry and Gerald Maclean (New York: Vintage, 1979).

Patrick Williams and Laura Chrisman, eds., *Colonial Discourse and Postcolonial Theory* (New York: Columbia University Press, 1994).

NOTES

I would like to thank Ellen Rooney for her generosity with insights and countless conversations about this essay.
    1. Quoted by Ngugi Wa Thiongo in *Homecoming: Essays on African and Caribbean literature, Culture and Politics* (London: Heinemann, 1972), p. 45.

2. See also Moira Ferguson's *Colonialism and Gender Relations from Mary Woll-stonecraft to Jamaica Kincaid: East Caribbean Connections* (New York: Columbia University Press, 1993), Firdous Azim's *The Colonial Rise of the Novel* (London: Routledge, 1993), among a host of other scholarly books on this topic.
3. Catherine Belsey and Jane Moore, eds., *The Feminist Reader: Essays in Gender and the Politics of Literary Criticism* (New York: Oxford University Press, 1987), p. 183.
4. See Nancy Armstrong *Desire and Domestic Fiction: A Political History of the Novel* (New York: Oxford University Press, 1987), p. 66. See also the chapter "The Authoritative Englishwoman: Setting up Home and Self in the Colonies," in my *The Politics of Home: Postcolonial Relocations and Twentieth-Century Fiction* (Cambridge: Cambridge University Press, 1996), pp. 35–64.
5. See Lata Mani, "Contentious Traditions: the Debate on Sati in Colonial India," in Kumkum Sangari and Sudesh Vaid, eds., *Recasting Women: Essays in Colonial History* (New Delhi: Kali for Women Press, 1989), pp. 88–126.
6. Gayatri Chakravorty Spivak, "Can the Subaltern speak?," in Patrick Williams and Laura Chrisman, eds., *Colonial Discourse and Postcolonial Theory: A Reader* (New York: Columbia University Press, 1994), p. 93.
7. That "subaltern" was the highest rank that an Indian could achieve in the British colonial army was a nice detail of not too much import.
8. See *Subaltern Studies*, 1, ed. Ranajit Guha (New Delhi: Oxford University Press, 1982). p. vii. In recent years such a "subaltern studies approach" has been taken up by historians in Latin America, Mexico, Japan, and other locations as a theory and methodology for reexamining disparate colonial and national histories.
9. See Shahid Amin, *Event, Metaphor, Memory: Chauri Chaura 1922–1992* (Berkeley: University of California Press, 1995).
10. Ibid., p. 3.
11. Ania Loomba, *Colonialism-Postcolonialism* (New York Routledge, 1998), p. 199.
12. See Gayatri Chakravorty Spivak, "Woman in Difference: Mahasweta Devi's 'Doulati the Bountiful'," *Cultural Critique* (Winter 1989–90), pp. 105–28.
13. Leela Gandhi, *Postcolonial Theory: A Critical Introduction* (New York: Columbia University Press, 1998), p. 2.
14. Gayatri Chakravorty Spivak, *In Other Worlds: Essays in Cultural Politics* (New York: Methuen, 1987), p. 179.
15. Ibid., p. 196.
16. Chandra Talpade Mohanty, Ann Russo, and Lourdes Torres, eds., *Third World Women and the politics of Feminism* (Bloomingon: Indiana University Press, 1991).
17. See Partha Chatterjee "The Nationalist Resolution of the Women's Question," Sangari and Vaid, eds., in *Recasting Women*, p. 233–53.
18. See Mrinalini Sinha "Potent Protests: the Age of Consent Controversy, 1891" in Sinha, *Colonial Masculinity* (1995; reprinted New Delhi: Kali for Women Press, 1997), pp. 138–80.
19. Deniz Kandiyoti, "Identity and its DisContents: Women and the Nation," in Williams and Chrisman, eds., *Colonial Discourse*, pp. 376–91. See also N. Yuval-Davis and F. Anthias, eds., *Women-Nation-State* (London: Macmillan,

1989); and Kumari Jayawardena, *Feminism and Nationalism in the Third World* (London: Zed, 1988).

20. Lila Abu-Lughod, "Introduction: Feminist Longings and Postcolonial Conditions," in Abu-Lughod, ed., *Remaking Women: Feminism and Modernity in the MiddleEast* (Princeton: Princeton University Press, 1998) pp. 3–31.

21. See Ama Ata Aidoo, *Changes: A Love Story* (London: The Women's Press, 1991); Tsitsi Dangarembga, *Nervous Conditions* (London: The Women's Press, London, 1988); Hanan al-Shaykh, *Women of Sand and Myrrh* (London: Quartet Press, 1989); and Shashi Deshpande, *That Long Silence*, (London: Virago, 1988).

22. See Salman Rushdie, "Damme This Is the Oriental Scene For You!," *New Yorker*, June 23 and 30, 1997, pp. 50–61.

23. See "Midnight's Orphans: How Indian is Indian Writing in English?" by the journalist Sheela Reddy in *Outlook*, February 25, 2002 (www.outlookindia.com/outlookarchive).

24. Shashi Deshpande, "English's Inter Alia: An Open-Letter to Some Fellow Writers," *Outlook* March 11, 2002 (www.outlookindia.com/outlookarchive).

25. See Rich's *Blood, Bread, and Poetry: Selected Prose, 1979–1985* (New York: Norton, 1986).

26. See Florence Stratton, *Contemporary African Literature and the Politics of Gender* (London: Routledge, 1994).

27. See Abdul JanMohammad, *Manichean Aesthetics: The Politics of Literature in Colonial Africa* (Amherst, MA: University of Massachusetts Press, 1983); and Fredric Jameson, "Third World Literature in the Era of Multinational Capitalism," *Social Text* 15 (1986), pp. 65–88.

28. See Jameson, "Third World Literature," p. 69 (emphasis in the original).

29. See Stratton, *Contemporary African Litrature*, p. 10.

30. Quoted in Carol Boyce Davis and Ann Adams Graves, eds., *Ngambika: Studies of Women in African Literature)* (Trenton, NJ: Africa World Press, 1986), p. xi.

31. Jacqui Alexander, "Erotic Autonomy as a Politics of Decolonization: An Anatomy of State Practice in the Bahamas Tourist Economy," in Alexander and Chandra Mohanty, eds., *Feminist Genealogies, Colonial Legacies, Democratic Futures* (New York: Routledge, 1997), pp. 63–100 (p. 65).

11

RASHMI VARMA

On common ground?: feminist theory and critical race studies

Feminist theory and critical race studies have often and long been considered to have separate and incompatible, indeed oppositional histories. This essay hopes to show that they not only share theoretical ground but offer critical interventions in the discourses and practices, both institutionalized and marginalized, of race and gender. This also means that both feminist theory and critical race studies are invested in analyzing the ground of representation, especially as it pertains to how we read literary and cultural texts. This essay will trace the contours of this common ground, highlighting the productive negotiations that have taken place between feminist theory and critical race studies. These interchanges have enabled the formulation of what I will refer to throughout as "feminist critical race studies."

Such a critical studies emerges out of two tendencies within theorizations of race and gender. Over the past fifty years, at least since the era of civil rights and women's rights struggles in the 1960s, race and gender have been variously represented as being "parallel," "intersecting," and "overlapping" systems of identity formation that structure social relations. Each of these ways of describing the relationship between race and gender persists in seeing race and gender as separate social systems. Feminist critical race studies challenges this distinctness and instead posits an articulation of race and gender. At the same time, against certain strands of postmodern skepticism of race and gender as "essential" categories of analysis in themselves, feminist critical race studies infuses readings of race and gender with theories of power that suggest that although gender and race categories are not fixed and innate, they nevertheless operate within systems that assign them value as categories of belonging and identification. Incorporating power into our analysis helps us to understand why certain races and genders obtain social prestige and wealth and thus the capacity to dominate other groups. This essay highlights how these systems of power are in fact historically interwoven with each other, forming a dense fabric that constitutes society itself and that shape how, through literature and art, we can understand our social predicament and imagine a different one. The task of a feminist critical race studies is precisely to help us to *read* the weave of race and gender in society, and to offer tools for dismantling embedded structures of domination and oppression. Studies that are informed by such a critical reading of race and gender highlight how, through literature and art, for example, we can both understand our social predicament and imagine a different, more just, society. For feminist critical race studies, a just society is not a utopian dream but is constituted in the continuous struggle for it.

The essay will also attempt to frame the interface between these thoroughly mutually implicated and interwoven theoretical terrains in a global context, asking the question: What happens to constructs of race and gender in the arena of not just national cultures but international and transnational struggles for rights and justice? A critical project that aims to open up space for thinking about justice would necessarily have to work against the prevailing and resilient Anglo-American centrism in feminist and race studies, while taking account of the long histories of genocide, slavery, and colonialism that created diasporas of black people in Europe and North America. Thus, while the nation states of the United States, France, or United Kingdom continue to be the troubled containers of our analyses, it is also important to see how national ideologies of race and gender shape transnational struggles to create a more equitable world order. This task seems especially urgent in the current context of a reconsolidation of national borders and identities along racial and cultural lines, even as the forces of economic globalization seek to cast the world as a global marketplace.

"Ain't I a black woman?": African American feminism and critical race theory

Sojourner Truth's question, "Ain't I a woman?," asked in nineteenth-century America represents an early and key moment recognizing the competing regimes of identification that black women have had to contend with historically: those of gender and race (see Ann duCille's essay in this volume). More than a century later, Anita Hill might have asked the same question with a variation: "Ain't I a *black* woman?" (my emphasis). Anita Hill is the lawyer who, in 1991, challenged the nomination of Clarence Thomas to the US Supreme Court, where he would become only the second black judge in the court's history. Anita Hill's charge that Thomas had sexually harassed her intensified the spotlight on an already controversial Thomas, well-known for his opposition to affirmative action policies and abortion rights. The explosive nature of Hill's accusation rested on the fact that she was a black woman accusing a black nominee to the Supreme Court of sexual harassment. What was most at stake, though it was largely unacknowledged, both in the nonstop media coverage of the Senate hearings and in academic and activist circles, was the question of black women's affiliations: should they rally behind the black nominee, or should they throw their weight behind a black woman who exposed not just Thomas's personal failings but the racist sexism of the entire political, juridical, and media establishment that sought to paint Anita Hill as a vindictive, unstable woman?

Many white liberals and conservatives, and many African Americans, too, expressed their support of Thomas's nomination in the light of continuing disparities in the representation of black people in important posts. On the other hand, opposition to Thomas came from both African American civil rights groups such as the NAACP (National Association for the Advancement of Colored People) and others who were repelled by his opposition to affirmative action, and from women's rights groups such as NOW (National Organization for Women) who opposed Thomas for his views on affirmative action and abortion, and who wanted the charge of sexual harassment to be taken seriously.

In the wake of the *Hill* v. *Thomas* case, many African American legal scholars, especially those committed to feminist politics, attempted to expose the narrow notions of racial solidarity that were harnessed (by blacks and whites) to rally behind a man who was, though black, fully committed to the "evisceration" of post-civil rights gains toward racial justice.[1] They pointed to the misguided belief that questions of gender power were irrelevant to the interests of the larger black community. Clearly, what had escaped comment in the understanding of this sensational case was that once again (as African American suffragettes had pointed out more than a century ago) it was the black man who came to represent black society as a whole, while the black woman's experience of sexual harassment became an unnecessary distraction from the opportunity of racial advancement. Thomas's highly charged statement that the attacks on him constituted a "high-tech lynching" itself encapsulated how a black woman's experience of exploitation could be rendered invisible. At the same time, in figuring the sexually harassed woman as race-neutral, mainstream women's groups failed to acknowledge, yet again, the complexity of black women's lives in the United States, in which racial justice is still an urgent priority. The false choice offered to black women in the *Hill* v. *Thomas* case – racial loyalty versus women's rights – in the end could not capture "the ways in which racial identities are lived within and through gendered identities," just as gender identities operate within and across race differences.[2]

Many of the African American feminist scholars (including many men) who responded to the *Hill* v. *Thomas* hearings were part of an intellectual movement in US law schools that began in the 1980s and brought together progressive scholars who were committed to radical social change. Coming out of a critique of traditional civil rights reforms that had emphasized formal equality and color-blindness in matters of law, they nevertheless understood the importance of the struggle for rights in general. The body of work and the theoretical perspective produced by these scholars, which drew significantly on literary studies and emphasized how law could be read as a social narrative, came to be known as Critical Race Theory (CRT). Taking on the study of law, race, and power in the United States, these scholars are particularly interested in examining how racial power becomes legitimate and acceptable in society. They argue that concepts such as "rule of law" and individual merit, which are often seen as universal givens, in fact obscure the question of how people of different races and sexes are unequally positioned within society. CRT scholars see racial power as systemic (and not simply the product of irrational individual prejudice), and they seek to highlight how law plays a key role in the construction and maintenance of social domination. Far from seeing law as operating above and beyond politics, CRT's work has focused on studying the historical centrality and complicity of law in upholding white supremacy (and embedded hierarchies of gender, class, and sexual orientation).

At the same time, their approach has signaled a departure from an easy racialism that views law as reflecting white interests. Law, in their analysis, is a site for ideological struggles around race and gender power, as can be seen quite sharply in the debates around affirmative action, abortion rights, and the recent gay marriage issue in the United States, each of which is articulated and struggled for in the language of rights and legality. Finally, although CRT scholars see race as socially constructed, they also emphasize its material reality, as in the experience of being "raced" in American society.[3]

The arguments over affirmative action serve to highlight the contested nature of such a formulation. For instance, affirmative action policies are considered to be racist by its opponents, who see racism in any perspective that deems someone's race to be important. Such a definition of racism presumes that in practical life one's race has little or no impact on one's chances of success and survival, and that the ideal and just state must be color-blind. Affirmative action is seen as "reverse discrimination" in which, for past prejudice, less meritorious black and other minority groups are given preference in jobs and admissions. In this view, white men are the new victims of racial prejudice. But progressive and radical proponents view the principle of affirmative action as acknowledging and deploying "race as a socially significant category of perception and representation," that has an effect on material life, in opposition to notions of merit that obscure the race and class privileges of whites and other dominant groups.[4]

The figuration of the white male as the new victim of a state reneging on race neutrality has an analogue in the black woman figured as the paradigmatic welfare queen (often a black unwed teenage mother) – uncontrollably fecund and manipulative of the beneficence of the state within whose belly she lives as a parasite. One can trace in such narratives of the black woman all sorts of anxieties about sexuality, race, class and the state in the United States in the aftermath of the 1960s when black women were emerging as key public figures, as theorists of power and writers and intellectuals in their own right. African American women such as Rosa Parks, who courageously refused to give up her seat to a white person on a bus in Mississippi and thus sparked off the civil rights movement; Fannie Lou Hamer and Ella Baker, who led southern black civil rights efforts through the involvement of SNCC (Student Nonviolent Coordinating Committee); poets and teachers such as Angela Davis, Audre Lorde, Pat Parker; the black lesbian members of the Combahee River Collective formed in the mid-1970s, to name only a few writers, artists, grassroots activists, and teachers, represented a powerful new voice in the United States that challenged deep-seated perceptions about the passive victimhood and malevolent parasitism of black female existence. While seeing themselves as giving shape to a new feminist consciousness, these intellectuals also saw their role as extending the work done by their nineteenth-century mothers such as Frances Harper, Anna Julia Cooper, Ida B. Wells, Sojourner Truth, and others.[5] Drawing upon, while also critiquing, the civil rights movement, the black liberation movement (including the Black Panthers), the Left progressive movements and the women's movement, which were all organized around their own singular axes of oppression, African American feminism became one of the most vibrant sites where an alternative political discourse of black womanhood was forged and where an unprecedented burst of creativity shaped a new black feminist consciousness.

Central to articulations of black feminist theory was a reconstruction of black women's intellectual and literary traditions by writers and literary critics such as Alice Walker, Barbara Smith, Barbara Christian, Hazel Carby, and others.[6] This process of creating something that could be gathered, published, read, and written about – that is, a body of creative and critical works by black women – was of course fraught with contradiction, and was to provide feminist critical race studies with important insights.[7] One key issue of contestation was the question of what constitutes black literary practice – a direct political engagement with racial and sexual oppression or a specific aesthetic form that spoke for black women's experiences? In her essay "Toward a Black Feminist Criticism", Barbara Smith made an impassioned case for making visible the presence of black women writers, especially black lesbian writers, and argued that a politicized black feminist consciousness was a prerequisite for black feminist literary criticism. Smith's radical voice burst through contemporaneous attempts to "recover" black women writers without placing them within a cultural and political history of silencing and resistance.

But Smith's essay came under criticism from other African American critics such as Deborah McDowell and Hazel Carby.[8] Carby criticized Smith's essay for "its assertion of an essential black female experience and an exclusive black female language in which this experience is embodied" (p. 9). Critics like Carby saw in this the danger of a narrow identity-based literary criticism in which only black women could write with authority about black women, a prospect that was seriously limited in its understanding of how ideology operates and shapes often very contradictory consciousnesses. What other critics found problematic as well was the assumption that a black feminist tradition was lying buried, only to be unearthed and pressed into visibility. Such an emphasis on recovering an "identifiable literary tradition" did not ultimately challenge prevailing paradigms and disciplinary boundaries, and indeed could be read as tacitly seeking acceptability within the mainstream academy.[9] The evocation of a separate black feminist tradition ultimately could not challenge canonical literature on its own terms. It could not, for instance, theorize, except as absence, what Toni Morrison refers to as "the four-hundred-year-old dark, abiding signing African presence" that had shaped "the body politic, the Constitution, and the entire history of (American) culture."[10]

A trenchant critique of white feminism, which positioned itself as dissident within the mainstream academy, took a central place in the evocation of a critical black feminist consciousness. In particular, Carly singled out "those strands of contemporary feminist historiography and literary criticism that seek to establish the existence of an American sisterhood between black and white women."[11] The history of racism in the early women's movement where white suffragettes made a historic compromise with white men in seeking to secure voting rights for themselves was seen repeating itself in the mid-twentieth-century women's movement. This lesson of history in which white women "allied themselves not with black women but with a racist patriarchal order against all black people" was important to acknowledge, expose and remember, before a more critical project of solidarity between white and black women could be forged.[12] But a larger failure of imagination and political will within the progressive and radical movements of the 1960s and 1970s also needed to be acknowledged to pave the way for a black feminist articulation of oppression and resistance. The Combahee River Collective Statement put it thus: "the liberation of all oppressed peoples necessitates the destruction of the political-economic systems of capitalism and imperialism, as well as patriarchy . . . We are not convinced, however, that a socialist revolution that is not also a feminist and anti-racism revolution will guarantee our liberation."[13]

So it is, as Deborah King writes, "in confrontation with multiple jeopardy that black women define and sustain a multiple consciousness essential for our liberation, of which feminist consciousness is an integral part."[14] Across disciplines, the formation of a critical black feminist consciousness was understood as the articulation of "multiple oppressions" of race, class, and gender, or what King calls "multiple jeopardy", with "multiple" refer-ring "not only to several, simultaneous oppressions but to the multiplica-tive relationships among them as well." (pp. 42–72 [p. 47]). Critiquing theoretical attempts by mainstream white feminists who had sought to construct parallels between racial and sexual oppression, King points out that such a view does not aid in the understanding of the condition of black women who suffer both, as well as other kinds of oppressions.[15] She argues that by looking at multiple sites of oppression in a context of both structure and agency one can see that gender, race, and class power do not always play out according to a predictable script, and that a critical black feminist theory is necessary in elaborating the complexities of both domination and resistance.

The growing complexity of black feminism's debate with mainstream (white) feminism can be illustrated in the differently understood "interrela-tionship between lives and social structure."[16] For instance, white feminist analyses of women's oppression within the family and their lack of equal job opportunities outside the home presumed the white patriarchal nuclear family to be the norm and did not take into account the fact that white women were often class oppressors to black men. Black women, who have historically been part of the labor force, especially in low-paid, low-status jobs in overwhelming numbers could not share white feminism's construc-tion of material liberation.[17] While many black women had levels of inde-pendence within the family that white women did not have, in the media and state-policy view black women who were heading households were pathologized as deviant, emasculating matriarchs or irresponsible and sexu-ally voracious women who posed a threat to family values and were morally unfit to receive state assistance.[18] What was obfuscated in this binarized figuration of matriarch or parasite was the systematic assault on welfare since the 1980s that was forcing black women into low-paid jobs and thereby increasing their workload both inside and outside the home. Under the neoliberal economic policies of Ronald Reagan that emphasized reduced state expenditure on education and health ("welfare") and increased privatization of public services, the quality of black women's lives was eroded by rising black male unemployment, and by spiraling rates of incarceration of black men. Even those black men who did manage to find employment found themselves in jobs that did not offer wages that could support a family.[19] A feminist critical race studies perspective allows us to locate the representations of black women as matriarchs or welfare queens within larger structural contexts of political economy and transformations in the role of the state.

The task of a feminist critical race studies must be to analyze the ways in which cultural constructs of race and gender intervene in and shape both the national and global economies wherein black women tend to be positioned at the bottom end of the spectrum in low-wage jobs that require the hardest, dirtiest labor. Their disproportionately high representation in the service sector, for instance, might be explained by pervasive and historically persistent cultural understandings of the role of black women's labor – emotional, reproductive and productive – that is extended into the public domain. Thus work of care as nurses' aides for the aged and the sick, as cooks, nannies, cafeteria workers, and housekeeping and janitorial staff is typically performed by black women.[20] The decade of the 1990s saw the rapid consolidation of free market global capitalism as never before with the passage of the North American Free Trade Agreement and the institution of the Wold Trade Organization to oversee and speed up economic globalization. Black women's presence in industry, where they are least likely to be unionized but most likely to lose their jobs as their companies look abroad in search of even cheaper, more flexible labor among Third World women (as seen in the continuing collapse of the textiles industry in rural North Carolina), is thus shaped simultaneously by the race, gender and class status of black women in the United States and that of black women and women of color globally.[21]

An important thread in the elaboration of a critical tradition of black women's lives has been the importance of black women's experience, their ways of knowing and being in the world, and of making that central to any theorizing about race in the United States.[22] Yet the project of a feminist critical race studies necessitates that experience should not be theorized in essentialist, ahistorical terms, but as embodied, material, and contingent. This can happen only when racism and sexism are understood as specific historical practices and systemic formations rather than as naturalized, innate prejudices that can either never be eradicated or can be "solved" if the torch of rationality can be shone on them. The question of how power operates in and through bodies, money, literature, and law must be central to a critical consciousness such that black and feminist are not static frameworks of analysis but are being constantly created and reshaped in the struggle for justice.[23]

A "bridge" between: multicultural feminisms in the United States

Both the possibilities and the limits of solidarity among black and white women, and among black women and women of color in the United States, especially those who are "not white enuf, not dark enuf," have been elaborated within the framework of what could be called critical multicultural feminism.[24] In the mainstream liberal view, multicultural feminism is essentially about the "diversity" and "difference" that women of color in the United States represent. In this view, multicultural feminism reflects the vast range of women from different ethnic groups and cultural backgrounds who participate in both the celebration of their differences and their commonalities as women of color. But, as CRT scholars have also argued, questions of diversity and difference have to be understood in structural and political terms; otherwise, they can take on the characteristics of commodities that are sold in supermarkets. In other words, it is not only vital to recognize that women are different from each other; it is also vital that we understand that different women occupy unequal positions in society.

It is also important to point out here that "women of color" is a very particular North American construction of women who are "not-white." Representing both local and global manifestations of power, the term also recalls the particular historical moment of the late 1970s and early 1980s when identity politics dominated modes of intervening in the hegemonic and homogenized national imaginary that figured the prototypical citizen as white. The term "women of color" came to designate a collectivity comprising immigrant women coming out of the experiences of colonialism and imperialism and subsequent decolonization in the Third World; Native American women with their long and tragic history of forced displacement and annihilation; African American women fighting the terrible legacy of slavery and segregation; Chinese and Japanese women carrying their histories of racist immigration policies and imprisonment in camps during the Second World War; and Chicanas' struggles with exploited labor in sweatshops, homes, factories and farms: all representing multiple sites and often contradictory histories of racism.

The main challenge for women of color has been to use this common history of different oppressions to forge a struggle for justice. Different histories – both in their circumstances and in their length – have sometimes led to racial fragmentation and provided a hierarchical mode of looking at oppression. These different histories are by no means to be dismissed. A Native American woman whose family has for generations been forced onto US reservations remembers a much older history of racial annihilation than perhaps a more recent immigrant woman whose labor is being exploited in Silicon Valley. A feminist critical studies emerges with this historical consciousness of difference to elaborate ways in which women of color in the United States, to use Stuart Hall's phrase, are "structured in dominance."

One of the important early attempts to articulate the project of a critical multicultural feminism was the publication in 1981 of *This Bridge Called My Back: Writings by Radical Women of Color*. Conceived by two young Chicana lesbian writers and teachers based in California, Gloria Anzaldúa and Cherríe Moraga, the book was a bold and exuberant collection of writings – poetry, essays, journals, letters, testimonials, and speeches – by Chicana, Native American, Asian American, and African American women. It announced the arrival of a movement of women of color that was gathering momentum so fast that just two years later, in 1983, Moraga, in her foreword to the second edition, was already expressing the need to make the movement much more international, such that it included women of color in the United States but also women in Chile, South Africa, the Philippines, and other places. Moraga recognized that "the *idea* of Third World women has proved to be much easier between the covers of a book than between real live women . . . Still, the need for a broad-based US women of color movement capable of spanning borders of nation and ethnicity has never been so strong."[25] Thus, even in the moment of the announcement of a movement of women of color, the very idea was under strain, subject to political constraints and confronting the limited capacity of language to capture the complexity of women of color.[26] Rosario Morales presents this struggle with language as a struggle for self-definition: "I want to be whole. I want to claim myself to be puerto-rican, and U.S. American, working class and middle class, housewife and intellectual, feminist, Marxist and anti-imperialist."[27]

In fact, one of the most salient contributions of the struggle to forge a "women of color movement" in the United States was the understanding that feminist theory could not presume a priori the subjects of feminism. The proper subjects of feminism had to emerge in the struggle that was articulated with a number of different and sometimes oppositional issues such as those present in feminist, nationalist, lesbian, antiracist, socialist, and anti-imperialist struggles. The key task that *This Bridge* set out for itself in its attempt to found a movement was the act of breaking the silence over the issue of women of color in the United States. In the shattering of the silence that enveloped the lives and experiences of women of color was also the hope of countering the "invisibility" of women of color, and of forging connections despite the divide-and-rule tactics of the establishment. In the acts of speaking and writing, these women were calling themselves into subjectivity. The process of giving voice to themselves, and making visible new communities of women, was understood as one of healing historical and psychic wounds created by internalized racism and self-hatred. In her poem "When I Was Growing Up," Nellie Wong writes of this as a feeling of being "crushed":

> when I was growing up, my sisters
> with fair skin got praised
> for their beauty, and in the dark
> I fell further, crushed between high walls
>
> (*This Bridge*, p. 7)

A new, alternative kind of creativity in poetry, art, and activism that integrated spirituality was to become an important ingredient of a women of color movement arising in the wake of, alongside, and in opposition to the mainstream, mostly white and middle-class feminism's slogan of "the personal is political." Such an expression of individualized oppression seemed to silence women of color whose individual lives were deeply entangled with those of their race and ethnic communities that were themselves subordinated within the larger US society. Also, for women of color, the identity of the white feminist was understood as constituting both the oppressed and the oppressor. However, the movement of women of color was not fighting to reject the personal altogether; the aim was to articulate a different understanding of the personal that was not wholly predicated on the individual, autonomous subject of liberal feminism. Moraga's own writings highlight how purportedly "personal" issues such as love, sexuality, and family, are in fact intensely political and deeply ideological domains of social power.[28] As part of the attempt to build a movement, women of color were organizing their own poetry workshops, participating in writing sessions around kitchen tables, and elaborating on older traditions of community in such activities as gardening and creating visual art. They sought to resituate creativity not as a bourgeois outlet for a generalized angst but as a matter of survival itself, alongside political work on issues such as housing, employment, access to legal abortion, and healthcare in general.

The body became an important site in the politics of empowerment of women of color. Feminist theory's imperative to answer to real experiences, to what Moraga calls "the flesh of these women's lives" (p. xviii) was elaborated in Moraga's "theory in the flesh," defined as a space where "the physical realities of our lives – our skin color, the land or concrete we grew up on, our sexual longings – all fuse to create a politic born out of necessity" (p. 23). Multicultural feminism's task was to anchor its analyses of individual oppression in real-life experiences of racism, oppression, homophobia, poverty, and sexism.

The theory that an analysis of racism and homophobia must emerge from the body is also present in the work of many white antiracist feminist writers. Minnie Bruce Pratt, describing her coming to feminist antiracist consciousness in the US South, writes of "identity" in terms of "skin, blood, heart."[29] Central to the contributions of white women writers like Pratt was an acknowledgment of whiteness as a racial category and a challenge to whiteness as the invisible but all-pervasive norm that shared features with heterosexism. In a moving and passionate account of her painful childhood in a racist family that she nonetheless shared a close and intimate relationship with, and her struggles against the Far Right-driven racist movements in the South in the 1980s, Mab Segrest concretely embodies her theoretical and political consciousness in the body.[30] She writes: "When racist violence in Alabama erupted like the lesions on my mother's arms, I was not surprised when it all came down to skin" (3). Yet, as an antiracist activist and feminist, Segrest is also aware that it should not all come down to skin, because beyond skin is the possibility of solidarity. But before skin ceases to matter, Segrest needs to tell of its devastating history of violence and pain, of disavowal and betrayal, as well as of healing and connection. It is only in laying bare the skin of racism, in finding a way to write about "race and family, the intimate and the historic, action and reflection," about Marvin Segrest, her racist white cousin, and the young black activist Sammy Younge who was killed by Marvin Segrest in an act of vicious hate, that she can infuse her political commitment with the will to change the world. In calling this act of affiliation with a nonracist, just, and humane world an act of "betrayal," Segrest is elaborating the limits of understanding identity purely in terms of skin.

The political role of multicultural feminism as expressed in Segrest's and Pratt's writings was also understood as a pedagogical imperative. Working against internalized self-loathing, alienation, and invisibility, it aimed to teach those who are living in/with contradictions – of class, color, and sexuality – ways to change the world. *This Bridge* appeared to inaugurate a consciously dissident and alternative curriculum struggling to make its way in the academy, while flourishing in the diverse everyday spaces that women of color inhabited. An answer to Audre Lorde's precept that "the master's tools can never dismantle the master's house," the book itself was described by its editors as a "revolutionary tool" that could be used to tear down existing structures of dominance.

Many of the same writers revisited these issues in what could be considered a sequel to *This Bridge: Making Face, Making Soul: Creative and Critical Perspectives by Feminists of Color* (1990).[31] If *This Bridge* was an attempt to break the silence, to turn the spotlight on the glaring absence of women of color in the national story, almost a decade later, *Making Face* was reacting to some of the (un)intended consequences of the initial stages of the women of color movement. Reframing "women of color" as "feminists of color" with a view to politicizing the movement, the collection of poetry, essays, and criticism attempted a revaluation of multicultural feminism and tried to engage institutional power and the critical establishment more directly. By 1990 multiculturalism was well established within the prevailing liberal framework that saw itself under siege by a decade of cultural conservatism and economic privatization under Reagan. But even within conservative thinking, multiculturalism was acknowledged as efficacious policy to keep the various class and race fractions contained within a hegemonic view of the American nation as homogeneous and dominantly white.

Thus, by 1990, multiculturalism had been transformed from an oppositional politics to official policy and came to dominate many US university campuses, making both student activism and curricular reform movements predominantly reactive in nature. In the slide from oppositionality to official endorsement, multiculturalism was typically reduced to the practice of tokenism and appropriation. Purporting to have "overcome the language of race and hence of racism," multiculturalism could be read, as Ien Ang argues, as "nothing more and nothing less than a more complex form of nationalism, aimed at securing national boundaries in an increasingly borderless world."[32]

Norma Alarcon writes that even *This Bridge*, a text that had announced itself as a "revolutionary tool," met a similar fate.[33] The book, she argues, became a "resource for the Anglo-American feminist theory classroom and syllabus," where the "tendency to deny differences that posed a threat to the 'common denominator' category" of women was still dominant (p. 359). Integral to the critique of the racism within the white women's movement was an analysis of the question of literary representations within feminist studies in which Third World women existed as subject matter.[34] Several contributors to *Making Face* pointed out that women's studies as a discipline, in spite of earlier critiques such as those offered by *This Bridge*, continued to thrive on institutional racism. While conferences, faculties, curricula, and feminist social science in general did open up to women of color, the category of race was consistently consigned to a subordinate position, and institutional structures that privileged white dominance remained in place. Feminists of color now saw multiculturalism as a politics that deflected emphasis from racism, appropriated by a liberal ideology that understood racial prejudice merely as something that could be outlawed by policies against race and sex discrimination and eliminated through token inclusions of women of color.

There were other equally important critiques to be made of that earlier 1980s moment of the announcement of multicultural feminism. Feminist theorists in *Making Face* sought to retheorize language not as a transparent medium for expressing experience, but as in itself a complicated and intensely contested site of struggle. The multivalent ways in which the subject of multicultural feminism came to name herself as an oppositional subject was now problematized, involving "both [a] theoretical and a political decision." Yet Alarcon sees even this construction of the subject in opposition as one with severe limitations. She writes:

> Current political practices in the United States make it almost impossible to go beyond an oppositional theory of the subject, which is the prevailing feminist strategy and that of others; however, it is not the theory that will help us grasp the subjectivity of women of color... each woman of color cited here, even in her positioning of a "plurality of self," is already privileged enough to reach the moment of cognition of a situation for herself. This should suggest that to privilege the subject, even if multi-voiced, is not enough. (p. 366)

Thus the organizing assumption in *This Bridge* that speaking, writing, and naming the subject into consciousness and agency was the main goal of multicultural feminism was now seen as politically limiting.

The 1990s, then, inaugurated a critique of the very identity politics that had provided an earlier "women of color movement" with a springboard. As Trinh T. Minh-ha observes: "The search for an identity . . . is usually a search for that lost, pure, true, real, genuine, original, authentic self, often situated within a process of elimination of all that is considered other, superfluous, fake, corrupted or Westernized."[35] Although a naturalized unity among women had for some time been understood as a convenient myth and a tool for domination, identity was now seen as an imprisoning box that was politically debilitating insofar as it posited difference over critical solidarity. Anticipating some of these critiques, Morales had written earlier:

'white and middle class' stands for a kind of politics. *Color and class don't define people or politics* . . . Racism is an ideology. Everyone is capable of being racist whatever their color and condition. Only some of us are liable to racist attack. Understanding the multiple and contradictory racist ideology – where and how it penetrates – is what is important for the feminist movement.

(*This Bridge*, p. 91)

In a related move, *Making Face* attempted to move away from representing black women and women of color as victims toward figuring them as agents of their lives. Emphasis was now placed on discovering the creativity of other black women and women of color in all realms of culture.[36] The focus on a more consciously political creativity also necessitated working against the binaries of black and white and challenging earlier articulations of a narrowly defined authenticity. In a landmark essay that conceptually closes off *Making Face*, Gloria Anzaldúa attempted to elaborate on this "new consciousness" as embodied in the figure of the *mestiza*.[37] Herself a product of racialized discourses that legitimized binary forms of thinking about race, the much-reviled figure of the *mestiza* allowed the theorization of a new feminism. This feminism located itself self-consciously in the "borderlands" of race, nation, and sexuality, refusing binary identifications and oppositional consciousness in favor of a hybrid, deliberately unstable identity. Advocating "a tolerance for ambiguity," the new consciousness entailed an epistemological shift toward a third element involving the breaking down of "the subject-object duality," of dualistic thinking in general (p. 379). This also involved critiquing culture from the inside out, "to unlearn the *puta/virgen* dichotomy" that dominates gender relations within Chicano/a communities, and to celebrate both sexual and cultural queerness that refuses binary thinking.

"I have no country": critical race feminism and the question of citizenship

In the same essay Anzaldúa reflects: "As a *mestiza* I have no country, my homeland cast me out; yet all the countries are mine because I am every woman's sister or potential lover . . ." (p. 380). While Anzaldúa is here attempting to work against narrow nationalist affiliations that center on the question of home, belonging, nationality, and ultimately of citizenship, she also wants to ground her feminism in a specific locale that is literally the borderlands between the United States and Mexico, whose local history is shaped by global forces. "This is home," she writes, "the small towns in the (Rio Grande) Valley, *los pueblitos* with chicken pens and goats picketed to mesquite shrubs. *En las colonias* on the other side of the tracks, junk cars line the front yards of hot pink and lavender-trimmed houses," evoking a specifically "Chicana architecture," as it were (p. 387). This is a landscape devastated by the *peso* devaluation in 1982 that destroyed the Mexican retail trade in the border area. (More than a decade later, the passage of the North American Free Trade Agreement was further to impoverish *mexicanos* on both sides of the border.) The memory of her father, a struggling farmworker who died at the tragically young age of 38, ushers in older memories of belonging and dispossession. She recalls in a poem:

> This land was Mexican once
> was Indian always
> and is.
> And will be again.

(p. 389)

The "geographical turn" within Anzaldúa's essay represented a crucial theoretical move to challenge racist constructions of US national identity that figured it as essentially white. It also attempted to bring the question of land rights to the issue of citizenship. Indigenous Native-American nations have throughout US history been subjected to forced inclusion and their sovereignty subordinated in the racialized, capitalist process of internal colonization. By drawing upon an older history of habitation and mobilizing the present everyday, vernacular experiences in architecture and culture to challenge the grand narrative of global capitalist development, Chicana and Native American feminist writers sought to carve out their own history and space within the national story, writing against the hegemonic frontier mythology of land conquest and racial domination.

Yet this geographical turn exposes one of the vexing contradictions of multicultural feminism. The contradiction centers on the unequal ways in which different women of color have access to what Jacqui Alexander and Chandra Mohanty call "the citizenship machinery" that is an integral part of the way in which the state assigns the population of different groups according to sexuality, class, national origin, and race and determines legal status.[38] One of the key theoretical challenges of feminist critical race theory is to untangle the discursive knot of nation, land, and race, and to undo the apparatuses of citizenship that include both exclusion and forced inclusion. A discourse that aligns racial identity with national identity, such that white people are rendered the true Americans, tends to fuse notions of homeland and nation; immigrants who are not white can be figured only as interlopers and perpetual outsiders. These aliens are seen as precipitating a crisis in and of the "West." The early twentieth-century discourse of the "yellow peril" of Chinese immigration, the current discourse against the "invasion" of Hispanics from Central and South America, and that arrayed against Muslims as dangerous to national security in the contemporary moment (here the dimension of religion is curiously mixed up with race and ethnicity), all show the ways in which the connections between land and nation have been periodically given prominence in response to varieties of racial panic and economic insecurity. A complex citizenship machinery, made all the more elaborate in the context of the "war on terror," is pressed into action to determine who is a legal citizen and who is illegal, who is a refugee and who is a temporary guest. These determinations create hierarchies of oppression and multiply axes of difference.

If the African American struggle through slavery and generalized systems of racism has been one about rights – the right to be recognized as a human being and as a citizen – then the struggle for various groups of people of color and immigrants has also been around the issue of citizenship. The question of citizenship is integral to feminist critical race studies as it situates local and national concerns about who belongs and who does not within a global frame of rights and justice. A related but equally important question is one about what happens to those women whose immigrant history cannot be narrated in terms of land and belonging in the past but only, as Ien Ang puts it, as an "eventual site of belonging" (*On Not Speaking Chinese*, p. 9). Anzaldúa's integration of a narrative of land as signifier of cultural belonging seems provocatively to challenge narrow legal discourses of citizenship. But it does not wholly address problematic notions of assimilation whose logic ensures that the immigrant could never be quite the same assimilating subject in the absence of an originary narrative of presence or of forced inclusion at the expense of indigenous sovereignty.

In *This Bridge* itself, feminists like Pat Parker emphasized the importance of anti-imperialist politics for multicultural feminism. Such an engagement entailed a rejection of US supremacy and a disavowal of the privileges afforded to US citizens.[39] The treatment of Iranians during the hostage crisis in the 1980s was a stark reminder to Parker that older understandings of the equivalence between whiteness and Americanness were persistent and hegemonic. Thus the very struggle to gain US citizenship is rife with contradictions when the United States is the world's only superpower. How should a critical feminist race politics work both toward the empowerment of women of color by agitating for citizenship (in terms of both legal status and participation in the national story), and toward a disaffiliation with the meaning and weight of what it means to be a US citizen and by extension the citizen of a global empire? It is on this terrain of contestations over national identity in the United States – of who belongs and who does not and of what it means to belong – that a feminist critical race studies can have a profound impact in articulating an agenda for social justice globally.

Subjects and citizens: black British feminism and the politics of the state

The question of citizenship is also key to the project of black British feminism that emerged in the late 1970s and early 1980s as a critique both of the postwar, postimperial British state and its discourses of race and nation, and of the Left-wing, antiracist and feminist movements formulating their own responses to the state. In addition to the historical legacy of slavery, black people in Britain are also inheritors of the complex history of European colonialism and capitalist recolonization. This layered history has led to the term "black British" being a generally inclusive term, incorporating former subjects of empire from Africa, the Caribbean, South Asia and elsewhere. Although sometimes critiqued for its homogenizing potential to obscure ethnic and religious differences, "black British" is mostly understood as a political category that identifies a common structural location shared by immigrants vis à vis the British state, involving the experience of marginalization, and signifying a politics of racial solidarity.[40] As Heidi Safia Mirza puts it in her anthology of black British feminism: "to be black and British is to be unnamed in official discourse."[41] One could be either black or British but not both. The question of whether black British is a "strategic political articulation," or is an instance of homogenizing identity politics, only underscores how blackness itself is a contested category in Britain even as it continues to function politically as a site of resistance.

Black British feminism became a recognizable political movement and critical entity in the late 1970s and early 1980s, in the intensely racialized terrain of politics that developed during Margaret Thatcher's Conservative rule (she was Prime Minister of Britain from 1979 to 1990). Black women organized against the sustained racist and fascist attacks of white police, Conservative politicians, street mobs, and an increasingly aggressive National Front, a far-Right white-supremacist organization. The politics of antiracism and the work of forging black-white alliances against the racist practices and rhetoric of both the state and of popular politics provided the background to the articulation of a black British feminist agenda that sought to understand black experience in Britain through gender difference and to forge a politics of gendered racial justice.

Such an agenda faced a major challenge when the local state (city councils and education authorities, for instance) adopted what then seemed like a radical policy of multiculturalism against the onslaught of Thatcherite nationalism and economic privatization predicated on purportedly "national" characteristics of thrift, enterprise, and hard work. While the Thatcher government openly promoted its xenophobic and racist view of Britain through its immigration policy and its erosion of state support for immigrants generally, progressive local authorities in cities such as London, Manchester, and Birmingham, where black Labour councilors played an important role, attempted to tackle issues of institutional racism and forge a multiracial politics. The practice and rhetoric of multiculturalism was thus paradoxically incubated within the logic of the free market.

A critical multiculturalism required an analysis that could respond to and explain the ways in which race structured the whole of British society, instead of simply focusing on the overt manifestations of racism. Such a critical understanding of race allowed for analyzing multiculturalism itself as a new type of racism, since it, too, relied on notions of essential racial and cultural difference. Multiculturalism privileged these cultural differences over issues of economic and social justice, and saw gender equity as a private matter to be left to the community.

There are at least three key and interrelated sites where black British feminism made important and transformative interventions during this time: the British state's immigration policy, multiculturalism as a political ideology, and struggles over work and the right to welfare. On the terrain of labor struggles, black British feminist politics has engaged with and challenged socialist theory's privileging of the white working-class male as the archetypal subject of struggle. Within trade union politics, class struggles were also typically pitted against cultural identity, even as factory owners exploited the lack of legal status or low social status of immigrant workers.[42] This arena continues to be of major significance to black British feminism. The contemporary conjuncture of global capitalism that has led to the opening of borders within the European Union, and New Labour's continuation of Thatcherite policies of increasing privatization of the public sector, is further exacerbating the status of immigrant women who are joining the ever-growing disposable workforce. The recent influx of poor white women from Eastern Europe into the sex work and housework sectors in a Britain enjoying an economic boom is only the latest challenge for feminist critical race studies and its analysis of women's labor and racial inequality.

Historically, British immigration policy has assumed migrant workers to be male, and women migrants as their dependants. For Caribbean women, this has been a particular problem, for in reality a majority of Caribbean women have come independently, and in equal numbers to men, beginning with the post-Second World War boom when workers from the colonies were recruited to low-paying jobs that allowed white upward mobility.[43]

During the 1960s and early 1970s, a major shift occurred. As Britain experienced economic instability, immigration acts restricting the entry of ex-colonial subjects from Asia, Africa, and the Caribbean were introduced and passed. Conservative politicians such as Enoch Powell unleashed a rhetoric of virulent racism amid calls to save white Britain from racial and cultural contamination.[44] The scandalous policy of conducting virginity tests on South Asian women to confim their marital status, instituted in the late 1970s and early 1980s, was only the most blatant example of how the state mobilized cultural assumptions about the status of women in South Asia and reinforced sexual subordination through its own policies. Issues such as domestic violence, honor killings, and forced marriages in the Asian community more generally, have highlighted the British state's problematic construction of gender rights as subordinate and even antithetical to its policy of multiculturalism which treats tradition as sacrosanct. Viewing cultural differences as inherent and immutable, the state ended up installing men as the natural spokespersons of their communities.

While a feminist critical race theory within Britain has had to confront, as in the United States, racist constructions of the black family as the site of social pathology, black British feminists pointed out that white feminist theory's often uncritical celebration of the Western nuclear family, romantic love, sexual freedom, and work as sites of liberation needed to be problematized. This complex of markers of women's emancipation has enabled the representation of black and Asian families in Britain as sites of female imprisonment. Such "exotic" practices as arranged marriage and the use of religious markers of identity are marshaled as evidence of the need to rescue black and Asian women by imposing progressive ideologies of the West such as secularism, sexual freedom, and individual choice in marriage.[45]

What emerged from this 1980s discussion of the state, white feminism, and multiculturalism was the critical position of family and community, in addition to the state, within black British feminist theory. A feminist critical race theory cannot afford to pit family against state, as the family itself is often the source of oppression of women, and is typically protected by the multicultural state. Gita Sahgal, in her account of the work of Asian feminist organizing in Britain, analyzes how alliances between the state and patriarchy are reinvigorated in the name of tradition and cultural difference, and shows that this traffic between the state and community can be traced back to British colonial policy in both India and Africa.[46] She looks at the work of three feminist organizations that helped to lay bare the contradictions within state policies of multiculturalism, a feminist politics of women's liberation, and antiracist politics, all of which tended to draw a line around community. Looking specifically at the work of the Southall

Black Sisters, a feminist organization based in a predominantly Asian borough in west London, the Brent Asian Women's Refuge in northwest London, and the group Women Against Fundamentalism that arose in the wake of the Rushdie affair, Sahgal points out how the main challenge for these groups was to provide a secular space for women who were victims of domestic violence, so as to enable them to name the multiple sites of their struggles and the contradictory locations of their affiliations. In particular, Sahgal reveals how even the politics of antiracism within the Asian community was not immune to subordinating women's rights to community rights. Responding to the calls of a community in danger from racist assaults, antiracist politics moved away from a socialist orientation and "became intimately bound up with questions of ethnic identity" ("Secular Spaces," p. 176). In its more dangerous manifestation, it enabled attacks on women who were seen as challenging tradition, and thus endangering community identity.

Paradoxically, the contradictions within the state policies of multiculturalism, the colonialist impulses within white feminism (or "imperial feminism"), and community-oriented antiracist politics have all created new spaces for a critical black British feminism to intervene in and reformulate itself. It takes seriously the imperative to reject the false choice of community rights versus women's rights. A feminist critical race studies project articulates the two, and works toward an understanding of justice that does not subordinate any aspect of a woman's being in order to win a particular political battle.

Empire's citizens

With the unleashing of the war on terror in the aftermath of the attacks on the World Trade Center in New York City and the Pentagon in Washington DC in September 2001, a new world order is being strengthened. The war on terror's organizing principle is the view that the globe is divided between a modern, "civilized," democratic, capitalist world (which happens to be also mostly Western and Christian), and a barbaric, fundamentalist, backward-looking world (which happens to be mostly Muslim, and one in which millions of poor people live in daily struggle against authoritarian and Western-supported regimes).[47] Such a view of the world as divided between the modern West and an uncivilized East has an older history in nineteenth-century imperialism's civilizational project, popularized in the global imagination as "the white man's burden." This view conceals powerful notions of racial superiority behind the more overt language of religious, ethnic, and cultural difference. Some of these terms of "difference" both deflect and displace race as a category that distributes power globally, and organize the world as one in which the civilized West is engaged in a "crusade" against the barbaric Muslim world's *jihad* against modernity, women's rights, and free market capitalism.

A growing Islamophobia in the West, even as Islam itself is flattened as an a historical and undifferentiated entity by those invested in politicizing it, is one of the problematic manifestations of this new imperialism. The rampant media frenzy about Muslims as backward, fanatical, and potential terrorists employs the logic of racism in the service of national security. At the national level, laws passed by the US Congress, such as the USA Patriot Act, and the establishment of the new Department of Homeland Security, make visible how this new global order is integrally linked to the question of citizenship, redefining the nation in terms of an increasingly homogeneous and culturally specific idea. In Britain, as in the Netherlands and France, there is a renewed call to Muslims to assimilate themselves fully into the dominant national culture, even as the state continues to collide with some of the more racial and conservative factions of the Muslim communities at the expense of addressing women's oppressions from within. These shifts in discourse and representation signal a rethinking of an older multicultural-ism as a strategy for containing racial and cultural differences within nation states, and within such new political entities as the European Union.

At face value, the war on terror seems to have little to do with gender difference.[48] But the West's desire to "smoke 'em out of their caves" and to bring the terrorists home "dead or alive" points to a pervasive masculinist style (drawing on a cowboy aesthetic recognizable through a manly swag-ger) of the conduct of global politics, even as preemptive military aggression that can "shock and awe" opponents into total annihilation heralds a new era of armed tactics. Militarism, always integral to the construction of US citizenship, and to the entrenched patriarchal gender arrangements, is now made more visible and complex.[49] The deep penetration of the culture of militarism blurs the spaces of policymaking and national sentiment. Emo-tion (tears, fear, panic, loss) and reason (strategy, planning, operation, mission accomplished) are used to bolster the creation of gendered national subjects who will maintain stability even as the terms of home and the world are inverted in the new order. The practices of masculinized brutality (perpetrated by women soldiers as well) in the Abu Ghraib prison in Baghdad and the ritualized beheadings of Westerners over the course of the war on Iraq since March 2003 are only the starkest examples of armed projects seeking to annihilate women who are seen as symbols of the "other" community, and to "emasculate" men of the opposing side in order to break their sense of being human. The image of a mother-to-be,

Lynndie England, engaged in acts of torture on the bodies of male Iraqi prisoners, defeats simplistic analyses of women as symbols of peace. The complex politics of race and gender infuses that image with the emotions of horror and sorrow, while providing evidence that war continues to be predicated on bodies that are gendered and raced in very material ways.

A feminist critical race studies project must now make itself relevant to this new global order. Ironically, it was in October 2001 that the world turned its attention to the women of Afghanistan. The war on Afghanistan was announced in their name, to enable them to read and thus free themselves from the repressive regime of the Taliban, who in 1996 had come to power on an ultraconservative Islamist platform, with the blessings of the Western democratic world.[50] On the eve of the invasion of Afghanistan in October 2001, our media-saturated worlds were flooded with images of Afghan women huddled in makeshift classrooms, trying to read by candlelight, against the orders of the Taliban. (We received no images of the millions of Iraqi women who read openly, and whose educational establishments, schools, colleges, libraries, and museums, were destroyed in a matter of weeks after the declaration of war on Iraq in March 2003.)

For some time before 2001, international feminist organizations had been mobilizing against the Taliban's policies of gender repression. But the situation of the women in Afghanistan now posed a great dilemma to progressive women everywhere: how could they simultaneously oppose the Taliban for its repression of women, and oppose the war on Afghanistan? The war, after all, was carried out by Western powers interested in advancing their own hegemony over the globe, even as they deployed, opportunistically and cynically, the rhetoric of moral agency.[51] What did it mean for US- and UK-based feminists to champion the women of Afghanistan in the context of this new imperialism? In their April 20, 2002 "Open Letter to the Editors of Ms. Magazine," the Revolutionary Association of Women of Afghanistan (RAWA) pointed out the contradictions within Western feminist positions. Denouncing the Northern Alliance, whom the US government was now supporting in the war against the Taliban, RAWA reminded Ms. Magazine readers that the women of Afghanistan wanted something more than the choice between the Taliban and the Northern Alliance.

Rejecting the construction of the war as a war for women's rights, RAWA's letter reveals that women as political agents inhabit multiple and contradictory sites within local communities, the state, the nation, and the global economy. What a feminist critical race studies needs is an ethical engagement with both global and local politics, making possible the analysis and critique of how the two are enmeshed in each other, and how even a "local" voice such as RAWA's cannot be made to represent the entire situation of Afghan women. Thus women in the United States and the United Kingdom would have to do the political work of learning about the world, and of mobilizing against their own country's imperialist positions, even if it means undermining, indeed disavowing, their own status as citizens so that women in other places can become citizens of the world.

The questions posed by the war on terror are not necessarily new questions, but they demand new answers. African American, black British, and postcolonial feminist theorists have demonstrated that location, economy, race, and nationality are crucial determinants of the ways in which feminist politics can be conducted. These feminists have looked at the ways in which the historical and geopolitical situatedness of women constricts, as much as it opens up, the possibilities for solidarity between feminists from the global North and South, from East and West. Rearticulating citizenship, gender, and race must be premised on understanding what solidarity means in the new global order.

Solidarity in its new formulation needs to be understood as not just a sharing of space and struggles, but also as having to work out the language and practice of a politics of justice. How can "our" language speak to "theirs" so that we can work together for a common goal is a question that must also consider the meaning and effect of solidarity when understood in those terms. Another way to ask the question now is: What role do US- and UK-based women have to play in the rights struggles of women in places like Afghanistan and Iraq? And what about those who have multiple geographical locations and affiliations, who teach, struggle, work, and write in multiple sites?

Perhaps a first step toward solidarity is to recognize its limits. US- and UK-based feminists must acknowledge their complicity as citizens and residents (however involuntarily) of a nation at war with Afghanistan and Iraq and with many other parts of the world. Solidarity entails questioning the power of the state and one's individual and group enmeshment in the system. In the new global order, it also means doing the theoretical and dissident work of explaining connections between racial and gender power and political economy, international politics and possible modes of transnational resistance. As the editors of *Critical Race Theory* pointed out, "generalized references to the North and the South" are often "metaphorical substitution for serious and sustained attention to the racial and ethnic character of the massive distributive transformations that globalization has set in motion" (p. xxx). This is a global order that is being reconstituted by new formations of economic and military power, but is being sustained and made legitimate by reiterations of racial and gender power. Another step toward a working solidarity, and by no means the final one, is to reengage the power of the idea of a common humanity in which differences can create a better understanding of the modalities of resistance. In other words, we need a project of universalism that can imagine a different global order, even as we remain simultaneously attentive to inequities and injustice. Perhaps, in another world, we can have a future without race and gender, but the urgent task on hand is to understand gender and race power within a project of justice.

A feminist critical race studies perspective can begin to create theoretical resources to analyze the contemporary conjuncture and to give birth to new ways of reading the languages and practices of justice.

Further reading

Zillah Eisenstein, *The Color of Gender: Reimagining Democracy* (Berkeley: University of California Press, 1994).

Cynthia Enloe, *Bananas, Beaches, and Patriarchy: Making Feminist Sense of International Politics* (Berkeley: University of California Press, 1990).

Ruth Frankenberg, *Displacing Whiteness: Essays in Social and Cultural Criticism* (Durham: Duke University Press, 1997).

Inderpal Grewal and Caren Kaplan, eds., *Scattered Hegemonies: Postmodernity and Transnational Feminist Practices* (Minneapolis: University of Minnesota Press, 1994).

bell hooks, *Talking Back: Thinking Feminist, Thinking Black* (Boston: South End Press, 1988).

Wahneema Lubiano, ed., *The House That Race Built* (New York: Vintage, 1998).

Valentine Moghadam, ed., *Identity Politics and Women: Cultural Reassertions and Feminisms in International Perspective* (Boulder, CO: Westview Press, 1994).

Chandra Talpade Mohanty, Ann Russo, and Lourdes Torres, eds., *Third World Women and the Politics of Feminism* (Bloomington: Indiana University Press, 1991).

Linda Nicholson, ed., *Feminism/Postmodernism* (New York: Routledge, 1990).

Andrew Parker, Mary Russo, Doris Sommer, and Patricia Yaeger, eds., *Nationalisms and Sexualities* (New York: Routledge, 1992).

NOTES

1. Kimberlé Crenshaw, Neil Gotanda, Gary Peller, and Kendall Thomas, eds., *Critical Race Theory: The Key Writings that Formed the Movement* (New York: The New Press, 1995), p. xxxi.
2. Ibid., p. xxxi.
3. Ibid., p. xxvi.
4. Ibid., p. xv.

5. See Hazel Carby, *Reconstructing Womanhood: The Emergence of the Afro-American Woman Novelist* (New York and Oxford University Press, 1987), for an important account and theorization of nineteenth-century black feminist intellectuals. A useful collection and sourcebook of black women's political and literary contributions by a white feminist historian is Gerda Lerner, ed., *Black Women in White America: A Documentary History* (New York: Vintage, 1973).

6. Alice Walker, "In Search of Our Mothers' Gardens," *Ms. Magazine* 1974; Barbara Smith, "Toward a Black Feminist Criticism," in *Conditions: Two* 1:2 (October 1977), pp. 157–75; and Barbara Christian, *Black Feminist Criticism: Perspectives on Black Women Writers* (New York: Pergamon Press, 1985).

7. Among the earliest anthologies coming out of second-wave black feminism was Toni Cade, ed., *The Black Woman* (New York: New American Library, 1970). This was followed by Mary Helen Washington, ed., *Black-Eyed Susans* (New York: Anchor Press, 1975); and Gloria T. Hull, Patricia Bell Scott, and Barbara Smith, eds., *All the Women Are White, All the Blacks are Men But Some of Us Are Brave* (Old Westbury, NY: Feminist Press, 1982).

8. Deborah McDowell, "New Directions for Black Feminist Criticism" (1980) in Elaine Showalter, ed., *The New Feminist Criticism: Essays on Women, Literature and Theory* (New York: Pantheon Books, 1985), pp. 186–99; Carby, *Reconstructing Womanhood.*

9. Smith, "Toward a Black Feminist Criticism," p. 163.

10. Toni Morrison, *Playing in the Dark: Whiteness and the Literary Imagination* (Cambridge, MA: Harvard University Press, 1993), p. xx.

11. Carby, *Reconstructing Womanhood,* p. 6.

12. Ibid.

13. Combahee River Collective, *Combahee River Collective Statement: Black Feminists Organizing in the Seventies and Eighties* (New York: Kitchen Table Press, 1986), pp. 12–13.

14. Deborah King, "Multiple Jeopardy, Multiple Consciousness: The Context of a Black Feminist Ideology," *Signs: Journal of Women and Culture and Society* 14:1 (August), p. 71, p. 47.

15. See also bell hooks, *Ain't I a Woman?* (Boston: South End Press, 1981).

16. Rose M. Brewer, "Theorizing Race, Class and Gender," in Rosemary Hennessy and Chrys Ingraham, eds., *Materialist Feminism: A Reader in Class, Difference and Women's Lives* (New York and London : Routledge, 1997), p. 238. See also Angela Davis, *Race and Class* (New York: Vintage, 1983).

17. This has been true historically. During slavery black female "participation" in the labor force was 100 percent, and until the 1980s it consistently exceeded that of white women.

18. See Daniel P. Moynihan, *The Negro Family: The Case for National Action* (Office of Policy Planning and Research, United States Department of Labor, Washington DC: Government Printing Office, 1965). For an early critique, see Robert Staples, "The Myth of the Black Matriarchy", in Staples, *The Black Family: Essays and Studies* (Belmont, CA.: Wadsworth, 1971); and Staples, *The Black Woman in America* (Chicago: Nelson Hall, 1973). For a different view, which represents black women as lacking in feminist consciousness, see Michele Wallace, *Black Macho and the Myth of the Superwoman* (New York: Dial, 1979).

19. For a really useful account of the entangled history of race and welfare policies, see Margaret B. Wilkerson and Jewell Handy Gresham, "The Racialization of Poverty," in Alison M. Jaggar and Paula S. Rothenberg, eds., *Feminist Frameworks: Alternative Theoretical Accounts of the Relations between Women and Men* (New York: McGraw Hill, 1993).

20. See Brewer, "Theorizing Race," p. 247.

21. See Barbara Ehrenreich and Annette Fuentes, *Women in the Global Factory* (Boston: South End Press, 1984), for an account of the ways in which global capitalism was exploiting labor along racial and gender lines, employing Third World women's labor in the export-processing zones and in sweatshops. For an early, pioneering account, see Maria Mies, *Housewives Produce for the World Market: The Lace Makers of Narsapur* (Geneva: International Labor Office, 1980); and Mies, *Patriarchy and Accumulation on a World Scale: Women in the International Division of Labor* (London: Zed Press, 1986). See also Swasti Mitter, *Common Fate, Common Bond: Women in the Global Economy* (London: Pluto Press, 1986).

22. See Patricia Hill Collins, *Black Feminist Thought: Knowledge, Consciousness, the Politics of the Women's Movement* (Boston: Unwin Hyman, 1990).

23. For interesting and challenging theorizations of experience, see Joan Scott, "Experience," in Judith Butler and Joan Scott, eds., *Feminists Theorize the Political* (New York and London : Routledge, 1992); and Paula Moya, *Learning from Experience: Politics, Epistemology, and Chicana/o Identity* (Ithaca: Cornell University Press, 1998).

24. Gloria Anzaldúa and Cherríe Moraga, eds., *This Bridge Called My Back: Writings by Radical Women of Color* (New York: Kitchen Table-Women of Color Press, 1983 [1981]), p. 5.

25. See *This Bridge Called My Back*, p. 5.

26. This idea was to prove further complicated because not all Third World women are women of color and not all women of color belong to the Third World. White women in the Caribbean and in Latin America, and women belonging to nonwhite nations that are advanced capitalist countries, such as Japanese women, occupy tenuous positions within the categories of Third World and women of color.

27. Rosario Morales, "We're All in the Same Boat," in Anzalduá and Moraga, eds., *This Bridge*, p. 91.

28. See, especially, Moraga's essay "From a Long Line of Vendidas" in Jaggar and Rothenberg, eds., *Feminist Frameworks*.

29. Minnie Bruce Pratt, *Rebellion: Essays 1980–1991* (Ithaca: Firebrand Books, 1991).

30. Mab Segrest, *Memoir of a Race Traitor* (Boston: South End Press, 1994).

31. Gloria Anzaldúa, ed., *Making Face, Making Soul: Creative and Critical Perspectives by Feminists of Color.* (San Francisco: Aunt Lute Books, 1990).

32. Ien Ang, *On Not Speaking Chinese* (London: Routledge, 2001); pp. 15–16.

33. Norma Alarcon, "The Theoretical Subjects of *This Bridge Called My Back* and Anglo-American Feminism," in Anzaldúa, ed., *Making Face*, pp. 356–69.

34. See Chandra Talpade Mohanty, "Under Western Eyes: Feminist Scholarship and Colonial Discourses," in Mohanty, Ann Russo, and Lourdes Torres, eds., *Third*

World Women and the Politics of Feminism (Bloomington: Indiana University Press, 1991).

35. Trinh T. Minh-ha, "Not You/Like You: Post-Colonial Women and the Interlocking Questions of Identity and Difference," in Anzaldúa, ed., *Making Face*, pp. 371, 317–5.

36. Michelle Cliff, "Object Into Subject: Some Thoughts On The Work of Black Women Artists," in Anzaldúa, ed., *Making Face*, pp. 271–90.

37. Anzaldúa, "La consciencia de la mestiza: Towards a New Consciousness," in Anzaldúa, ed., *Making Face*, pp. 377–89.

38. Jacqui Alexander and Chandra Mohanty, eds., *Feminist Genealogies, Colonial Legacies, Democratic Futures* (New York: Routledge, 1997), p. xiv.

39. Pat Parker, "Revolution . . . It's Not Neat, or Pretty, or Quick," in Anzaldúa and Moraga, eds., *This Bridge*, pp. 239–40.

40. See Beverley Bryan, Stella Dadzie, and Suzanne Scafe, eds., *The Heart of the Race – Black Women's Lives in Britain* (London: Virago, 1985).

41. Heidi Safia Mirza, ed., *Black British Feminism: A Reader* (London and New York: Routledge, 1997), p. 3.

42. See Amrit Wilson, *Finding a Voice – Asian Women in Britain* (London: Virago, 1978).

43. Amina Mama, "Black Women, the Economic Crisis and the British State", *Feminist Review*, Special Issue "Many Voices, One Chant," 17, July 1984, pp. 22–34.

44. See Stuart Hall, "A Torpedo Aimed at the Boiler-Room of Consensus," *New Statesman*, April 1998, pp. 14–19. Writing on the thirtieth anniversary of Conservative politician Enoch Powell's racist speech given in Birmingham in April 1968, Stuart Hall led a series of reflections on Powell's speech and its political fallout. Powell's speech was reproduced alongside the critical reflections in the magazine.

45. From September 2004 the French government has banned the wearing of all visible religious symbols in public schools in France. While this technically applies to all religious markers of faith, the controversy has centered overwhelmingly on the figure of the young Muslim schoolgirl wearing a headscarf. See Norma Moruzzi, "A Problem with Headscarves: Contemporary Complexities of Political and Social Identity," *Political Theory* 22:4 (November 1994), pp. 653–72.

46. Gita Sahgal, "Secular Spaces: The Experience of Asian Women Organizing," in Gita Sahgal and Nira Yuval-Davis, eds. *Refusing Holy Orders: Women and Fundamentalism in Britain* (London: Virago, 1992), pp. 163–97.

47. For an elaboration of this view much before September 11, 2001, see Samuel Huntington, *The Clash of Civilizations* (New York: Simon and Schuster, 1996).

48. Feminist critics of war have for some time now drawn attention to the war crimes against women in the rape camps of Bosnia and Bangladesh, of the rape and mutilation of minority Muslim women in the communal carnage in Gujarat, India, in 2002; and in the genocidal wars and refugee camps in Rwanda and Darfur. But the challenges for feminist critical race studies offered up by the contemporary moment are understandably still not fully clear.

49. See Catherine Lutz, *Homefront: A Military City and the American 20th Century* (Boston: Beacon Press, 2001). See also Cynthia Enloe, *The Morning After:*

Sexual Politics at the End of the Cold War (Berkeley: University of California Press, 1993). It is also important to take into account how Third World, postcolonial states are mediating this complex of global capitalism and militarism. The global sex trade organized around militarized masculinities is only the most vivid instance of this.

50. Speaking in a radio presidential address on November 17, 2001, First Lady Laura Bush declared: "The fight against terrorism is also a fight for the rights and dignity of women." See *The News and Observer*, Sunday, November 18, 2001, p. 16A.

51. This question was central to the forum "Women Fight Fundamentalisms After September 11" that I co-organized with Miriam Cooke at the University of North Carolina and Duke University on November 1 and 2, 2001. We invited three feminists whose work critically engaged this question: Gita Sahgal from London, Nawal el-Sadaawi from Cairo, and Mab Segrest from Durham, North Carolina. I owe many of my insights to the work of these three courageous women; to Miriam Cooke, Catherine Lutz, and Ranjana Khanna; and to the numerous other interlocutors who participated in the forum.

12

ELIZABETH WEED

Feminist psychoanalytic literary criticism

Excitement

In 1987 Janet Malcolm wrote an animated, enthusiastic review essay for the *New Yorker* on the recently published *In Dora's Case: Freud, Hysteria, Feminism*: "The new writings – feminist, deconstructive and Lacanian, for the most part – have a wild playfulness and a sort of sexual sparkle that flicker through their academic patois and give them extraordinary verve . . . The New Critics of psychoanalysis worry Freud's text as if it were a metaphysical poem."[1]

Rather than a metaphysical poem, the essays address, of course, Freud's notorious handling and mishandling of an early case of female hysteria. But if (with a few brief exceptions) literature is absent from the volume, literary reading practice is not. Of the seventeen contributors, thirteen are academic literary critics. Although the presence of literary practitioners does not guarantee the literariness of the readings, the volume has enough essays that do worry over the workings of the texts – their power and their treachery – to give it the flavor of a serious encounter between Freud and the literary deconstructionists.

Two other elements make the collection stand out for Malcolm. The first is its "sexual sparkle," the sheer pleasure the critics take in "using Freud's own weapons against him, find[ing] example upon example of unconscious self-betrayal" (p. 306), as when Jane Gallop looks closely at Freud's defense of his daring to talk to young girls about delicate subjects: "I call bodily organs and processes by their technical names, and I tell these to the patient if they – the names, I mean – happen to be unknown to her. *J'appelle un chat un chat.*" Gallop "charmingly," as Malcolm says, points out the following:

> At the very moment he defines nonprurient language as direct and noneuphemistic, he takes a French detour into a figurative expression. By his terms, the French sentence would seem to be titillating, coy, flirtatious. And to make matters even more juicy (less "dry"), *chat* or *chatte* can be used as a vulgar

(vulvar) slang for the female genitalia. So, in this gynecological context, where he founds his innocence upon the direct use of technical terms, he takes a French detour and calls a pussy a pussy.

(In Dora's Case, pp. 208–9)

Malcolm is clear about the pleasures of such critical sharp-shooting. The "sex-playful" readings she invokes, and her explications of the explications of Jane Gallop, Toril Moi, Neil Hertz, and others all carry a transferential charge: "Like the Rat Man's dead father, the dead father of psychoanalysis still 'lives' in our imagination as a sort of superstar professor, whose classes are so big that in order to attract his attention we practically have to make public nuisances of ourselves" (p. 308).[2]

Along with the critical verve and sexual sparkle of the essays, there is something else that Malcolm draws our attention to: "*In Dora's Case*, largely devoted to writings of the past ten years by young and youngish literary critics who teach English and Comparative Literature at American and English universities, put me in mind of a scene in Virginia Woolf's *The Years* – the scene that forms the novel's symbolic center – where two little girls excitedly dance and leap around a bonfire for the older girl's birthday" (pp. 305–6). In expressing her enjoyment of the emancipated glee of Woolf's girls, Malcolm acknowledges her appreciation of the *feminist* nature of the writings in this collection; if not all the essays are feminist, the ones she prefers are.

Malcolm's essay, then, represents a collection that brings together literary critical readings, psychoanalysis, and feminism in a work that is as irresistible as it is transferentially invested. Perhaps one might say that all feminist criticism – all but the most disciplined and domesticated – carries a transferential charge much greater than that of routine academic criticism. One might even argue that it was the unabashedly transferential nature of early feminist criticism more than its political character that opponents found disconcerting. At least until Harold Bloom's "Anxiety of Influence," literary criticism, probably the least detached of the critical disciplines, performed its work at a reassuring remove. Academic feminism changed that. This is not to say that all feminist criticism of the 1970s through to the late 1980s shone forth with an irresistible, gleeful energy. But there was a general excitement in that early work. What are the particular forms of excitement found in the feminist psychoanalytic criticism of those decades, and what stands in the place of that excitement today?

Reading difference

Feminist psychoanalytic reading of literature does not easily lend itself to description. That is the case not simply because it is not one practice but multiple practices with complex histories, and not simply because all the players – feminism, psychoanalysis, reading, literature – are themselves multiple with complex histories. The difficulty in capturing it stems especially from the way the four players are related: they are all *implicated* in one another; they *traverse* one another, to borrow language from Shoshana Felman.[3] Let us see how the four might be said to be implicated at the simplest and most straightforward level. Feminism is traversed by psychoanalysis: there, in the language of Freud, far from its own emancipatory frame, feminism finds its own questions – What does a woman want? What *is* a woman in a world defined by men? – in forms at once uncannily familiar and alien. Second, feminism is traversed by literature. Literature is one of the privileged sites for the congealing of notions of femininity and masculinity and, at the same time, the site of their perpetual disturbance. For these reasons literature inhabits feminism's imagination of itself. And feminism is implicated with reading. In fact, reading is the indispensable tool of its practice if we think of "reading" as an inescapable engagement with meaning – meaning that has interests and ruses of its own.

Psychoanalysis is traversed by feminism. In his famous letter to Marie Bonaparte, Freud writes: "the great question that has never been answered, and that I have not been able to answer, despite my thirty years of research into the feminine soul, is 'What does a woman want?'"[4] This question provokes Freud's work as if it *were* a feminist question, ultimately refusing all answers because all answers seem addressed to the wrong question. Indeed, this nagging provocation is already embedded in Freud's early work with female hysterics, the limitations and failures of which contributed to the birth of psychoanalysis. Psychoanalysis is also traversed by literature and by reading. Among the many allusions to literature in Freud's writing, there are the brilliantly successful encounters, as with the myths of Oedipus and Narcissus, through which he formulates and reformulates some of his most difficult theories; and the more problematic encounters, as with E. T. A. Hoffmann's "The Sand-Man," which he uses to evoke the uncanny, and with Wilhelm Jensen's Gradiva, employed as an allegory of psychoanalysis. Freud is indebted to narrative throughout his work, particularly in his case studies. And above all, there are Freud's own theories as to how to *read* the unconscious. From *The Interpretation of Dreams* on, Freud sees the folly of hermeneutics for his project. There is no unconscious to be discovered, only the unconscious effects seen in dreams and jokes and parapraxes and symptoms. Moreover, even these effects can never be apprehended directly. In reading dreams, for example, it is not in the "latent" meaning of the dream – that more cryptic meaning lying behind the dream's "manifest" content – that the analyst finds the effects of the unconscious, but in what Freud calls the "dream-work," psychic operations of condensation, displacement, and overdetermination.

The catalog is not finished; we have yet to consider how reading and literature can be said to be traversed by feminism and psychoanalysis. But rather than continuing to review what we know about these mutual implications, I would like to turn to some implications that are harder to see. To begin again: in what way can the practice of psychoanalysis be connected to the practice of feminist literary criticism? Literary criticism is the reader's engagement with texts. Psychoanalysis is a clinical practice, in which an analyst treats a patient who is in one way or another unable to be, as Freud put it, a normally unhappy person. In the ideal course of treatment, by means of transference and counter-transference, the analyst and patient engage with the workings of the patient's unconscious in such a way as to bring about psychic change. Clearly, on this level there is no connection between the two practices. Yet the relationship between literary criticism and psychoanalysis is a long one. Elizabeth Wright offers an admirably thorough and intelligent analysis of this relationship in her *Psychoanalytic Criticism: A Reappraisal.*[5] Wright shows how – starting with Freud – both analysts and literary critics have been fascinated by the challenge of applying psychoanalytic theories to authors and their texts. Although the types of fascination are different, it is evident that the relative compliance of the literary author and text has been a common attraction. No resistant Doras here.

Literature and Psychoanalysis: The Question of Reading, Otherwise, a special issue of *Yale French Studies*, set out to challenge this relationship in which literature deferred to psychoanalysis and psychoanalysis used literature to rediscover what it already knew. In her introduction, Felman explores the ways in which literature and psychoanalysis are implicated in each other, traverse each other. While the intent is not to reverse the master-slave relation so that psychoanalysis might submit to literature, the aim of the volume is to open up and reinvent the relationship between the two by looking at it from the literary point of view (p. 6). Accordingly, of the dozen contributors to the volume, all but three are literary critics, one of the three being Lacan. But Lacan, of course, occupies a special place in the volume by virtue of his having already brought into view the relationships among psychoanalysis, language, and reading. Since the late 1950s Lacan had borrowed freely and loosely from structural linguistics, particularly from Ferdinand de Saussure and Roman Jakobson, to develop his own theories of signification and ways to read unconscious effects. Thus it might appear as if by the time the *Yale French Studies* volume appeared in 1977, Lacan had preempted the project, reinventing the relationship of psychoanalysis and literature, but with the old transferential relationship securely in place.

While some readers were – and still are – tempted to deliver the passive literary text over to a powerful Lacanian theory that knows its truths, this approach requires one to ignore or forget Lacan's own thoughts about transference, particularly his notion of the analyst as the "subject-supposed-to-know." Transference starts, according to Lacan, as soon as the analysand begins to think that the analyst actually *knows* his truths, his secret meanings, his desires. As Dylan Evans explains:

> It is a particular relationship to knowledge that constitutes the unique position of the analyst . . . [T]he analyst must realize that he only occupies the position of one who is presumed (by the analysand) to know, without fooling himself that he really does possess the knowledge attributed to him. The analyst must realize that, of the knowledge attributed to him by the analysand, he knows nothing.[6]

What the analyst does is listen to the analysand, intervening with interpretations. But it is not a question, for Lacan, "of fitting the analysand's discourse into a preconceived interpretive matrix or theory (as in the 'decoding' method) but of disrupting all such theories. Far from offering the analysand a new message, the interpretation should serve merely to enable the analysand to hear the message he is unconsciously addressing to himself" (p. 89). The interpretation will most likely have to do with a meaning in the analysand's words that is other than that of the consciously communicated meaning, so to open up the analysand's language, to make it other to itself, the analyst must work at *not* understanding. As Evans puts it, the analyst is not seeking an "imaginary intuitive grasp" of the patient's "hidden message"; on the contrary, his task is "simply to read the analysand's discourse as if it were a text, attending to the formal features of this discourse, the signifiers that repeat themselves" (p. 89).

The "reading" that Evans describes is not a fully technical term for Lacan but it is for literary critics, and it is that notion of reading that helps to bring literature and psychoanalysis together in a new relationship. To follow Barbara Johnson, the question is actually one of *rereading*. Her essay "The Critical Difference: BartheS/BalZac" begins: "Literary criticism as such can perhaps be called the art of rereading."[7] She takes as her point of departure Roland Barthes's consideration in *S/Z* of the question of rereading, which he sees as a practice running counter to the marketplace, to the ideology of consumable pleasure in which one moves from story to story. For Barthes, rereading is crucial, for only by returning to the text can one avoid repetition: "those who fail to reread are obliged to read the same story everywhere" (*The Critical Difference*, p. 3). Johnson's understanding of Barthes's paradoxical comment leads us to see how the reading of a literary text might be compared with the listening of the analyst. What Barthes implies, she says, is that a single reading is made up of the "already-read": "that what we can see in a text the first time is already in us, not in it; in us insofar as we ourselves are a stereotype, an already-read text; and in the text only to the extent that the already-read is that aspect of a text that it must have in common with its reader in order for it to be readable at all." (p. 3) To reread the same, moreover, is to engender the text's own difference from itself, a difference that is central to the deconstructive project of rereading.

What enables psychoanalysis and literary criticism to have a new sort of interaction, then, the kind of interaction that Felman calls for, is their shared relationship to knowing and not-knowing, repetition and difference. The essay in the *Yale French Studies* volume that most strikingly displays these relationships is Johnson's own, "The Frame of Reference: Poe, Lacan, Derrida." A reading of Derrida's reading of Lacan's reading of Edgar Allan Poe's "The Purloined Letter," the essay never ceases to consider the knotted dramas of knowing and not knowing, insight and blindness, difference and repetition. In the end, Johnson deconstructs Derrida's critique of psycho-analysis (via Lacan's reading of Poe). It is not that Derrida is wrong, Johnson suggests, when he objects that psychoanalysis is only "capable of finding itself wherever it looks" (p. 136)[8]; it is that his objection to psychoanalysis turns out to be a disclosure of the very essence of psychoanalysis:

> Psychoanalysis is, in fact, the primal scene it seeks: it is the first occurrence of what has been repeating itself in the patient without ever having occurred. Psychoanalysis is not the interpretation of repetition; it is the repetition of a *trauma of interpretation* – called "castration" or "parental coitus" or "the Oedipus complex" or even "sexuality" – the traumatic deferred interpretation not *of* an event, but *as* an event that never took place as such. The "primal scene" is not a scene but an interpretive infelicity whose result was to situate the interpreter in an impossible position. And psychoanalysis is the recon-struction of that interpretive infelicity not as its interpretation, but as its first and last act. Psychoanalysis has content only insofar as it repeats the discontent of what never took place.

(p. 142)

If psychoanalysis is the repetition of the trauma of interpretation, of the "interpretive infelicity" – not to say impossibility – that is sexuality, litera-ture, Johnson argues, is one of the scenes of the impossibility. "If human beings were not divided into two biological sexes, there would be no need for literature" is the opening line of her essay on Stéphane Mallarmé's "The White Waterlily." It is not that literature is able to produce any deep truth of the mysteries of sexuality, Johnson writes, nor is it even a question simply of literature being able or unable to speak that truth. It is rather that literature is thoroughly implicated in sexuality: "It is not the life of sexuality that literature cannot capture; it is literature that inhabits the very heart of what makes sexuality problematic for us speaking animals. Literature is not only a thwarted investigator but also an incorrigible perpetrator of the problem of sexuality."[9] Seen this way, there can be little wonder that in the 1970s literature and psychoanalysis came to see themselves as inextricably connected.

Sexual difference

"Sexual Difference" is a term rarely encountered today outside a psychoanalytic context and even there it is sometimes used interchangeably with "gender." While both terms take their distance from anatomy, "sexual difference" has its own history and particular uses. It is not a formal psychoanalytic term, as Debra Keates points out: "Freud concentrated on the 'distinction' (*Entscheidung*) between the sexes, and Lacan on the 'relation' (*rapport*) between the sexes."[10] The term first took on life and flourished in the context of the deconstructive exploration of difference, where it called attention to the very *exclusion* of difference. In her *Fictions of Feminine Desire* (1982), Peggy Kamuf writes of the logocentric reduction of sexual difference: "The legacy of the enclosure of difference within oppositional hierarchies can be traced through any one of the many privileged terms that are signaled in neologisms such as logocentrism, phonocentrism, phallocentrism, and androcentrism. As to why we might need such manifestly contrived terms, cf. J. Derrida, *De la grammatologie* . . . chapter 1."[11] In feminist psychoanalytic thinking, this deconstructive "sexual difference" refers to the *sexuation* that Lacan points to when the human subject enters the "symbolic order," as he calls it, a *psychic* sexuation into masculine and feminine.

As is almost always the case, Lacan's thinking grows out of Freud's. Freud locates the multiple meanings of "masculine" and "feminine" in at least three registers, according to Laplanche and Pontalis: the biological, the sociological, and the psychosexual. The realm of the biological for Freud offers a certain scientific clarity in the delineation of primary and secondary sex characteristics but cannot account for psychosexual behavior. The sociological domain comprises both the real and the symbolic functions of the male and female in a given culture. And the psychosexual register connects with both, but primarily with the sociological. "In other words," as Laplanche and Pontalis caution, "these notions are highly problematic and should be approached with circumspection."[12]

Whereas Freud uses the term "castration" to elaborate the phantasmatic relationship[13] of the psychosexual to the biological and the sociological, Lacan uses the "phallus." In his formulation the Oedipus complex can be grasped by looking to the different positions occupied by the phallus – which he calls a "signifier of desire" – in the desires of the players in this triangular scene of child, mother, phallus/father. How the child finds its way through this complex determines its assumption of a sexual position of masculine or feminine. Whichever way the child goes, this assumption of a sexual position is made at a price, the price Lacan calls "lack," which is experienced as a lack in and of being, and which is a psychic response to the (phantasmatic) loss of an imaginary wholeness before sexual differentiation, before entry into the symbolic realm.

This taking up of a sexual position, this becoming a sexed subject, is not an anatomical assignation – anatomical males can take up a feminine position and females a masculine – it is a *psychic* positioning. But the work of the phallus in the "knot" of the biological, the sociological (real and symbolic), and the psychosexual is asymmetrical work. Here is Jane Gallop's representation of that asymmetry:

> In question here is some "whole" which is made up of two parts, like humanity is divided into two sexes. The phallus is both the (dis)proportion between the sexes, and the (dis)proportion of any sexed being by virtue of being sexed (having parts, being partial) and human totality. So the man is "castrated" by not being total, just as the woman is "castrated" by not being a man. Whatever relation of lack the man feels, lack of wholeness, lack in/of being, is projected onto the woman's lack of the phallus, lack of maleness. Woman is then the figuration of phallic "lack"; she is a hole. By these mean and extreme phallic proportions, the whole is to man as man is to the hole.[14]

The subject is thus constituted by "lack" and it is the subject's – that is to say, the individual, asymmetrically positioned psychic subject's – (mis)apprehension of lack that fuels desire.

Freud's revolutionary insight that the relationship between the sexual aim and the sexual object is a consequence not of nature but of unconscious drives becomes newly available through Lacan's theory of desire. "Desire" (Lacan's elaboration of Freud's "wish") must be seen as distinct from "demand." "Demand" is the helpless infant's call to have biological needs met. But as the needs are met, they cease to be simply one with the infant; they are cleft by the very demand to the place of the Other, which, according to Lacan, comes to signify absolute "love." While physical needs can be met, the absolute demand for love cannot. What is left over, what is unsatisfied, is desire.[15]

Feminist critics who engaged with Lacanian theory found much there to work with. Psychoanalytic theory could only repeat over and over that the assumption of either psychic position – masculine or feminine – was an imaginary feat, never fully achieved by real human beings. That is to say, "sexual difference" became a term that could signify *at the same time* the coercive psychic positioning in the symbolic and the *impossibility* of ever fully taking one's sexual place. Moreover, as indicated earlier, Lacan's turn to language in his theorization of psychic operations helped to make psychoanalysis productive for feminist criticism. The early years of feminism had produced important work on two of the sites of masculinity and femininity – the biological and the sociological (real and symbolic) – including important critiques of the historical collapsing of meanings onto one another. But over the years these two sites had themselves become locked into an ever more closed – and already known – relationship. Psychoanalysis offered something else. At stake was not so much the inequity of men and women, nor the avowal or disavowal of the biological in gender, but a welcome understanding of the *impossibility* of sexual difference.

Johnson exposes this impossibility in a discussion of the following very difficult statement of Lacan's: "The phallus is the privileged signifier of that mark where logos is joined together with the advent of desire."[16] "The important word in this definition," Johnson comments, "is *joined*. For if language (alienation of needs through the place of the Other) and desire (the remainder that is left after the subtraction of real needs from absolute demand) are neither totally separable from each other nor related in the same way to their own division, the phallus is the signifier of the articulation between two very problematic chains." Johnson further develops this tricky joining by looking at another of Lacan's difficult formulations: "A signifier is what represents a subject for another signifier." What does this mean, Johnson asks, except the subversion in the second half of the sentence of the very distinction that is established in the first half, rendering the two terms neither fully merged nor fully distinct. The "signifier" is differentiated from itself in the very process of definition, with the second "signifier" seeming to take on the place of the word "subject": "The signifier for which the other signifier represents a subject thus acts like a subject because it is the place where the representation is 'understood.'" It is this signifier, then, that "situates the place of something like a reader." We are again in the unsettling neighborhood of the "interpretive infelicity" referred to earlier. Here there is no masculine or feminine truth to be found but only places from which to seek those tantalizing promises. The signifier in this sentence of Lacan situates the place of the reader and, Johnson goes on, "the reader becomes the place where representation would be understood if there were any such thing as a place beyond representation; the place where representation is inscribed as an infinite chain of substitutions whether or not there is any place from which it can be understood" (p. 141).

This was the "sexual difference" that feminists found in Lacan, a sexual difference born of treacherous signification, which, thanks to its very treachery, offered a way to read the insistence of its effects.

Feminocentric reading

Feminist psychoanalytic criticism of the late 1970s and the 1980s was, of course, by no means limited to literature. Many feminist critics brought literary analysis to bear on nonliterary texts such as those of Lacan and Freud, Luce Irigaray and Julia Kristeva. The enormously influential British journal, *m/f*, published between 1978 and 1985, brought literary critics together with political philosophers, sociologists, film theorists, and psychoanalysts, to theorize the intersection of representation, social theory, and psychoanalysis from a Marxist-feminist perspective.[17] Also during this period, feminist film theory drew on psychoanalytic paradigms to transform film criticism.

Within literary studies, psychoanalytic approaches were not limited to the Lacanian and Derridean. During the 1980s there was a lively interest in representations of oedipal – mostly mother-daughter – relationships in literature. Two of the most influential books for this approach were Dorothy Dinnerstein's *The Mermaid and the Minotaur: Sexual Arrangements and Human Malaise* (1976) and Nancy Chodorow's *The Reproduction of Mothering: Psychoanalysis and the Sociology of Gender* (1978).[18] Both helped to introduce object relations theory into feminist criticism and both take up the question of the mother, so underdeveloped in Freud, and so neglected in favor of the father in Lacan. It is not surprising that feminists would be eager to pursue the maternal path, yet object-relations criticism had its limitations, limitations that might account for the fact that its influence seems to have waned after the 1980s.[19] According to Claire Kahane, the problems lay not with Melanie Klein, whose work engendered British object relations theory, but with successors of Klein who displace Klein's theorization of reality and phantasy onto a notion of external versus internal reality. The result is a focus on the development of the self in terms of its "real relations with external objects." What is lost is the force of unconscious phantasy and the work of language. As Kahane comments: "If not rejecting outright Klein's emphasis on the drives, aggression and fantasy . . . object relations theory nevertheless downplays it and situates fantasy as an ego function, an effort to deal with the drives rather than a representation of them."[20] To leave out psychic representation is to leave out a key player in Freud's notion of the unconscious and to flatten the very relationship of the literary to the psychoanalytic.

In one of the more animated feminist debates of this period, which concerned this problem of representation, Lacanian-oriented feminist critics took on the challenge of exposing the blind spots of other feminist approaches. One example is Mary Jacobus's "An Unnecessary Maze of Sign-Reading" from her 1986 volume, *Reading Woman: Essays in Feminist Criticism*.[21] What strikes one about Jacobus's title, *Reading Woman*, is how strange it sounds to today's reader, awkward even. Does it refer to a woman who is reading? Does it refer to something that is being read, like woman-as-image? In fact, Jacobus's title is hard to read because the theoretical term "woman" has all but disappeared from critical language. Jacobus makes explicit her theoretical use of the term in the introduction to her volume: "In their different ways, all the essays included address both the question of a feminist reading and the related (for me, inseparable) question of reading 'woman' as a figure for sexual difference" (p. ix). "Woman" is a figure, then, but its work is to represent not something relatively concrete and knowable, like "a woman," but rather something called "sexual difference." A figure, or figurative language, can be seen as something that takes us away from a word's proper meaning. The "angel in the house," for example, takes us to places that the "woman of the house" does not, and even those critics who see all language as inescapably figural will agree that in those two phrases "woman" has a more "proper" function than "angel." But here, in Jacobus's comment, the question seems to be something other than that of the relative degree of distance between the figure and some proper sense of what is figured. The question Jacobus raises with her use of the theoretical term "woman" is where, if anywhere, does proper sense reside?

In "An Unnecessary Maze of Sign-Reading," Jacobus addresses this question through a reading of Charlotte Perkins Gilman's story *The Yellow Wallpaper*, a text in which both literal and nonliteral figures loom large.[22] A favorite among US feminist critics, *The Yellow Wallpaper* rapidly became a canonical feminist text and, in the process, spawned readings that Jacobus finds too closely wed to the work's expository dimension. She takes as an example Annette Kolodny's "A Map for Rereading: Or, Gender and the Interpretation of Literary Texts," which portrays the novel's protagonist as imprisoned in a man's world and destroyed by her very efforts to make meaning of this world. For Jacobus, such a reading has an incoherence of its own: in rejecting the tendency to see women as basically unstable or hysterical, it "simultaneously (and contradictorily) claim[s] that women are not mad and that their madness is not their fault" ("Unnecessary Maze," p. 233).[23] Jacobus sees this contradiction as symptomatic, arguing that thematic readings such as Kolodny's that look to find the social world reflected in the psyche and vice versa cannot but tie themselves in contradictory knots in that they manage to leave out both the unconscious and language. Such readings, she writes, end up "translating the text into a cryptograph," (p. 233) simply substituting latent content for manifest content, with no regard for the "formal features" that make such substitution possible. To expose the effects of the unconscious, Jacobus looks to what she characterizes as the unconscious of the text: "specifically . . . its literariness, the way in which it knows more than it knows (and more than the author intended)" (p. 233).

To offer a somewhat more extended example of the feminocentric reading of the period, I turn to Naomi Schor's "Female Paranoia: The Case for Psychoanalytic Feminist Criticism." The essay is, as the title tells us, a theoretical manifesto. First published in 1981, it reappears in Schor's 1985 collection *Breaking the Chain: Women, Theory, and French Realist Fiction* as the final essay of the volume and the only essay in a section entitled "Theory's Body."[24] It is a dazzling, witty piece that succeeded in its aspirations as a manifesto (see Wright's *Feminism and Psychoanalysis: A Critical Dictionary* for "Clitoral Hermeneutics"). It is also the least paraphrasable of the feminist readings offered here, perhaps because Schor's style of argumentation is the most literary and the least philosophical of American feminist theorists'. There are a number of ways to characterize that literariness. If we take a philosophical style to be primarily a metaphoric mobilizing of textual elements into theoretical concepts, Schor's style can be seen as exuberantly metonymic. That is, its arguments are born from felicitous meetings and couplings, from the interplay of the contingent and the contiguous. This mode of reading is not unrelated to the way the psychoanalyst "reads" the analysand's discourse. Just as the analyst avoids "understanding" common meaning so as to make the analysand's language Other to itself, Schor is wary of the "already read" text. Moreover – and here is where the "exuberance" comes in – Schor's style frequently plays with irony, albeit a particularly feminist form of irony, about which more shortly. Indeed, in some of Schor's readings, irony is the *only* signal of her argument's "ignorance" of some weighty and commonly understood meaning. Not only are all these literary aspects of Schor's style at work in "Female Paranoia," but they have, as will be seen, a strikingly mimetic relationship to the subject matter of the essay.

"Female Paranoia" is about the possibility of the very existence of femi-nist – not to say female – theory, a question related to the problem of whether or not there can be said to be a female paranoia. Freud frequently likened elaborate intellectual work to the intricately constructed delusions of paranoiacs. The problem is that Freud sees paranoiac system-building as a paradigmatically male condition that expresses a repressed homosexual desire on the part of the paranoiac for his persecutor. It is no surprise, Schor says, that when Freud does encounter a female paranoiac who seems to challenge his theory, he succeeds at the end in reconciling her case to the paradigm. For, as Schor points out, it is not only his particular theory of paranoia that is at stake, but (masculine) theory itself.

In her reading of Freud's "A Case of Paranoia Running Counter to the Psychoanalytic Theory of the Disease," Schor points to the element of his analysis that saves theory. Having determined in the first half of his paper that the patient's paranoia has to do ultimately with the woman's repressed homosexual desire for her mother, thereby bringing it in line, he devotes the rest of the discussion to the question of a noise the woman heard when embracing her lover (a fellow worker about whom she is ambivalent) – "a kind of knock or tick" – that frightened her and caused her to flee the man's house. This noise becomes the foundation of her paranoid theory, for in fleeing the house she passes two men, one of whom is carrying an object that she takes to be the camera that her lover is using to blackmail her. After establishing that accidental noise is an intrinsic trigger to phantasies of the primal scene, Freud then makes his final point: "I do not believe that the clock ever ticked or that any noise was to be heard at all. The woman's situation justified a sensation of throbbing [*Klopfen*] in the clitoris. This was what she subsequently projected as a perception of an external object" (*Breaking the Chain*, p. 154).

If, as Schor comments, we take the patient's "delusions as an exemplary case of female theorizing," then the implications of Freud's audacious and "possibly quite mad hypothesis" are evident: "The first of these implications can be stated quite simply: female theorizing is grounded in the body" (p. 154). Schor continues: "Indeed it may well be that female theorizing in-volves at least as much asserting the body's inscription in language, as demonstrating the female body's exclusion from language, a more widely held view . . . The question then becomes: is there any evidence to support my hypothesis that female psychoanalytically based and oriented theory is, by definition, a materialism riveted to the body?" (pp. 154–5). Schor finds her question complicated by the second implication of Freud's possibly mad hypothesis: not only is female theory grounded in the body, it is clitoral.

A review of the thinking of Kristeva and Irigaray persuades Schor that their theories valorize the vaginal, which is clearly seen to be associated with *jouissance*, that enjoyment that escapes the limits of the pleasure principle. But consider the dangers of the vaginal, Schor says. It is bound up with the female avant-garde of *écriture feminine* and its preoccupation with the ineffable, the unnamable. On the other hand, the enterprise of valorizing the clitoris is also a risky business, she admits. What resolves her dilemma and provides the support she needs for her hypothesis is, as she says, "the place of the clitoris in contemporary theory" (p. 159). Turning to the famous "Purloined Letter" exchange, Schor points to a moment in Derrida's argument where, eager to expose Lacan's errors, he mobilizes evidence to show what Lacan did not see when describing the location of the purloined letter. Referring to the fireplace, Derrida writes: "We have here, in fact, what is almost an anatomical chart, from which not even the clitoris (or brass knob) is omitted."[25]

This is the comment, Schor says, that exposes the clitoris as "coextensive with the detail." "The clitoral school of feminist criticism might then well be identified by its practice of a hermeneutics focused on the detail, which is to say on those details of the female anatomy generally ignored by male critics and which significantly influence our reading of the texts in which they appear"(p. 159). Illustrating her claim with a deft reading of Poe's "The Mystery of Marie Roget," a tale of rape and murder, she inaugurates clitoral theory and declares its rhetorical figure as synecdoche, "the detail-figure." It is no accident, she says, that Roman Jacobson subordinates synecdoche to metonymy and Lacan does away with it entirely. Concluding, she writes: "Clearly in Lacan's binary structural linguistics, with its emphasis on the perfect symmetry of metaphor and metonymy, there is no room for this third trope, just as in his . . . [analysis] of Poe, there is no room for the knob-clitoris. Now let us praise synecdoche!" (pp. 162–3).

A word finally on Schor's irony. In "Fetishism and Its Ironies," Schor argues that "irony and not metaphor is the trope of fetishism" and conversely that the much-vaunted modernist irony is fetishistic in its operations.[26] Irony is what allows the writer both to discredit and to reappropriate what is discredited, as in Flaubert's case, for example, where he can at once distance himself from Romanticism and "reactualize" it in his text. But this presents a problem once again for women: "If irony is the trope of fetishism and if female fetishism is a rare, if not nonexistent, perversion, then it would seem to follow that irony is a trope absent from women's writing" (p. 106). What Schor calls for is a feminist irony that departs from modernist irony with its accompanying anxiety about sexual difference: "What needs to be appropriated by women is irony, but an irony peeled off from fetishism, a feminist irony that would divorce the uncertainty of the ironist from the oscillations of the fetishist . . ." (p. 106). Now let us ironically praise synecdoche.

Incitement

It is commonly understood that in the mid- to late 1980s feminist critical attention shifted from "woman" to "women," thereby signaling a salutary correction of what had been a blindness to difference, something of what Johnson called earlier and in another context "the difference within." There is, of course, a truth in this narrative of feminist critical history. What is true is that mainstream feminist theory, including psychoanalytic criticism, was virtually oblivious to the notion that its own white, bourgeois preoccupations were exclusionary, a historical oblivion that even now, after all that has been written, is inadequately understood. To attribute the phenomenon to racism is not to answer the question but only to ask once again how it is that racist blindness works. Some feminist critics have been quick to attribute the blindness to a perceived political deficiency in poststructuralist and psychoanalytic theories, an argument that seems less persuasive when one considers that liberal mainstream feminist theory, which was fully embedded within the emancipatory tradition of American liberalism, was just as blind. Indeed, the blindness of deconstructive feminism is more troubling in part because the latter at least took as its very foundation a critique of the imaginary inclusiveness of liberalism.

In the case of feminist psychoanalytic criticism, the question becomes even more complicated because here it is misleading to speak of a shift from "woman" to "women." As we have seen, "woman" as a theoretical term has as its very problematic a distance from anything that could be seen as a flesh-and-blood referent. That is, "woman" is an impossibility, uninhabitable by real women. What does it mean, then, to see the critical move from "woman" to women as progressive? Does it mean that the problematic of sexual difference has disappeared? That "woman," whose ineluctable phantasmatic life draws its very power from the way it plays with referentiality, is no longer?[27] Rather than try to sweep away theoretical questions with sociological answers, it is better to keep two truths alive at once: that "woman" was and is a critical deconstructive and psychoanalytic term, and that feminist deconstructive psychoanalytic criticism was blind to differences among and within women. Without being able here to explore the specificity of that blindness, I would suggest that the very inability to see the

ELIZABETH WEED

differences within women had to do with the power of the theoretical and
deconstructive insights. Feminist critics were not so much in thrall to the
theory – witness their vigorous critiques – as to the exhilarating possibility
that "woman" and "sexual difference" were assailable. It is not entirely
clear that quite the same blindness was at work, as some have suggested,
with regard to   sexuality. Because the critiques of woman and sexual
difference were constitutively critiques of heterosexual closure, heterosexual power was to various degrees acknowledged, as was not the case with
racialization.

What is clear is that the *particular* form of excitement characterizing the
feminist psychoanalytic criticism of the 1980s is gone. One has only to
consider two of the prevalent themes of current psychoanalytic criticism –
trauma and melancholy/mourning – to see how differently charged the
critical register is. One might say that today's psychoanalytic criticism is
fueled rather by a kind of incitement or provocation. It is, for example,
entangled in numerous debates across the fields about the relative adequacy
of explanatory models.[28] Take as an example the case of current work
on psychoanalysis and race. Part of the provocation here is an impatience
with psychoanalysis itself. If the earlier meeting of feminism and psychoanalysis was troubled, the meeting with the critics of racialization is even
more so because of psychoanalysis's own relative neglect of the question of
race. Yet, for all of its limitations, psychoanalytic criticism is seen by some
critics as crucial in offering insights not found in other explanatory models.
The knottiness and seeming intractability of the problems of racialization
and racism draw these critics to the psychoanalytic approach.

I offer as an example Claudia Tate's 1998 *Psychoanalysis and Black
Novels: Desire and the Protocols of Race*, which brings together questions
of race, sexual difference, and representation.[29] Like Jacobus, Tate is concerned to rescue her texts from what she sees as the weight of prescriptive
readings, including the reading of the black novel as necessarily emancipatory. To ask that black novels prove that racism exists in the world, Tate
argues, is to underwrite racism, to subordinate "expressions of private
longing to racial politics" (*Psychoanalysis*, p. 11) and to deny black subjects
the complexity afforded to whites. Her "Desire and Death: Seducing the
Lost Father in *Quicksand* by Nella Larsen" takes on a text that labors under
a weight of many readings.[30] White readers of the period (it was published
in 1928) tended to see it as "free from the curse of propaganda" (p. 125)
and refreshingly psychological. Reviewers for African American periodicals
acknowledged that the mulatta protagonist, Helga, has preoccupations not
limited to racial discrimination but, like W. E. B. Du Bois, they celebrated
that richness as a way of universalizing race, of "incorporat[ing] race within

broader human concerns so as to mitigate its power to determine the lives of African Americans" (p. 126).

When *Quicksand* was revived in the 1970s, some critics attended to its psychological complexity but even they failed, Tate observes, to integrate that complexity with what was now taken to be the story of a "tragic mulatta." Not surprisingly, Tate finds the black feminist readings of the 1980s to be perhaps the most "prescriptive" in that they are both closer to and more distant from the dynamics she sees at work in the text. For these critics, Helga is seen to be caught in a trap formed by female sexuality, biology (a rapid series of pregnancies takes her life), race, and a black bourgeois patriarchal economy. Ultimately, Tate finds that none of the readings that cast Helga's dilemma in terms of an entanglement of race, gender, and bourgeois class codes does justice to the novel's "irrational causality"(p. 127).

Tate traces Helga's downfall not to the social repression of female sexu-ality but to a powerful desire that takes her to her death, a "wild internal repulsion like 'rank weeds' that repeatedly overpowers her" (p. 123). What makes the protagonist of *Quicksand* so interesting and puzzling to readers is that she is an attractive, educated middle-class woman who repeatedly refuses opportunities that could be seen to promise happiness. In her wan-derings she moves back and forth between the real and imagined white world of her mother and those of her black father, only at the end to propel herself into a marriage with a black southern minister who shares nothing of her class background and sensibility. Her fourth pregnancy almost kills her and, like a death sentence, the closing words of the novel tell us that, barely able to walk, she begins to bear her fifth child. Understandably, the reader looks to external causes to try to fathom why this woman would become so seemingly powerless, like a victim of quicksand, but to do so, Tate says, one has to ignore the forces of Helga's unconscious desire. What is crucial for Tate's reading is where she turns to find the signs, indeed, the symptoms, of this desire. She does acknowledge, of course, the fictional details of the character – deserted by her father at a young age, psychologically abused by her white mother and viciously racist stepfather and siblings – but Helga is a fictional character, Tate argues, not a person to be mined.

Tate turns to the text, to its rhetorical strategies, language, and figures. She points, for example, to the instability, or even treacherousness, of the narrator. Throughout most of the novel, the narrative technique of free, indirect discourse gives the reader the impression that Helga is telling her story. Yet, at the same time, the narrator never disappears into the character; a distance is maintained and, as Tate says, there is "little intimacy" between them (p. 120). Indeed, following Tate's reading, the narrator becomes increasingly detached until, at the end, the character is – chillingly – left alone.

For Tate, "[t]he compulsion driving the novel to this conclusion is the enigma of the text" (p. 120) and that enigma has to do with Helga's desire. The desire that propels the character from one place to another, from one sexual relationship to another, is enigmatic not only because it appears at once all-consuming and irrational but because the text both reveals it and conceals it. It is by an accumulation of textual effects – repetitive words and narrative incidents, plays of language and details – that Helga's desire is put into play, and, by careful attention to the text, Tate traces the enigma. For Tate, it is an insatiable longing for the fantasized, abandoning father that consumes Helga. Unlike some readers who look to the abusive mother as the figure that fuels Helga's desire, Tate argues that everything in the text produces a fantasy of paternal loss. But the mother is not absent; the daughter repeats the mother's desire, though the maternal legacy does not stop there. Helga's psychic economy is masochistic: "Like the abused child, she perceives pain where pleasure should be" (p. 133).

If the longing for the father propels Helga from place to place and lover to lover, the internalization of the racist "repulsion associated with her black-ness" drives her to masochistic self-destruction. In the text's play of masking and revelation, both elements – desire for the father and masochism – are offered up to be read at various points but in ways that only enhance the enigma. Until Helga returns to Harlem from Copenhagen, the text aligns Helga's undefined longing with race, with a desire to identify with her father; after that, Tate argues, the novel loses whatever interest it seemed to have in "staging racial protest," and the vague force that is the nexus of desire and a masochistic drive to destruction takes over. And that force is nowhere better read, she says, than in the narrator's changing relationship with Helga, a "narrative transition from the sympathetic free-indirect dis-course to the sadistic domination of the detached third-person narrator, who seems to sentence Helga to death" (p. 135).

Reading on

If the conceit of moving from "excitement" to "incitement" has any truth, it is one of tone, which, while not insignificant, can be misleading. It might be better to think of certain psychoanalytic literary readings – feminist, antiracia-list, queer – as being joined by a common, continuing desire: that of evading the already read, the already known. In the crucial convergence of theory and politics during the past decades, literature has occupied a somewhat dubious if not suspicious position in relation to philosophy or history or sociology. There is no question but that the latter fields can discover and expose important truths. Yet, as Tate or Jacobus or Schor show, those truths are not always the whole story and what is left out often has to do with the very intractability of the misogyny or the racism or the homophobia that has been exposed. To engage with the impossibility of reading, that is to say, to reread, is the psychoanalytic political project.

Further reading

Elizabeth Abel, Barbara Christian, and Helene Moglen, eds., *Female Subjects in Black and White: Race, Psychoanalysis, Feminism* (Berkeley: University of California Press, 1997).

Rachel Bowlby, *Still Crazy After All These Years: Woman, Writing, Psychoanalysis* (London and New York: Routledge, 1992).

Teresa Breunan, ed., *Between Feminism and Psychoanalysis* (London and New York: Routledge, 1992).

Judith Butler, *Bodies That Matter: On the Discursive Limits of "Sex"* (New York: Routledge, 1993).

Cathy Caruth, *Unclaimed Experience: Trauma, Narrative, and History* (Baltimore and London: The Johns Hopkins University Press, 1996).

Anne Anlin Cheng, *The Melancholy of Race: Psychoanalysis, Assimilation, and Hidden Grief* (Oxford and New York: Oxford University Press, 2000).

Rey Chow, *Women and Chinese Modernity: The Politics of Reading between East and West* (Minnesota and London: University of Minnesota Press, 1991).

Tim Dean, and Christopher Lane, eds., *Homosexuality and Psychoanalysis* (Chicago: University of Chicago Press, 2001).

Shoshana Felman, *Writing and Madness: Literature/Philosophy/Psychoanalysis*, trans. Mantha Noel Evans and Shoshana Felman (Ithaca: Cornell University Press, 1985).

What Does a Woman Want? Reading and Sexual Difference (Baltimore and London: The Johns Hopkins University Press, 1993).

Shirley Nelson Garner, Claire Kahane, and Madelon Sprengnether, eds., *The (M)other Tongue: Essays in Feminist Psychoanalytic Interpretation* (Ithaca and London: Cornell University Press, 1985).

Marianne Hirsch, *The Mother/Daughter Plot: Narrative, Psychoanalysis, Feminism* (Bloomington and Indianapolis: Indiana University Press, 1989).

Diane Hunter, ed., *Seduction and Theory: Readings of Gender, Representation, and Rhetoric* (Urbana and Chicago: University of Illinois Press, 1989).

Mary Jacobus, *Psychoanalysis and the Scene of Reading* (Oxford and New York: Oxford University Press, 1999).

Barbara Johnson, *The Feminist Difference: Literature, Psychoanalysis, Race, and Gender* (Cambridge, MA, and London: Harvard University Press, 1998).

Julia Kristeva, *Desire in Language: A Semiotic Approach to Literature and Art*, ed. Leon S. Roudiez (New York: Columbia University Press, 1980).

Christopher Lane, ed., *The Psychoanalysis of Race* (New York: Columbia University Press, 1998).

Hortense Spillers, "Mama's Baby, Papa's Maybe: An American Grammar Book," *Diacritics* 17:2 (Summer 1987), pp. 65–81.

NOTES

1. Reprinted in Charles Bernheimer and Claire Kahane, eds., *In Dora's Case: Freud-Hysteria-Feminism*, 2nd edn. (New York: Columbia University Press, 1990), p. 306.
2. Malcolm compares the relationship between Freud and his readers to the transferential relationship between an analyst and a patient. The term "transference" is used to evoke the way unconscious elements emerge in psychoanalysis with a strong feeling of immediacy. The "Rat Man" refers to Freud's "Notes upon a Case of Obsessional Neurosis" (1909), in which the patient's morbid dread of rats is connected to his relationship to his dead father.
3. See Shoshana Felman, ed., introduction to *Literature and Psychoanalysis: The Question of Reading, Otherwise*, special issue of *Yale French Studies* 55/56 (1977), pp. 5–10.
4. Quoted in Ernest Jones, *The Life and Work of Sigmund Freud*, 3 vols. (New York: Basic Books, 1955), II, p. 421.
5. Elizabeth Wright, *Psychoanalytic Criticism: A Reappraisal* (New York: Routledge, 1998).
6. Dylan Evans, *An Introductory Dictionary of Lacanian Psychoanalysis* (London and New York: Routledge, 1996), p. 197.
7. In Barbara Johnson, *The Critical Difference: Essays in the Contemporary Rhetoric of Reading* (Baltimore: The Johns Hopkins University Press, 1980), p. 3.
8. I quote from the slightly revised version of the essay that appears in Johnson's *The Critical Difference*. Derrida's reading of Lacan's reading of Poe, entitled "Le Facteur de la Vérité," is in Derrida's *The Postcard: From Socrates to Freud and Beyond*, trans. Alan Bass (Chicago and London: University of Chicago Press, 1987). An English translation by Jeffrey Mehlman of Lacan's "Seminar on the Purloined Letter" is in *Yale French Studies* 48 (1972).
9. Johnson, *Critical Difference*, p. 13.
10. See Debra Keates, "Sexual Difference, " in Elizabeth Wright, ed., *Feminism and Psychoanalysis: A Critical Dictionary* (London: Blackwell, 1992), p. 403.
11. Peggy Kamuf, *Fictions of Feminine Desire: Disclosures of Heloise* (Lincoln and London: University of Nebraska Press, 1982), pp. xvi, 150 n6. That queer theorists can today condemn "sexual difference" along with "gender" for its narrow disregard for difference attests to the limits of how much theoretical work any term can do. "Sexual difference" has long since been subsumed by the known.
12. J. Laplanche and J.-B. Pontalis, *The Language of Psychoanalysis*. trans. Donald Nicholson-Smith (New York and London: W.W. Norton, 1973), pp. 243–4.
13. "Phantasy" is commonly spelled with a "ph" to indicate that it is an unconscious activity.
14. Jane Gallop, *The Daughter's Seduction: Feminism and Psychoanalysis*. (Ithaca: Cornell University Press, 1982), p. 22.

15. "Love" is, of course, not experienced as an emotion in this work of the unconscious. The word is used partly to underline that what is at stake is not simply a developmental process but a structural one in which what comes to be desire will never cease to be driven by the unconscious. Similarly, the union of being that is represented by "lack" is not something "experienced" at some early pre-oedipal stage but rather something that is retroactively formed; that is, it does not precede the symbolic but is the effect of the symbolic.

16. In *The Critical Difference*. Johnson quotes from Lacan's *Ecrits* (Paris: Seuil, 1996), p. 692 (her translation).

17. See Parveen Adams and Elizabeth Cowie, eds., *The Woman in Question* (Cambridge: MIT Press, 1990).

18. Dorothy Dinnerstein, *The Mermaid and the Minotaur: Sexual Arrangements and Human Malaise* (New York: Harper and Row, 1976); and Nancy Chodorow, *The Reproduction of Mothering: Psychoanalysis and the Sociology of Gender* (Berkeley: University of California Press, 1978).

19. For an analysis of this influence, see Marianne Hirsch, "Object-Relations Oriented Criticism," in Wright, ed., *Feminism and Psychoanalysis*, pp. 280–4.

20. Claire Kahane "Object-Relations Theory," in Wright, ed., *Feminism and Psychoanalysis*, pp. 285–6.

21. Mary Jacobus, *Reading Woman: Essays in Feminist Criticism* (New York: Columbia University Press, 1986).

22. Charlotte Perkins Gilman, *The Yellow Wallpaper*, ed. Elaine R. Hedges (Old Westbury: The Feminist Press, 1973).

23. Annette Kolodny, "A Map for Rereading: Or, Gender and the Interpretation of Literary Texts," *New Literary History* 11:3 (Spring 1980), pp. 451–67, cited in Jacobus, *Reading Woman*, pp. 231–3.

24. Naomis Schor, *Breaking the Chain: Women, Theory and French Realist Fiction* (New York: Columbia University Press, 1985). "Feminocentric" is Schor's term (see p. ix).

25. Jacques Derrida. "The Purveyor of Truth," trans. Willis Domingo et al., *Yale French Studies* 53(1975), p. 69.

26. Naomi Schor, *Bad Objects: Essays Popular and Unpopular* (Durham: Duke University Press, 1995), p. 106.

27. For an example of the dominant narrative of the turn from woman to women, see Elizabeth Abel's "Black Writing, White Reading: Race and the Politics of Feminist Interpretations," in Elizabeth Abel, Barbara Christian, and Helene Moglen, eds., *Female Subjects in Black and White: Race, Psychoanalysis, Feminism* (Berkeley: University of California Press, 1997). Abel gives a number of reasons why in the mid-1980s white feminist attention turned to texts by women of color: "The new attentiveness was overdetermined [in part] . . . by the internal logic of white feminism's trajectory through theoretical discourses that, by evacuating the referent from the signifier's play, fostered a turn to texts that reassert the authority of experience, that reinstate political agency, and that rearticulate the body and its passions" (p. 107). The rather stunning theoretical condensations and displacements of such a statement invite analysis of its own overdetermination. To turn to a different critical context, it is similarly misleading to claim, as some queer theorists do, that there has been a progressive move away from sexual difference to multiple sexualities. It is not that the positing of

multiple sexualities is not a productive move: it most certainly is. But "sexual difference" does not represent the dystopic pole of this progressive narrative.

28. See, for example, Cynthia Marshall's "Psychoanalyzing the Prepsychoanalytic Subject," *PMLA* 117 (October 2002), pp. 1207–16, for the current debate between new historicist and psychoanalytic critics.

29. Claudia Tate, *Psychoanalysis and Black Novels: Desire and the Protocols of Race* (New York and Oxford: Oxford University Press, 1998).

30. See Nella Larsen, *Quicksand* (New York: Collier Books, 1971).

13

BERTHOLD SCHOENE

Queer politics, queer theory, and the future of "identity": spiralling out of culture

Any attempt to map the political complexities of the queer movement must begin with an acknowledgement of its theoretical indebtedness to the first volume of Michel Foucault's *The History of Sexuality* (1976) which, mainly owing to its radical reconception of sexuality and power, has become "the text that, everyone now says, you can't even begin to practice queer politics without reading."[1] Foucault dismantles traditional views of sexuality as an instinctual quality and encourages us to conceive of it instead as a discourse, arguing that the ways in which sexuality expresses and manifests itself are subject rather than, as previously assumed, impervious to the specificity of their historical and cultural context. As Angela Carter, doubtlessly Foucault's queerest English contemporary, expressed it so pertinently in *The Sadeian Woman*:

> our flesh arrives to us out of history, like everything else does. We may believe we fuck stripped of social artifice; in bed, we even feel we touch the bedrock of human nature itself. But we are deceived. Flesh is not an irreducible human universal. Although the erotic relationship may seem to exist freely, on its own terms, among the distorted social relationships of bourgeois society, it is, in fact, the most self-conscious of all human relationships, a direct confrontation of two beings whose actions in the bed are wholly determined by their acts when they are out of it.[2]

In this constructionist view of sexuality, no sexual desire or act ever comes "naturally" to anybody. Rather, our sexualities operate as dependent variables within a vast complexity of macro-political equations of power which for the most part are entirely beyond our control. In this context, so Foucault explains, one would err greatly to conceive of power as a solidly embodied establishment of executive authority or political oppression; neither ought it to be mistaken for a wieldy set of governmental implements administering the imposition of "a pure limit set on freedom."[3] According to Foucault, power is apprehended accurately only if we learn to grasp it not in terms of an extraneous influence but as a force at once constitutive of, immersed in, and emanating from culture's processual interplay of innumerable internal force relations. Power must never be regarded *simply* as diametrically opposed to powerlessness, that is, as discretely isolated from its alleged counterpart by a neat hierarchical chasm; rather, power and powerlessness are intimately entwined and always of necessity implicated in one another.

For instance, Foucault suggests, if the political efficacy of a system of control is gauged most appropriately by the extent to which it succeeds in obfuscating its oppressive agency, people may in fact be most oppressed whenever they deem themselves most free. As long as perfect concurrence prevails between institutional expediency and individual desire – that is, as long as what everyone ought to be finds itself in perfect unison with what everyone wants to be – dissent remains an inconceivable political disposition. Consequently, to envision the end of systemic oppression in terms of an emancipatory self-extrication from power is misleading and delusive. One cannot ever liberate oneself from one's socio-historically determined frame of being and thus accomplish a triumphant jump out of culture. According to Foucault, the best one can hope to achieve is a first tentative step out of a position of remote control into a position of self-conscious unruliness and resistance.

The first volume of Foucault's *The History of Sexuality* is dedicated to an analysis of the intimate relationship between discourses of sexuality and discourses of power, using as an example the rise of nineteenth-century sexology and its scientific categorization of human sexuality into the normal and the deviant. As Foucault demonstrates, the nineteenth century instigated rather than merely recorded "an explosion of unorthodox sexualities" (*History of Sexuality*, p. 49). Instead of detecting "difference" in nature, sexology invented and then allocated it, mainly in order to accentuate the hegemony of the one and only normative standard – that is, reproductive heterosexuality within marriage – of which all other sexual practices or orientations were understood to be inferior aberrations. Moreover, instead of marveling at the astonishing heterogeneity of human sexuality that their investigations brought to light, Victorian sexologists examined sexual diversification only in order to catalog, curb, and condemn it. Thus "wrapp[ing] the sexual body in its embrace" (p. 44) and rendering "scattered sexualities rigidified [and] stuck to an age, a place, a type of practice" (p. 48), sexology propagated "the solidification . . . of an entire sexual mosaic" (p. 53) which, not without irony, resulted in the proscription of any "natural" development of sexuality.

Surely, the evocative poignancy of Foucault's choice of words in *The History of Sexuality* could not fail to appeal to the emergent queer movement of the early 1990s and add to its resolve to reclaim the sexual body from its containment within sexology's apparatus of definitive description. Resisting hegemonic heteronormativity by rubbing new life into "the frozen countenance of the perversions" (p. 48), the queer movement set out to release sexuality's subversive power – its original vivacity, mobility, and color – from sexology's imposition of categorical fixity. Picking up on the distinction Foucault himself makes between the different *modi operandi* of an *ars erotica* ("art of love"), on the one hand, and a *scientia sexualis* ("science of sexuality"), on the other, the queer movement is perhaps best described in terms of a politically inspired eroticism – a libidinal politics, or a politics of desire – whose celebration of sexual diversity proliferates in defiant disrespect of the intellectually retentive, pathologizing parameters of Victorian sexology's *scientia sexualis*.

But the queer movement resists not only the condescension inherent in sexology's neat nomenclature of sexual deviancy. In typically queer fashion, it also confronts the homophobic insult expressed by the word "queer" itself, not in order to defuse it, but proudly to cultivate its evocation of an ostracized outlaw existence. Thus "queer" has undergone a tremendous semantic transformation "from taunt to flaunt, from a hurtful slur to an emblem of positive identification."[4] As "a signifier of attitude, of a refusal to accept conventional sexual and gendered categories, of a defiant desire *beyond* the regular confines of 'heteronormativity,'"[5] "queer" designates the new democratic virtues of nonconformity, civil disobedience, and political defiance. Intent on disrupting anything too smoothly commonsensical or straightforward, "queer" stands for recalcitrance and strategic fractiousness, forever positioning itself at cross-purposes with what Michael Warner has called the "regimes of the normal."[6] To be "queer" in this sense means to be a transgressor, to go against the grain and trespass onto forbidden ground, aiming thereby to expose the fraudulent artifice of mainstream society's most centrally constitutive taboos and prohibitions. "Queer" also signals a strong and heartfelt commitment to collective politics and, at the same time, a deliberate pose of individual detachment.

To the exasperation of its critics, "queer" remains prone to bouts of embarrassing flippancy, political ineptitude, and frivolous self-indulgence, which are sometimes quite hard to justify in Foucauldian terms as bold, carnivalesque expressions of a previously suppressed "power asserting itself in the pleasure of showing off, scandalizing, or resisting" (*History of Sexuality*, p. 45). However, even if the exact intentions of queer activism are not always immediately transparent, its principal impetus and motivation remain profoundly political. Originally constituted in response to "the AIDS national emergency and the pervasive institutional backlash against queers of all sexes"[7] which began in the mid-1980s, the very existence of "queer" reveals the failure of the integrative gay equal rights campaigning that preceded it.

As Warner states in his introduction to *Fear of a Queer Planet*, unlike gay and lesbian politics, "queer struggles aim not just at toleration or equal status but at challenging [mainstream] institutions and accounts" (p. xiii). From a queer perspective, so-called "liberation" movements, be they gay and lesbian or feminist, only ever succeed in facilitating access to an intrinsically oppressive system, whilst leaving the system itself intact. Willing to surrender their revolutionary potential in exchange for social integration, liberation movements ultimately not only embrace but actively perpetrate their own systemic containment in a shockingly opportunistic renunciation of difference. To fit in, gay men and lesbians often seem quite happy to see their sexual difference extinguished in heteronormative role play while, within the basically unreconstructed order of postfeminist patriarchy, women's masculine self-fashioning – that is, their mimicry of masculine behaviour in the name of equality – significantly thwarts the possibility of any enduring manifestation of female distinctiveness or "difference."

By contrast, queer politics confronts the system with an alternative set of lifestyles, which are not only incommensurate but utterly alien to bourgeois heteronormativity. Queer activism clings to the hope that its attitude of anti-assimilationist resistance and deliberate disidentification from mainstream culture, as well as its provocative championing of the sexual, will guard it against systemic fixation and political "neutering." By repudiating all attempts at identification – be they derogatory or affirmative, systemic or counter-discursive – queer politics insists on its essential *anti*-identity, protesting that, as David Halperin puts it, it is "defined not by the struggle to liberate a common, repressed, pre-existing nature but by an ongoing process of self-constitution and self-transformation" (*Saint Foucault*, p. 122). "Queer," then, designates at once an indeterminate and open signifier, which is both singular and infinitely plural, and a quite definitive political stance, which is grassroots-political and pragmatic as well as utopia-bound.

The terminological indeterminacy of "queer" must certainly be regarded as both its greatest asset and its most disabling drawback. Thus Simon Watney praises the term for "its gender and race neutrality," highlighting the capacity of "queer" to bring together and, at least momentarily, unite all people of (any kind of) difference, that is, anybody who, for whatever reason, has ever suffered discrimination.[8] In Halperin's words, queer represents "*whatever* is at odds with the normal, the legitimate, the dominant.

There is nothing in particular to which it necessarily refers. It is an identity without an essence [which] demarcates not a positivity but a positionality vis-à-vis the normative" (*Saint Foucault*, p. 62). While this relativity of "queer" enables declarations of solidarity and the forging of political alliances across a broad spectrum of hitherto mutually isolated, diasporic, and disempowered identities, it also deflects the sexual specificity of the queer movement's original engagement and thereby seriously impairs its political clout and consistency. The definition of "queer" as anyone opposed to the normal and normative seems in fact prone to elicit certain theoretically astute, yet otherwise quite unhelpful statements, such as Kate Chedgzoy's categorical excommunication of (closeted) gay men from intercommunal queer bonding. In *Shakespeare's Queer Children* Chedgzoy distinguishes shrewdly, albeit with little political sensitivity, between "black people and women [who] have sought to highlight their exclusion from cultural privilege and authority," on the one hand, and "gay men [who] have always had access to those things – have, indeed, played a central role in defining and maintaining them," on the other.[9]

Yet, albeit evidently susceptible to (mis)appropriation and often acutely self-contradictory, "queer" somehow contrives to maintain itself as an all-encompassing umbrella at the same time as it claims to epitomize a new politics of strict nonsubsumption. Rather than translating scattered voices of individual difference into a uniform chorus of group assertion, queer politics makes a point of drawing attention to the often conveniently overlooked sexual heterogeneity within the gay "community" itself and, by logical extension, the invariably makeshift body of affiliated identities that together compose society at large. Hence the most crucial difference between the queer movement, on the one hand, and feminism or gay liberation, on the other, is the refusal of "queer" ever to characterize itself definitively, or to advertise a specific profile of eligibility for its members. The queer movement retains "the ability to escape definition."[10] Thus it not only circumvents what Judith Butler describes in *Gender Trouble* as feminism's foundational paradox – namely "that it presumes, fixes, and constrains the very 'subjects' that it hopes to represent and liberate"[11] – it also successfully avoids the apparently inevitable pitfall of "every single theoretically or politically interesting project of postwar thought" which, according to Eve Sedgwick in *Epistemology of the Closet*, "has finally had the effect of delegitimating our space for asking or thinking in detail about the multiple, unstable ways in which people may be like or different from each other."[12] Providing the comfort and empowerment afforded by group affiliation without requiring its members to yield their autonomy as individuals, queer politics sets out to problematize the vicissitudes of collective

BERTHOLD SCHOENE

identification in order to expose what it regards as the contempt for individual difference that facilitates traditional forms of belonging. As Sedgwick points out, "there are important senses in which 'queer' can signify only when attached to the first person,"[13] a proposition that finds further authentication in Warner's observation that "nearly every lesbian or gay remembers being such before entering a collectively identified space" (*Fear of a Queer Planet*, p. xxv).

Queer politics finds its roots in the AIDS activism of the 1980s and early 1990s, which saw the emergence of nationwide direct-action groups like ACT UP and Queer Nation in the United States and Outrage! in Britain. As Halperin has suggested, it is in certain forms of resistance cultivated by AIDS activists that "Foucault's strategic reconceptualization of sex, knowledge, and power has found . . . its most original, intelligent, and creative embodiment" (*Saint Foucault*, p. 122). Halperin thus champions ACT UP ("AIDS Coalition To Unleash Power") as the most "genuinely queer" initiative (p. 63) because it set out to voice the concerns of everybody affected by the AIDS epidemic and not just gay men's. Governmental AIDS-education campaigning proved fatefully handicapped by the conservative policymakers' anachronistic notions of sexuality as expressive of a specific identity rather than expressing itself in acts often quite indifferent to sexology's exacting demarcations between the "deviant" and the "normal." Mistaking the gay community for a closed, neatly self-contained circuit of sexual activity, conservative governments erroneously identified gay men as exclusively afflicted by the outbreak and rapid spread of the disease. However, queer suspicion of traditional conceptions of identity must be seen to derive not only from a fundamental opposition to systemic attempts at ghettoizing political minorities but also, far more poignantly, from the realization that systemic allocations of identity can, and do, in fact prove lethal. Clearly, the queer policy of radical group indeterminacy must be welcomed for the very simple reason that sexual deviance is never homogeneous.

On the other hand, however, what Halperin refers to as the "suspiciously non-homosexually specific" openness of "queer" renders the movement vulnerable to hijacking attempts by "trendy and glamorously unspecified sexual outlaws who . . . claim the radical chic attached to a sexually transgressive identity without, of course, having to do anything icky with their bodies in order to earn it" (*Saint Foucault*, p. 65). In other words, "it provides a means of de-gaying gayness" (p. 65) and thus significantly contributes to the depoliticization and systemic containment of the queer movement. "Queer" is reduced to little more than a fashion that will no doubt pass, hampered by a glitzy clutter of expensive merchandise (loud

T-shirts, in-your-face body piercings, *risqué* club- and gymwear) and expressive not of Foucauldian resistance but of exactly its opposite: a desire molded and remote-controlled by the *zeitgeist* of late capitalist consumer culture which cherishes such hyperbolic gestures of individuality as humanity's most precious and exquisite gift.

The question of the political efficacy of "queer" is compounded further by what Joshua Gamson calls "the queer dilemma" of appearing unable to decide as a group on the exact trajectory and purpose of its sexual politics: is it primarily geared toward winning minority rights or – more fundamentally, if also far less pragmatically – is it aimed at combating the hegemony of bourgeois culture's profoundly heterosexist epistemology of sex? Torn between the apparently irreconcilable *modi operandi* of an ethnic-essentialist and a deconstructionist politics of resistance, "queer" either dons the guise of "a quasi-ethnicity, complete with its own political and cultural institutions, festivals, neighbourhoods, even its own flag,"[14] or it defies the treacherous comforts of such identitarian solidification only to face the impossible task of "haphazardly attempting to build a politics from the rubble of deconstructed collective identities" (Gamson, "Must Identity Movements Self-Destruct?," p. 395). As Gamson illustrates, the problem is that "fixed identity categories are both the basis for oppression and the basis for political power" (p. 395). Therefore the question of what is ultimately more pressing remains: the fight against cultural oppression or the fight against institutional oppression? According to Watney, queer culture can "never settle for 'equality,' since it is so apparent that this involves total subjection to the rationality of 'normal' sexuality and its identities" ("Queer Epistemology," p. 25). Yet, by obstinately sticking to its radical principles, the queer movement is at risk of calcifying into an inflexible ideology, whereas ironically, by opting for an ostensibly self-defeatist politics of expediency, it remains true to its ideal of a forever freely shape-shifting mobility of identity.

Since, according to Foucault, "resistance is never in a position of exteriority in relation to power" (*History of Sexuality*, p. 96), the kind of political purity envisioned by the deconstructionist constituencies of the queer movement is ultimately unsustainable. Perhaps the dilemma caused by the (compromising) ins and (radical) outs of queer politics is best exemplified by the conspicuous and far from merely semantic ambivalence inherent in the statement of "coming out." Within the framework of lesbian and gay liberation, coming out invariably coincides with a demand for integration and is thus perceived as a self-assertive step out of the political no-man's-land of society's obscure margins into the very center of mainstream decisionmaking. As Diana Fuss explains: "to be out, in common gay parlance, is precisely to be no longer out; to be out is to be finally outside of exteriority and all the exclusions and deprivations such outsiderhood imposes. Or, put another way, to be out is really to be in – inside the realm of the visible, the speakable, the culturally intelligible."[15] By contrast, viewed from a radically queer perspective, a deliberate, ostentatiously displayed cultivation of outsiderhood deserves to be valued as a political statement in its own right. Within a queer framework, coming out never represents a feat of liberation but instead works as a strategic gesture of defiance. Visibility within the system does not necessarily mean complicity with it; nor, however, does emancipatory self-assertion guard against enmeshment in mainstream politics. According to Halperin, as "coming out puts into play a different set of power relations" (*Saint Foucault*, p. 30), it lays the foundation for future change rather than representing change in itself.

Owing to its commitment to a politics of radical anti-identity, the queer movement is at risk of winding up trapped and paralyzed by its own painstakingly theoretical self-consciousness. Thus Leo Bersani's reminder in *Homos* that "the power of [oppressive] systems is only minimally contested by demonstrations of their 'merely' historical character," and that "to demystify them doesn't render them inoperative,"[16] seems a perfectly justified critique. However, his proposition that "we have erased ourselves in the process of denaturalizing the epistemic and political regimes that have constructed us" (p. 4) appears unnecessarily dramatic. Neither deliberately nor inadvertently does queer politics ever perpetrate a "de-gaying [of] gayness" which – according to Bersani – brings about "the elimination of gays" (p. 5). Aiming to render heteronormativity's hold over it slippery and uncertain, the queer movement refuses "gay" as a label, but the evacuation of the term is by no means equivalent to discursive or actual self-annihilation. Rather, presented only with signifiers that are perceived as oppressive, queer individuals choose not to "come out" in any clear-cut, definitive manner and, by thus deliberately eschewing tangibility, they make a virtue out of their categorical homelessness, which suspends their agitated mode of being somewhere halfway between the visible and the hidden. As Alan Sinfield writes, "by inviting us to perceive ourselves as *settled* in our sexuality, the ethnicity-and-rights model releases others from the invitation to re-envision theirs."[17] Accordingly, by opting to *un*settle itself, the queer movement demonstrates that "the problem of sexuality" resides ultimately not with itself but with mainstream society which, once deprived of an easily identifiable Other against whom to assert itself, comes seriously unstuck.

Neatly corresponding with this imagery of homelessness and a subversive underground existence is Sinfield's concept of subculture – chosen over "community" for its reassuring lack of "cosy, togetherness connotations"[18] – which opens up navigable territory between the ethnic-essentialist and deconstructionist branches of the queer movement. As Sinfield explains, "subculture does not mean establishing a party line, but working questions out" (*The Wilde Century*, p. 206) while at the same time "retaining a strong sense of diversity, of provisionality, of constructedness" ("Diaspora and Hybridity," p. 289). Building a bridge between queer politics and queer theory, Sinfield's pragmatic understanding of the queer impulse as continuous subcultural agitation also aggregates smoothly with Butler's utopian envisioning of sexual politics as "an open coalition [which] will affirm identities that are alternately instituted and relinquished according to the purposes at hand; it will be an open assemblage that permits multiple convergences and divergences without obedience to a normative telos of definitional closure" (*Gender Trouble*, p. 16).

Because it seems like an opportunistic sell-out of the anti-assimilationist principles of queer resistance, any institutionalization of "queer" in the form of "queer theory" or "queer studies" must be utterly anathema to radical queer activists and campaigners. In fact, any attempt to capture the unruly ambivalence of queer sexual politics within the statutes of an academic discipline must appear as an unforgivable betrayal. However, while some argue that the systemic confinement of academia renders it unsuitable as a forum for making people recognize the fraudulent artifice of "het culture" (Warner, *Fear of a Queer Planet*, p. xxi), others are more optimistic. Halperin, for instance, envisages academic queer studies as "a gay science without objects" (*Saint Foucault*, p. 122), evidently understanding "gay" in this context to denote not only sexual difference but also the indestructible spirit of antidisciplinary playfulness and carnivalesque subversion. Queer theory seeks to explain and justify why queer politics so passionately rejects society's "administrative labels for the management of sexual difference" (Petersen, *Unmasking the Masculine*, p. 97) and also why, despite many a vociferous protestation to the contrary, these normative appellations have always already been internalized by lesbians and gay men. However, since its inauguration in an essay by Teresa de Lauretis, in which it was "intended to mark a certain critical distance from the . . . by now established and often convenient formula" of lesbian and gay studies ("Queer Theory," p. iv), queer theory has also shown a proclivity for attempting to reach beyond the mundanely political toward the as yet inconceivable sexual configurations of utopia. Thus, in de Lauretis's words, what primarily drives theoretical queer engagement is the desire "to recast or reinvent the terms of our sexualities, to construct another discursive horizon, another way of thinking about the sexual" (p. iv).

To date, queer theory's concerted effort at deconstructing the hetero/homo binary, which has dominated Western sexology since the mid-nineteenth century, must stand as its most incisive and epistemologically consequential recasting of sex. In *Epistemology of the Closet*, Sedgwick points at the sheer paucity and one-dimensionality of sexology's description of sexual orientation. After the categorical segregation of humanity into the allegedly complementary halves of the male/masculine and female/feminine, the body of sexuality has been equally dissected, leaving us with two distinct species of human beings locked into two rigidly demarcated and mutually exclusive circuits of desire. Despite the fact that humanity might just as arbitrarily have been sorted into the celibate, the monogamous, and the promiscuous, Sedgwick finds to her bemusement that "the gender of object choice . . . has remained . . . *the* dimension denoted by the now ubiquitous category of 'sexual orientation'" (*Epistemology*, p. 8). In evident agreement, Butler makes short shrift of "the heterosexual logic that requires that identification and desire be mutually exclusive," which she dismisses in *Bodies That Matter* as "one of the most reductive of heterosexism's psychological instruments." And indeed, how much sense does it make that "if one identifies *as* a given gender, one must desire a different gender."[19]

What queer theory's deconstruction of the hetero/homo binarism reveals is the fact that heterosexuality is as systemically constructed and controlled an orientation as homosexuality. Although Arlene Stein and Ken Plummer's conclusion that "queer theory normalizes homosexuality by making heterosexuality deviant"[20] seems far-fetched, there is certainly a tendency among queer critics to read heterosexuality's homophobic paranoia as symptomatic of its essential constructedness and fragility. According to Calvin Thomas in *Straight with a Twist*, for example, "because there is no final 'proof' of heterosexuality, heterosexuality must constantly set about trying to prove itself, assert itself, insist on itself" (p. 28) whereas, once "out," homosexuality appears far more at ease with itself. Contrary to how it is occasionally construed, queer theory is most emphatically *not* equivalent to the study of homosexuality. Rather, queer theory dedicates itself to an investigation into the plights and pleasures of sexual orientation in general. As Steven Seidman explains, it is "a study of those knowledges and social practices that organize 'society' as a whole by sexualizing – heterosexualizing or homosexualizing – bodies, desires, acts, identities, social relations, knowledges, culture, and social institutions" (*Queer Theory/Sociology*, p. 13).

However, the question of what exactly queer theory does, or ought to be doing, remains problematic. No doubt the most pressing issue is whether, in terms of both its political engagement and its academic import, queer theory – as a historical offshoot of feminism – has grown into the latter's partner or rival. Much has been made in this context of the proposition by the editors of Routledge's bestselling *The Lesbian and Gay Studies Reader* to define lesbian and gay studies in analogy to the study of women's history. Accordingly, queer theory becomes the field of academic study that "does for *sex* and *sexuality* approximately what women's studies does for gender,"[21] bringing about a disciplinary split between feminism and queer theory that continues to be highly controversial. While some critics, such as Biddy Martin, deplore and warn against the tendency "to construct 'queerness' as a vanguard position that announces its newness and advance over against an apparently superseded and now anachronistic feminism with its emphasis on gender,"[22] others (most prominently Butler in her essay "Against Proper Objects") doubt if such an analytic separation is at all feasible. After all, what would such a "split into univocal dimensions in order to make the claim that the kind of sex that one *is* and the kind of sex that one *does* belong to two separate kinds of analysis" accomplish other than a facile and profoundly unsophisticated erasure of "the ambiguity of sex as act and identity"?[23] Apart from threatening to produce what Butler anticipates as "the academic version of breaking coalition" ("Against Proper Objects," p. 21), the methodological separation of women's studies from lesbian and gay studies would harm both disciplines by desexualizing and thus effectively castrating feminism while overdetermining "queer," which, by definition, can successfully exert its subversive power only as long as it remains indeterminate.

Taking the debate on the discrete disciplinarity of queer studies a significant step further, in *Epistemology of the Closet*, Sedgwick experiments with the possible effects of a momentary suspension of mutual accountability between studies of gender and studies of sexuality. Rather than endorsing a disciplinary split between feminism and what she terms "antihomophobic enquiry," she suggests that "in twentieth-century Western culture gender and sexuality represent two analytic axes that may productively be *imagined* as being distinct from one another" (p. 30, my emphasis). Nowhere does Sedgwick deny that the study of sexuality and the study of gender are interrelated. However, she does suspect them to be not invariably or of necessity coextensive, though, so she writes, "we can't know in advance how they will be different" (p. 27). If Sedgwick's theoretical inquiry can be said to perpetrate a separation, it is a separation not between feminism and queer theory, or sexuality and gender, but between politics and theory. While this separation is purely experimental and strategic, its results are expected to benefit politics in the long run because "a great deal depends – for all women, for lesbians, for gay men, and possibly for all men – on the fostering of our ability to arrive at understandings of sexuality that will respect a certain irreducibility in it to the terms and relations of gender" (p. 16). Sedgwick's reflections on sexuality deliberately exploit the fact that a disintegration of sexuality from gender is feasible while retaining an acute awareness that it is feasible *only*, and never for very long, in theoretical terms. Her critical fascination with sexuality is due to the fact that unlike sex and gender, which she regards as more or less equally determined by "the bare choreographies of procreation" (p. 29), sexuality strikes her as impervious to essentialization. True, sexuality is to a certain extent physically preordained as well as socially constructed, yet it also has a completely different side to it – a side that is redolent of freedom and the unpredictability of the queer.

The ultimate queer objective is to intervene in both gender and sexuality studies by dissolving all traditional sexology's normative categories, including, in the final instance, the oppositional anticategory of the queer. As Peter Tatchell explains: "we queers are . . . destined to be the agents of both our salvation and our supersession . . . This, then, is the great paradox: queer liberation eradicates queer."[24] This demise of "queer," which accomplishes its perfect political fulfilment, is an inevitable corollary of its infinite indeterminacy. As Sedgwick declares, absolutely everybody is invited to become involved in the queer movement's "open mesh of possibilities," that is,

> [the] gaps, overlaps, dissonances and resonances, lapses and excesses of meaning when the constituent elements of anyone's gender, of anyone's sexuality aren't made (or *can't be* made) to signify monolithically. The experimental linguistic, epistemological, representational, political adventures attaching to the very many of us who may at times be moved to describe ourselves as (among many other possibilities) pushy femmes, radical faeries, fantasists, drags, clones, leatherfolk, ladies in tuxedoes, feminist women or feminist men, masturbators, bulldaggers, divas, Snap! queens, butch bottoms, storytellers, transsexuals, aunties, wannabes, lesbian-identified men or lesbians who sleep with men, or . . . *people able to relish, learn from, or identify with such.*
>
> ("Queer and Now," p. 8, my emphasis)

Sedgwick's generous definition of "queer" encompasses not only all gender rebels and sexual nonconformists, but also those potentially capable of becoming or fancying themselves as such, which renders "queer" a universal human trait or, in other words, an utterly unremarkable noncharacteristic. Evidently aware of this impending eclipse of meaning, Sedgwick warns that the queer trend towards mass inclusivity must not erase the specificity of same-sex desire and object-choice "from the term's definitional centre [because that] would be to dematerialize any possibility of queerness itself" (p. 8). The whole problem of definition is compounded even further when one realizes that the seemingly commonsensical equation of "queer" with "nonheterosexual" is no longer valid either because, so Thomas notes in *Straight with a Twist*, "straights, who would be definitionally barred from the terms gay, lesbian, or bisexual, could not be excluded from the domain of the queer except by recourse to the very essentialist definitions that queer theory is often at pains to repudiate" (p. 14). Consequently, it seems as if in order not to betray its most fundamental principles, "queer" cannot but compromise its self-consistency and political resolve by perilously opening up to ever greater appropriation and neutralization.

But what if the profoundly pessimistic notion of "queer" as an act of inevitable self-evaporation is solely to do with our lack of faith in its power to affect, enlighten, and win over those who come into contact with it? Must the influx of straights into the queer movement really of necessity signify an appropriation or (re)colonization? What if, instead, the exposure of straights to an exclusively queer ambience were to have a permanently queering or, to borrow Thomas's term, "twisting" impact on them? The chief opponent of "queer," it has to be remembered, is after all not hetero-sexuality but the system of heteronormativity. So, what if, at long last, heterosexuals began to feel seriously uncomfortable about being identified with what is clearly an oppressive regime of sexual normativity? What if they started to worry about the odd privilege, as well as the cost of that privilege, that is commonly attached to what they get up to in bed, which, after all, is not so far removed from what the majority of us do, and may even bear, at least potentially, the same internal diversity of both desire and practice? What, in Thomas's words, "would it mean for straights really to understand (and not just theoretically toy with) the queer argument that the normative regimens they inhabit and embody are ideological fictions rather than natural inevitabilities, performatives rather than constatives?" (p. 13). Might heteronormativity eventually come to be recognized as an unaccept-ably oppressive order of sexual apartheid? And, as a result, might the queer movement come successfully to fulfil its greatest ambition, which, according to Peter Tatchell, is "the evolution of a new eroticism" catalyzing "a far-reaching sexual revolution to transform sexuality in ways that ultimately benefit both homosexuals *and heterosexuals*" ("It's Just a Phase," pp. 47–9)?

The new queer identity, projected by critics such as Thomas and Tatchell, emerges from the utopian fantasy of a perfect reassemblage of our original sexual "self-and-otherness," or hetero/homo hybridity, which we have come to unlearn under heteronormative pressure. Hence Bersani's depiction of "queer" as "a kind of ghetto . . . based on the assumed superiority of queer culture to what is stigmatized as compulsory heterosexuality" (*Homos*, p. 10) appears to be missing the point. Of course, the first imperative in any queer deconstruction of sexology's hetero/homo binarism must aim at a

reversal of the implied hierarchical opposition. Thus Bersani himself specu-
lates that "lurking behind heterosexuality is a more 'original' . . . same-sex
desire that the invention of homosexuality helped to repress" (p. 36).
Following a similar train of thought, Fuss regards homosexuality as a
heterosexual projection symptomatic of heterosexuality's enforced repression of its own internal alterity. "To protect against the recognition of the
lack within the [heterosexual] self," so Fuss writes, "the self erects and
defends its borders against an other which is made to represent or to become
that selfsame lack" (*Inside/Out*, p. 3). Thomas similarly identifies straightness (and importantly, by implication, gayness) as "an effect of constitutive
exclusion" (*Straight with a Twist*, p. 31), hinting that originally, before the
institutionalization of heteronormative splitting, there may have existed a
kind of queer *ur*sexual potential to which perhaps, eventually, we will be
given leave to return.

Hence the second imperative in the queer deconstructive effort is not to
misconceive of "queer" as the mere opposite to straight (the way "gay" is);
rather, "queer" stands for all sexual distinctiveness rolled into one, thereby
rendering "queer" an expression of our desire "to move beyond the artificial
and constricting divisions that centuries of homophobia and puritanism
have imposed on us all" (Tatchell, "It's Just a Phase," p. 48). Reuniting
straight and gay in an act of radical decategorization, "queer" effects a
dissipation of heteronormative pressure at the same time as it alerts us to the
existence of an equally insidious *homo*normativity. As Tatchell shrewdly
points out: "many of us love to say that inside every straight there is a queer
bursting to come out [whereas] few are prepared to admit that inside every
lesbian and gay man there might be an element of repressed straightness"
(p. 52).

In *Epistemology of the Closet*, Sedgwick states that "people are different
from each other," expressing amazement at "how few respectable, conceptual tools we have for dealing with this self-evident fact" (p. 22). Incredulous
at "the number and *difference* that 'sexual identity' is supposed to organize
into a seamless and univocal whole" ("Queer and Now," p. 8), Sedgwick
calls for every individual to be granted exclusive "propriodescriptive authority" (*Epistemology*, p. 27) because, she emphasizes, "to alienate conclusively,
definitionally, from anyone on any theoretical ground the authority to describe and name their own sexual desire is a terribly consequential seizure"
(p. 26). Everyone must be free to devise their own sexual identity even, or
especially, if their desire finds no matching counterpart in sexology's catalog
of "perversions." Sedgwick aims to abolish the violence of definition
and categorization by reconceptualizing identities as "projects of nonce
taxonomy" (p. 23): although marked by similarity and hence displaying

classifiability, identities always remain distinctly singular, resembling spontaneous, momentary and nontransferable coinages that possess validity only within the context of their most immediate employment.

In line with Butler's understanding in *Gender Trouble* of gender identity as the result of performative enactment, queer theory views all traditional forms of identity as coercive assignments that, regardless of people's individual specificity, subject everybody to the regulatory imperatives of unequivocal cultural intelligibility. The queer argument is that since no two individuals are ever perfectly alike, identity as we know it often distorts rather than illuminates individual difference, thus rendering queer theory the only epistemological approach intent upon accommodating "difference" without discriminating against it by inevitably freezing it into a definitional cluster. Yet what if there existed an identity from whose perspective "queer" itself was experienced as a harmful, dystopian imposition? Could there possibly be someone who would perceive the queer insistence on fluidity and indeterminacy as an imperative of such excruciating interference that they would find it necessary to disassociate themselves radically from the queer movement? In other words, is there perhaps somebody out there longing to be "fixed"?

As a parallel reading of Jay Prosser's study of transsexual autobiography, *Second Skins*, and Judith Halberstam's *Female Masculinity* indicates, the question of what exactly is authentically queer (or "queerer") – "gender variance that retains the birth body" or "gender variance that necessitates sex reassignment"[25] – is by no means easy to answer. The comparatively simple question of how queer is transsexuality turns out to be equally fraught with difficulties. In a chapter dedicated to what she introduces as "the butch/FTM border wars" (*Female Masculinity*, p. 143), Halberstam delves into the manifold conflictual tensions between queer masculine-identified lesbians perfectly at ease with their sexual and gender hybridity on the one hand and female-to-male transsexuals desperate for corrective surgery on the other. At a first glance, because it drives a wedge between chromosomal sex and its gender-specific realization, transsexuality appears to expose the invariably inaccurate arbitrariness of any univocal gender assignment. However, this parodic quality is ultimately owned only by transsexuals who are happy to inhabit a body/mind conglomerate of indeterminate transitionality; it does not extend to all those who feel trapped inside "the wrong body" and thus subscribe to a discourse of transsexual embodiment "in terms of an error of nature whereby gender identity and biological sex are not only discontinuous but catastrophically at odds" (p. 143). As Halberstam highlights, any manifestation of transsexuality impatient to pass through what it perceives as an awkward and extremely painful phase of transition is at risk of assuming the markedly unqueer appearance of "a homophobic restoration of gender normativity" (p. 144). Refuting the queer ideal of endless sexual fluidity, transsexuality that is geared toward corrective sexual reassignment testifies to "the ways in which desire and gender and sexuality tend to be remarkably rigid" (p. 147). Equally unqueer is transsexuality's reliance for self-authentication on the sexological treatment of sexual difference as a potentially curable mental affliction.

Practically the whole of transsexuality's trajectory – "not only [its] reconciliation between sexed materiality and gendered identification but also [its desire for] assimilation, belonging in the body and in the world . . . without trouble"[26] – goes against the grain of queer theory's fervently desired recasting of gender and sexuality. Conversely, queer theory seems at risk of assuming the appearance of an oppressive ideology which not only seeks to delegitimate transsexuality's quest for harmonious somatic closure but, in uncanny imitation of one of traditional sexology's favourite maneuvers, threatens to pathologize it as a severe case of neurotic self-delusion triggered by an internalization of heteronormative principles and structures. Thus, so Halberstam notes, "lesbians have tended to erase FTMs by claiming transsexual males as lesbians who lack access to a liberating lesbian discourse" (*Female Masculinity*, p. 149).

From a queer perspective, transsexuality is seen as symptomatic of a homophobic homosexuality unable to bear a body perceived to be at odds with its "natural" desire. While queer theory welcomes transsexuality's resignification of sex, it remains embarrassed by the latter's desire for a literal reconciliation of sex and gender, thus giving rise to the impression that queer impatience with transsexuality may at least partly be to do with the apparent threat that transsexual unorthodoxy poses to queer dogma. As Prosser writes: "in transsexuality sex returns [as] the queer repressed" (*Second Skins*, p. 27). Protesting an inalienable inner essence of sex, which demands stable accommodation within "the right body," transsexuality exemplifies a vigorous refutation of Butler's claim that "sex does not precede but is an effect of the cultural construction of gender" (p. 26). Convinced of "the material reality of the imaginary and not, as Butler would have it, the imaginariness of material reality" (p. 44) and, moreover, profoundly dissatisfied with the prospect of consigning itself to the sometimes-adventure, sometimes-ordeal trajectory of a life of queer mobility, the transsexual subject cannot wait to be "fixed" in order to, at long last, cease to be queer.

It is often assumed that a radical deconstruction of identity, such as that promoted by queer theory, must inevitably lead to disempowerment and political incapacitation. For how might a self without tangible contours and of little definitive substance ever be expected to muster the resolve required to take the initiative and effect a change in its living conditions or, in fact, be changed itself? On the other hand, a constructed and hence deconstructible self, subject to and easily undone by change within its socio-cultural context, is clearly far more open to strategic manipulation than a self immutably fixed within a preordained, transhistorical essence. So, whereas the self of queer theory is endowed with the malleability necessary for change, it appears to lack the faculty of autonomous agency, which is generally regarded as indispensable for effective political engagement. It is precisely this prejudice of the queer self's assumed political incompetence that Butler tackles in "From Parody to Politics," the concluding chapter of *Gender Trouble*. In this often overlooked coda to her most influential work, Butler devises an ingenious blueprint for queer identity politics after deconstruction. Inspired by Foucault, she conceives of the self not as an autonomous entity that takes charge and wields power over an objectified world to which it is exterior, but as an irrevocably integral constituent of the world's multitudinous networks of power relations. In Butler's view, genuine, lasting change can be effected only gradually and from within the existing cultural and political frame. "If subversion is possible," she argues, "it will be a subversion from within the terms of the law" (*Gender Trouble*, p. 93). Accordingly, within queer politics, liberation or emancipatory change is not accomplished by a sudden revolutionary seizure of power, but by dint of subtle, intricate processes of unraveling, reconnecting, and evolving which contribute, slowly but surely, to humanity's gradual spiralling out of one set of power relations into another, hopefully less oppressive, set of power relations.

Within this queer dynamic of political change, individual identity is perhaps most aptly pictured as an elastic spiral rather than a neatly encapsulated role. Although within any cultural context individual self-identification is controlled by imperatives of performative imitation of the socially acceptable and systemically requisite, there is always leeway for maneuver. This is the case because, as Butler explains, "signification is not a founding act, but rather a regulated process of repetition," suggesting that agency might be "located within the possibility of a variation on that repetition" (p. 145). Or, put differently, "the task is not whether to repeat, but how to repeat or, indeed, to repeat and, through a radical proliferation of gender, *to displace* the very gender norms that enable the repetition itself" (p. 148). For example, while within a given culture all males may find themselves coerced into repeating the given behavioural scripts of masculinity – without the strict observance of which masculinity would lose its univocal intelligibility within that culture – for these scripts to be successfully perpetuated they depend on being *interpreted* by a multitude of *different* men. Similarly, although there are no doubt cultures within which circulate quite strictly fixed concepts of what constitutes a socially acceptable rendition of femininity, and thus room for individual interpretation may be extremely limited, it is nonetheless conceivable for a female to get away with a relatively unfeminine impersonation of femininity, provided that within her culture she continues to remain identifiable as a "woman." And, as cultural history amply demonstrates, what one generation is prone to frown upon as a taboo-breaking and scandalously deviant impersonation of gender may come to be viewed as nothing out of the ordinary or, in fact, a most desirable innovation in the eyes of the next.

It is in this way that individuals – constructed, but never entirely determined by cultural and socio-historical circumstance – are given the opportunity to intervene productively in history, not so much by forging a counterdiscourse against systemic coercion as by subversively, "queerly," modulating discourse itself. The most promising proponents of this kind of discursive modulation are no doubt Thomas's queer heterosexuals who, in order to preempt being mistaken for representatives of a system of heteronormative oppression, have not utterly discarded "those institutional, compulsory ideals, those compulsory performances [of heterosexuality]" but begun to "work to mitigate, or militate against [them]" (*Straight with a Twist*, p. 31). Thus, by daring to repeat differently, Thomas's "straights with a twist" have become unruly queer subjects embarked upon a gradual emancipatory process, not so much of spiralling out of culture as of expanding and recasting the regulatory limits of cultural signification.

In conclusion, it ought not greatly to surprise us then that despite its evident preoccupation with what are predominantly socio-political concerns, "queer theory has been dominated by literary theorists" (Seidman, *Queer Theory/Sociology*, p. 13) rather than, as one might perhaps be led to expect, constituting an area of research reserved mainly for the attention of sociologists. It seems crucial not to forget that, inspired by Foucault's reconception of sexuality as a discourse, queer theory finds its roots in a "literary" rather than literal understanding of the human, grasping our existence in time not as a natural, homeostatic fact impervious to cultural change but conjuring it instead as a historical process propelled by quasi-textual dynamics that ensure its fruitful susceptibility to resignification. Thus the queer subject's response to a regulatory tradition of discursive pressure can be likened to a dissident reader's subversive reinterpretation of the literary canon. In both instances, a position of allegedly powerless exposure and merely passive recipience reveals its potential as a site of resistance and subversive political agency. Similar to the way in which every individual reading is always also an act of rewriting, every performative act of cultural repetition is invested with the promise of subjective resignification.

What becomes evident here is the curious Foucauldian ambiguity of the term "subject" itself, which appears to hold connotations of both subjugation and (admittedly limited) agency and control. Since, according to Foucault, power and powerlessness are never pure opposites but invariably locked into a relationship of mutual interdependence, any exertion of power never wholly incapacitates the subject but in fact, if only for the sake of its own effective realization, must endow the latter with the power to react – either to succumb or to resist, to internalize power or to reflect it, or anything in between – and this is where the cultural production of the subject and its "identity" – both in sexual/gendered and in more general terms – ceases to be straightforward.

Further reading

Judith Butler, *Gender Trouble: Feminism and the Subversion of Identity* (New York and London: Routledge, 1990).

Michel Foucault, *The History of Sexuality*, 3 vols., trans. Robert Hurley, *Volume I: The Will to Knowledge*, (London: Penguin, 1978 [1976]).

Diana Fuss, ed., *Inside/Out: Lesbian Theories, Gay Theories* (New York and London: Routledge, 1991).

David Halperin, *Saint Foucault: Towards a Gay Hagiography* (New York and Oxford: Oxford University Press, 1995).

Jay Prosser, *Second Skins: The Body Narratives of Transsexuality* (New York: Columbia University Press, 1998).

Eve Kosofsky Sedgwick, *Epistemology of the Closet* (London: Penguin, 1994 [1990]).

Steven Seidman, ed., *Queer Theory/Sociology* (Cambridge, MA: Blackwell, 1996), pp. 1–29.

Calvin Thomas, ed., *Straight with a Twist: Queer Theory and the Subject of Heterosexuality* (Urbana and Chicago: University of Illinois Press, 2000).

NOTES

1. David Halperin, *Saint Foucault: Towards a Gay Hagiography* (New York and Oxford: Oxford University Press, 1995), p. 26.
2. Angela Carter, *The Sadeian Woman: An Exercise in Cultural History* (London: Virago, 1979), p. 9.
3. Michel Foucault, *History of Sexuality*, 3 vols., trans. Robert Hurley, *Volume I: The Will to Knowledge* (London: Penguin, 1998 [1976]), p. 86.
4. Calvin Thomas, ed., *Straight with a Twist: Queer Theory and the Subject of Heterosexuality* (Urbana and Chicago: University of Illinois Press, 2000), p. 18.
5. David Glover and Cora Kaplan, *Genders* (London and New York: Routledge, 2000), p. 106.

6. Michael Warner, ed., *Fear of a Queer Planet: Queer Politics and Social Theory* (Minneapolis and London: University of Minnesota Press, 1993), p. xxvi.
7. Teresa de Lauretis, "Queer Theory: Lesbian and Gay Sexualities – An Introduction," *differences* 3:2 (1991), pp. iii-xviii, (p. v).
8. Simon Watney, "Queer Epistemology: Activism, 'Outing', and the Politics of Sexual Identities," *Critical Quarterly* 36:1 (1994), pp. 13–27 (p. 15).
9. Kate Chedgzoy, *Shakespeare's Queer Children: Sexual Politics and Contemporary Culture* (Manchester: Manchester University Press, 1995), p. 190.
10. Alan Petersen, *Unmasking the Masculine: "Men" and "Identity" in a Sceptical Age* (London: Sage, 1998), p. 118.
11. Judith Butler, *Gender Trouble: Feminism and the Subversion of Identity* (New York and London: Routledge, 1990), p. 149.
12. Eve Kosofsky Sedgwick, *Epistemology of the Closet* (London: Penguin, 1994 [1990]), p. 23.
13. Eve Kosofsky Sedgwick, "Queer and Now," in *Sedgwick, Tendencies* (London: Routledge, 1994), pp. 1–20 (p. 9).
14. Joshua Gamson, "Must Identity Movements Self-Destruct? A Queer Dilemma," in Steven Seidman, ed., *Queer Theory/Sociology* (Cambridge, MA: Blackwell, 1996), pp. 395–420 (p. 396).
15. Diana Fuss, *Inside/Out: Lesbian Theories, Gay Theories* (New York and London: Routledge), p. 4.
16. Leo Bersani, *Homos* (Cambridge, MA: Havard University Press, 1995), p. 4.
17. Alan Sinfield, "Diaspora and Hybridity: Queer Identities and the Ethnicity Model," *Textual Practice* 10:2 (1996), pp. 271–293 (p. 273), (my emphasis).
18. Alan Sinfield, *The Wilde Century: Effeminacy, Oscar Wilde and the Queer Moment* (London: Cassell, 1994), p. 206.
19. Judith Butler, *Bodies That Matter: On the Discursive Limits of "Sex"* (New York and London: Routledge, 1993), p. 239.
20. Arlene Stein and Ken Plummer. "'I Can't Even Think Straight': 'Queer' Theory and the Missing Sexual Revolution in Sociology," in Seidman, ed., *Queer Theory/Sociology*, pp. 129–144 (p. 135).
21. Henry Abelove, Michèle Barale, and David Halperin, eds., *The Lesbian and Gay Studies Reader* (New York and London: Routledge, 1993), p. xv.
22. Biddy Martin, "Sexualities Without Genders and Other Queer Utopias," *Diacritics* 24:2/3 (1994), pp. 104–21 (p. 104).
23. Judith Butler, "Against Proper Objects," *differences* 6:2/3 (1994), pp. 1–26 (p. 4).
24. Peter Tatchell, "It's Just a Phase: Why Homosexuality is Doomed," in Mark Simpson, ed., *Anti-Gay* (London: Freedom Editions, 1996), pp. 35–54 (p. 54).
25. Judith Halberstam, *Female Masculinity* (Durham and London: Duke University Press, 1998), p. 143.
26. Jay Prosser, *Second Skins: The Body Narratives of Transsexuality* (New York: Columbia University Press, 1998), p. 59.

INDEX

Abel, Elizabeth, 281
Abu-Lughod, Lila, 222, 223
academic feminism, 74, 113; and feminism,
    81, 94; and literary criticism, 10, 11,
    262; politics of, 74–5, 80–1, 86;
    success of, 10–11, 12, 13; as
    transferential, 262
Adams, Parveen, 87–8
Adorno, Theodor, 173–4
agency, 53, 89, 100, 108, 114, 156, 246
Aidoo, Ama Ata, 226
Alarcon, Norma, 244, 245
Aldington, Richard, 148
Alexander, M. Jacqui, 227, 247
Althusser, Louis, 79–80, 89
Amin, Shahid, 217
Ammons, Elizabeth, 35
Ancrene Wisse, 60–1, 62–7
Anderson, Linda, 19–20
Anderson, Margaret, 142
Anderson, Steve, 186
Ang, Ien, 244, 248
Anzaldúa, Gloria, 220, 241, 246–7, 248
Armah, Ayi Kwei, 226
Armstrong, Nancy, 19, 88–9, 109,
    207, 215
Asian American women, 240, 241; critique
    of feminism, 109, 112
Aspinall, Sue, 184
Augustine, Saint, 126
Austen, Jane, 5, 99, 103
autobiography, 19–20, 21, 121–2,
    124–7, 129–31; confession model,
    121–4; non-Western, 127–32; politics
    of, 121–2; representation in, 124,
    126, 134; and the subject, 120–1,
    127–8; testimonial mode, 128–9,
    131–2, 213

Bâ, Mariama, 226
Baker, Houston, 46
Bambara, Toni Cade, 39–40, 41, 220
Barney, Natalie, 142
Barrett, Michèle, 175, 188
Barrios, Domitila, 128
Barthes, Roland, 261
Beach, Sylvia, 142
Beasley, Chris, 198
Benstock, Shari, 138, 139
Berlant, Lauren, 108
Berry, Mary Frances, 42
Bersani, Leo, 290, 295, 296
Bielby, Denise D., 173–4
black British feminism, 249–52, 255; black
    British, meaning of, 228
black feminism, 5, 35, 42–3, 238–9, 255,
    277; 19th-century black feminism, 30,
    32, 34, 38, 44, 45; black feminist
    lesbian criticism, 43–4; and black
    studies, 42, 47; black womanhood,
    discourse of, 236; and canon, 8, 18, 22,
    35, 39, 42, 43, 44–5, 232, 236–7; on
    category of woman, 35, 37, 39; and
    critical race studies, 236; and politics of
    experience, 44, 239; and white feminism,
    29, 30–1, 37–8, 39–40, 111, 112, 237–9
black women, 5, 236, 238–9, 240, 241, 257;
    race and gender alliances of, 234, 240;
    racial and gender inequality, experience
    of, 29–31, 35, 36, 239
Blamires, Alcuin, 57
Blau DuPlessis, Rachel, 137, 138
Bloom, Harold, 78, 100–1, 262
body, 18–19, 203–4, 273, 274;
    French feminism's account of
    the, 153–4, 156, 162
borderlands, 246–7

Felman, Shoshana, 121, 132, 263, 264, 266
Felski, Rita, 121, 122
feminism(s): and abolitionism, 29; and
    antiracism, 29, 81, 251–2; and
    capitalism, 81–2; category of woman, 3–
    4, 5–6, 12, 15, 29, 39, 82–3, 84, 85–6,
    111, 112–13, 221, 271, 275, 276, 281;
    divisions within, 9–10, 12, 13–14, 15,
    82–3; early 20th century, 139–41;
    lesbian feminism, 48; and narrative of
    femininity, 73; and new imperialism, 3,
    254, 255–6; politics of, 13, 14, 19, 73–4,
    75–7, 80, 159, 83–4, 85–6, 93, 94;
    postfeminism, 184, 187; on sexual
    difference, 269; and slavery, 29–30,
    38; subject of, 16–17, 22, 82–3, 84,
    214–15, 227, 241–2; see also academic
    feminism; black feminism; black British
    feminism; critical race studies, feminist;
    French feminism; multicultural
    feminism; postcolonial feminism; white
    feminism
Ferrante, Joan, 55
Fielding, Helen, 187–8
Fielding, Henry, 99, 102
film, 172, 176, 182–4, 188; feminist film
    theory, 270
Fisher, Shelia, 55
Ford, Ford Madox, 145
Foster, Frances Smith, 33, 46
Foucault, Michel, 203–4, 207, 288; on
    anthropocentrism, 202, 203–4; on
    cultural history, 106; on discourse, 158,
    180; poststructuralism, influence on,
    204–5, 206; on power, 283–4, 285, 289,
    299, 301; on sexuality, 23, 202–3, 283,
    284–5, 300; on the subject, 195, 202, 301
Fox, Pamela, 111, 112
France, Marie de, 55, 57
French feminism, 20, 146, 205; criticisms of,
    154; de Beauvoir, influence of, 156; and
    essentialism, 166, 167; Sigmund Freud,
    103; and hysteria, 162–3; on hysteria,
    162, 261–2; on literature, 263, 264; on
    the mother, 270; on Oedipus narrative,
    101, 166; on paranoia, 273; on reading,
    263–4; on sexual difference, 267–8; on
    sexuality, 202; on subjectivity, 158, 159;
    and US feminism, 153–5, 157; on the
    wish, 268; on women, 263
Friedan, Betty, 176
Friedman, Susan Stanford, 125–6
Fuss, Diana, 75, 289, 296

Gage, Matilda Joslyn, 37
Gagnier, Reginia, 121
Gallop, Jane, 17, 261–2, 268
Gamson, Joshua, 289
Gandhi, Leela, 217–18
Gates, Henry Louis Jr., 33, 46–7
gender, 8, 112, 286; and class, 111, 212,
    238–9; culture, gender produced in
    56–7, 88–9, 105–7, 175, 299–300; and
    race, 18, 35–6, 111, 212, 213, 232–3,
    234, 238, 239, 256; and sexual difference,
    267, 280; and sexuality, 227, 292,
    293–4, 297–8; and the subaltern,
    217–18; as topic of feminist theory, 13,
    17, 21, 22, 82, 292
George, Rosemary Marangoly, 22
Gilbert, Sandra, 146; The Madwoman in the
    Attic, 46, 100–1, 102, 107, 214
Gilman, Charlotte Perkins, 44, 271–2
Gilroy, Paul, 131
Goldman, Emma, 53, 61
Gormly, Kathleen, 198, 206
Gramsci, Antonio, 173, 216
Greer, Germaine, 172
Gubar, Susan, 80–1, 146; The Madwoman in
    the Attic, 100–1, 102, 107, 110, 214;
    "What Ails Feminist Criticism," 11–12,
    13–14, 16
Guggenheim, Peggy, 142
Guha, Ranajit, 216
Guilbert, Georges-Claude, 186–7

Haaken, Janice, 123, 124
Hagedorn, Jessica, 228
Halberstam, Judith, 297–8
Halley, Janet E., 55
Hall, Stuart, 241
Halperin, David, 286, 288, 290, 291
Hanscombe, Gillian, 138
Harper, Frances, 34, 35, 45, 46
Harrington, C. Lee, 173–4
Harris, Joel Chandler, 45
Hartman, Saidiya, 111
H. D., 147–8
Heap, Jane, 142
Heng, Geraldine, 18, 55, 57, 58
Hennessy, Rosemary, 86
Hermann, Judith, 123
heterosexism, 3, 43; heteronormativity, 82,
    285, 286, 295; homophobia, 243
Hill, Anita, 233–4
Hill, John, 183
Hollows, Joanne, 175–6

homosexuality, *see* queer
Hopkins, Pauline, 45–6
Horkheimer, Max, 173–4
Hudson, Barbara, 180
Hull, Gloria T., 41
Hurston, Zora Neale, 41, 44, 45,
    46, 47
Huyssen, Andreas, 139, 143

identity politics, 12, 15, 245, 299
ideology, 9, 79–80, 177, 178, 181,
    198, 213; of gender, 73–4, 175, 180;
    ideology critique, 6–7, 53; of romance,
    179, 180
images of women, 175–7
imperialism, 3, 18, 57, 214–15, 240, 248;
    new imperialism, 252
Irigaray, Luce, 160, 166, 167; on desire,
    165–6; on the imaginary, 167–8; on
    language, 161, on mimicry, 162–3, 165

Jacobs, Harriet, 33, 111
Jacobus, Mary, 271–2, 276
Jakobson, Roman, 274
Jameson, Fredric, 226
Jardine, Alice, 146, 164
Johnson, Barbara, 112, 261, 266–7; *The
    Critical Difference*, 1–2, 3, 4, 17,
    265–6, 269–70; *The Feminist Difference*,
    7, 11; *A World of Difference*, 83–4,
    86–7, 91, 105, 111, 112
Jones, Gayl, 41
Joyce, James, 142, 149
Julian of Norwich, 55

Kahane, Claire, 270–1
Kamuf, Peggy, 6, 267
Kandiyoti, Deniz, 222
Kane, Cheikh Hamidou, 212
Kaplan, Amy, 109
Kaplan, Cora, 111
Karmi, Ghada, 131
Kauffman, Linda, 26
Keates, Debra, 267
Kempe, Margery, 55, 57
Kenner, Hugh, 138
King, Deborah, 238
Klein, Melanie, 270–1
Kolodny, Annette, 271–2
Kristeva, Julia, 85, 160, 161, 167; on the
    avant-garde, 163, 164; on the semiotic
    163–4, 166, 167, 168
Krueger, Roberta, 57

Lacan, Jacques, 160, 265, 268; on the
    father, 166, 168, 270; on language, 158,
    161, 202, 269–70, 274; on literature,
    264–5, 266, 274; on sexual difference,
    159–60, 267, 268; on subjectivity,
    159, 163
Lane, Michael, 195–6
language, 20, 87, 90, 195–6, 205, 269; and
    sexual difference, 89, 269; as site of
    struggle, 153, 245; and the subject, 158,
    161, 203; vernacular, 47, 224–5
Laplanche, J., 267
Larsen, Nella, 276, 278
Lawrence, D. H., 139, 144
Lefanu, Sarah, 178
lesbian and gay studies, 291, 293; lesbian
    and gay politics, 286
Levenson, Michael, 136
Lévi-Strauss, Claude, 196–7
Lewis, Wyndham, 137
Lochrie, Karma, 57
Loomba, Anita, 217, 222
Lorde, Audre, 244
Lovell, Terry, 104
Loy, Mina, 145–6

MacKinnon, Catherine, 82
Madonna, 186, 187
magazines, 172, 178–80, 184–6, 187, 188;
    feminism in, 184–5, 186
Making Face, Making Soul, 244–7
Malcolm, Janet, 261–2
Mani, Lata, 215–16
Mansfield, Katherine, 145
Marcus, Sharon, 89–92
Marinetti, F. T., 137, 139, 143
Marsden, Dora, 138, 142
Martin, Biddy, 293
Marxism, 173–4; materialism, 86, 94
masculinism, 206, 253–4; and modernism,
    20, 137–9, 141–2,
    143–4, 148
Mason, Mary, 125
Mayhew, Henry, 129–30
McDowell, Deborah, 39
McNamer, Sarah, 57
McNay, Lois, 204
McRobbie, Angela, 178–9, 180,
    184–6, 187
Meulenbelt, Anja, 122, 124
Messer-Davidow, Ellen, 19
mestiza, 246
Miller, Daniel, 187

psychoanalysis, 23, 176, 202; and feminism, 263; hysteria, 162–3, 165, 261, 263; literature in, 23, 261, 263–7; object relations theory, 270–1; paranoia, 273; politics of, 275, 278, 279; on race, 276, 278; on sexual difference, 5, 159, 165, 267, 269, 270; on subject, 103, 119, 158, 164; transference, 262, 265

queer movement
coming out, 289–90; and liberation movements, 286; politics of, 285, 286, 287–91, 298–300; "queer," meaning of, 285, 286–7, 288–9, 290, 293, 294–6, 296
queer theory, 23, 57, 291; black lesbian feminism, 43–4, 237; and feminism, 112, 286, 287, 288, 292; and lesbian and gay studies, 291, 293; and literary theory, 300–1; queer feminism, 17, 18; on sexual difference, 280, 281; on transsexuality, 298

race, 7, 17, 18, 19, 246, 286; in American fiction, 110; in Britain, 251; emergence of race in medieval period, 57, 58, 60, 66, 67–8; in feminism, 3, 237–8, 244–5, 275; and gender, 3, 5, 18, 22, 35–6, 111, 212, 232–3, 234, 238–9, 256; and law, 235; and nation, 247, 253; in new imperialism, 252; psychoanalysis on, 276, 278; racism, 12, 33, 67, 235, 239, 243; whiteness, 58, 82, 243, women of color's experience of, 29–31, 36, 240, 242
Rappaport, Erika, 141
Rawlinson, Mary C., 203, 204
reading, 3, 4–5, 6, 17, 18, 56, 179–80, 264; active, 7–8, 16; the novel, 4, 19, 99–100; and psychoanalysis, 23, 261, 263–7; resisting readings, 18, 53–4, 56, 58, 62, 67, 300; symptomatic reading, 53, 54–5
representation, 19, 21, 22, 89, 211, 232; in autobiography, 124, 134, 126; politics of, 84–5, 86, 87–8, 92; and rape, 90
Rhodes, Jane, 34–5
Rhys, Jean, 145, 214–15
Rich, Adrienne, 121, 124, 134, 225
Richardson, Dorothy, 143, 146–7, 149
Richardson, Samuel, 99, 102, 104, 109
Riley, Denise, 25, 85
Robinson, Lillian, 11, 14, 19

romance fiction, 172, 177, 185
roman de la Rose, 54
Rooney, Ellen, 18–19
Rushdie, Salman, 224, 252
Russo, Ann, 220

Sahgal, Gita, 251–2
Said, Edward, 213
Saussure, Ferdinand de, 196
Sawhney, Sabina, 4
Schenk, Celeste, 120
Schoene, Berthold, 23, 112
Schor, Naomi, 76, 105–6, 167, 207, 272, 275
science fiction, 172, 178
Scott, Bonnie Kime, 138, 148
Scott, Joan, 204–5, 206, 207
Scott, Patricia Bell, 41
Scott, Sir Walter, 99, 104
Sedgwick, Eve, 287, 288, 292, 293, 296–7
Segrest, Mab, 243
Seidman, Steven, 292, 300
Selden, Raman, 198
sentimentalism, 46, 99, 104, 109
sexuality, 7, 165–6, 227, 246, 266–7, 283; as discourse, 23, 283, 300; feminism's account of, 4, 13, 17, 23, 276; and gender, 5, 292, 293–4, 297–8; heterogeneity of, 284–5, 296–7; hetero/homo binary, 290, 292, 295; politics of, 77, 79, 88, 93, 293; transsexuality, 297
sexual difference, 5–6, 13, 23, 87–8, 91–2, 207; psychoanalysis on, 5, 159, 165, 267, 269, 270; poststructuralism on, 205; queer theory on, 280, 281
Sharpe, Jenny, 207
Showalter, Elaine, 8, 39, 100, 177
Silverman, Kaja, 207
Sinclair, May, 145
Sinfield, Alan, 290–1
Sinha, Mrinalini, 222
slavery, 29–30, 38, 249, 257; role of gender in, 30, 36
Smith, Barbara, 41, 43, 44, 47, 48, 237
Smith, Sidonie, 128
Smyer, Virginia L., 138
Snitow, Ann, 84, 85
Sommer, Doris, 128–9, 131–2
Spelman, Elizabeth, 35–6
Spencer, Linda, 185
Spender, Dale, 178
Spillers, Hortense, 11

CAMBRIDGE COMPANIONS TO LITERATURE

CAMBRIDGE COMPANIONS TO CULTURE